KNOWLEDGE-BASED MANUFACTURING MANAGEMENT

Applications of artificial intelligence to the effective management of manufacturing companies

KNOWLEDGE-BASED MANUFACTURING MANAGEMENT

Applications of artificial intelligence to the effective management of manufacturing companies

Roger Kerr

The University of New South Wales

ADDISON-WESLEY
PUBLISHING
COMPANY

Sydney · Wokingham, England · Reading, Massachusetts
Menlo Park, California · New York · Don Mills, Ontario
Amsterdam · Bonn · Singapore · Tokyo
Madrid · San Juan

HD
9720.5
K45
1990

To Therese and Katherine, and in memory of my parents.

Cover designed by Text & Cover Design, Singapore
Typeset by Times Graphics.
Printed in Singapore.

First printed 1990.

National Library of Australia Cataloguing-in-Publications Data
Kerr, Roger.
  Knowledge-based manufacturing management.

  Bibliography.
  Includes index.
  ISBN 0 201 41622 0.

  1. Production management – Data processing. 2. Manufacturing processes – Technolgical innovations – Management. 3. Expert systems (Computer science). I. Title.

658.500285

Library of Congress Cataloging-in-Publication Data
Kerr, Roger.
  Knowledge based manufacturing management : applications of artificial intelligence to the effective management of manufacturing companies / Roger Kerr.
  p. cm.
  ISBN 0-21-416622-0 :
  1. Manufactures—Management—Data processing.   2. Maufacturing processes—Automation. I. Title.
  HD9720.5.K45 1990
  658.5'0028'5633--dc20

89–18617
CIP

Preface

This book is aimed at industrial and manufacturing engineers at postgraduate and professional level, providing an introduction to the potential applications of knowledge-based systems technology to manufacturing management. The concept of the book originated from the author's experience that, although engineers at postgraduate level are usually computer literate to the extent of having a good working knowledge of languages such as FORTRAN, and of having used simple CAD systems and spreadsheets, their knowledge of data modelling, artificial intelligence and knowledge-based systems is often virtually non-existent. With the increasing emergence of knowledge-based systems from the research laboratories into practical application, and with the enormous surge of interest in this field by manufacturing industry, it would seem that swift action is required to rectify this state of affairs, particularly since it is industrial and manufacturing engineers who will play a leading role in the development and implementation of such systems.

The book assumes no prior knowledge of either data modelling or artificial intelligence, and as such it is self-contained. It does, however, assume that the reader has some basic familiarity with modern techniques of production management, although current trends in this field are summarised in Chapter 2. The coverage of the basic principles of knowledge representation goes somewhat beyond that found in the 'Introductory AI for Managers' type of book, and should provide sufficient grounding for an appreciation of some of the more critical issues raised in relation to the detailed examples. It assumes that the reader has a sound technical background with some basic computer knowledge. The chapter on data modelling has been included as this specific technology will play a fundamental role in the design of manufacturing information systems for many years to come, and a good grounding in the structuring of data and databases is invaluable for a better appreciation of the structuring of knowledge and knowledge bases.

Throughout the book there is a strong emphasis on the contribution of knowledge-based systems to the achievement of manufacturing *integration*. Thus, although the book is primarily about knowledge-based manufacturing management, the applications of knowledge-based systems to the technological activities of product design, process planning, GT, etc. are considered in some detail because the proper management and computer support of these tasks are absolutely critical to the achievement of overall conceptual integration. The nuts and bolts of the computer integration of manufacturing (such as computer interfacing and robotics) have been omitted deliberately. The treatment throughout attempts to view integrated manufacturing from an organisational rather than a technical perspective. Also omitted, or treated very peripherally, are considerations relating to the business functions of a manufacturing organisation, such as finance and marketing, as these are not considered quite so central to the solution of the current problems of manufacturing integration as are production management and engineering.

The very recent emergence of knowledge-based technology onto the factory floor has inevitably meant that fully-documented operational systems are few and far between. The documented systems that do exist tend to be confined mostly to the computer industry. I have resisted the temptation to examine the standard examples of knowledge-based systems such as XCON in order to stress the fact that such systems are as applicable to the down-to-earth environment of the small job shop as they are to the large computer manufacturer. I have favoured examples of applications (or possible applications) to manufacturing in the metal trades which produce somewhat less sophisticated products, but nevertheless constitute a major sector of industry. The examples chosen for examination in depth are either prototype systems or systems under development whose techniques or principles are of more interest than the fact that they have proved themselves in practice.

The field covered in this book is changing very rapidly. It is hoped that sufficient coverage is given to the more enduring general principles of knowledge representation and knowledge-based manufacturing integration that the book will outlast at least some of the systems it describes.

Roger Kerr
The University of New South Wales

Publishers acknowledgement

The publishers wish to thank the following for permission to reproduce figures and tables: Figures 15.14: K. E. Hummel and S. L. Brooks, 'Symbolic representation of manufacturing features for an automated process planning system', ASME Winter meeting: Knowledge-based expert systems in manufacturing, Anaheim, December 1986. Figure 16.13: Lu S. C-Y, 'Knowledge-based expert systems: a new horizon of manufacturing automation', ASME Winter meeting: Knowledge-based expert systems in manufacturing, Anaheim, December 1986. Figure 17.6: C. C. Koo and P. Cashman, 'A commitment-based communication language for distributed manufacturing', ASME Winter meeting: Knowledge-based expert systems in manufacturing, Anaheim, November 1986. Reprinted with permission of The American Society of Mechanical Engineer. Figures 2.9–10: C. G. Gallagher and W. A. Knight, *Group technology methods in manufacture*, © 1986, Ellis Horwood Limited, Chichester. Figures 16.9 and 16.11: Donald Michie, *On machine intelligence*, 2nd edition (page 248–9), Ellis Horwood Limited, Chichester. Figure 11.3: Reprinted by permission of the publisher from Integration of computer integrated manufacturing databases using artificial intelligence In *Expert systems and intelligent manufacturing*, (Michael D. Oliff, ed) © 1986 by Elsevier Science Publishing Co. Inc. Figures 13.9–11 and 13.13: Browne et al, *An approach to the design of PAC Systems*, © Dr Jimmie Browne, Ireland. Figure 17.4: M. Brodie and J. Mylopoulos (eds), *On knowledge base management systems*, © 1986, Springer-Verlag, New York. Figures 15.3–5: S. Luby, John R. Dixon and M. K. Simmons, Creating and using a features data base. In *Computers in mechanical engineering*, © 1986, Springer-Verlag, New York. Figure 2.14: E. H. Davis and J. L. Goedhart, Integrated planning frontiers, In *Intelligent manufacturing*, (Michael Oliff, ed) Benjamin/Cummings, Menlo Park. Reprinted courtesy of The Society of Manufacturing Engineers © 1985. Figure 12.21: S. F. Smith, A constraint-based framework for reactive management of factory schedules In *Intelligent manufacturing*, (Michael Oliff, ed) Benjamin/Cummings, Menlo Park, © 1988, S. F. Smith. Figure 2.13: Davis and J. L. Goedhart, Integrated planning frontiers In *Intelligent manufacturing*, (Michael Oliff, ed) Benjamin/Cummings, Menlo Park, © Dr T. E. Vollman, 1988. Figure 13.5: A. Kuziak, EXGT-S: A knowledge-based system for group technology, *International Journal of Production Research* 26(5), © 1988, Taylor-Francis, London.

Trademark notice

UNIX™ is a trademark of AT&T; KnowledgeCraft and SIMPAC are trademarks of Carnegie Group Inc.; PDP11™, VAX™ and XCON™ are trademarks of Digital Equipment Corporation; KEE™, KEE Connectum™ and Simkit are trademarks of Intellicorp; IBM™ is a trademark of International Business Machines Corporation.; PROLOG™, MPPROLOG™ and ARITY PRO-LOG™ are trademarks of Logic Programming Associates Limited; OPS83™ is a trademark of Production Systems Tech Inc.; Rulemaster™ is a trademark of Radian Corporation; ZETALISP™ is a trademark of Symbolics Incorporated; POPLOG™ is a trademark of University of Sussex; OPS5™ is a trademark of Verac Inc.; SMALLTALK80™ and INTERLISP™ are trademarks of Xerox Corporation.

Contents

Part I
BASICS

Chapter 1
Introduction

1.1 The crisis facing western manufacturing industry

In the past few years, a revolution has started to occur in the Western world in traditional concepts of manufacturing, whose eventual implications are likely to be more profound than those of the first industrial revolution of the early eighteenth century. As in the case of the first industrial revolution, some of the causes of this new industrial revolution are the result of a technology push. New production technologies, computer-aided design systems, computer-controlled machine tools, computer systems for automatic process control, robots, automatic guided vehicles for transporting goods between work stations and in and out of store, are becoming increasingly available at decreasing cost. The introduction of such technologies into modern manufacturing organisations is already resulting in substantial savings in direct labour costs, but the overall results of this technology push have not met original expectations. Overall increases in productivity have so far been disappointing, particularly in those companies engaged in small batch production, in which there has been a failure to coordinate effectively the operations of the individual pieces of advanced technology to form a synergistic whole.

3

Ironically, the increasing complexity and shorter life cycles of modern consumer products are increasing the strategic significance of small batch manufacturers, who now find themselves competing with high quality Japanese products manufactured at a cost which cannot be matched by Western countries with existing levels of productivity. Therefore, in addition to the current technology push, there is a very real need for advances in manufacturing information technology which allow the achievement of this missing synergy.

As a number of simple but robust analyses have shown, the solution of the current problem in Western manufacturing industry does not lie in the reduction of the direct labour burden by increasing the level of automation. Direct labour typically represents only 5% to 20% of total manufacturing cost. The only way of achieving higher levels of productivity is to attack what is commonly called the 'hidden overhead' present in the excessive quantities of inventory, work-in-progress, scrap and rework that is a normal feature of most manufacturing companies. The Japanese have had considerable success in achieving this by means of an underlying philosophy and a collection of techniques which have come to be known as 'Just-in-Time' production. A number of organisations in the West have tried to emulate the Japanese methods with varying degrees of success. The Japanese concept of JIT is not necessarily directly transferable to all types of Western manufacturing company, because of product-market and/or cultural differences. However, the aims of JIT (that is, the elimination of all forms of waste in the manufacturing process, from excess scrap to excess stock) can be realised in a variety of ways, all of which require a vastly increased degree of lateral coordination of the activities of different dependent parts of the manufacturing organisation, rather than selective local refinement of any one aspect without regard to its place in the whole. Thus to invest in the latest $400,000 machining centre will be futile if the increased output, coupled with the necessity to justify the expenditure by keeping the machine running, results in a pile up of work-in-progress on the downstream side due to poor coordination with assembly requirements.

1.2 The need for integration

The key to achieving coordinated goal-directed activity in any purposeful organisation lies in combining effective initial organisational design, in which relevant dimensions are chosen for the division of the organisation into groups of related activities, with the existence of techniques or systems which achieve the required degree of coordination or integration both within and between such groups.

Traditional manufacturing has tended to attack the problem through division by function, and has simplified the coordination problem by the build-up of inter-process stocks between functional divisions, allowing them to proceed quasi-independently of each other. But it is such inter-process stocks that now account for the major part of the 'hidden overhead', and which the Japanese have learnt almost to eliminate.

The technique of Material Requirements Planning, introduced to American industry in the 1970s, represented a step forward in terms of an attempt to achieve improved lateral coordination of different functional production activities and so cut interprocess stocks. MRP2, an evolution of MRP, was ostensibly intended to achieve, in addition, coordination of physical production with other activities such as marketing, distribution, purchasing and accounting. However, limitations in the design and flexibility of such systems, together with their rather ad hoc imposition on existing manufacturing organisational frameworks, has again lead to a rather disappointing improvement in productivity.

In spite of this, the MRP approach was correct in the sense that it regarded the sharing or transmission of information as the essential agent or 'glue' which achieved the necessary binding or coordination of different manufacturing activities to achieve synergistic operation of the whole. MRP was intended to force an explicit recognition of the key role of information transfer in the manufacturing enterprise. Despite these noble ideals, the results of MRP have been disappointing. Although this failure has been due in large part to the fact that MRP did not address the fundamental problems of rationalisation and simplification of the manufacturing process, it can be also ascribed to limitations in the information processing technology employed. Even today, many MRP systems in use are grounded in the information and data-base technology of the 1970s, with most of the associated (and well documented) problems of the large information systems of the time: predominantly batch (in the computer sense) rather than real-time operation; inadequate filtering of unnecessary information; high cost and low flexibility, leading to the organisation having to freeze its operational concepts to 'standard MRP' for the (necessarily long) lifetime of the system.

MRP was basically concerned with integration of materials flow, along the 'production management' axis of the organisation. Other moves towards integration have been in the domain of manufacturing technology. The computer integration of design and manufacture (so called CAD/CAM) is an objective that is being increasingly pursued world wide. Initially, this was a regarded as primarily a computer hardware problem, that of enabling different types of computer to communicate with one another. Although most of the technical obstacles to inter-computer communication in CAD/CAM have been overcome, the systems have not given the hoped for instant gains to overall organisational productivity. More enlightened manufacturing engineers now realise that the only problem to have been solved is that of computer interfacing. The problems of true integration of the different areas of manufacturing technology are, in fact, far more than the mere interfacing of different computer systems. The decision of how knowledge of the overall manufacturing problem should be distributed between individual systems, and what type of information should flow through the interface, presents the second, and much more intractable problem. It has also proved to be a problem that cannot be easily solved from the narrow technical perspective of the computer specialist.

The key to alleviating these problems lies in combining the latest advances in information and knowledge engineering technology with completely new forms of manufacturing management philosophy and organisational design. Neither approach on its own is likely to be sufficient to make a significant difference to today's levels of overall productivity. Management techniques and organisational forms which support decentralised decision making on all aspects of a particular group of products by small, highly integrated autonomous groups are already making an appearance in Western industry. Information technology in the West has already received a major boost from the challenge posed by the Japanese Fifth Generation Computer Project, the results of which are starting to find their way to the factory floor. The synergistic effect of these two types of change can together provide the productivity boost that allows the West to remain competitive.

1.3   The changing role of the computer

The current revolution in Information Processing technology is essentially concerned with changing the computer from a mere number cruncher performing numerous repetitive computations relating to a limited set of highly structured tasks, into a machine that is capable of storing symbolic knowledge and performing sophisticated symbolic manipulation and reasoning. This includes making intelligent inferences about the meaning and significance of various patterns existing in flexibly structured data, and deducing appropriate actions in response to such patterns which are consistent with some set of predefined goals. Essentially, computers are now capable of having artificial intelligence built into them.

To many people, the logical conclusion of this prospect is a factory of the future in which humans are replaced by a hierarchical network of intelligent computers, each with carefully structured access to subsets of a hierarchically partitioned common database, and with connections to robots which perform the physical operations of material movement, machine loading, assembly and inspection. In a highly structured and bounded environment, these would no doubt outperform their human counterparts in terms of efficiency, and this is already the direction being taken by computer-controlled flexible manufacturing cells. The human brain will nevertheless remain superior to any intelligent computer of the forseeable future by virtue of our ability to adapt to new, unforseen and unprogrammed situations in ways that are consistent with higher level and more general goals that would be very difficult to represent in a computer. If we assume that a rapidly changing environment will from now on be the norm for manufacturing industry, it would seem that human intervention at some stages of the manufacturing process will be essential for some time to come, even if only to keep the direction of change relevant to society's needs.

In the short term, there is much to be gained from incorporating the latest advances in information and knowledge engineering into Manufacturing Information Systems which achieve a synergistic integration of human and computer decision making. A departure from the conventional management information systems (MIS) approach to supporting decision making started in the late 1970s with the emergence of the Decision Support Systems (DSS) movement. This movement aimed to foster the development of systems that provided more than just the volumes of frequently irrelevant numbers that were generated by the more traditional types of MIS. A DSS is a system which makes some attempt to convert this mass of data into useful, decision relevant information by providing such things as simple filters, ad hoc query capabilities, data condensation techniques, graphics displays, extrapolation, and simple modelling capabilities.

A very important feature of DSS is the attention paid to developing representations and models that fit naturally into the user's individual perspective of the decision-making environment. We thus see a strong trend away from both complex mathematical models which are incomprehensible to the user, and from systems that generate reams of numbers through which the user has to sift to find the information required.

The DSS movement is still active and is exploiting recent developments in underlying enabling computer technologies, which are allowing the original concepts of DSS to come to fruition. Currently, a reasonable definition of DSS would be 'systems that use all available and relevant computing technologies to improve the quality and timeliness of human decision making'. These technologies include Database technologies, Computer Modelling technologies, User Interface technologies, and increasingly, Artificial Intelligence. The latter is particularly important to DSS because of its emphasis on representation of problem spaces in ways which map easily on to the forms of representation naturally used by the human brain. Although many of the ideas of DSS are finding their way gradually into the manufacturing information systems being marketed by some of the larger computer companies and software houses, progress in this area is still rather slow. The most effective implementation of DSS ideas still tends to be in one-off prototypes or smaller off-the-shelf systems based on personal computers.

However, it could be argued that as long as humans remain in control of the decision-making process in manufacturing organisations, it is by the adoption of philosophies derived from the DSS movement with their emphasis on flexible and human-oriented problem representation, and man-machine synergy, that will be of most signifance for better coordination of manufacturing operations through improved decision making. Developments in the enabling technologies of Data Modelling, Database Management Systems (DBMS) and Artificial Intelligence (AI) are of critical importance to the current and future directions of DSS.

1.4   The impact of database technology

Changes in database technology are leading to an increased emphasis on representing the semantics (meaning) of data, and on allowing flexible data retrieval based on the real information needs of the user, rather than the mere provision of preprogrammed standard reports. New developments in data modelling are resulting in data structures which map directly onto the objects and constructs employed naturally by humans in thinking about their data environment. Effective management of the *meaning* of data can facilitate the development of integrated data models of the entire enterprise, resulting in the potential for company-wide common databases with common logical structures. It can thus be ensured that all departments of the organisation base their current and planned activities on the same data.

This contrasts strongly with information systems of the 1970s and early 80s which relied on computerisation within functional boundaries. The payroll system was set up independently of the inventory system; the design system independently of the production planning system. The rationale was to make the system more manageable by minimising the relationships between data. However, any attempts by managers to retrieve information rather than data from the system were doomed to frustration, as the data they required was usually distributed between functional areas with often incompatible data structures. Use of a single centralised database, or distributed databases with a common logical structure, allows relationships between functional areas to be explicitly represented in the data structures, and provides for the availability of information based on data spread across the entire organisation.

Management of the meaning of data is not, however, a trivial problem. The additional data relationships that must be represented creates a new class of problems concerned with 'semantic integrity'. Relationships between data items implicitly embody its semantics, and the requirement for semantic integrity demands that the stored data be mutually consistent and complete. The data structures needed to store engineering and geometric data about product designs and their associated manufacturability constraints incorporate many complex relationships whose adequate representation poses difficulties for data models, such as the relational model which is limited in its semantic constructs. The semantic and logical integration of this type of data with manufacturing management data is not an easy problem.

1.5 From databases to knowledge bases

The techniques of artificial intelligence are concerned with the computer representation and application of *knowledge*, and the application of knowledge is intimately connected with making interpretations of the meaning of data. Recent developments in AI techniques not only provide a powerful means of modelling the semantics of data. They also allow us to go beyond the passive data structures of conventional database technology, and provide stored general rules and active inference mechanisms for making logical deductions about data, thus opening the possibility of generating new facts from existing data. In the context of manufacturing tasks, this can allow the automatic development and evaluation of alternative courses of action using versatile heuristics (production planning and scheduling), the making of intelligent inferences about the current state of affairs in the factory and its possible causes from patterns in current and historical data (production control) and the automatic *search* for and evalution of different configurations of individual functional entities which are intended to operate together as a functional whole (design). All of these activities imply an automatic *search* of a conceptual space represented by a semantically meaningful set of data structures, in terms of which the problem can be described.

The key role of search in artificial intelligence is of critical importance to its applicability in manufacturing. AI systems contain active components (which may vary from simple IF-THEN rules to quite complex procedures) which are 'fired' by predefined patterns in a dynamic database, and perform manipulations on other data items in search of some goal (a particular configuration of the database which satisfies some predefined criteria). Rather than being 'blind', the search is guided by a strategy (usually defined by a set of domain dependent rules or heuristics) which chooses the most appropriate rule or procedure for next application. This type of problem-solving technique is effective for messy and ill-defined problems which are underconstrained in their definition, or for which no unique optimal solution exists and which involve considerable combinatorial complexity.

In manufacturing, there are many tasks of this nature, and many of the current difficulties in manufacturing management stem from the existence of combinatorially complex, underconstrained problems (or problems in which the constraints are difficult to represent in numerical terms). Starting with product design, there are clearly a large number of different configurations that will satisfy the constraints defining the required product functionality. Allowable configurations must also obey the constraints of the laws of physics and of good engineering design, but the design problem is still basically a problem of constraint directed search. Process and facilities design likewise are strongly interactive tasks in which many solutions will be feasible, and which must be solved by intelligent search for satisfactory solutions rather than algorithmic determination of the optimal solution. Production planning and control, traditionally one of the most problematical areas of manufacturing, is a task which has enormous combinatorial complexity, and in which problem solutions are subject to many different types of constraint, some of which are qualitative or preferential in nature. The representation of these types of constraint and the associated problems of constraint-directed search can both be facilitated by the use of AI techniques.

AI concepts likewise have strong implications for production control. The lifetime of a given valid operational schedule is inherently very short, due to the inescapable presence of randomness on the shop floor caused by such things as machine breakdowns, missing tools, absent operators, late deliveries, and other unplanned contingencies. An important part of operational control is the ability to react effectively to unanticipated shop floor events and this requires a search mechanism for a recovery plan to the original schedule. The programming of intelligent search methods using domain-specific knowledge to diagnose the problem and develop a recovery plan can greatly assist in solving this problem. The number of control points can also be enormously increased by this means. Background intelligent monitoring systems can not only be used for real-time control of automated systems at shop floor level, but can also assist in managerial control by monitoring patterns in operational data to detect deviations and also to diagnose their causes and suggest strategies for recovery.

Perhaps, however, the most important potential contribution of AI is the possibility of allowing manufacturing decisions to be made not simply on the basis of shared common data (whose meaning and significance may still be open to alternative semantic interpretations), but also on shared common *knowledge*. The division of knowledge about the product and the manufacturing environment into separate watertight compartments, as encouraged by the traditional functional organisation of manufacturing companies, has proved to be one of the major stumbling blocks in the achievment of manufacturing integration. The way in which knowledge-based systems can be used to facilitate the sharing of organisational knowledge, and hence the making of better organisational decisions, is one of the main themes of this book.

1.6   The objectives and organisation of this book

The main objective of this book is to provide a guide for the key people who must work together in the process of designing and implementing knowledge-based manufacturing management systems. On the manufacturing side these include industrial and manufacturing engineers, manufacturing managers, production planners and controllers, and shop floor supervisors, all of whom are presumed to have little knowledge of advanced database technology or AI. On the Data Processing side, they include DP professionals who may have little familiarity with modern techniques of manufacturing management, and only a peripheral knowledge of AI.

Part 1 gives an overview of the systemic nature of manufacturing and the critical role of information and knowledge in manufacturing management; this is followed in Part 2 by a brief review of the basic concepts of modern database theory, data modelling techniques, and artificial intelligence (with a strong emphasis on knowledge bases and knowledge-based systems). Part 3 covers specific applications to production management and production systems design of the techniques described in Part 2, whilst Part 4 looks at applications to manufacturing technology. In both these parts, a general review of application areas is followed by a detailed examination of some selected existing systems. In Part 5, problems of implementation are discussed, both from a technical and a human perspective.

Chapter 2
Changing Concepts of Manufacturing Management

2.1 Manufacturing management in the pre-computer era

2.2 Early forms of computer support for manufacturing management

2.3 The era of MRP

2.4 Alternatives to MRP — rationalisation and simplification

2.5 The quest for computer integration

Many of the problems currently facing manufacturing industry can only cbe fully understood by examining the way in which manufacturing management and organisation have evolved since the turn of the century. This has been influenced in part by the corresponding evolution in information processing technology, and the ways in which successive waves of new technology have been applied (or misapplied) to the task of improving manufacturing efficiency. The purpose of this chapter is to give a brief overview of the recent evolution of manufacturing management. This will enable current key issues to be better understood in the context of a historical perspective, and the potential role of current and future information and knowledge processing technology to be examined from a critical stance which draws on the lessons accumulated during the course of this evolution.

2.1 Manufacturing management in the pre-computer era

Traditional approaches to manufacturing management originating in the pre-computer era have been heavily oriented towards the achievement of manufacturing efficiency through the unquestioning application of the maxims of scientific management, introduced by Frederick Taylor at the beginning of this century. These maxims were based on the philosophy of *reductionism*, and rely heavily on the 'machine analogy' for the organisation, in which the overall operation of the factory is decomposed into its basic indivisible component subtasks. These are analysed separately and the most efficient way of performing each subtask is scientifically determined.

This strong emphasis on optimising individual subtasks is often at the expense of satisfactorily coordinating and integrating them in a harmoniously functioning whole. Manufacturing operations have had a tendency to become complex and interdependent, leading to severe coordination problems. These are invariably solved by the introduction of slack into the system in the form of high interprocess inventories and long lead times. Large inventories are used as buffers to decouple individual production processes from each other so that each process can proceed at its own pace, virtually independently of the remainder of the system. The effects of breakdowns and other irregularities occurring in a process can be localised by inserting buffer stocks that, in the event of such contingencies, can be drawn on by the downstream processes, thus avoiding halts in production (Figure 2.1). The padding of manufacturing lead times, by giving the production foreman generous time allowances within which to adjust schedules to cope with unexpected interruptions to production, can further help to create environments in which the necessity for tight coordination between different production stages is minimised.

The characteristic emphasis of traditional manufacturing on dividing the organisation by function also encourages the use of slack, in the form of extended lead times to decouple manufacturing activities to which physical inventories do not apply. Thus, product design and process planning activities may occur in functionally separate departments in isolation both from each other, and from the production environment. By allowing wide time margins for the completion of these activities, the need for tight coordination between them, at least from a temporal point of view, can be reduced.

A great deal of effort has gone into the development of scientific methods to determine the optimal amount of slack in a manufacturing system, especially the amount of buffer stock that should be carried. For a particular production process, a statistical analysis of the frequency and duration of interruptions to the process, together with the fluctuations on the downstream demand, can in principle allow estimates to be made of

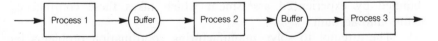

Figure 2.1   Interprocess stocks as buffers.

the degrees of 'protection' afforded by buffers of varying size. In practice, however, the production foreman will usually estimate buffer sizes, using judgement based on experience, and will invariably err on the 'safe' side, since disruptions to production causing late deliveries have much more visible and immediate effects than the hidden cost of high inventories.

An additional encouragement to the creation of buffer stocks comes from the requirement to minimise the effects of predictable interruptions caused by machine set-ups. The set-up frequency, and the resulting lost production time, can be reduced by manufacturing in larger batches giving longer uninterrupted production runs. These in turn produce excess inventory, which has carrying costs associated with storage and the opportunity cost of the capital thus tied up. The economic size of the batch is that which results in a trade-off between the cost of lost production due to set-ups and the excess inventory caused by manufacturing more than is immediately required. This can be determined by the so called Economic Batch Size formula which relates to a simple ordering situation in which both the set-up and the inventory carrying costs are known, and gives the relationship between the economic batch size Q, the set-up cost per batch s, the inventory carrying cost per unit time per unit stock i and the demand per unit time d as:

$$Q = \sqrt{\frac{2sd}{i}}$$

The economic batch size is that which gives the minimum value of the total cost function per unit time, as shown in Figure 2.2. This formula gained a great deal of visibility because of its simplicity, and generations of students of production management were brought up being able to quote it and its numerous extensions. It has, nevertheless, been heavily critized. One criticism is that the formula as such encourages the acceptance of long set-up times as manufacturing 'givens' rather than as factors to be reduced or eliminated, and this inevitably leads to production in large batches. Another criticism is of the basic assumptions that demand is continuous and steady, and cost parameters are measurable. In a large number of manufacturing situations, these assumptions are highly dubious. The best batch size in a given situation will usually depend on many contingency factors not included in this formula, such as the current loading on the plant, the urgency with which the batch is required, and forecasts of the future demand. Thus, rather than abiding by the application of standard formulae, better results can usually be obtained by experienced assessment which takes these contingency factors into account.

The attempt to solve manufacturing coordination problems by introducing generous amounts of slack, with the associated human

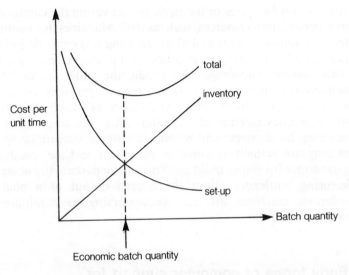

Figure 2.2 The economic batch quantity.

tendency to err on the safe side, has lead Western manufacturing industry into a situation in which inventory levels tend to be excessively high and manufacturing lead times excessively long. The former leads to higher manufacturing costs arising from the overheads in carrying large stocks. The latter leads to sluggish response to the market and lost market opportunities. It is now commonly realised that the hidden costs of inventory represent a higher proportion of total manufacturing costs than do direct labour costs, and are in fact the greatest single source of reducible cost in the average manufacturing company.

Unfortunately, standard methods of cost accounting do not illuminate this fact clearly, nor do they provide any incentives for inventory reduction. First, all overhead costs not directly associated with the manufacture of a product (such as cost of storage space and administrative overhead) are often allocated to the unit cost of the product in proportion to the direct labour hours required per unit. As direct labour hours are reduced by an increasing degree of automation, and indirect overhead resulting from provision of additional storage areas and stock handling equipment increases, then merely loading the direct labour cost to recover this overhead can present individual manufacturing cost centres with a distorted picture of how best to achieve cost reductions. An individual manufacturing cost centre can reduce its apparent costs only by concentrating on reducing the direct labour hours per unit of product, which does not attack the main sources of real cost. The opportunity cost of money invested in inventory is not even regarded as a 'cost' at all in traditional accounting terms, with inventory itself actually being regarded as an 'asset'.

Another problem lies in the habit of recovering the capital cost of expensive production resources such as NC Machines by assuming a fixed depreciation cost per year and distributing this over the individual items produced by the machine in proportion to the machining time per item. This method encourages the production of as many items as possible in a given time in order to reduce the cost per item and has given rise to excessive emphasis on maximisation of machine use (keep expensive machines running at all costs). This encourages both larger manufacturing batch sizes, and a tendency to go on producing items whether they are actually required or not ('Just in Case' production), leading to further inventory build up. This can be particularly acute when manufacturing bottlenecks limit the overall output of a plant, but non-bottleneck machines are still kept running to maximise their utilisation.

2.2   Early forms of computer support for manufacturing management

The attempt, in the pre-computer era, to solve manufacturing coordination problems by setting up quasi-independent functional subunits, decoupled from each other by buffer stocks and long lead times, was largely a consequence of the information processing limitations of the unaided human brain. Manufacturing operations were sufficiently complex that, in the absence of a computer, it was not possible to institute the centralised storage, manipulation and retrieval of detailed information required to achieve tight centralised coordination of a plant, and the instant transmission of this information to relevant staff. The only practical solution was a 'divide and conquer' approach in which each subunit made its own local decisions on the basis of the local information available, which was stored and manipulated manually. Thus, the decision made at a particular work centre as to what item to produce in what quantity and by what date was based on the current buffer inventory level of the item and the standard manufacturing batch sizes used to replenish it, rather than any master plan which coordinated detailed individual production schedules with end product requirements.

During the 1950s the first attempts were made to improve manufacturing planning and control by the installation of computer systems. These were initially introduced simply to perform well-defined functions that had hitherto been performed manually, such as inventory control, purchasing and accounting. Such systems were mostly transaction processing systems which recorded transactions (such as stock withdrawal) in a transaction database, updated any required cumulative totals (such as stock on hand) and automatically generated requirements for new transactions (such as stock reorder) if certain conditions were met (such as stock below reorder level). Basically, they took some of the existing manual procedures of a given functional area, and automated them. This provided the potential for increased efficiency within functional areas, but there was little attempt to use the computer to help achieve a higher degree of coordination between functional areas, either by vertical or horizontal transmission of information. At the same time, the increasing instability of the manufacturing environment made the achievment of close coordination all the more important. Technological change, the requirement to satisfy customer demands for increasingly sophisticated products with ever shorter lifecycles, rapidly fluctuating economies and the emergence of global competition, meant an end to the period of relative stability of the 1950s and 60s. Means had to be sought of using the information processing power of the computer to make companies more responsive to change.

The first documented approach to the use of the computer to assist with the *global integration* of different manufacturing activities appeared in the mid 1960s, when IBM produced a conceptual outline of what they called a Production, Inventory and Control System (PICS — IBM, (1968)). This system evolved from IBM'S work on data structures for storing manufacturing bills of materials, the so-called Bill-of-Material processor (BOMP) program which heavily influenced all IBM's subsequent work in the production and inventory control area. This allowed products to be represented in the form of tree structures which explicitly detailed the composition, in hierarchical form, of the end product and the various levels of subassemblies, components and subcomponents of which it was composed.

The PICS system called for the use of the computer to support eight different functional areas of the manufacturing company: sales forecasting, requirements planning, capacity planning, engineering data control, shop floor control, operations scheduling, purchasing, and inventory control. The PICS concept was presented by IBM in the form of a wheel configuration, shown in Figure 2.3, which emphasised the degree of commonality of data requirements, and hence the degree of necessary coordination, between each area.

2.3   The era of MRP

2.3.1   The principles of MRP

The PICS concept lead to the evolution of what came to be known as Material Requirements Planning (MRP), the principles of which are comprehensively described by Orlicky (1975). MRP is an attempt to use the 'number-crunching' power of the computer to develop a production plan for an entire plant in which the production of each individual item

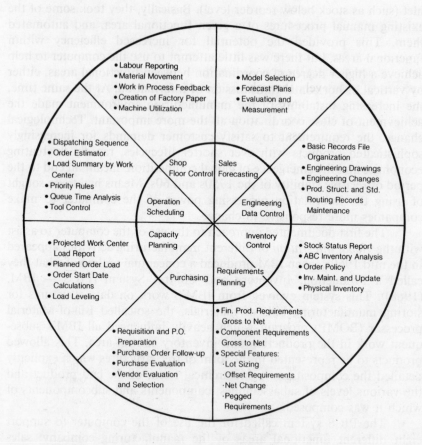

Figure 2.3 The PICS 'wheel'.

is coordinated with a master production schedule for the production of end products. It was realised that, if such an end product master schedule could be fixed in advance, and suitable lead times were allowed for each stage of the manufacturing process, this would in turn fix the quantities and timings of requirements of sub-assemblies, components and raw materials that would be required to meet this schedule. If these requirements were transmitted to the individual work centres responsible for producing each item, work centres could produce to a build schedule that was directly linked to requirements for end products rather than being determined merely on the basis of periodic replenishment of buffer stocks.

MRP operates by a computer generated 'explosion' of the master production schedule for end products into the implied requirements for individual components and raw materials, by referring to the stored bill of materials for each item to obtain the identity and number of the constituent items needed to produce it. It then performs a netting and time phasing calculation in which, after making allowance for current inventory levels and the average manufacturing lead time allowed to produce each item, net production quantities and timings of constituent items needed to meet the end product build schedule are computed. This is repeated recursively through the bill of materials on a level by level basis, until at the lowest level the computation finishes with the generation of purchasing requirements for bought-in raw materials. A summary of this process is shown in Figure 2.4.

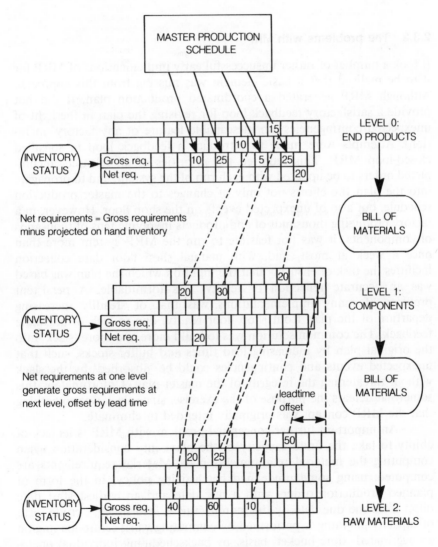

Figure 2.4 Typical MRP 'explosion'.

The principle behind MRP was that the necessity of large buffer stocks could be virtually eliminated (or at least reduced to some residual level providing a cushion against real uncertainties, such as machine breakdowns), since the requirement for an individual component item could now be predicted from the end product master production schedule combined with the bill of materials, and precise coordination between supply and demand for each individual item in the plant could, in principle, be achieved. Uncertainty in demand and the associated requirement for buffer stocks could be confined to the end product level.

2.3.2 The problems with MRP

It took a number of rather unsuccessful early implementions of MRP for it to be realised that a basic element was missing from this approach. Although MRP generated a coordinated production plan, it did not provide a satisfactory feedback loop for revising the plan in the light of unexpected contingencies (an inescapable feature of any factory operation). Attempts were made to introduce a feedback loop in so-called closed-loop MRP. This required the priorities of all released, incompleted orders to be updated with each run of the system, and to propagate into the plan the effects not only of changes to the master production schedule, but also of unexpected events on the shop floor. However, in a factory producing thousands of end products involving tens of thousands of components, it was not feasible to run the MRP system more than once a week at most, and, with manual shop floor data collection facilities the task of ensuring that the input on which the plan was based was an accurate reflection of reality, was formidable. A persistent problem of many implementations was that of steadily increasing departure of the plan from shop floor reality, due to lack of adequate feedback. The common solution was to build more and more 'slack' into the original plan by increasing lead times and buffer stocks, such that unexpected events and contingencies could be 'absorbed' by the slack without threatening the integrity of the master plan. Unfortunately, this somewhat defeats the purpose of the exercise, since slack was something that the MRP concept was originally intended to eliminate.

An important further conceptual problem with MRP is its lack of ability to take the finite capacity of the plant into consideration when computing the material requirements plan. Material requirements are computed, using some predefined batch-sizing policy, in the form of planned production orders with a due date and an earliest start date offset from the due date by the manufacturing lead time. A crude form of capacity planning is performed by computing work centre loading on an aggregated 'time bucket' basis, by backscheduling individual operations from the due date of the order with allowance for queue time between operations. The loading of a work centre to greater than its capacity in a particular time bucket is supposed to indicate the presence of a 'capacity problem' which must be solved by some means such as planning to work an extra shift, or by subcontracting work out. In fact, this approach neither indicates whether a capacity problem really exists, nor does it provide any indication of whether the problem could be avoided by simple adjustments to the plan that do not threaten the integrity of the master production schedule. For example, apparent capacity problems might be solved merely by pulling in a job from an overloaded to an underloaded time bucket, or by using a more flexible lot sizing policy, as shown in Figure 2.5. Real capacity problems may involve the selective slippage of due dates. However, standard MRP systems provide the user only with a very restricted capabilty to experiment interactively with alternative options. The solution of problems is conveniently left to the judgement and local knowledge of personnel on the shop floor.

The fact that the material requirements plan is developed prior to and independently of any capacity check, and uses standard lead times which have slack already incorporated in them, and are input to the system rather than being computed from the basis of a feasible production schedule, is an important reason why MRP has generally failed to have the hoped-for effect in terms of tighter coordination and reduced slack. The further fact that standard MRP systems lack the ability to perform crisp what-if analyses in real time, is a failing that, as

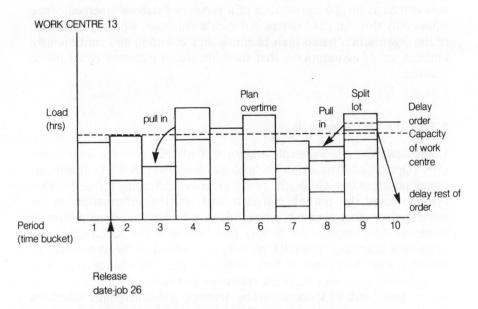

Figure 2.5 MRP infinite loading profile.

Kanet (1986) has pointed out, can lead to missed strategic opportunities as well as lack of effective control over shop floor operations.

2.3.3 MRP2

In spite of many MRP failures, an increasing number of companies installed MRP systems throughout the 1970s and 80s, and the MRP concept was extended to cover more of the activities of the organisation. In the same way that the master production schedule combined with bills of materials could be used to determine material requirements, other records could be used to establish labour, machine, capital, purchasing, marketing and shipping requirements. In other words, the full range of manufacturing resources needed by the organisation to implement a particular master plan could be established by a similar set of computations to the basic MRP requirements explosion technique. Facilities were provided to raise the top level of planning from an end product build schedule to the level of an overall business plan, with rough-cut checks on associated resource requirements and costs before the end product MPS was finalised. The meaning of the MRP acronym changed from Material Requirements Planning to Manufacturing Resources Planning, and was referred to as MRP2 to distinguish it from the original and more restricted usage (Figure 2.6). This concept was, of course, contingent on all the necessary master data on manufacturing resource characteristics and availability being stored and kept current. Hence a new emphasis on the importance of a **common database** emerged, since it was only through the existence of such a database, whereby each part of the organisation based their planning on a common and continuously updated set of assumptions, that such integrated planning could prove feasible.

2.3.4 The OPT approach

Coincident with the widescale adoption of MRP2, a new system called OPT (Optimised Production Technology) developed by Eli Goldrath, an Israeli physicist (see Goldrath, 1981), received increasing publicity. This system stores the bill of materials and routing information in an integrated product network, which allows a better conceptualisation of materials flow through the factory and facilitates the identification of bottleneck resources. The OPT philosophy emphasises the importance of maximally efficient usage of bottleneck resources. Scheduling activity is thus concentrated on bottleneck resources and resources involved in an order's post-bottleneck operations by developing detailed finite schedules for these resources, using variable size 'transfer' batches, (which are

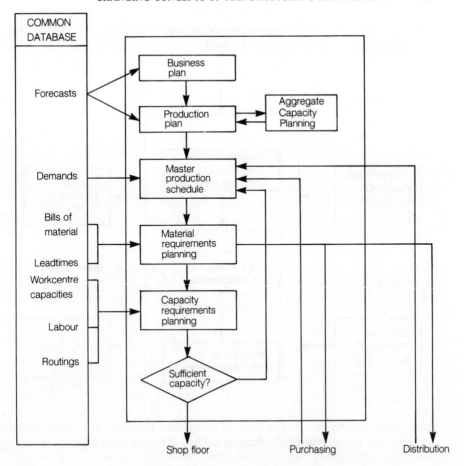

Figure 2.6 Schematic of MRP2.

integral multiples of some predefined minimum allowable transfer batch size) for increased flexibility, and a proprietary scheduling algorithm (colloquially known as the brain of OPT). Non-critical pre-bottleneck operations of an order are backscheduled from the time of the bottleneck operation using a procedure similar to MRP. However, because of the finite capacity scheduling of bottleneck resources, the lead time of an order is an output of this process, rather than having to be an estimated input as in the case of MRP. A block diagram of the OPT approach is shown in Figure 2.7.

So far there have been two main criticisms of OPT. First, it relies on the existence of a fairly well defined bottleneck for its principles to be valid. In many plants the bottleneck is not clearly defined, and manufacturing contingencies may cause it to wander within the timescale of an OPT schedule. The second objection is concerned with the tightness of the OPT schedules, which must be precisely adhered to if the plan is

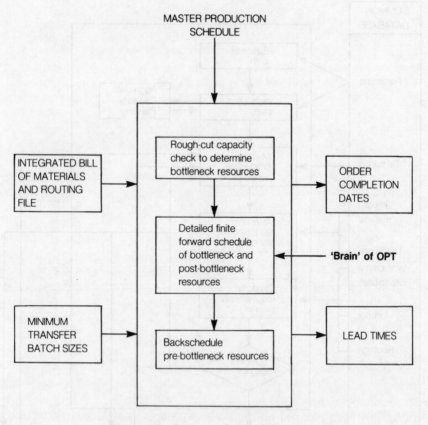

Figure 2.7   Schema of the OPT system.

to retain its integrity, and make little allowance for the familiar interruptions caused by Murphy's law. Although these can be minimised for bottleneck resources by preventative maintainance and buffer stocks, it is unlikely they can be completely eliminated, and when they occur OPT gives no guidance on schedule recovery, short of a rerun of the entire plan.

2.4   Alternatives to MRP — trends towards rationalisation and simplification

2.4.1   The need to contain complexity

The concept of MRP2 was a bold attempt to provide a system of integrated manufacturing management with all activities centrally coordinated, and with different functional sections of the organisation obtaining information from a common database. The comparative lack of success of MRP in relation to the high expectations set for it may largely be ascribed to the fact that it was trying to solve a problem made unnecessarily complicated by the high variety, complex product and component interdependencies, and complex material flow patterns that were a common feature of many manufacturing companies. The MRP approach accepted the problems of manufacturing variety and complexity as givens, and proceeded to try and solve these problems by massive amounts of computation and information transfer. The centralised approach, and use of predominantly early 1970s computer technology in most MRP systems, which were strongly oriented towards batch rather than interactive information processing, simply did not provide the flexibility and real time feedback and control that was required to cope satisfactorily with the enormous complexity of many real world manufacturing operations.

The main reasons for the proliferation of complexity in manufacturing have been the functional separation of, and lack of standardisation and systematisation in, the activities of product design, factory layout design and process planning, and the lack of clear visibility of the implications of these activities for production scheduling. Products tend to be designed without regard for the implications of the design on the variety of components and complexity of the manufacturing processes required. Lack of easy access to previous similar designs leads to an unnecessary proliferation of new designs and part numbers. Manufacturing processes are planned without regard for the potential complexity they might cause for the production scheduler, and factory layouts have invariably been planned on the basis of grouping machines by function, without considering how alternative product-oriented layouts might be used with rationalised process plans to simplify both production scheduling and material flow through the factory. A very important dimension of manufacturing integration and one that was not addressed at all by MRP2 (which was concerned solely with the integration of the different logistical and financial activities) is the integration of the technical activities of product design and process planning in such a way as to *rationalise and simplify* the critical operational tasks of production planning and scheduling. This approach is shown conceptually in Figure 2.8.

During the 1980s, increasing emphasis started to be placed on rationalisation and simplification of operations (in order to simplify the problems of managing them), rather than mere computerisation (which, without the first two, tended to produce only a faster executing 'mess'). For many companies this meant a large scale rethink of their existing manufacturing operation, with a rationalisation of existing designs, process plans and factory layout, from a new and more integrated perspective. The application of the principles of Group technology, Just-in-Time Production with Total Quality Control, and Design for Manu-

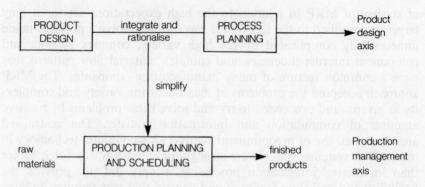

Figure 2.8 Simplification of production planning and scheduling by rationalisation/integration of design and process planning.

facture, all presented conceptual frameworks in which this integrated perspective could be achieved, at least during the reorganisational phase.

2.4.2 Manufacturing rationalisation using group technology

Group Technology (Gallagher and Knight, 1986) is concerned with discerning underlying similarity in products, parts, processes, and production resources by structuring these entities into clusters based on common attribute values. Through the application of Group Technology (GT) groups of similar set-up parts can be identified.

Rationalisation of product range and design with reference to GT considerations can enhance the degree of standardisation and interchangeability of parts which in turn introduces greater simplicity into the manufacturing process. Use of GT coding and classification schemes in conjunction with production flow analysis can assist in the identification of part or product 'families' that flow through, or could flow through the same clusters of machinery. These clusters of machines can then form the basis for manufacturing cells which are capable of performing all the operations required to produce a given family of parts (Figure 2.9). Provided the capacity of such cells is reasonably matched to the demand for individual part families, cells can be dedicated to families and hence become self-contained and autonomous in their operation. Thus, the term 'group' in Group Technology can (and has) been applied not only to groups of similar parts but also to groups of machines that form manufacturing cells, and the groups of people who are responsible for them.

The approach of GT is to solve a large part of the problem of manufacturing coordination by the creation of independent subtasks. Since manufacturing cells are autonomous in operation, close coordina-

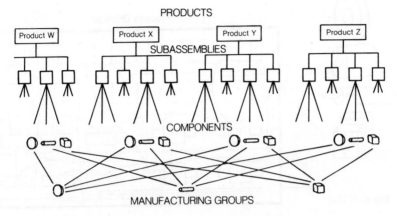

Figure 2.9 Formation of groups.

tion between cells is not required, and the activities of each cell can be planned independently of the others. The concept has been expressed in a variety of forms by different authors. For example Skinner (1978) writes of the 'focused factory' concept in which a manufacturing organisation is divided into a number of autonomous 'subfactories' each making their own family of products. The effect of unexpected contingencies within a subfactory are localised, not through buffer stocks but through autonomy of operation.

Physical grouping of machines into cells devoted to part or product families means a product rather than a process-oriented factory layout which can drastically reduce the distances travelled by items in their progress from one operation to the next. In the process-oriented layout of the traditional factory, items tend to follow complicated routings and travel large distances. The paths they follow have frequently been compared to 'bowls of spaghetti' (Figure 2.10a). Long and uncertain throughput times result, with the physical separation of sequential processes increasing the difficulty of inter-process coordination. A change to product-oriented layout can result in much simpler material flow patterns, as shown in Figure 2.10b, since sequential processes are performed in physically adjacent locations. Stock handling costs are reduced, and coordination greatly improved.

2.4.3 Just-in-Time manufacture

The concept of autonomous manufacturing cells with their greatly simplified work-flow characteristics is closely related to the Japanese concept of Just-in-Time production, which was pioneered by Toyota, and first comprehensively described in English language texts by Schonberger (1982) and Hall (1983). The original thrust of the JIT approach went beyond mere

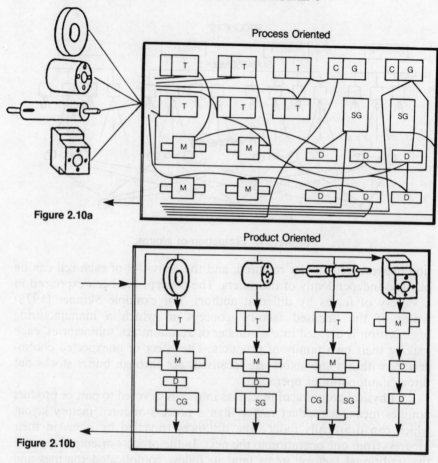

Figure 2.10a

Figure 2.10b

Figure 2.10 Process versus product-oriented layout.

simplified work flow, to find ways of increasing the material velocity through the factory by only producing items just-in-time to be moved to the subsequent process. This implies the reduction of lead times to something approaching the physical production time, and the elimination of long queues of work-in-progress, by each work station producing items only in the quantity required by the next work station, neither more nor less, coupled with the immediate movement of the production batch to the next process. The extent to which a JIT program was successful was measured by the residual buffer stock required between processes. The ideal buffer stock is zero, implying that all material spends 100% of its time in productive, value adding operations, with no time spent waiting for processing. This represents an ideal that is not usually realizeable, yet when regarded as a goal to be strived for, it can result in drives towards continuous improvement rather than a complacent acceptance of current standards as defining the required level of performance.

A number of prerequisites are necessary for JIT production to be achieved. First, it requires a group of production facilities to be dedicated to a relatively small group of products with low variability on the total demand, and with a slight excess of productive capacity; (this must be achieved, if necessary by redesign of product/market strategies). Second, assiduous attention to set-up engineering must ensure that quick set-up changeovers between items are possible, so that very small batches can be produced economically. This allows a mix of finished products to be produced whose composition can be varied according to the varying demand patterns for the individual products. Third, potential disruptions to production must be minimised through high levels of preventative maintainance and reduction of scrap and rework by quality control at source.

The JIT philosophy rejects the obsession with maximising machine use prevalent in Western industry, which tends to lead only to higher work-in-progress and longer lead times. Items are produced only if the next process signals it needs them, not merely to maximise utilisation. The resulting increased machine and operator idle time is employed constructively by a multi-skilled workforce in preventative maintainance and searching out causes of poor quality. This in turn reduces the number of unplanned interruptions to production, and so further reduces work-in-progress and lead time build up.

The JIT concept is basically concerned with the conversion of discrete batch production processes into continuous flow processes, in which it is only necessary to keep a cumulative count of the number of items produced, rather than tracking each individual work order. Planning and scheduling of continuous flow processes on dedicated production lines are relatively trivial compared to scheduling the batch production of a large number of different items through a number of capacity constrained production facilities. JIT is thus an excellent example of the problem simplification approach to manufacturing management. Rather than attempting to solve complex problems with complex tools such as MRP, the JIT philosophy is to simplify the problem by appropriate redesign of the manufacturing operation, and then use simple techniques for its solution. As the planning and control of production are commonly regarded as one of the most difficult problems faced by manufacturing management, and one of the largest sources of waste, the solution presented by JIT is to redesign the whole manufacturing operation and simplify planning and control as much as possible.

2.4.4 Quality

An important trend in the 1980s has been the return of quality to a position of pre-eminence in manufacturing. There had been a tendency in the 1960s and 70s to try and increase profitability by using low cost materials, labour and equipment. In the 1980s, the hidden costs associated with the resulting poor quality started to become increasingly exposed. These hidden costs include material loss, rework time, warranty costs, inspection time and the hard-to-measure costs of customer disatisfaction. As part of a strategy for attacking such costs, we see the emergence of drives for quality at source, as exemplified by the philosophy of Total Quality Control (TQC), which may be regarded as complementary to JIT production.

Rather than relying on detection of defects *after* production with traditional statistical sampling techniques, TQC emphasizes the elimi-nation of the problems that lead to poor quality at source by constant analysis of the causes of all observed defects, and the continuous search for ways to redesign products and processes such that the causes of poor quality are eliminated, and the ideal of 'zero defects' is achieved. TQC complements JIT in that a reduction of production interruptions caused by quality problems enables the ideal JIT target of 'zero inventory' to be achieved more closely.

Japanese success in improving the quality of their goods using TQC techniques, and their ability to cut product costs by the near elimination of work-in-progress inventories have made it urgently necessary for the West to follow suit both in improving quality and decreasing cost.

Both JIT and TQC can be subsumed into a broader manufacturing philosophy that has been termed **waste elimination**. Excessive stock levels, long lead times, defective items, and non-value-adding operations such as material movements and set-up times are all examples of manufacturing waste. The waste elimination approach aims to encourage the participation of each member of the workforce, usually in the context of small group problem-solving sessions, in analysing the causes of waste in whatever form it may take, and designing ways of reducing it. This contrasts the approach of traditional manufacturing organisation, in which these forms of control are centralised, and placed in the hands of specialised departments. The rationale behind encouraging workforce involvement is based on the observation that those closest to the shop floor problems that result in waste will often be able to suggest the best means of prevention, provided they are given sufficient training and incentive.

This clearly involves raising the levels of knowledge and problem-solving ability of the workforce to far above that normally expected in Western industry. However, the resultant system of distributed problem solving in semi-autonomous work groups or cells has much to commend it, from both pragmatic and theoretical perspectives, over the monolithic centralised control model of traditional manufacturing, as will be seen in Chapter 3.

2.4.5 Design for manufacture

In the traditional manufacturing operation, product designers give designs to manufacturing with little understanding of the associated manufacturing problems. This can result in needlessly complex processing requirements, which can result in poor quality, increased lead times, and more complex scheduling requirements. A number of companies have realized that competitiveness would require an integration of product design and process planning into one activity. This implies the identification, *during the early part of the design phase*, of product concepts that are inherently easy to manufacture. The requirements and constraints imposed by machining, assembly and materials handling need to be included as part of a functional optimisation of the design process. This resulted in the emergence of the concept of Design for Manufacture (DFM), which involves an iterative process of the type shown in Figure 2.11.

Whereas the traditional design cycle starts with the optimisation of the product design itself, followed by the detailed design of each component prior to the planning of individual processes, the DFM approach starts with a simultaneous conceptual optimisation of both product *and* process. This is refined in a series of iterative subtasks concerned with simplification (eg, designing components for ease of

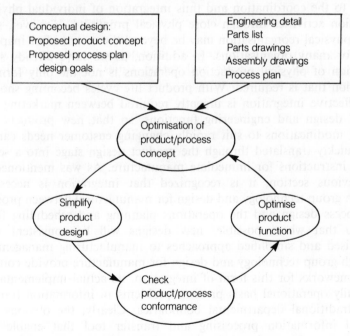

Figure 2.11 Design for manufacture — continuous optimisation of product and process.

assembly and handling), conformance of design to processing needs and constraints, and functional optimisation which considers the choice of materials and parameters to maximise the design objectives.

A number of specific conceptual methodologies have been developed to implement the concept of Design for Manufacture. The Design For Assembly (DFA) method developed by Boothroyd and Dewhurst (1983), seeks to minimise costs of assembly within the constraints of other design requirements. The Taguchi method (Taguchi, 1986) is concerned with producing robust designs using statistical experimentation, and based on a so-called loss function, which is a measure of the loss experienced either to the customer or the company in deviations of parameter values from the design intent. These and similar methods require the close integration of different types of knowledge normally the province of different functional departments. The role of the computer in achieving this integration will be seen during the course of this book.

2.5 The Quest for Computer Integration

The division of a manufacturing organisation into a number of autonomous, focussed subunits with simplified material flow patterns provided the key to the coordination and thus integration of individual physical production activities through close physical proximity. However, such drastic physical reorganisation may be beyond the means of or inappropriate for many organisations. In addition, as we have already seen, integration of physical production operations is not the only form of integration that is required. With product life cycles becoming shorter, more effective integration is urgently required between marketing and product design and engineering functions, so that new products and product modifications to suit rapidly changing customer needs can be more quickly translated through the product design stage into a set of process instructions for immediate manufacture. As was mentioned in the previous section, it is recognized that integration is necessary (through group technology and design for manufacture) between product and process design and the operations planning and scheduling function, so that where possible, new designs will be consistent with rationalised and simplified approaches to manufacturing management. Although group technology and design for manufacture provide conceptual frameworks for this form of integration, its actual implementation on a daily operational basis presents problems in information transfer across traditional departmental boundaries. Clearly, the obvious and essential information processing and transfer tool that enable this integration to be achieved is the computer. Hence the concept of 'Computer Integrated Manufacturing' (CIM), a term originally attributed to Joseph Harrington Jr. in his book of the same name (Harrington, 1973), has became an increasingly discussed topic throughout the 1980s.

2.5.1 The COPICS concept

As early as the beginning of the 1970s, IBM had published a conceptual framework for an approach to computer-based integrated manufacturing control which they called COPICS (Communications Oriented Production Information and Control System). COPICS was not a software package. It merely provided a detailed view of the data flow and functional integration required between the eight functional areas that had already been defined in the PICS system. Cross functional communication and a common central database were important features of the COPICS system as indicated in one of the diagrams from the COPICS document reproduced in Figure 2.12. The importance of the master production schedule and feedback from capacity planning was also stressed in this schema.

The COPICS concept coincided with the proliferation of interest in MRP systems and the MRP 'crusade' of the mid 1970s. As MRP evolved into MRP2, an increasing number of the functional areas defined by COPICS were incorporated, albeit with a limited degree of success in

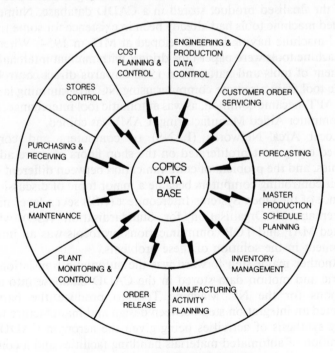

Figure 2.12 The COPICS concept.

terms of the achievement of any significant improvements in manufacturing performance. However, the failures were put down by MRP advocates to an overly narrow, technical view, and an insufficient degree of integration of the material requirements planning with the other functions (see for example Wight, 1981).

2.5.2   The computer integration of design and manufacture

A notable omission from the leading MRP2 systems was the integration of design, process planning, and numerical process control with the other functions. MRP2 systems were oriented towards operations planning and control with a fixed set of products and processes, rather than towards providing facilities for the continual introduction of new products and processes.

In fact, the individual functions of product design, process planning and automatic process control were receiving independent attention as the rapid proliferation of microcomputers in the 1980s brought increasing degrees of automation or computer assistance to these tasks. Computer Aided Design and Drafting (CADD) systems enabled product designs to be interactively conceptualised on screen, analysed in terms of such techniques as Finite Element Analysis, and the resulting geometric and motion data of the finalised product stored in a CADD database. Numerically-controlled machine tools had already been in existence for some time, the first NC machine having been developed at MIT in 1954. Whereas the early machine tools were paper tape driven, with manual interchange and adjustment of tools and parts, from 1970 onwards direct control of the machine tool from a remote computer using NC programming languages such as APT, became common, as was automatic tool interchange, and the term Computer Aided Manufacturing (CAM) was coined.

Local Area Networks (LANS) of computers and computer-controlled equipment proliferated on the shop floors of more advanced companies, and the problem of communication between different devices and their controlling computers became a major topic of discussion. The emergence of the Open Systems Interconnect (OSI) seven layer model of the International Organisation for Standardisation (ISO) with the associated MAP and TOP communications protocols was an important development in the solution of these problems.

Another major step forward was the automatic translation of the geometric and motion data stored in the CADD database into a set of instructions for the NC Machine Tool to produce the part. This represented an integration step between design and manufacture with the resulting synthesis of activities being given the acronym CADD/CAM. The addition of automated materials handling facilities and a computer-based hierarchical control system lead to the formation of the Flexible

Manufacturing System in which part designs were automatically translated into computer instructions for an NC Machine, the appropriate raw materials were automatically retrieved from storage, machined and returned to store.

To many people, the flexible manufacturing system became the embodiment of the concept of computer integrated manufacturing. However, in the context of the overall operation, this type of integration really only represented a very limited subset of the type of company wide computer integration that was the conceptual ideal of writers such as Joseph Harrington Jr. For example, the integration of machining and assembly operations, of design and marketing, physical production and planned requirements, process planning and production scheduling were all areas in which little progress was made. The term 'islands of automation' was coined to describe the highly efficient automated functions such as machining, and assembly, whose potential could not be realised because they required manual interfacing to each other and to the remainder of the organisation.

2.5.3 Islands of integration

The 'islands of automation' syndrome caused the precise nature of the term 'integration' to come under increasing debate. Investigations of the varying states of integration that typically existed in different manufacturing companies lead Miller, Rosenthal and Vollman (1986) to classify three different types of integration which they termed **technical** integration, **procedural** integration, and **goal** integration.

Technical integration involves the act of establishing physical communication (i.e., data coding, transmission and interpretation) between different functional areas.

Procedural integration occurs when different functional areas using common data have a consistent view of the interpretation of that data and thus can operate on the data with appropriate procedures that are in line with its meaning.

Goal integration occurs when the same information is used by different functional areas to achieve common goals.

Miller, Rosenthal and Vollman asserted that at least the first two, and depending on the organisational context perhaps the third, type of integration must be established before an integrated manufacturing system can be said to exist. Thus the establishment of physical communication channels and protocols between a CADD system and an NC machine tool does not mean integration of the two functions unless common data structures exist which are consistently interpreted by each. The design function cannot be said to be integrated with the marketing function unless common goals are established concerning reasonable trade-offs between such things as cost and quality, and satisfactory communication links exist between them.

Whereas in the second half of the 1980s technical integration problems were rapidly diminishing with the emergence of MAP and TOP protocols as increasingly accepted standards, procedural and goal integration provided a much more intractable set of problems. Independent computerisation of separate functional areas usually resulted in incompatible data structures in each area so that the meaning and significance of the data became distorted on transfer. The rigid divisions and lack of communication that frequently existed between functional areas also meant that goal integration problems were prevalent.

Miller *et al* also provided some empirical data in their study on the progress of a sample of 264 American companies in the extent of integration achieved at the time of the survey (1984). The study indicated the common existence of five islands of integration or areas within which the majority of companies had made progress in integrating the individual functional activities. These islands were classified as financial reporting, inventory status, sales and market planning, manufacturing engineering, and quality control (Figure 2.13). The 'bridges' between the islands represent the major efforts that were underway in order to integrate these islands.

Integration of activities within the inventory control island correspond quite closely to the integration aimed for by MRP packages. MRP2 clearly represents an attempt to integrate the financial reporting, inventory status and strategic planning islands. However, they found that, unlike the broad and comprehensive notion of integration conceptualised by Harrington, or by the COPICS picture, actual efforts were somewhat disjointed and incremental. This lead them to conclude that 'CIM is far into the future'.

2.5.4 Enterprise integration based on information technology

Whereas to the manufacturing engineer, integrated manufacturing meant the integration of CADD and CAM, and to the shop floor it meant a communications and interfacing exercise, to management, true integration was more concerned with a global information systems concept in which *all* parts of the organisation base their operations on common and current data in a shared database. This is basically a re-affirmation of the original COPICS concept. Shared data has been called the integration 'glue' that binds the system together and allows it to operate as a coordinated whole. Integation on an **enterprise** level rather than on a narrow technology level confined to the shop floor or drawing office, is the objective of the information systems view of integration.

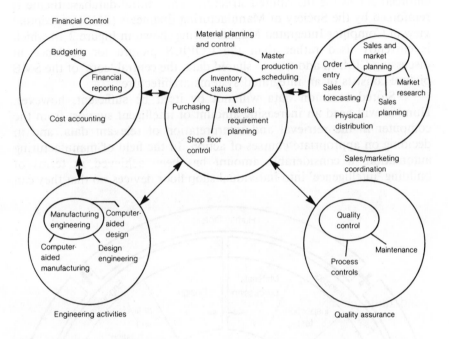

Figure 2.13 Islands of integration.

Database and information systems technology therefore have a crucial role to play in modern manufacturing management. Relational databases which allow flexible, ad hoc retrieval of data using powerful query languages will be a very important part of this technology. Rigorous and consistent structuring of data that describe products and the flow of associated product data through the various stages of the manufacturing process from design to final shipment can potentially allow anyone within the organisation to access the particular items of data they require for their decision making. Currently, most individual functions of a manufacturing organisation maintain their own private databases. Rather than dispense with these separate databases in favour of a single common database, it is possible that individual databases will be retained, but given a common, relational form (see Melkannof, 1984).

The resulting 'distributed' relational database could then perform the same integrating function as a single central database, provided that integrity constraints ensuring the consistency of the data are effectively enforced across the distributed structure. The central database theme is reinforced by the Society of Manufacturing Engineers (SME) conceptual view of Computer Integrated Manufacturing shown in Figure 2.14 which is currently used rather than the COPICS picture for guidance in discussing CIM. In addition to shared data, the central 'core' of the SME picture consists of an integrated systems architecture.

Stored common data will not by itself be sufficient, however. Humans will need an increasing amount of intelligent support from the computer in the retrieval and interpretation of relevant data, and in deciding on appropriate courses of action. In the field of manufacturing automation, a considerable amount has been achieved in terms of building 'intelligence' into individual shop floor devices, so that they can

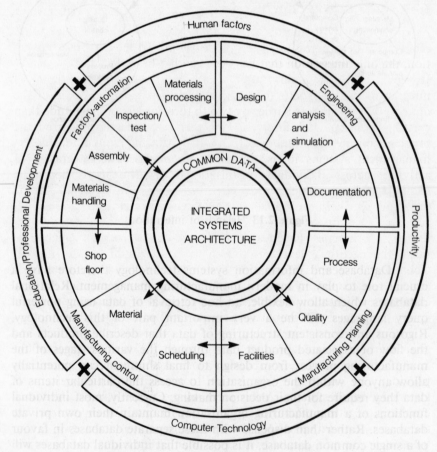

Figure 2.14 The SME view of CIM.

perform a flexible range of operational tasks such as materials handling, machining, assembly and inspection with minimal human intervention (see Wright and Bourne, 1988). The next logical stage is to build in distributed intelligence at higher levels of the enterprise, by capturing and structuring the knowledge employed by humans in making technical and operating decisions at higher levels of abstraction, and incorporating this into knowledge bases. In the same way that distributed databases of consistently structured and current data can contribute to integration by the provision of common data for decision making, distributed knowledge bases can contribute to integration by performing automatic inferences over this data, alerting appropriate parts of the organisation to data patterns which require investigation, and working out and recommending options for current or future action.

2.5.5 Barriers to integration

As discovered by a number of researchers, among them Miller *et al*, relatively little progress has been made towards true enterprise integration; the only integration that has occurred has been confined to islands. It seems that the main problems are in linking these islands of integration. Many experts (e.g., Davis and Goedhart, 1987) are of the opinion that this task is harder by two to three orders of magnitude than creating the islands themselves. This seems to stem largely from the problems of integrating modern technology with the often old-fashioned management systems in use in many companies. The integration of activities across individual organisational departments is becoming technologically possible, but is not occurring, mainly due to people problems. Furthermore, rather short-sighted financial justification criteria based on short term outlook rather than strategic benefits and long term competitiveness have lead many companies to become reluctant to make the necessary level of investment and commitment, either in technology or people. Davis and Goedhart state: '. . . the challenges to effective integrated systems today lie more in the domain of the organisational behaviourist and the management scientist, than the systems technologist, computer scientist, or software specialist.'

One way to surmount these problems is through a synthesis of the simplification/rationalisation approach offered by Group Technology and Just-in-Time production, combined with the integrating technology provided by relational databases, comunication protocols, and knowledge-based systems. A key focus of the future will be a renewed emphasis on getting the basics right first: by reorganising and simplifying the manufacturing scenario (which will involve solving many of the 'people' problems associated with functional integration) *prior* to laying the technology on top of the process. A case study of how this type of approach is being used in the 3M corporation has been documented by Butcher (1987). The renewed emphasis on and understanding of basic manufacturing principles associated with the rationalisation process provides an excellent opportunity to systematise and document much of this understanding in the form of knowledge bases that will contribute further to the integration process. The remainder of this book is concerned with a detailed examination of this approach, and some of the key underlying technologies.

Chapter 3
Manufacturing Organisations as Systems

3.1 Brief synopsis of the systems approach

3.2 Systemic models of manufacturing organisations

3.3 Organisation for changing environments

In the previous chapter we saw how the linking of manufacturing functions through the physical interfacing of the various 'islands' of automation has mostly failed to provide true integration in the sense of a genuine and close coordination of different activities towards a common set of goals. In many cases, this can be attributed to the narrow and overly technical perspective of integration being taken by those tasked with its implementation. The purely technical problems of integration have mostly been solved, in the sense that interfaces have been developed to allow different islands to share data and exchange messages. It is the organisational and conceptual problems associated with integration which have emerged as the main barriers to further progress. However, these types of problem are neither new, nor unique to the field of integrated manufacturing.

Issues of coordination and integration of different organisational activities have been studied over a number of years within the wider context of **systems** thinking, which has been comprehensively described by writers such as Ackoff and Emery (1972), Beer (1966, 1979) and Churchman (1971). Systems thinking leads to a contrasting view of the problems of coordination and control within organisations to that generated by machine age thinking, as exemplified in the theories of Taylor and the philosophy of reductionism. It is the latter that has encouraged the growth of the specialisms that we have so much difficulty in integrating.

Because of the key importance of systems thinking in understanding these issues, this chapter provides a brief overview of the systems approach and its relevance to manufacturing management.

3.1   Brief synopsis of the systems approach

3.1.1   General characteristics of a system

The conventional definition of a system is 'a collection of entities which are connected in some way to form a unified and coherent whole'. Thus, a system is not a randomly assembled set of elements but consists of elements that can be identified as belonging together because of some common purpose or goal.

A system is characterised in terms of an input, a process, and an output (Figure 3.1). Inputs to a system may consist of materials, money, energy, humans, information or a mixture of these, and are the start-up force that provide the system with its operating necessities. The **process** transforms inputs to outputs, and may be a machine, a human, a computer, tasks performed by members of an organisation, etc. The features which define and delineate a system form its **boundary**. The system is that which lies inside the boundary, and the environment of the system is that which lies outside the boundary. In some cases it can be difficult to decide what is inside and what is outside a system boundary. For example, suppliers of raw materials who are very closely coordinated with a particular manufacturing company may for some purposes be regarded as part of the system of the manufacturing company, and for other purposes as part of the environment of that system.

A process which is designed by humans and is fully understood in detail (for example a machining process) is often termed a **clear box**. If the inputs and outputs are fully defined but the process is not (as in the case of a group of people producing creative solutions to a problem) the process is termed a **black box** (Figure 3.2). The process of one system may be a black box from the point of view of another system. For example, machining processes are black boxes from the point of view of production control, which is only concerned with the inputs and outputs.

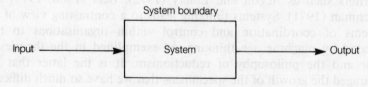

Figure 3.1 A simple system.

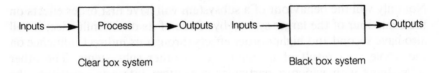

Figure 3.2   Clear and black box systems.

3.1.2 Subsystems

A system is composed of subsystems, and may in turn be part of a larger system. For example, machines, operators and work-in-progress may be regarded as subsystems of a particular production department. This in turn may be a subsystem of a manufacturing division, which is a subsystem of a manufacturing company. The company itself is a subsystem of the industry in general. This nesting of systems within systems forms a **hierarchy** (Figure 3.3) The precise definition of which subsystems are members of a given system and which are not is subjective, and depends on the context in which the system is being defined. It is clearly possible for a system to be a member of more than one larger system, as in the case of the company employee who is also a member of the local football club.

3.1.3 Subsystem interactions

Subsystems of a larger system generally interact with each other. A change occurring in one subsystem will affect the other subsystems in some way. Thus, subsystems cannot generally be analysed in isolation, but must be considered in relation to each other as well as to the whole.

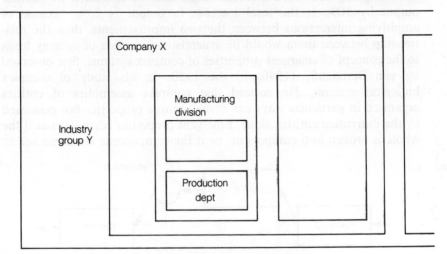

Figure 3.3   Contained systems.

Not only will the behaviour of a subsystem will have first order effects on the behaviour of the larger system by virtue of its direct influence; it will also have second and higher order effects through its indirect influence on the whole as a result of its influence on other subsystems. The other subsystems with which a particular subsystem interacts constitute the **environment** of that subsystem.

The interconnections and interactions between subsystems are called **interfaces**. These occur at the boundaries between two systems, when part or all of the output of one subsystem becomes part or all of the input to another subsystem (Figure 3.4). When the output of one subsystem provides the input to another subsystem, it will often be necessary to standardise it in some form that will be acceptable to the receiving system. Parts produced as a result of one production process must meet a certain set of specifications before they can be accepted by another production process. Information generated by one organisational department may have to be presented in a certain way before it is comprehensible to another department. It is sometimes necessary to interpose an additional subsystem to act as a 'transducer' between two interacting systems to ensure compatibility of their inputs and outputs.

Interactions or relationships between subsystems can be of several types. A **symbiotic** relationship between two subsystems exists when they are dependent on each other for their existence (e.g., the production and sales subsystems of a manufacturing company). A **synergistic** relationship between two subsystems exists when the cooperative action of the two subsystems produces a total output which is greater than the sum of their outputs taken independently. For example, buying a new machine might be estimated to increase the output of a process by 10% and designing new work methods might also be estimated to increase output by 10%. If the total increase in output is 25%, because of amplifying interactions between the two improvements, then the relationship between them would be synergistic. The idea of synergy leads to the concept of **emergent** properties of complex systems, first observed by von Bertalanffy (1940) in the 1920s in his study of complex biological systems. He noticed that complex assemblies of entities organised in particular ways can reveal unique properties not possessed by the individual entities alone. Emergent properties cease to exist if the whole is broken into components or if the components are organised in

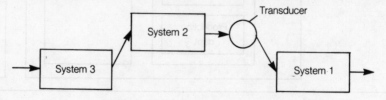

Figure 3.4 System communication.

a different way. Thus, emergent properties cannot be understood by study of the components in isolation.

3.1.4 Factoring of subsystems

In order to understand the processes by which a system converts its inputs to outputs (i.e., to change one's perception of a system from a black box to a clear box) it is usually necessary to factor the system out into its constituent subsystems to examine their behaviour and interactions. These are factored out further, as a recursive activity, until a set of systems is obtained whose processes are understandable without further factoring. The subsystems resulting from this factoring process generally form hierarchical structures as shown in Figure 3.5.

The boundaries and interfaces between subsystems need to be clearly defined. Each subsystem needs to be specified in terms of its inputs and outputs and the other subsystems which generate or receive them. If all subsystems interconnected with each other, a very large number of such interfaces would need to be defined, the number of interconnections in general being $(n(n-1))/2$ where n is the number of subsystems. In general, however, not all subsystems interconnect, and various methods of systems design are available to minimise the number of interconnections that are necessary.

3.1.5 Simplification of subsystem interactions

There are a number of methods for simplifying subsystem interactions. These are as follows:

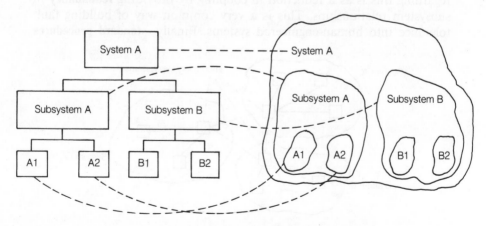

Figure 3.5 Hierarchical structuring of systems.

(1)   By forming clusters of subsystems which interact with each other through an interfacing system that looks after the interactions. Interactions between clusters are guided by interactions between the respective interfacing systems (Figure 3.6). Hierarchical organisations tend to structure interactions between their subsystems in this way. The interfacing system is the manager of a department whose job is to handle the interactions between departmental members by insisting that they only communicate through him, and by representing his department in interactions with other departments.

(2)   By decoupling subsystems to make detailed interaction analysis unnecessary. This is often done in cases where, to produce synergy, a very tight degree of coordination between two systems is required, but the continued existence of the subsystems as separate entities makes this difficult to achieve. Decoupling of subsystems may be achieved by the use of **buffers**, **slack resources**, or **standard procedures**.

Examples of these three types of decoupling are shown in Figure 3.7.

An example of the use of **buffers** is where inventory is used to decouple the components of a multi-stage production system. These are difficult to coordinate with respect to materials flow because of random events which impede effective synchronisation of output availability from one stage with input requirements at the next stage. The buffer stocks may themselves be regarded as **decoupling systems**. An example of the use of **slack resources** is where excess machine capacity is available in a multi-stage production process, so that if a machine breaks down and threatens the timely arrival of materials at the subsequent process, a parallel backup machine can be brought into action. Another way of regarding this is as a reduction in coupling by providing **redundancy** in subsystem relationships. This is a very common way of building fault tolerance into human-engineered systems. Finally, **standard procedures**

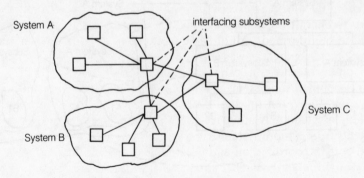

Figure 3.6 Clustering of subsystems.

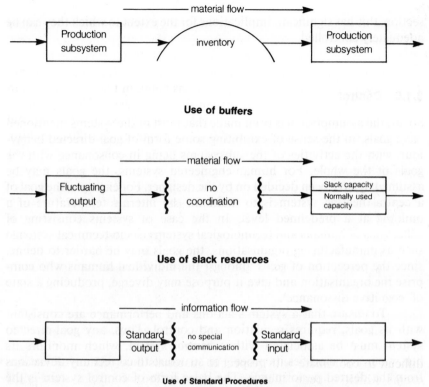

Figure 3.7 Methods of decoupling subsystems.

can enforce greater predictability on the behaviour of a subsystem, and thereby simplify the nature of its interaction with other systems. For example, a set of process instructions prepared by manufacturing engineering may need to be in a prescribed format so as to be easily intelligible to production, and to eliminate any sources of ambiguity or misunderstanding. The various decoupling methods described here can reduce the need for communication between subsystems, and allow them to communicate on an exception basis only (i.e., only when one subsystem starts to operate outside a set of prescribed limits do the other subsystems need to be informed). All of these methods have been used in manufacturing management, as was shown in the previous chapter. However, the decoupling mechanisms can themselves be expensive. Another problem is that decoupled subsystems acting independently may perform their own tasks optimally, but the sum of their actions may not be optimal for the system as a whole. A move to tighter coupling between subsystems gives benefits from a more system-wide optimisation of tasks, but at potentially high cost in coordination and communication. Perhaps the most significant impediment to the effective performance of tightly coupled systems is the enormous complexity they can exhibit. As will be seen in the next section, this has significant implications for the extent to which they can be adequately controlled.

3.1.6 Control

So far, the assumption has been made that most of the systems mentioned have goals, in the sense of exhibiting some form of goal-directed behaviour, with the activities of the subsystems being in consonance with the goals of the whole. For human-engineered systems, the goals may be assumed to have been decided on by the designer. For example, the goal of a central heating system is to maintain the internal temperature of a building at a predefined level. In the case of systems consisting of collections of humans and technological systems (socio-technical systems) such as manufacturing organisations, the goals may be harder to define, since the perception of goals amongst the individual humans who comprise the organisation and give it purpose may diverge, producing a state of 'cognitive dissonance'.

To ensure that a system's actions and performance are consistent with its goals, requires regulation and control. Thus, any goal-directed system must be associated with a **control system**, which monitors its behaviour and modifies its process or structure to correct any deviations from the desired performance. The basic form of control system is the closed loop feedback system, shown in Figure 3.8.

This forms one of the building blocks of the subject of Cybernetics, which was initiated by Norbert Wiener in the 1940s and is concerned

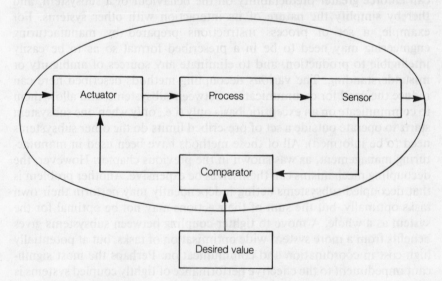

Figure 3.8 A simple closed loop feedback system.

with the study of feedback and control in systems. The components of a closed loop system are a sensor to measure the current state of affairs, a comparator to measure any discrepancy between the current state and the desired state, and an actuator to respond to the discrepancy. This simple loop is used in control engineering, in a negative feedback sense, as the basis for such things as achieving stability of output of a device given a variable input, by feeding the output signal back to control the way in which the device responds to the input.

There can be confusion about the separability of the control system from the system being controlled. In control engineering, the process being controlled is usually a physical process, whereas the control process itself is an **informational** process (i.e., its inputs and outputs both consist of information rather than material or energy). The control system is thereby separated from the physical system. In a manufacturing organisation, the basic flow of materials, operation of machines, etc. are physical processes, with inputs and outputs consisting of energy and matter. Control of these physical processes is achieved by separate control systems which process information, and these may be either humans or computers. These control systems can themselves be subject to control. Since humans (and also computers) are capable of monitoring their own actions and changing their own behaviour, they are often regarded as 'self-controlling' systems. No distinction is made in this case between the controller and the system itself. Only when control is exercised at a higher systemic level (e.g., by a foreman over a machine operator) is a distinction usually made, although this can have the effect of blurring some important control issues, as will be seen in the next section.

All control processes in the manufacturing operation (from control of physical operations upwards) process information. Since these control systems are the subsystems of the organisation, it follows that all organisational subsystems, with the exception of the basic indivisible physical manufacturing processes themselves, are concerned exclusively with the processing of information.

3.1.7 Orders of feedback

The closed loop feedback system shown in Figure 3.8 is a feedback system of the **first order**, since the system is monitored against a single external goal and there is no choice available to the system other than to correct the deviation from that goal, irrespective of changes in the environment. For example, in the case of a thermostat, a thermal equilibrium is maintained, regardless of external weather conditions.

If a system can initiate alternative courses of action in response to changed external conditions, and can choose the best alternative for a given set of conditions, it is said to be a feedback system of the **second**

order. The systems must be able to make a choice, in a given set of environmental conditions, whether to reduce the difference between the current goal, or change the goal, which implies having a goal of a higher order and being capable of monitoring, in an additional feedback loop, the progress towards this higher order goal, and making a decision. This is shown in Figure 3.9.

If a system is capable of changing its goals by reflecting on past experiences, it is called a feedback system of the **third order**. This implies ability to redesign the types of feedback it receives according to their success in guiding the system towards higher order goals, and therefore represents a **learning** ability. This type of feedback system is shown in Figure 3.10.

Second and third order feedback are associated with systems that are capable of proactive as well as reactive decision making. Such systems can **plan** alternative methods of reaching their goals, by simulating various alternative sequences of actions, and choosing the most appropriate. Any form of manufacturing planning and control system involves notions of second and third order feedback.

3.1.8 The law of requisite variety

Problems can arise with control as the complexity of a system, and the environment in which it operates, increase. The cybernetician Ross Ashby pointed out in 1958 that in order to achieve effective control of a system, the control mechanism itself must be capable of matching the complexity (or variety) of the system being controlled. Ashby defined

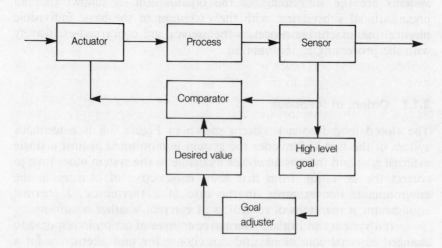

Figure 3.9 Second-order feedback.

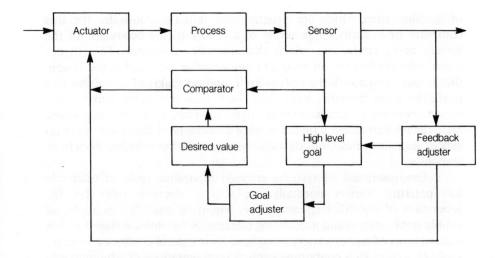

Figure 3.10 Third-order feedback.

variety as 'the number of different discriminable states a system can exist in' and stated his conclusion as the 'law of requisite variety'. A controller possessing requisite variety must in principle be capable of (a) discriminating every possible state of the system, and (b) generating an appropriate control response for each state.

For example, if we have a stock control system of 1000 different types of unit, the number of possible states in the system would be all the possible combinations of stock levels for every unit. Any controller designed to regulate this system fully would need to be capable of discriminating each of these states and reacting appropriately.

In a very complex system, with many subsystems and many possible interactions between them, the number of possible states that the system can take up can be vast. Many states, however, will not require corrective action and much of the data potentially available about each state will be irrelevant to the control action to be taken, or will contain more detail than is required. Thus the control system would normally contain a set of attenuators which filter, condense or otherwise reduce the data describing the system to that currently relevant to its control. In the inventory example, the inventory manager might have stock levels stored in a database with retrieval functions enabling selective viewing of items near or below some preset reorder point. He would not need any information about the other items.

Likewise, in terms of control responses, the controller must either possess either a set of *explicitly* stored control responses for each system state, or the capability of *generating* a response for each state. Control systems in organisations usually rely on the latter, either in terms of a set of decision rules which are programmed into the controller (be this computer or human), or in terms of a theory of the behaviour of the system being controlled, which the controller possesses. This theory would take the form of an abstract **representation** or model of the system that is isomorphic with the system itself, and is capable of explaining any deviation from intended behaviour, how such deviations can be corrected, and how system behaviour can be modified to achieve new goals. Such theories represent a higher level of knowledge of the system than do sets of decision rules, and are capable of generating a higher variety of responses.

Organisational subsystems engaged in routine tasks of relatively low potential variety normally use sets of decision rules for the generation of control responses. This would be true, for example, of simple stock control and accounting systems. Subsystems engaged in less routine tasks of higher variety must base their control responses on more sophisticated models containing explicit representations of structural and causal relationships within the system, and between the system and its environment, which allow complex chains of reasoning to occur. It is important to realise, however, that the controller is basing its behaviour on its **model** of the system. A controller cannot regulate anything more complex than the real world projection of the model it contains. One must remember that 'as soon as the system to be regulated adopts a state not allowed for in the model embraced by the controller, regulation fails' (Beer 1979).

3.2 Systemic models of manufacturing organisations

3.2.1 Functional organisation

Traditional manufacturing organisation has been based on the assumed efficiency of the division of labour. This relies on the identification of specialised resources (functional task areas), and the structuring of the organisation around the tasks performed by these resources. Thus, each group of specialised resources becomes a subsystem of the organisation. This results in the typical arrangement shown in Figure 3.11.

The problem with such an arrangement is that it involves a high degree of interaction between individual subsystems. The interactions required, together with some rough indication of their relative strengths, are shown on the diagram. Because of the number and complexity of these interactions, and consequently the enormous variety capable of being generated by the system, any attempt at centralised control, based on a single unified model of the system held by any central management group, is highly problematical. The way in which this

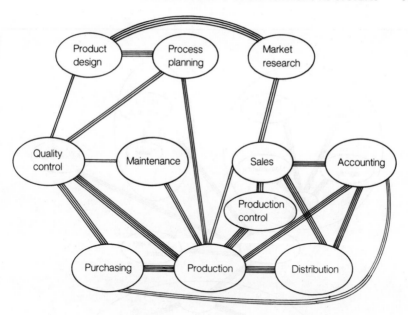

Figure 3.11   Subsystems of a manufacturing organisation.

problem has traditionally been tackled is to attempt to reduce variety by standardisation. In relatively simple and stable manufacturing environments, (e.g., the repetitive production of cars on an assembly line), a simple way of coordinating subtasks is to specify a set of standard operating procedures to be followed by each subsystem. This effectively removes the necessity for a high degree of communication between subsystems, since the operating procedures themselves are designed in such a way as to integrate individual activities. Operating groups need have no skills other than those required to implement these standard procedures. The residual coordination required is implemented through a clearly defined hierarchical authority structure, in which specialised control subsystems (managers) are set up to coordinate the individual components of individual subsystems, and a restriction is placed on inter-system links, so that subsystems can only communicate with their controlling system (Figure 3.12).

This reduces the number of inter-system links, and hence the potential variety of the system. A manufacturing company relying on this method of coordination will have a strongly mechanistic flavour. Its intended mode of operation will have much in common with mechanical systems. However, this method will only succeed in environments where nearly all possible events and contingencies can be anticipated in advance and rules and procedures provided which cater for them.

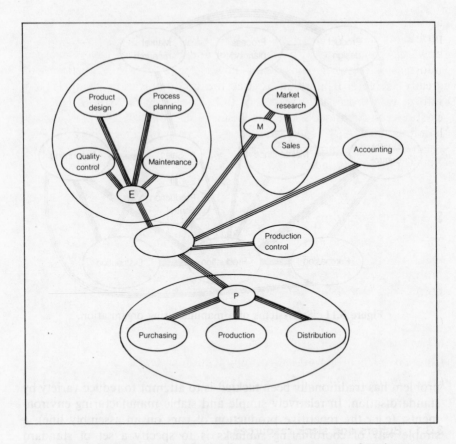

Figure 3-12 Grouping of manufacturing subsystems by function.

3.2.2 The effect of unstable environments on functional organisation

As situations occur that have not been experienced before and are not covered by standard procedures (e.g., a sudden increase in orders for a particular model that exceed production capacity) a set of contingency procedures must be developed which take into account how all the individual subsystems will be affected and will respond to the unexpected situation (e.g., should orders be delayed, extra capacity be obtained, or can alternative processes or subcontracting be used?). These procedures will usually require coordination between subsystems, and must therefore be performed by the controlling subsystem (the manager).

An increase in the unpredictability and uncertainty of the environment will result in more situations occurring which have no precedent and therefore have no rules or procedures to cater for them. A proliferation of variety results. These situations must all be referred upwards to managers at a higher level and this in turn means that the information between subsystems flowing in a vertical direction will greatly increase. The result is that the communication channels and information processing capacity of subsystems become overloaded, and existing control models become insufficient in terms of their variety handling capability. Increasing delays start to happen between the occurrence of the problem and its resolution, and resolutions are often suboptimal due to lack of requisite variety in the control models.

3.3   Organisation for changing environments

The increasing instability of the manufacturing environment has meant that, since the early 1970s, many companies have experienced a proliferation of the type of problem mentioned above. Galbraith (1973) proposed a number of solutions to this problem, namely:

(1)   Creation of buffers or slack resources.
(2)   Creation of independent tasks.
(3)   Investment in vertical communication systems.
(4)   Investment in lateral communication systems.

3.3.1   Buffers and slack resources

The creation of buffers or slack resources is the alternative that tends to be adopted by default, in the absence of any other active response. This frequently takes the form of time buffers in which the time taken for the organisation to respond to any situation is lengthened. Poor coordination in materials flow leads to a build up of interprocess stocks which themselves act as buffers, reducing the need for such coordination. Eventually, the buffers themselves may become formalised in a set of decoupling subsystems with their own control mechanisms. Inventory control systems are basically performing this function, as are MRP systems which allow time buffers in the form of planning lead times which are considerably longer than the physical production time.

3.3.2   Self-contained tasks

The creation of self-contained tasks represents a different form of partitioning of the total manufacturing system into subsystems in such a way that interactions between subsystems are reduced. This can be achieved by creating subsystems based on common **objectives** rather than a common **function**, as shown in Figure 3.13. Subsystems which group together the different skills and resources required to manufacture individual product groups will require much less coordination with each other, than will subsystems based on function. In the production area, self-contained tasks may take the form of group-technology based manufacturing cells at the shop floor level, and product divisions at the corporate level. The creation of self-contained tasks implies a greater degree of distribution of control to subsystems themselves rather than imposing it from above. Rather than having control centralised at the apex of the organisation, each subsystem is responsible for its own control and has a considerable degree of autonomy. Thus, individual subsystems will require their own control models which are high variety with respect to their own internal operations. As a result, since they have ownership of the model, they can be much more adaptive to local problems and contingencies than if the model were part of a centralised control system based on company-wide standardisation.

3.3.3 Investment in vertical communication systems

The third alternative suggested by Galbraith is an increase in information processing capacity. Increased vertical information processing capacity has been used to support functional organisational divisions. For example, in many manufacturing companies centralised MRP systems are basically concerned with coordination between functional subsystems by vertical information transfer.

The method of hierarchical planning has been introduced as an additional means of coordinating functional areas, and devolving more responsibilty for self-control to functional subunits. Hierarchical planning involves a succession of plans at progressively more detailed levels of decomposition, each of which places a set of constraints on plans at the lower level. A typical hierarchical planning approach given by Anthony (1965), and still commonly quoted, divides planning into the strategic, or long range level, the tactical planning or intermediate range level, and the operational control or short range level (Figure 3.14).

At the **long range** level, an aggregate plan might be made for the entire plant over a year or more, to coordinate purchasing, production, sales and engineering through the development of an aggregate Master Production Schedule to meet forecast demand for product groups. This will establish purchasing policies for long lead time or bulk raw materials, establish any major product or process modifications that will become effective over this period, and establish aggregate production resource capacity levels and target inventory levels to meet the plan. This will be decomposed at the **intermediate range** level to a set of tactical

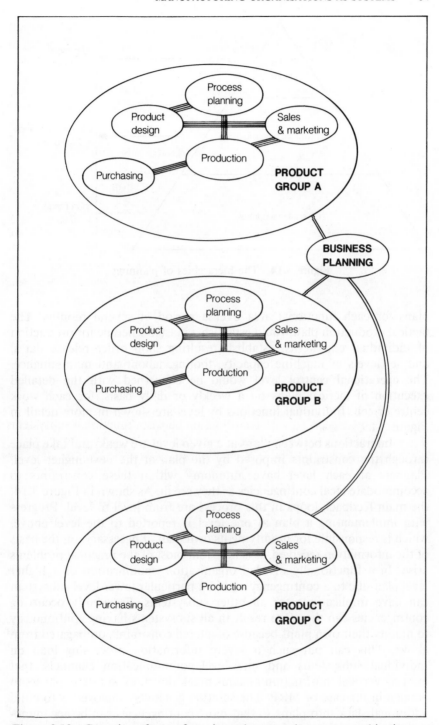

Figure 3.13 Grouping of manufacturing subsystems by common objectives.

Figure 3.14   The hierarchies of planning.

plans for each functional area over a period of several months. The tactical production plan would establish a master schedule for production of individual end items, establish resulting shop order release dates, and set levels of machine capacity, tooling, labour and maintainance. The **operational control** level would be concerned with the detailed execution of tactical plans on a weekly or daily basis, for each work centre or cell. Individual functions by level are shown in more detail in Figure 3.15.

Interactions between plans at a given level are weak, and take place through the constraints imposed by the plan at the next higher level. Planners at each level have autonomy within these constraints to accommodate local contingencies as they see fit. As shown in Figure 3.14, the main feedback loops in this process are from level to level. Progress with implementing a plan at one level is reported to the level above, which is responsible for modifying its own plan, if necessary, on the basis of the information received. It is here that most of the practical problems arise. In a functionally divided organisation, modification of a higher level plan due to a contingency within a particular lower-level subsystem can have implications for all other subsystems. Frequently occurring contingencies can therefore result in all subsystems having continuously to modify their own plans because of altered constraints propagated from above. This can put such a severe information processing load on individual subsystems and inter-level communication channels, that existing vertical information systems break down, as so often appears to happen in the case of MRP. The solution generally employed is to build additional slack into plans so that more contingencies can be accommodated at a given level before necessitating replanning at the higher level.

Planning level	Functions
Strategic planning	Product design
	Aggregate resource management
	Aggregate forecasting
	New product planning
	Long lead time ordering
	Manufacturing engineering
	Systems design
Tactical planning	Master production scheduling
	Due-date setting
	Requirements planning
	Capacity planning
	Purchasing
	Aggregate inventory management
	Preventative maintenance planning
Operational control	Shop order release
	Shop floor scheduling
	Dispatching
	Receiving
	Capacity control
	Tool control
	Inventory control
	Diagnostic maintenance
	Quality control
	Cost control

Figure 3.15 Planning and control functions by level.

3.3.4 Investment in lateral communication systems

Lateral communication systems can be used as an alternative method to resolve the effects of such contingencies. These often take the form of informal relationships between subsystems (for example, the insidious informal system that often runs in parallel with formal MRP systems). These can cause difficulties when used in conjunction with formal hierarchical planning based on a vertical information system, if they result in actions of which the formal system is not aware. Provision for formalised lateral communication is not generally provided as part of a vertically oriented information system. Conceptually, the task of lateral coordination could be assigned to a subsystem whose sole task would be to maintain the area of overlap of two interacting subsystems by mediating between them. This concept is demonstrated in the use of product managers, or task forces in a 'matrix management' framework.

3.3.5 Synthesis of approaches

None of the techniques suggesed by Galbraith are mutually exclusive, and it seems that current trends may be in favour of a combination of all four, employed at different levels of the organisation. Partitioning of a manufacturing operation into self-contained, mission-oriented subsystems is clearly finding increasing favour, as shown by the increasing tendency of companies to reorganise themselves on a product basis, making use of focused factories and group technology oriented layouts. The weak interactions between such subsystems, being of relatively low variety, could be handled by lateral communication through further subsystems specially designed for that purpose. The individual product-oriented subsystems would at some level have to decompose to individual functions (e.g., sequential production processes) requiring tight coordination. However, close physical proximity and simplified work flow, coupled with a small degree of buffering, should reduce the variety generated by any group of tightly coupled functional subsystems to a level that could be matched by a single controller (e.g., a Kan-Ban system, or the control software of a flexible manufacturing cell). Vertical communication could then occur between aggregations of these subsystems to encourage a form of overall hierarchical planning that would be minimal in terms of its constraints consistent with ensuring **overall** organisational cohesiveness and identity. A typical arrangement is shown in Figure 3.16. In this diagram, it will be seen that interactions between subsystems at higher levels is minimal. The role of individuals associated with these subsystems (e.g., production director and engineering director) is not to *direct* as in the functional model, but merely to provide this minimal intervention referred to above (e.g., maintenance of common engineering and accounting standards and personnel policies).

This type of approach is characterised by a strong emphasis on decentralised non-programmed problem solving, relying on localised integration of different types of specialist knowledge (e.g., design and manufacturing knowledge) previously associated with separate functional departments. These localised packets of integrated knowledge (which we might term 'knowledge bases') are assumed embedded in a framework in which the manufacturing system itself has been decomposed into minimally interacting subsystems. The amplifying power of

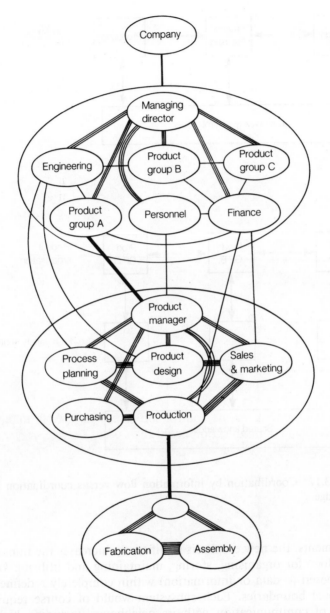

Figure 3.16 High variety lateral, interactions forced down to lowest level where they are within capability of single controller.

the computer, and its ability to store knowledge as well as data, can then be used to develop a control model of very high variety for each subsystem (Figure 3.17). Whereas in the past the main concentration has been on technology for facilitating information flow between functional

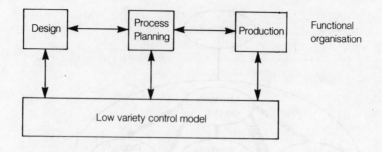

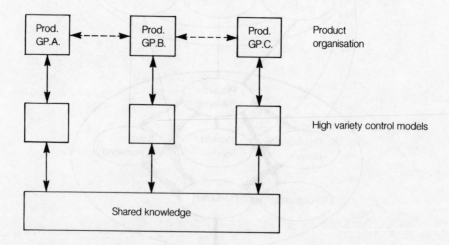

Figure 3.17 Coordination by information flow versus coordination by shared knowledge.

departments, the new emphasis significantly increases the importance of technology for organising, storing, maintaining and utilising *knowledge* (as opposed to data or information) within completely redefined sets of functional boundaries. Each subsystem would of course require some degree of communication with its neighbours, including higher level subsystems responsible for formulating and maintaining strategic goals. This would cause updates in local knowledge bases to reflect changes in the subsystem environment. Each subsystem might also be expected to increase its knowledge base by the internal processes of *experimentation* and *learning*. The requirement for these knowledge bases to be dynamic and adaptable serves to stress the importance of developing adequate technologies for their management.

In this chapter, the terms *data, information* and *knowledge* have been used without a clear definition of their differences. The next chapter examines in some detail the nature of these three concepts, and serves as a link to part 2 of the book which is concerned with the technology of their computer representation.

Chapter 4
Data, Information and Knowledge

4.1 The distinction between data, information and knowledge

4.2 The communication of knowledge: messages, syntax and semantics

4.3 Information theory

4.4 Knowledge, information and data processing in manufacturing organisations

The previous chapter introduced the notion of a manufacturing organisation being divided into a number of weakly interacting subsystems, each of which regulates its own internal activities by means of a *knowledge-based* control model which will be a partial model of the whole enterprise, but will be of requisite variety with respect to the states that can be generated within the subsystem itself. This implies that individual subsystems will have access to current and valid *data* about the states of their own operations, and the *knowledge* to interpret this data, so as to establish what actions are required to achieve their goals. Subsystems can be coordinated laterally by other subsystems whose sole concern is the maintenance of the interfaces. Their activities must also conform to the goals of the enterprise as a whole, and, to achieve this, some degree of vertical communication must take place with higher level systems which are responsible for overall corporate plans. Thus subsystems must communicate *information* to each other both laterally and vertically.

4.1 The distinction between data, information and knowledge

Humans receive **data** from their environment in the form of various types of sensory stimuli. Over an extended period of time, and on a continuing basis, the brain establishes patterns and categories of data which are generalised into aggregate groupings, forming higher level entities or constructs which are explicitly interrelated. This system of interrelated constructs defines human understanding of the nature of the environment, and provides a frame of reference for the interpretation of further stimuli (Figure 4.1). One of the reasons for this organising activity within the brain is to be able to make predictions about how the world is likely to evolve, so that the human organism can adapt to it. The brain is essentially a control system displaying third order feedback.

The set of organised constructs possessed by an individual at any particular time in relation to a particular environment or domain may be regarded as constituting the **knowledge** possessed by that individual about that environment or domain. Any new data which modifies the knowledge structures of the recipient in some way may be regarded as constituting **information**. Note that both knowledge and information are entirely subjective attributes. Different individuals may develop an entirely different set of mental constructs to make sense of the same set of stimuli, depending on the level and nature of their pre-existing constructs, which in turn have arisen in response to their previous sensory experiences. This set of constructs will then define their reactions to further stimuli. The following quotation illustrates this point:

> ...consider the implications to various people of a train whistle penetrating the evening dusk. To the saboteur crouching in the culvert, it might signify the failure of his mission because the whistle indicates the train has already passed over his detonating charge without causing an explosion. To the playboy, it might presage the imminent arrival of the transgressed husband. ... To the lonely wife it means the return of the travelling husband. To the man with his foot caught in the switch down the track, it preshadows doom... In brief, the nature and the significance of any information is fundamentally and primarily functions of the attitudes, situations and relevant responsibilities with respect thereto of the people involved with it...'

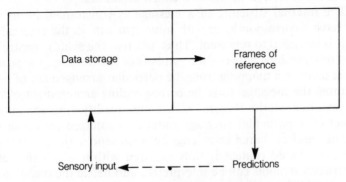

Figure 4.1 A simple model of human cognitive behaviour.

Edward D. Dwyer, *Some observations on management information systems: advances in EDP and information systems (New York: American Management Association 1961) pages 16–17.*

4.2 Communication of knowledge: messages, syntax and semantics

Knowledge is communicated between individuals in the form of **messages**. Humans convey knowledge in the form of strings of symbolic surrogates (words) which **represent** the abstractions the individuals have developed and which form part of their knowledge. These strings of symbolic surrogates are received by other humans in the form of data, which, like direct sensory input, must be interpreted within the frame of reference provided by the existing knowledge structures of the receiver. An important class of data is thus the symbols used to represent knowledge and communicate it in the form of messages.

For symbols to be interpreted, it is necessary for both the sender and receiver of the message to agree on the concepts to which the individual symbols or groups of symbols refer. A particular set of symbols which are surrogates for an agreed set of objects, concepts or constructs constitute the vocabulary of a **language**. For commumication to take place effectively, certain rules are established to restrict combinations of symbols to those that are permissable within the language. The set of agreed symbols, and the rules defining permissable symbol sequences collectively define the **syntax** of the language. Thus part of the knowledge (or set of constructs) possessed by both sender and receiver must be knowledge of the syntax of the language being used for communication.

A set of data symbols can only be converted into knowledge (i.e., ascribed meaning) through some process whereby the symbols and the patterns inherent in the symbols can be interpreted and matched against some pre-existing set of constructs. The process of ascribing meaning to a valid combination of symbols is called **semantics**.

The internal structure of a message as constrained by its syntax should have a correspondence with some structure in the external world which it is intended to represent. Thus, whereas the syntax constrains the internal relationships between the symbols of the message, the semantics takes the form of a mapping from the particular arrangement of symbols constituting the message, to some corresponding arrangement of objects in the external world (Figure 4.2). Consequently, the semantics (or meaning) of a particular message cannot be inferred from the syntax alone, but requires shared knowledge between sender and receiver of this mapping. A shared **context** is thus required within which the relationships between symbols can be interpreted, and hence the meaning of the message established.

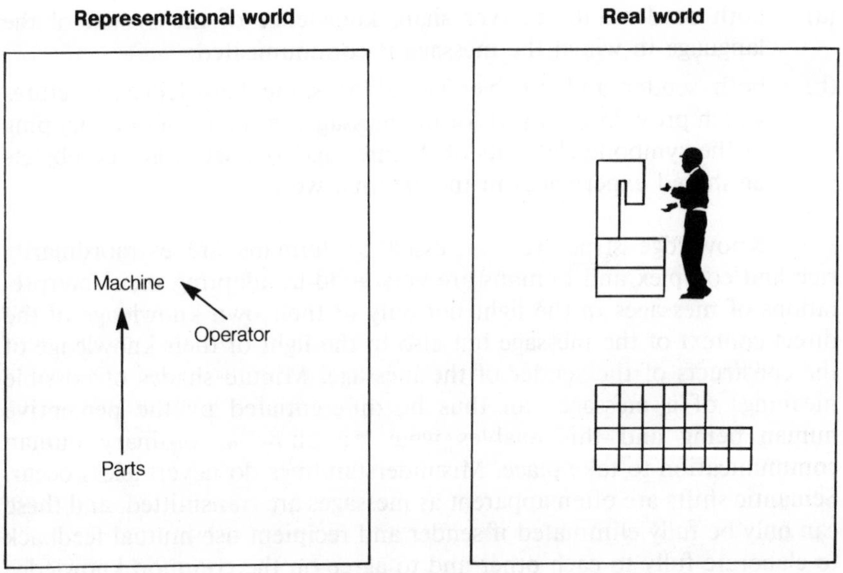

Representational world   **Real world**

Figure 4.2 Mappings from representational to real world.

Consider, for example, the following string of word symbols:

Machine M316b has broken down

This is a sentence which obeys the laws of English grammar, in other words if the sentence is a message, the syntax of the message is well defined. However, in the absence of any knowledge structure in the receiver to which this combination of words relates, the sentence conveys no intrinsic meaning. The reader of this book will recognise the sentence as a syntactically correct message, but the message itself will not lead to any increase in knowledge, because 'Machine M316b' is unlikely to be part of the reader's current experience. There is no pre-existing context to which the message relates. Yet to the production controller in a manufacturing company possessing a particular machine of identity M316b, the message has an immediate and important meaning. The current knowledge of the production controller may be that the company possesses a machine of that identity, that it was working, and that a backlog of work is waiting to be processed. The message is interpreted in the context of this pre-existing knowledge and adds to it the knowledge that the machine needs repair and that jobs waiting to be processed are likely to be late.

The ascribed meaning of a message by the receiver is the same as the intended meaning of the message by the sender only to the extent that:

(a)   both sender and receiver share knowledge of the syntax of the language in which the message is communicated;

(b)   both sender and receiver share the same knowledge structures which provide a context for the message, in the form of a mapping of the symbolic elements of the message to a set of agreed objects or shared experiences in the external world.

Knowledge structures possessed by humans are extraordinarily rich and complex and humans are very good at adapting their interpretations of messages in the light not only of their own knowledge of the direct context of the message but also in the light of their knowledge of the constructs of the sender of the message. Minute shades of possible meanings of a message can thus be differentiated by the perceptive human being and this enables what we know as ordinary human communication to take place. Misunderstandings do nevertheless occur. Semantic shifts are often apparent as messages are transmitted, and these can only be fully eliminated if sender and recipient use mutual feedback to elaborate fully to each other and to agree on the common knowledge structures which provide context to the message, or if they tightly restrict the types of messages that can be exchanged.

4.3   Information theory

We have defined information as data that in some way modifies the knowledge structures of the recipient of the data. Shannon, in his mathematical theory of communication (1948), has elaborated on this definition. According to his theory, the information content of a message is the extent to which that message reduces any uncertainty that may have previously existed in the knowledge of the recipient of the message. Consider the production controller sitting in his office, unaware of the current status of machine M316b, who receives an informal message to the effect that machine M316b has broken down. Because he can understand the syntax and semantics of the message, and because its interpretation reduces his uncertainty about the status of machine M316b, we can say that the message conveys information. Consider now the same production controller a few hours later when he receives a computer generated report on the status of all machines in the shop. This report may indicate that machine M316b has broken down. But since the production controller is already aware of this, the message does not in any sense reduce his state of uncertainty about the status of machine M316b, even though he may correctly understand its syntax and semantics. The message is therefore devoid of information.

Shannon developed this particular view of information in terms of probability theory. A simple exposition of this may be given again in terms of the broken machine example. Assume that the probability that the machine is operating correctly has been determined (by some means or other) as being 0.95; the probability that the machine is broken down and is repairable is 0.045 and the probability the machine is broken down and is irrepairable is 0.005. Assume that at some point in time a message is received that the machine is running normally, and at some later point in time, a further message is received to say it is irrepairably broken. To someone who is aware of the probablilities of the machine being in various states, we might intuitively feel that the message indicating the machine is irrepairably broken conveys more information than the one which indicates it is running normally, since the latter condition is what one would *expect* with a fairly high probability. Hence more information is conveyed by the least expected message. Shannon formally defined the information content I of a message which indicates a system to be in some state i by the formula:

$$I = -\frac{\log P_i}{2}$$

where P_i is the prior probability that the system will be found in state i. For the broken machine example, the information content of the first message (machine running) is 0.07 and the information content of the second message (machine irrepairably broken) is 7.6.

Shannon's theory of communication, originally developed out of an analysis of physical data transmission problems, has since been generalised into a so-called 'theory of information' which is again heavily based on probability theory, and is beyond the scope of this book. However, for the practical purposes of understanding the relationship of information to data and knowledge, we can generalise Shannon's definition to agree with our previous definition of information as a message which adds to or modifies in some way the knowledge level of the recipient. We must assume, of course, that for this to occur, the existing knowledge structures of the recipient are sufficient for him to interpret the semantics of the message. The production controller new to his job who receives a computer printout of the status of all machines on the shop floor may not derive any information from the report because he is unaware that the code "1" means the machine is operable and the code "2" means it is broken. Messages may be devoid of information because they are expressed in a syntax which is not known to the recipient, as might be the case if the machine status codes were displayed in binary form.

The conversion of data to information is therefore an act that itself requires knowledge. The recipient of a message requires knowledge of the syntax of the message, and sufficient knowledge of the context of the message to make an appropriate semantic interpretation. In addition, the semantic content must be such that it modifies the original knowledge in some way.

4.4   Knowledge, information and data processing in manufacturing organisations

The notion of the importance of requisite variety in the control model by which the behaviour of organisational subsystems are regulated underlines the importance of the efficient collection of data and its conversion into information that modifies the knowledge of the recipient. The current state of any subsystem is only determinable by the continuous collection and monitoring of data, and decisions concerning appropriate corrective action usually demand the application of sophisticated knowledge structures for the interpretation of the data.

4.4.1   Vertical information flow

Data originates at the basic operational levels of a manufacturing organisation, and the data which is collected and stored must possess sufficient variety for the basic tasks of detailed operational control. Decision making at higher systemic levels must also rely on basic operational and environmental data originating at the lowest level. The stored data used for detailed operational control will, however, contain more variety than can be assimilated or is necessary for the essentially coordinating role fulfilled by higher levels. Therefore, these levels must have access to a condensed form of this data. This can be achieved by filtering and summarising operational data in a predefined way, and providing it to higher levels in the form of standard reports (Figure 4.3).

However, experience has shown that the information content of such standard reports is very low (Ackoff, 1967). The filtering and summarising of data in any *predetermined* way involves a presupposition about the types of data and data patterns and relationships which are significant. This means that unexpected data patterns which are highly important may be inadvertantly filtered out by the blind application of standard reporting procedures. The frequently adopted solution of reducing the level of filtering results in reports of such voluminosity that it becomes impossible for any individual to extract information without many days' analysis. The result becomes a reliance on informal word-of-mouth reporting rather than formally collected data (see for example Mintzberg, 1973). This has the added advantage that the data can generally be relied on to be **current**. However, one of the problems with informal reporting is that it is more open to semantic misinterpretation and distortion than a set of formally documented summarising processes.

A potential solution to this problem is to provide higher levels of the organisation with their own set of filters so that they can obtain, in a flexible manner, the types of reports and dissections they require from the detailed operational database. This involves the provision of a

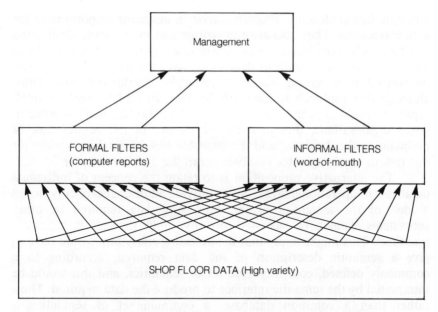

Figure 4.3 Variety filtering in manufacturing organisations.

flexible and easy-to-use query language with appropriate summarising facilities. There are number of such languages eg, *SQL* and *Query-by-Example* which are used in conjunction with relational databases; these will be discussed in Chapter 5.

One of the main problems arising from this approach is that it requires **semantic consistency** of all the operational data likely to be accessed in this way. If operational units are responsible for maintaining their own local databases, even if they all form part of a distributed relational database, it is frequently found that they will store common items of data in different semantic contexts, according to the way in which the data is to be used. For example, a bill of materials used by the production department would reflect how a product is put together, whereas the same bill of materials maintained by the design department would reflect the design discipline according to which the product was developed, and might be structured in a very different way. A job may have one release date for the purchasing department, which reflects when the raw materials should be planned, and another release date to the production department which reflects when work is actually scheduled to start.

Much has been written about the problems of integrating these different views across separate databases. One proposed solution is to have a single database maintained centrally so as to ensure total semantic consistency of all the data stored in it. This has been criticised as unfeasible (e.g., Pels and Wortmann, 1985) on the grounds of the immense complexity of the task of catering to the needs of all users in terms of their required semantic interpretations. Problems arise in assigning responsibility for data correctness. They also arise in writing and maintaining application programs, when the insistence on semantic integrity has caused a shift in semantic meaning of items of data which have traditionally always been interpreted in a certain way in a particular operational area. Thus, although this approach is *rationally* feasible, and might work in small organisations, it appears that it would not be *organisationally* feasible in larger organisations, due to excessive variety in the *control* task of maintaining the database, and the probable lack of requisite variety for this task in any imaginable database controller or administrator.

The alternative proposition is to retain the concept of individual databases in operational areas, but to provide additional explicitly stored models of the semantics of the data. Any data required by other subsystems cannot be accessed directly, only through a 'semantic interface'. This might imply that the accessing subsystem would have to give a semantic description of the data required, according to a commonly defined, company-wide set of semantics, and this would be interpreted by the semantic interface to produce the data required. Thus, rather than a common database, a common set of semantics is maintained to enforce proper interpretation of data stored in separate (but remotely accessible) operational databases (Figure 4.4). There are a number of alternative semantic datamodels available, some of which are described in Chapter 5. Issues involved in the design and maintenance of semantically consistent manufacturing databases are examined in Chapter 17.

4.4.2 Lateral information flow

Many of the same problems concerning the vertical flow of information also relate to horizontal information flow. However, whereas higher

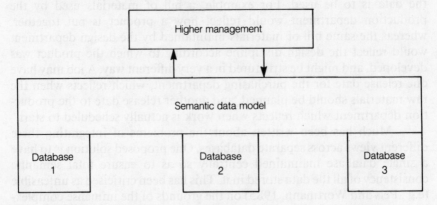

Figure 4.4 Integration of databases by common set of semantics.

organisational levels are more concerned with data summaries not requiring immediate action, subsystems communicating with each other on the operational level will usually be concerned with detailed coordination, and hence in the transmission of messages that require a fast response. When communication is at a human-to-human level the usual techniques of redundancy (e.g., following up a verbal request with a written request) and feedback (e.g., checking the receiver's interpretation of the message by asking him to rephrase it in his own words) can be used to minimise semantic distortion. However, when for example communication is between two databases, potential semantic distortion must be eliminated by other methods, such as the semantic interface. If the lateral interaction between subunits is reasonably clearly defined, in terms of the area of operational overlap if not in its detail, then particular attention can be paid to controlling the semantic consistency of the overlapping concepts (Figure 4.5). Thus more freedom may be given to modify data structures which are not part of the overlapping set, whereas those that are common can be more closely controlled, and possibly maintained by an intermediary subsystem.

4.4.3   Information processing for decision making

Subsystems must not only be capable of converting raw data from their immediate environment into information, and interpreting the meaning of messages from other subsystems. They must also be capable of using their knowledge to make decisions about alternative courses of action that might need to be taken, based on the information they have received. We have already seen how each subsystem needs to have a control model of its own operation which is of requisite variety with respect to the detail of that operation to ensure that adequate regulation can occur. Problems arise in this process from the limited capacity of the unaided human brain to sustain such requisite variety models, particularly with regard to the control actions to be taken. It is difficult for humans to enumerate, let alone evaluate all the alternative ways in which

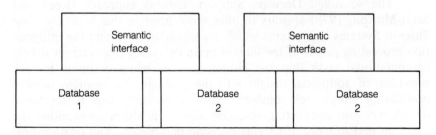

Figure 4.5 Integration of databases by overlapping semantics.

realistically complex organisational subsystems can be brought into a state of control.

Herbert Simon (Simon, 1960) coined the term 'satisficing' to describe what he saw as the decision making behaviour actually employed by most managers in realistic situations. Rather than evaluating all possible alternatives and choosing the best, as would be prescribed by theories of rational choice, Simon suggested that lack of time and information processing ability meant that managers could do little more than sequentially evaluate alternatives and choose the first alternative that was good enough in the sense of conformance with the basic constraints that a viable solution should satisfy. This is termed 'satisficing' behaviour.

A number of other limitations exist on humans' ability to process information. For example, the short term memory of the human brain is very limited, making it difficult for it to process numerical information and make computations. The ability of humans to detect differences in stimuli appears to be a function of the magnitude of the stimuli being compared (Woodworth and Schlosberg, 1955), often resulting in difficulty in discriminating between what is normal and what is abnormal. Humans also have difficulty in interpreting probabilistic data, such as a lack of intuitive understanding of the effect of sample size on sampling variance, and a lack of the intuitive ability to identify correlation and causality (Tversky and Kahneman, 1971). The fields of Management Science and Operations Research have attempted to provide managers with tools in the form of mathematical models to enable them to overcome some of their limitations, and to examine a wider range of alternatives than would otherwise be possible. However, the frequently unstructured nature of managerial decision making has hampered the utility of such approaches. In many cases, courses of action have to be evaluated against multiple criteria, often with lack of sufficient data or time to obtain it, or complete knowledge of the structural relationships which would enable the results of an action to be computed in terms of these criteria. The models provided by the management scientist are often naive in their represention of problems and oversophisticated in the techniques used to obtain solutions (see for example Ackoff, 1979).

The so called Decision Support Systems approach (Keen and Scott-Morton, 1978) appears to offer more hope in this area. Decision Support Systems are systems which are intended to extend the information processing power of the human brain by taking over certain simple computational tasks that the human sees as being desirable for the provision of additional insight into the problem. These often involve postulating simple relationships between decision and performance parameters and conducting so-called what-if analyses to examine the effect on performance of varying decision parameters. The relationships between parameters can be made increasingly sophisticated as the analysis proceeds. However, the emphasis is not on reaching an optimum solution in the model, but in raising the degree of the manager's insight into the way in which the effects of certain actions may propagate in the real world, thus raising the quality of his decisions.

Perhaps the most important future influence on providing assistance in the achievement of requisite variety in the models of the enterprise that are used in its control, will lie in the representational techniques of Artificial Intelligence. The flexible representation of knowledge, rather than mere data or predefined models, opens up new possibilities in the elaboration of current human-based models, as will be shown in subsequent chapters.

Part II
TECHNIQUES

Chapter 5
Fundamentals of Data Modelling

Planning and controlling the activities of a manufacturing organisation requires the storing, accessing and updating of a vast amount of data, for eventual conversion to information and knowledge. The premising of actions on common and consistent sets of data is an essential part of any attempt to integrate manufacturing activities (see for example, Melkannof, 1984). A manufacturing organisation's database contains not only a 'snapshot' view of the current state of the organisation and all its resources at a particular point in time, but also selected aspects of the organisation's historical states, and possibly certain projections of its future states.

A frequently cited ideal is that all the functions of an organisation should share a common database which can be accesssed by independent application programs. This would allow decisions at all stages of the manufacturing process to be taken on the basis of data that is not only common, but is ensured to be current by continuous real time update using automatic data collection systems. In practice, however, this is far from reality in the majority of existing organisations. It is common practice for companies utilizing computers to use separate databases for each computerised function, often implemented with different and incompatible software and hardware. Not only do such databases contain redundant data, but data transfer between them usually entails writing complex programs.

For an organisation which has its data distributed over many separate databases, the aggregation from scratch of these databases into a single common database is likely to prove a formidable and time-consuming task. Since millions of data items are likely to be involved, the task if performed manually could take many years of effort. As a result, this has very rarely been attempted. The problem of data being stored in incompatible forms has been cited as one of the major existing barriers to achieving effective integration between 'islands' of automation.

There are three possible solutions to this problem:

(1)   To modify each individual database to conform to a common logical structure which will ensure consistency of data meaning between each database.

(2)   To develop programs which have embedded knowledge of the interpretation to other parts of the organisation of the data stored, and which can access each database and extract the semantic meaning of the data according to the frame of reference of the party who is accessing the data.

(3)   To develop programs which are capable of automatically transfer-ring the data stored in each individual database into a centralised common database, having restructured it into a consistent and common logical form.

Each of these three methods requires knowledge of the various data structures that might be used in different parts of the organisation to store data. In addition, any form of data structuring involves the implicit attribution of a certain amount of semantic meaning to the data and as such may be regarded as a simple form of factual knowledge representation.

The purpose of this chapter is to examine in more detail how data can be structured, with particular emphasis on the relational data model. This is an important basis for the study of true knowledge bases and for the integrated storage and management of data and knowledge which will be examined later in the book.

5.1 Elements of data modelling

5.1.1 Specification of data objects

All computer databases depend on some underlying data 'model'. This is an abstraction that allows the meaning of the data to be partially captured by placing restrictions on the relationships that can exist between data items, and the values they are allowed to take.

An individual data item normally refers to some attribute or property of a real world object or entity (such as a machine, a tool, or a customer account) which has a value. A convenient working definition of a data item is an 'object-attribute-value triplet' of the form

<object name, object attribute, attribute value>

The object name is actually an attribute of the object that allows us to identify it unambiguously (e.g., a production job may have a job number J219 which is the identifying attribute of that job). If this job has a further attribute *due date* with the value '7/5/88', an attribute *item* with the value 'widget', and an attribute *quantity* with the value '12', these facts could be expressed as the object-attribute-value triplets:

<J219 *Item 'Widget'*>
<J219 *Due-Date '7/5/87'*>
<J219 *Quantity '12'*>

A pictorial representation can be seen in the form of bubble diagrams in Figure 5.1a, where each bubble contains an attribute-value pair related to the name attribute of a single object (J219). Since each bubble diagram contains the name of the job in common, they can be aggregated as in Figure 5.1b. A job, in the generic sense, is described in terms of the following attributes: *job name, item, due-date* and *quantity*. An individual job is characterised by giving values to these attributes. Furthermore, if we stipulate that no two jobs can have the same name (i.e., the name uniquely identifies the job), then the values of the remaining three attributes will be determined by the job name, which is referred to as the 'key' attribute, and whose bubble is half shaded in the diagram. A given job name identifies a job with one due date, for one specific quantity, of one specific item. This can be shown on the bubble diagram in Figure 5.1b by drawing a bar adjacent to the attributes whose values are uniquely determined by the job name. This type of link

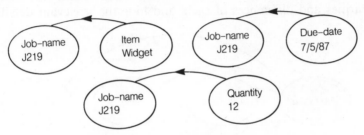

Figure 5.1a Attributes and values.

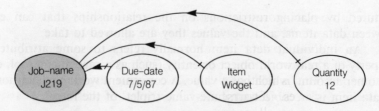

Figure 5.1b   Keys and functional dependency.

represents a **one-to-one** or **functional** relationship between the job name and the remaining attributes.

By grouping objects with similar attributes into categories (e.g., all individual jobs may be grouped into the general category '**job**') and placing restrictions on all individual data objects belonging to the same category so that they have the same set of attributes, then the individual attributes of a particular data object become the attributes of the category. For an object to be a member of the category, it must possess the attributes of the category. Abstraction of a category from a set of similar objects defines a **type**, whereas a particular instance of a member of the category is called a **token**. A description of data categories in terms of their attributes defines the **intensional** properties of the data. The intensional properties of the **job** category would be the following attributes: *job-name* (the key), *item, quantity* and *due-date*. These could be represented in the bubble diagram shown in Figure 5.2. A data model is generally specified in terms of a set of object categories and their attributes. A description of the data objects themselves in terms of their attribute *values* defines the **extensional** properties of the data. Henceforth, unless otherwise stated, we shall be referring to the intensional properties of categories of data (i.e., object categories and attributes rather than individual objects and attribute values).

Data typing, or restricting data to belong to specifically defined categories, enforces the objects described by the data to be represented in a uniform, homogeneous manner. As such, the representation is sometimes rather inflexible. However, when we are dealing with a very large number of similar objects it is extremely useful to be able to abstract out a set of basic common characteristics which define the *essential* similarities and differences of each, and hide the irrelevant detail. For

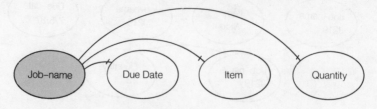

Figure 5.2   Intensional properties of a data category.

example, if we were storing information on a very large number of jobs, and if each job were characterised by an entirely different set of attributes, it would be very difficult to extract any meaningful information from the data concerning commonalities, differences or comparisons between jobs. This is relatively easy if we restrict all jobs to having the same set of attributes. Of course this becomes less important when we are dealing with very small numbers of objects. If the objects are also fundamentally different, then untyped data models are more appropriate. These will be encountered in later chapters.

5.1.2 Data relationships

Relationships can exist between data categories to reflect how the corresponding real world objects are related. Consider, for example, the data categories **machine** and **machine-operator**. Since, in the real world, a machine-operator is assigned to a particular machine, a corresponding relationship should exist between the data category **machine-operator** and the data category **machine**. This can be represented in a network diagram by drawing a link between the two data categories as shown in Figure 5.3a. The link may be labelled in a way that gives some semantic meaning to the nature of the relationship. This particular link has been labelled 'assigned to', interpreted in the direction implied by the arrow.

The link itself (although not its semantic interpretation) may be represented in the data in a variety of ways. For example, we may have as an attribute of **machine-operator** a data value that identifies the machine with which the operator is associated. Thus an attribute of **machine-operator** is '*machine-id*' which matches the attribute of '*id*' of machine. Individual instances of the data category **machine-operator** will be linked to individual instances of the data category **machine** by the existence of this common attribute.

5.1.3 Integrity constraints

In addition to definitions of the categories or types that are allowed to exist in a data model, together with their attributes and relationships, it

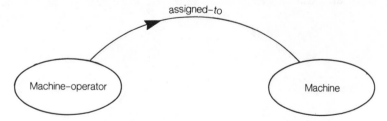

Figure 5.3a A relationship between two objects.

is also common to specify an explicit set of constraints that can restrict the types of objects and relationships that are allowed to exist. These are sometimes referred to as **semantic integrity** constraints and are basically concerned with the compliance of data values with our knowledge of what is and what is not allowed to occur in the real world. The types of constraints that can be applied are as follows:

(1) **Existence constraints**

These constrain the range of values that attributes can take; since the values of the attributes define a particular instance of an object type, this constraint restricts the objects that can be permissably represented. For example, the *type* attribute of **machine** may be restricted to take on a value from the range of recognised machine types such as lathe, drill and milling machine.

(2) **Dependency constraints**

These enforce certain relationships between objects by making a particular object's existence conditional on some other object's existence. For example, if the set of permissable values of the attribute *machine-id* of the object **machine-operator** is constrained to be a member of the set of values of the attribute *id* of the object **machine**, then this enforces a relationship between specific machine operators and specific machines. The existence of a machine-operator assigned to a particular machine is made dependent on the existence of that machine.

(3) **Mapping constraints between entities**

Constraints can be imposed on the number of instances that can exist of a particular object type with the same value of a given attribute. For example, it may be specified that for a given machine instance, only one machine-operator instance can exist with the value of that machine id. This is constraining the relationship between operator and machine to the extent that a machine can only have one operator. Constraints such as this can be represented diagramatically, as shown in Figure 5.3b.

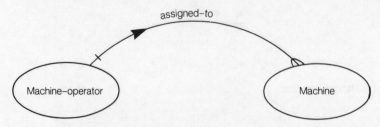

Figure 5.3b Mapping constraints on the relationship.

The bar drawn across the link to **machine-operator** indicates that a machine can have only one operator. The operator is functionally (uniquely) determined by the machine. The 'crow's foot' on the link to **machine** indicates that one operator can be assigned to many machines. Hence, the machine is not functionally (uniquely) determined by the operator.

Some of these constraints may be automatically enforced by the types of data structure allowed, depending on what that structure is. These are called **inherent** constraints. Other constraints are termed **explicit** constraints because they must be specified externally to the permissable data structures and enforced by external procedures that check data for constraint violation and prevent the entry of any data that would cause such violations.

5.1.4   Operations on a data model

Specification of the allowable data categories, attributes and explicit constraints on data values and combinations of values defines the **static** part of a data model, which allows us to capture the static features of the world. The data model is a snapshot which maps allowable features of the world on to allowable combinations of data items in the model. However, before a data model can be regarded as being fully defined, we must also capture some of the dynamic features of the world by specifying the operations allowed on the data to change it. Typical operations that might be performed are:

- retrieval of a data object instance
- creation of a data object instance
- deletion of a data object instance
- changing attribute values of a data object instance

A good data model will be structured in such a way that it is posssible to define a comprehensive set of operations which can be applied to the data without causing any inherent integrity constraints to be violated. Restrictions can also be placed on these operations by specifying, for example, that changing the *date-of-birth* field of **employee** is not permitted. Certain operations which would create a set of data that violated the explicit constraints of the data model should obviously also be forbidden. These restrictions are normally enforced by independent constraint checking.

Specification of the data categories or types that are allowed to exist in a particular data model, together with their attributes, the explicit constraints that exist, and the data operations that are allowed are referred to as a **schema**. A collection of data structured according to a particular schema is termed a **database**. A system that provides a language for defining a data schema, a method for specifying and enforcing explicit constraints on data values, and a set of operations for retrieving and manipulating data values is called a **Database Management System** (DBMS).

5.2   Mappings and levels of database schemata

A database schema may be described at varying levels of detail, with a set of mappings existing between levels as shown in Figure 5.4. The **conceptual schema**, at the top level, is a general (though concise) description of the data objects, attributes and relationships of importance in the particular application environment being modelled. Production of a conceptual schema is an important intermediate step in database design since it provides a link between abstract data structures and the real world, which can clarify and resolve various design issues by providing a quick reference to the 'meaning' of the data structures, and by facilitating communication with end users.

The conceptual schema is next mapped on to what is commonly called the **logical** schema. This is in many respects similar to the conceptual schema in that it is a description of the objects, attributes, relationships and constraints that exist. However, whereas the conceptual schema is primarily a description of the real world, the logical schema is primarily a description of the data. Thus, it will consist of a detailed specification of individual data item types in terms of objects and attributes and a complete and formal description of all constraints that exist on attribute values and relationships. It will also contain definitions of the allowable operations on the data including the various levels of access and update authority by end users.

The final mapping that takes place is from the logical to the **physical** schema, which is a description of the physical structure of the database. This physical structure may be defined in terms of such things as indexed sequential files, arrays, hash tables, trees, inverted files, etc. It contains details of the pointers that exist to link items of data, the access paths used to retrieve data and how explicit constraints are enforced. Modern database management systems normally relieve designers of database applications from the necessity of having to specify the physical schema. Once the logical schema has been fully specified, the DBMS will automatically make the necessary mappings on to the physical schema. Hence the designer can view the application entirely in terms of the logical model. Therefore we will not examine the physical schema in any further detail, but will confine ourselves to a more detailed examination of the conceptual and logical schemas.

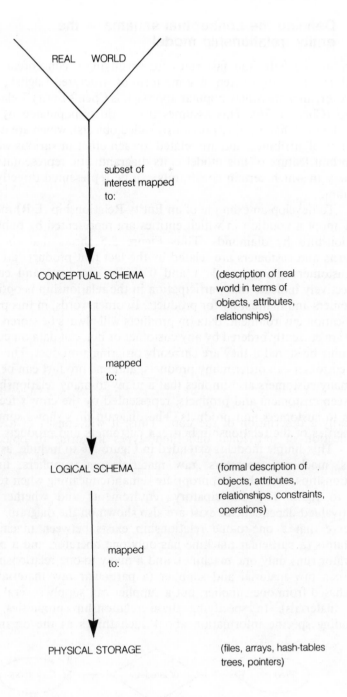

REAL   WORLD

subset of
interest mapped
to:

CONCEPTUAL SCHEMA   (description of real
world in terms of
objects, attributes,
relationships)

mapped
to:

LOGICAL SCHEMA   (formal description of
objects, attributes,
relationships, constraints,
operations)

mapped
to:

PHYSICAL STORAGE   (files, arrays, hash-tables
trees, pointers)

Figure 5.4 Mappings and levels of database schemata.

5.3   Defining the conceptual schema — the entity- relationship model

There are no hard and fast rules for specifying a conceptual schema, which is frequently written in some form of structured English, if at all. However, an increasingly popular approach is Chen's Entity-Relationship model (Chen, 1976). This assumes the world is populated by entities (eqivalent to what we have previously called objects), which are described in terms of attributes, and are related to each other in various ways. The important feature of this model is its diagrammatic representation, and the way in which certain constraints can be represented directly on the diagram.

To develop an example of an Entity-Relationship (E-R) model, we shall adopt a notation in which entities are represented by bubbles and relationships by diamonds. Thus Figure 5.5 shows that the entities **products** and **customers** are related by the fact that products are *ordered by* customers. The symbols 1 and 0 against products and customers respectively indicate that participation in the relationship is optional for customers and mandatory for products. In other words, in this particular application environment, data on products will always be stored whether they are currently ordered by any customer or not, but data on customers will only be stored if they are currently ordering a product. The fact that one customer can order many products, and one product can be ordered by many customers also implies that a many-to-many relationship exists between customers and products, represented by the crow's feet on the links to customers and products. The diagram thus shows some of the properties of the relationship between customers and products.

This simple model is extended in Figure 5.6 to include, as entities, parts, machines, operators, raw materials and suppliers, linked by relationships which have appropriate semantic meaning when read from left to right. The participatory requirements and whether or not multivalued dependencies exist are also shown on the diagram. Thus we observe that a one-to-one relationship exists between machines and operators (a particular machine has only one operator, and a particular operator runs only one machine), and a many-to-one relationship exists between raw material and supplier (a particular raw material is only purchased from one supplier, but a supplier can supply several different raw materials). In specifying these relationship properties, we are encoding specific information about such things as the organisation's

Figure 5.5   A simple E-R diagram.

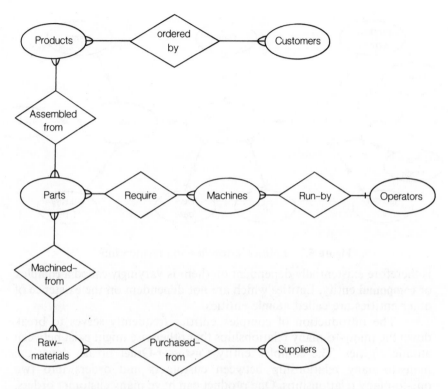

Figure 5.6   A more complex E-R diagram.

purchasing policies, and are therefore imparting a degree of meaning to the data.

The attributes of each entity must now be decided, and can be drawn on the diagram as bubbles connected to the entities as shown in Figure 5.7. It will be seen, however, that not only entities but also relationships can have attributes. For example, there will be many separate instances of the *orders* relationship between different customers and different products, each of which will have an identifying set of attributes such as the date of the order, the quantity, and the required delivery date. In many senses, the relationship between customer and product can be regarded as an entity in its own right. We thus create the new entity **customer-order** with attributes as indicated, to replace the *orders* relationship. This entity is *dependent* on the prior existence of both customers and products for its own existence, with the identities of each being required as attributes (an order must be by a specific customer for a specific product). This is an example of a **dependency constraint** (see section 5.1.3), and can be represented by drawing arrows on the links between entities in the direction of the dependency. An entity which is created to represent a relationship between two other entities and which

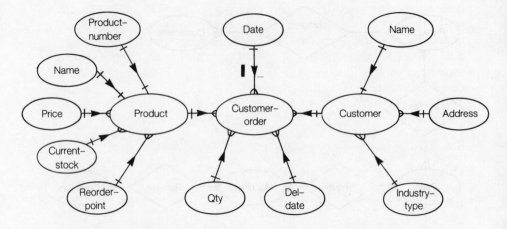

Figure 5.7   Entities, attributes and relationships.

is therefore existentially dependent on them is varyingly called a **complex** or **compound** entity. Entities which are not dependent on the existence of other entities are called **atomic** entities.

The introduction of complex entities frequently serves to break down the many-to-many relationships that otherwise might exist between atomic entities. The complex entity **Customer-Order** breaks down the many-to-many relationship between customers and orders into two one-to-many relationships. One product can have many customer orders, but one customer order can only be for one product; one customer can have many orders, but one order is associated with only one customer. The breaking down of many-to-many relationships by the creation of complex entities is an important step in reducing relationships to representing functional dependencies between entities. The importance of this will be seen in the context of the relational data model described in section 5.4.

An entity relationship model can provide a convenient method of systematically describing the application environment by identifying the important entities and the relationships between them, and in specifying *some* of the constraints on the relationships. Additionally, more detailed constraints on values of attributes etc. can, if required, be specified adjacent to the attribute name, but this is perhaps going beyond the level of detail that should be incorporated in a conceptual schema. Its pictorial representation and natural language descriptions of entities and relationships make it convenient as a first-cut description that retains a direct semantic association with the application environment, and should be intelligible to end users. It does not specify the detailed data structures that will be used to store individual instances of these entities and relationships, and how the specified constraints will be enforced, and therefore does not imply any particular computer implementation. This takes place at the next level of modelling (the so-called logical level), in which the conceptual schema is mapped into a form that more directly matches its final representation in the computer. A number of alternative data models are appropriate for modelling at this level, each of which is associated with a different type of computer implementation. These are described in the next section.

5.4 Data modelling at the logical level

There are many data models which can be used in the development of a database schema at the logical level. The four that will be considered here are:

(1)   The Hierarchical Model
(2)   The Network Model
(3)   The Relational Model
(4)   The Binary Relational Model

All these models regard the universe as being populated by entities which have attributes and relationships. However, they differ in the types of constraint they enforce in the inherent sense on the way in which entities can be described, on the types of relationship that exist, and on how they are represented.

Most commercially available DBMSs use one or more of these data models on which to base the data structuring, query and update facilities they provide. They each have particular advantages and limitations and a modern trend has been to develop hydrid DBMSs which can use more than one. The first two are mainly of historical interest for the purposes of this book and will only be treated briefly. The data model with most significance for the themes developed here is the relational model and some of its extensions; these will therefore be treated in greater detail.

5.4.1 The hierarchical and network models

Both the hierarchical and network data models assume that the world is populated by entities and relationships, with the entities being described in terms of sets of attributes. In the hierarchical model, entities are constrained to be related to each other in the form of a tree structure, specified in terms of a set of parent-child relationships where a parent entity can have any number of children, but a child entity can have only one parent. Entities at the top of the tree are termed roots. In the network model, entities can be linked to each other without this restriction, and links may be two-way, giving a generalised network rather than a tree structure. Examples of data structured according to these two models are shown in Figure 5.8.

In both models, entities are stored in the form of records, and links between entities are stored either by physical structuring of the data, or in the form of pointers from one entity to another. Although very efficient data access can result from traversing these predefined links, the fact that the links (and hence access paths) are 'hard-wired' into the physical structure of the database means that it is more difficult to access data in a flexible, ad hoc manner, since all data has to be retrieved via these predefined access paths. Data retrieval normally entails writing special programs which need detailed knowledge of the access paths and of how they can be most efficiently used.

Certain types of integrity constraint can be enforced automatically by these data models allowing the constraints to be inherent in the structure of the data. For example, physically structuring data to represent a set of hierarchical relationships can make it impossible for a machine to exist without the existence of a department to which it belongs, assuming these entities have a parent-child relationship in the database. However, if the department is deleted from the database, all the machines belonging to it will also be deleted, even though in reality they might have been merely moved to another department.

The motivation for the use of either of these data models comes largely from their efficiency, rather than from their versatility in modelling complex data environments. In addition, neither model has a well-defined set of operations for manipulating the data in such a way that inherent integrity constraints are guaranteed to be preserved. These limitations prompted the definition of a third data model, the relational model.

5.4.2 The relational model

The most important model for the purposes of this book is the relational model and its extensions (Codd, 1970). Like the hierarchical and network models, this model also sees the world as populated by entities, attributes and relationships. However the relational model is based on the mathematical theory of 'sets' and the notion of a 'relation'. Before looking any closer at this model, it is necessary to define these two terms.

A **set** is defined as a collection of objects or symbols, each of which is uniquely identified and has a specified membership condition. Members of the set can either be specified exhaustively, or through the membership condition. For example, a set A containing the numbers 1, 3, 7, 10 could be defined by:

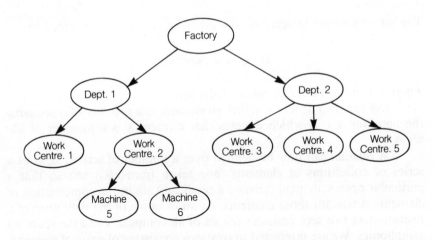

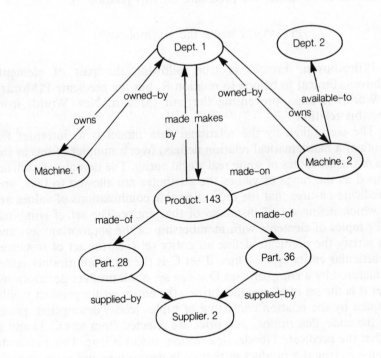

Figure 5.8 Hierarchical and network data models.

$$A = \{1, 3, 7\ 10\}$$

The set of positive integers on the other hand could be specified by:

$$B = \{x{:}x \text{ is positive}\}$$

where x is an arbitrary element of the set.

We can also denote whether an element is a member of a set using the notation: $x \in A$ which denotes that element x is a member of the set A.

A **relation** can now be defined over a number of sets A, B, C as a series of collections of elements, one taken from each set, so that a particular open statement (termed a predicate) about the combination of elements is true for those elements. As an example of the definition of a relation over two sets, consider the set of all composers and the set of all symphonies. We are interested in relations consisting of pairs of elements {x, y}, x being taken from the set of composers and y from the set of all symphonies. If we define the predicate for this relation as:

$$P(x,\ y) = \text{'x wrote the y symphony'}$$

then P(Beethoven, Eroica) is true, allowing the pair of elements {Beethoven, Eroica} to belong to relation R, but the predicate P(Mozart, New World) is false, preventing the pair {Mozart, New World} from joining this relation.

The step taken by the relational data model is to interpret the elements of a mathematical relation defined over a number of sets as the values of the attributes of some real world entity. The domain of each set is defined as the range of values the attributes are allowed to take, and the predicate ensures that the only allowable combinations of values are those which define actual instances of that entity. The set of combinations or **tuples** of elements with membership of the appropriate sets and which satisfy the predicate define an entity set (i.e., the set of instances of a particular entity type). Thus, if set C is the set of all product codes manufactured by a company, set D is the set of all product descriptions, and set P is the set of all product prices, the entity set for product would be defined by the relation consisting of tuples {code, description, price} where the code, description, and price are selected from sets C, D and P such that the predicate P(code, description, price) is true. This predicate is defined as true if a product of that code description and price actually exists.

Tuples representing instances of an entity are represented in the form of tables, in which the table name is the name of the entity set, columns correspond to attributes, and rows correspond to the tuples which form the actual entity instances. An example of this is shown in Figure 5.9 for the entity set **Process-times**.

Process-times

Machine–id	Part–id	Set-up-time	Run-time
M1	P12	4.6	16.4
M1	P23	1.9	8.3
M1	P30	1.4	20.6
M2	P6	4.3	10.1
M2	P26	4.1	8.3

Figure 5.9 Example of a relation.

Certain constraints exist on the structure of these tables which derive from the theory of sets on which the representation is based. In particular, no repeating or null values of attributes are allowed, and the order of appearance of the tuples is not significant. Retrieval from the database is on the basis of data values rather than pointers. A tuple does not have to be uniquely determined by a single identifying attribute. It is merely sufficient that the tuples themselves are all different. The key which enables unique access to a record is the minimum set of attribute values whose combination uniquely defines that record. If more than one attribute is required the key is said to be **composite**. In the example in Figure 5.9 the key would be the combination of attribute values *machine-id* and *part-id*.

Conventional implementations of relational databases have a reputation for having rather long access times. This is, however, rapidly being overcome by using new forms of computer technology such as content addressable memory.

The relational model does not provide explicit support for the representation of relationships between entities in the form of the pointers provided by the hierarchical and network models, nor for enforcing constraints on those relationships. Relationships must be expressed by including the key of one entity type as an attribute of another. In the case of Figure 5.10 a relationship between the entity type **part** and the entity type **machine** would have to be represented by having, for example, the identifying attribute of **part**, (Part-id) as an attribute of the entity **machine** to indicate the fact that a part is made on a specific machine.

Machine–id	Part–id	Set-up-time	Run-time		Part–id	Qty

Figure 5.10 Representing a relationship in the relational model.

The operations allowed on a relation have an important set of characteristics:

- they operate on entire relations (sets of tuples) rather than individual records;
- they are independent of the order of the tuples or of the fields; that is they are dependent only on the structure of the relation itself;
- taken together, they constitute a formally defined relational algebra, which means they are defined mathematically rather than by convention.

These will be discussed in more detail in Section 5.4.4.

5.4.3 Normalisation

One of the most important features of the relational model is that, provided each of the relations that comprises the database conforms to a well defined set of characteristics, the internal consistency or integrity of the data is guaranteed to be preserved by the permitted update operations. This can avoid so-called update anomalies. An example of an update anomaly is where relations are structured in such a way that the same item of data is stored in several relations. If the item is updated in one relation only, a state of inconsistency will exist in the database. A set of relations structured according to certain rules will avoid this anomaly by storing each data item in only one place.

The process of structuring relations to preserve their integrity under update operations is called 'normalisation'. Starting with a trial set of unnormalised relations, it is possible to restructure them progressively through a number of 'normal forms' each of which eliminates a group of possible anomalies. There are five normal forms (first, second, third, fourth and fifth). Ill-structured relations are frequently in 1st or 2nd normal form, and the objective of normalisation is to convert them to third, fourth or fifth normal form, depending on the degree of integrity preservation required. Normalisation generally increases the number of relations (and hence entity sets) in the data representation, which can thus change from that which was conceptualised initially.

To illustrate the process of normalisation, consider the following example. Assume that we have identified **assembly process** as an entity and have identified attributes of this entity leading to the relation, as shown in Figure 5.11.

This relation is initially in unnormalised form. The key attribute is *Ass-id*. The first thing to note is that the attributes *Cpt-id* and *Qty* are repeating, or multi-valued attributes. Since an assembly may in general consist of any number of components, these attributes have been repeated to cater for the appearance of several components in the

Assembly–process

Ass–id	Cpt–id	Qty	Cpt–id	Qty	Cpt–id	Qty	Std.Time	Work–Stn	Loc
A1	P23	2	P29	1	P108	3	10.4	WC3	Dept 1
A2	P43	4	P16	2			11.6	WC3	Dept 1
A3	P104	1	P29	1	P101	2	23.1	WC1	Dept 1
A4	P45	2	P29	3			15.4	WC4	Dept 2

Figure 5.11 Unnormalised data.

assembly. The condition for a table to be in first normal form is:

Rule 1 For a table to be in first normal form, there must be no repeating attributes (each attribute must be single valued).

If we restructure the relation so that the attributes *Cpt-id* and *Qty* only appear once, it takes the form of Figure 5.12. This relation is now in first normal form, but we see that in order to eliminate the repeating attribute *Cpt-id* we must introduce an extra tuple for each component, repeating all the other data items for each tuple. The relation now has a composite key of two attributes: *Assembly-id* and *Cpt-id*, values of both of which are required to uniquely identify a record. This actually represents a step backwards, since we have increased the data redundancy and made update more difficult. However, this problem is eliminated by further normalisation.

Assembly–process

Ass–id	Cpt–id	Qty	Std.Time	Work–Stn	Location
A1	P23	2	10.4	WC3	Dept 1
A1	P29	1	10.4	WC3	Dept 1
A1	P108	3	10.4	WC3	Dept 1
A2	P43	4	11.6	WC3	Dept 1
A2	P16	2	11.6	WC3	Dept 1
A3	P104	1	23.1	WC1	Dept 1
A3	P29	1	23.1	WC1	Dept 1
A3	P101	2	23.1	WC1	Dept 1
A4	P45	2	15.4	WC4	Dept 2
A4	P29	3	15.4	WC4	Dept 2

Figure 5.12 First normal form.

Rule 2 For a relation to be in second normal form, each attribute must be functionally dependent on all attributes of the key.

It will be recalled that for one attribute to be functionally dependent on another (see section 5.1.1), a particular value assigned to one attribute will uniquely determine the value of the dependent attribute. Taking the first normal form relation we have just constructed, if we examine the functional dependence of each non-key attribute on the composite key *Ass-id*, *Cpt*, it will be observed that, although the attribute *Qty* depends on the whole key (i.e., values must be assigned to both *Ass-id* and *Cpt* to uniquely determine Qty), the non-key attributes *Std.Time*, *Work-Stn* and *Location* depend only on the part of the key *Ass-id*. In other words, the value of *Ass-id* uniquely determines the values of these attributes, regardless of the value of the *Cpt* part of the key. This is indicated by the arrows in Figure 5.12, which represent functional dependencies. We can only restructure this relation for second normal form by splitting it into two relations: **Assembly-BOM**, and **Assembly-Proc**, as shown in Figure 5.13.

Assembly–BOM

Ass–id	Cpt–id	Qty
A1	P23	2
A1	P29	1
A1	P108	3
A2	P43	4
A2	P16	2
A3	P104	1
A3	P29	1
A3	P101	2
A4	P45	2
A4	P29	3

Assembly–Proc

Ass–id	Std.Time	Work–Stn	Location
A1	10.3	WC3	Dept 1
A2	11.6	WC3	Dept 1
A3	23.1	WC1	Dept 1
A4	15.4	WC4	Dept 2

Figure 5.13 Second normal form.

We have now stored the components that form an assembly, and their quantities in a separate relation to the other details of the process. *Qty*, the only attribute of the first relation, is now dependent on the whole of the key (*Assembly-id, Cpt*). The second relation has only one attribute (*Assembly-id*) as key, and all non key attributes are dependent on it.

To check whether the relation is in third normal form, we must apply rule 3.

Rule 3   A relation is in third normal form if conditions for first and second normal forms are satisfied and if values of all attributes depend directly on the key, with no transitive dependencies through other attributes.

Examination of the **Assembly-Proc** relation shows that the attribute *location* is functionally dependent on another attribute, *work-centre*. In other words, the location is determined by the work-centre and only indirectly by the *ass-id* in so much as this determines work centre. This is indicated again by the arrows representing functional dependencies in Figure 5.13. This dependency can be removed by splitting the

Assembly–BOM

Ass–id	Cpt–id	Qty
A1	P23	2
A1	P29	1
A1	P108	3
A2	P43	4
A2	P16	2
A3	P104	1
A3	P29	1
A3	P101	2
A4	P45	2
A4	P29	3

Assembly–Wkstn

Ass–id	Std.Time	Work–Stn
A1	10.3	WC3
A2	11.6	WC3
A3	23.1	WC1
A4	15.4	WC4

Wkstn–Loc

Work–Stn	Location
WC1	Dept 1
WC3	Dept 1
WC4	Dept 2

Figure 5.14   Third normal form.

Assembly-Proc relation into two further relations, **Assembly-Wkstn** and **Wkstn-Loc** as in Figure 5.14.

Data on the location of work stations has been separated out from data on the assembly process, and the resulting set of relations are now in third normal form (sometimes referred to as Boyce-Codd normal form). An entity relationship diagram of this set of relations is shown in Figure 5.15, in which it will be seen that the normalised relations correspond to complex entities (relationships), with the atomic entites of assembly, work station, component and department merely being attributes in this representation. Links are represented by the key of one entity (e.g., Wkstn-Loc) being an attribute of another (**Assembly-Wkstn**). The optional or compulsory participation of entities in relationships and dependency constraints are not enforced by the relational representation.

In the majority of cases, the structuring of relations in third normal form is regarded as being sufficient for the maintainance of integrity constraints in the majority of applications. Two other normal forms (fourth and fifth) do, nonetheless, exist. The structuring of relations into these further normal forms are concerned with avoiding possible update anomalies resulting in loss of data that can occur when a relation is split into sub-relations, which are then joined again to form the original relation. This possible loss of data can be caused by the presence of so-called join dependencies. Details of these additional normal forms are beyond the scope of this book, but may be found in advanced texts on data modelling, for example Tsichritzis and Lochovsky (1982) and Date (1981).

Normalised data relations can be mapped onto physical storage structures with relative ease. However, one disadvantage is that data access can take considerably longer if strict normalisation is observed. For example, postcodes are normally stored as an integral part of an address of a customer. Yet postcode will often be transitively dependent on customer name through another attribute such as street number,

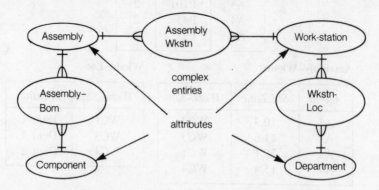

Figure 5.15   E-R diagram of normalised entities.

implying that addresses should consist of two relations. In practice this would severely increase access times and addresses are stored in unnormalised form. The practical design of relational databases usually requires a number of compromises to be made between the degree of normalisation and reasonable access times. When unnormalised relations are retained, the designer is responsible for independent actions being taken to check and maintain data integrity, since this can no longer be guaranteed by the structure.

5.4.4   Relational operations

The advantage of a normalised relational representation is that it is possible, by performing a well-defined set of operations, to construct any desired view consistent with the way any particular individual wishes to aggregate, partially aggregate, or subdivide the entities arising from a normalised model. A relational database is, therefore, highly suitable for a situation in which the database will have multiple users whose requirements cannot be predicted in advance. The operations that may be used to construct different user views while preserving data integrity are formally defined as the operations of a **relational algebra**. The main operations which allow 'view construction' are as follows; examples of their use are shown in Figure 5.16:

(1)   **Selection**: this creates a new relation from an existing relation by selecting those tuples (or rows) having specified attribute values (a subset of the rows of a relation is selected).

(2)   **Projection**: this creates a new relation by selecting only specific columns from an existing relation and removing any redundant tuples from the new relation.

(3)   **Join**: this creates a new relation by joining together two existing relations having attributes (columns) in common, and concatenating tuples with the same value of that attribute.

By using combinations of the above operations, it should be possible to view a set of normalised relations which might represent entities having no correspondence with the user's view of reality, in terms of a new set of entities which correspond closely to the user's view.

5.4.5   Relational query languages

A number of query languages have been developed specifically to extract information from relational databases in a more convenient and understandable form than by application of relational algebra operations. The language that we shall consider briefly here, and which has become

SELECTION
SELECT (ASSEMBLY–Wkstn) WHERE (Work–Stn = '3')
This would generate from the Assembly–Wkstn relation the table:

Assembly–id	Std.Time	Work–Stn
A1	10.3	WC3
A2	11.3	WC3

PROJECTION
PROJECT (Assembly–Wkstn) OVER (Assembly–id, Std.time)
would generate the table:

Assembly–id	Std.Time
A1	10.3
A2	11.6
A3	23.1
A4	15.4

JOIN
JOIN (Assembly–Wkstn, Wkstn–Loc) OVER (Work–Stn)
would generate the table:

Assembly–id	Std.Time	Work–Stn	Location
A1	10.3	WC3	Dept 1
A2	11.6	WC3	Dept 1
A3	23.1	WC1	Dept 1
A4	15.4	WC4	Dept 2

Figure 5.16 Relational algebra operations.

the de facto industry standard, is Structured Query Language (SQL)
developed by IBM (Astrahan and Chamberlin, 1975).

SQL is based around the command SELECT which has syntax of
the form:

SELECT(attribute names)FROM(relation name)WHERE(attribute conditions)

This command has the effect of scanning a relation and selecting those
tuples whose attributes follow the conditions stated in the WHERE part,
and then displaying only the values of the attributes selected in the first
clause of the command. Thus the command:

SELECT(Assembly-id,Std.Time)FROM(Assembly-Wkstn)
    WHERE(Std-Time>15)

SELECT (Assembly–id,Std.time) FROM (Assembly–Wkstn) WHERE
(Std.time >15)
would generate the table:

Assembly–id	Std.Time
A3	23.1
A4	15.4

a

SELECT (Assembly–id,Location) FROM (Assembly–Wkstn,Wkstn–Loc)
WHERE (Assembly–id.Work–Stn = Wkstn–Loc.Work–Stn)
would generate the table:

Assembly–id	Location
A1	Dept 1
A2	Dept 1
A3	Dept 1
A4	Dept 2

b

Figure 5.17 Tables generated by SQL retrievals.

would generate the table in Figure 5.17a displaying the *id* and *standard times* of all assembly operations with a time longer than 15 units.

Attributes can be selected from multiple relations as though the relations had first been joined on the common value of an attribute.

Thus, it would be possible to retrieve data on the locations (departments) where assemblies are processed using the command:

SELECT(Assembly-id,Location)FROM(Assembly-Wkstn,Wkstn-Loc)
WHERE(Assembly-id.Work-Stn = Wkstn-Loc.Work-Stn)

This would generate the table in Figure 5.17b.

The SELECT command here has performed an implicit join of the relations **Assembly-Wkstn** and **Wkstn-Loc** on common values of the attribute *Work-Stn* (which appears in both relations) and has then made a projection of the resulting relation on the two attributes *Assembly-id* and *Location*. The result is to show the location of each assembly operation.

Quite complex queries can be formulated in this way, enabling data which is distributed over many different relations to be meaningfully collated and displayed using a single command.

5.4.6   The binary model

One disadvantage of the relational model is that the decision on what are entities, what are attributes and what are relationships is often difficult, and somewhat arbitrary decisions must frequently be made. Complications are also introduced by the frequent need to compromise between degree of normalisation and access efficiency. A recent type of data model which tries to eliminate this inhomogeneity is the binary relational model. This makes no distinction between attributes, entities, and entity instances. All are regarded merely as entities linked together in pairs as a set of binary relations. Thus the **Assembly-Wkstn** and **Wkstn-Loc** relations of Figure 5.14 would be encoded in binary relational form as the three binary relations shown in Figure 5.18a.

The **Assembly-Bom** relation, which has a composite key, *Ass-Bom* and *Cpt-id*, must be handled by introducing an artificial entity to represent the composite key. If we call this entity **Ass-part** and stipulate it must have a unique value for each valid combination of assembly and part, then the Assembly-Bom relation would be encoded as the three binary relations in Figure 5.18b.

By creating suitable artificial entities, any type of data environment can be represented as a set of binary relations. Each relation will give the identifier of an entity and one of its descriptive attributes. Some versions of the binary view (see for example Frost, 1982) advocate the naming of each different type of relation explicitly. In this case, the binary relations are stored as 'triples' of the form <entity-id, relation name, entity-id>. Thus the binary relations between assembly-no and standard time and between assembly-no and workstation might have a

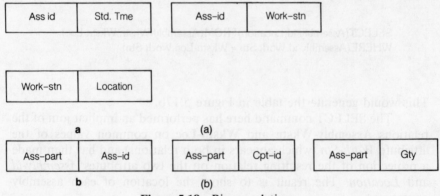

Figure 5.18   Binary relations.

set of instances which would be stored as follows:

assembly-1 has time	16.4	
assembly-2 has time	7.8	
assembly-1 on workstation	WC1	
assembly-2 on workstation	WC1	

These are, in fact, just the <object-attribute-value> triples that were identified as the elementary item of data in section 5.1.

Membership of an entity set and relationships between entity sets can also be stored as binary relations:

assembly-1	is-a	assembly
assembly	has	stnd.time

Retrieval of data from this type of binary relational model can be effected by specifying the retrieval pattern required: Thus the request: (assembly-1 has time ?) would return the value '16.4'. The request: (? on-workstation WC1) would return the value 'assembly-1'. More complex queries could be handled by relational algebra operations to form any user view of the data required, however complex.

The binary view has the advantage of being a uniform, simple to understand representation which is sufficiently flexible to represent any type of relationships between data items, and hence can be used to provide a consistent framework for the design of conceptual schemas in which the transition to the logical schema is relatively trivial since the necessity for file design is removed. Furthermore, this type of representation can readily accommodate changes: the addition of further relations will have no effect on the remainder of the structure (whereas in the standard relational model renormalisation might be needed). Another very important advantage is that the user of the database need have no knowledge of any underlying file structure to make ad hoc queries.

It has been argued that binary relations are unrealistically small, and that applications will almost invariably want to access multiple attributes of an entity. In the binary model, these must all be accessed separately. On the other hand, different applications will need to access different and overlapping subsets of the attributes, and the mere fact that attributes are identified separately indicates an intention to use them separately. If a group of attributes are always used together, such as the individual lines of an address (street, suburb, postcode, etc.) they can generally be aggregated into a single attribute.

5.5   Modern trends — Semantic and fifth generation database management systems

A major limitation of conventional database management systems lies with the problems that arise in making the connection between the conceptual schema (model of the world) and the logical schema (model of the data). One of the purposes of defining a conceptual schema is to produce a description of the world which is structured so that it can be conveniently translated into a logical model which is mappable onto physical storage structures, and yet at the same time conveys the semantic meaning of the structures being described in a way that is understandable to database users. This requires a language which is precise and formally defined, yet sufficiently rich in its semantic constructs to capture the meaning required. The conceptual schema should be independent of the logical representation used. Unfortunately, most conventional DBMSs do not provide such a language. The conceptual schema must often be developed (if at all) externally to the DBMS and tediously translated into a logical schema before it can be accepted by the DBMS. Ad hoc queries to the database therefore require knowledge of the semantics of the logical schema. For example, *ad hoc* queries of a relational database require knowledge of the relations into which the data is structured and their meaning, some of which, through normalisation, may not correspond to any familiar object in the user's world. Similarly, application programs accessing the database require knowledge of the logical schema, and this causes difficulties in communication between two databases with different logical structures.

Furthermore, conventional DBMSs do not support automatic data integrity checking, other than on those constraints which are enforced by the allowable data structures. Although the user may specify a number of integrity constraints in the conceptual schema (for example ER diagrams can conveniently display optional or compulsory participation of entities in relationships) these also must be translated into the corresponding constraints in the logical schema, and generally speaking, separate programs must be written to enforce them, and these must be modified when constraints change.

The main thrust in development of future generation DBMSs is in the provision, not only of formal languages for the definition of conceptual schemas including all the integrity constraints that can be identified at this level, but also of facilities for the automatic translation of a conceptual schema as defined in such a language, to the logical and thus to the physical level. The conceptual schema, rather than existing merely as a series of diagrams on sheets of paper, or in the head of the designer, now becomes the complete specification of the database. Updates, queries, and changes to database structure, are all addressed at the conceptual level which is the focal point of communication with and about the database.

Contrasting methods of achieving this are being investigated. A number of researchers (e.g., King and McLeod, 1985) are investigating the use of so-called semantic data models. These seek to provide a set of general semantic constructs which repeatedly appear in different problem domains, and which can effectively express the meaning and structure of data captured from those domains. Some of these efforts are based on the ER modelling approach and seek to provide a language in which the entities, relationships and associated constraints can be specified, prior to the automatic translation of this specification into a logical schema. In order to ensure the preservation of the semantic integrity of the schema on interpretation to the logical level (which may involve automatic data normalisation) the constraints need to be fully specified. Since the individual who is specifying the conceptual schema may not be aware of all the constraints that need to be specified, considerable effort is going into developing systems which have embedded knowledge of the general types of constraint that need defining before a schema can be regarded as sufficiently specified for translation to the logical level, and can prompt the designer accordingly. A typical example of such a system is described by Hawryszkiewycz (1985).

Semantic constructs can be provided as part of the language available for defining the conceptual schema, and allow data to be structured in semantically richer ways than is permitted in the relational model. The semantic data modelling work of King and McLeod, for example, introduces the constructs of aggregation (combination of individual object classes to form a composite class), generalisation, specialisation, and inheritance (allowing the combination of object categories into super-categories at higher levels of abstraction, with inheritance of characteristics of a category from its super-category). Objects are also divided into concrete objects, events (point and duration), abstractions, and names, each with an explicit set of associated constraints that map onto the real world behaviour and relationships of these constructs. These types of construct can, of course, be defined in conventional data modelling by the explicit declaration of the relevant constraints. But whereas in the context of the conventional DBMS, design decisions are required as to the method of representation of these constructs in the logical schema, in a semantic database they can be explicitly specified in the formal language provided at the conceptual level, and automatically implemented in lower level schema. By providing sometimes quite complex abstractions, semantic databases can enforce a greater number of integrity constraints than can be supported by structures of lower semantic content. A good overview of semantic database modelling is given by Hull and King (1987).

An alternative to providing predefined semantic constructs, which are sometimes restrictive in their representation capability for application areas for which they were not designed, is to use conceptual schema definition languages which are lower in their level of implied semantics, but have the expressive power to define explicit constraints (which are to a large extent *inherently* represented in the data structures of the models relying on semantically complex constructs) in addition to data structures. In other words, both the data structures and the explicit constraints are expressible in the same formal language. The schema definition languages used to achieve this tend to be based on the notion of the elementary fact (Kent, 1983) or the primitive sentence (Nijssen, 1984). Nijssen has described these types of data model as fifth generation data models. They are in fact the natural language equivalents of the binary relations described earlier. The user defines the conceptual schema in terms of a large number of simple sentences consisting of noun-verb-adjective triplets. The idea is that by passing an analyser over this natural language description, the elementary sentences can be parsed into nouns, verbs and adjectives corresponding to entities, relationships and attributes, and that these can be mapped onto some convenient logical schema such as the relational or binary relational schema.

Inferential retrieval is another feature attracting considerable research. In conventional databases the only facts or data that can be retrieved from the database are those which are already stored. A system with formal logical reasoning capability can, however, report inferred facts which are consistent with those already stored. This will be explored in more detail in the final section of the book, in which the integration of knowledge bases and databases is examined.

Chapter 6
The Computer Representation of Knowledge

This chapter discusses in somewhat greater depth than Chapter 4 what is meant by the concept of knowledge and how **knowledge** (rather than merely data) may be stored in a computer. The following three chapters look at three different knowledge representation paradigms in more detail.

6.1 Categorisation of knowledge

In Chapter 3 we defined the knowledge of a person as a system of related facts, abstractions, theories and models or procedures existing in that person's mind, enabling them to interpret, predict and respond to their environment in a manner consistent with their general goals (which must themselves be definable within the same knowledge framework). The representation of knowledge is thus concerned with the representation of facts, the abstraction of patterns within these facts, and the generalisation of patterns to form theories. It is also concerned with the ability to apply these theories in an interpretive and predictive sense, to infer the existence of new facts or conclusions, or to plan intelligent, goal-directed actions. The aim of knowledge represention is to capture both the facts about a particular domain of interest, and the ways in which the facts can be used in reasoning and problem solving within this domain. A systematically organised collection of stored knowledge is referred to as a **knowledge base**.

109

In order to discuss the computer representation of knowledge, it is convenient to divide knowledge (somewhat arbitrarily) into the following categories (shown schematically in Figure 6.1):

(1)   Knowledge of the current facts known or thought to be true of a particular environment, general relationships between these facts, and any constraints on allowable facts and relationships. This type of knowledge may be termed **declarative**, or more colloquially, what knowledge.

(2)   Knowledge about procedures for the inference of new facts or relationships, or heuristics for the finding of solutions to specific problems within the environment. This type of knowledge may be termed **procedural**, or more colloquially, 'how to' knowledge.

6.1.1   Declarative knowledge

Declarative knowledge about a factory environment might include knowledge of such things as the jobs currently in progress on the shop floor, the identity, location and capabilities of the various production facilities available, the range of products made by the company and their material and processing requirements and stock levels currently held. These facts could be stored in a computer by making use of one of the data models described in the previous chapter. This involves organising

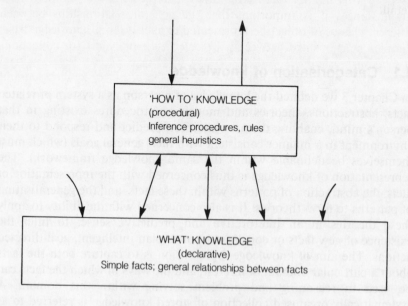

Figure 6.1   Types of knowledge.

facts into groups pertaining to similar classes of object, identifying the attributes of the object that are thus represented, and storing groups of facts about an object as object instances. Conventional databases may, in fact, be regarded as stores of declarative knowledge.

Declarative knowledge may also consist of general relationships between facts. In a data model, these relationships are usually represented implicitly in the way in which the data is structured. For example, consider the situation where both a tool and an operator are required for a job to be processed on a machine: this may be implicitly represented in a relational database by setting up a relation called 'job-assignment' possessing the identities of the machine to be used and the operator and tool to be assigned to the job as attributes. The database, by insisting on non-null attribute values, would then ensure that a job could not be assigned to a machine without an operator and a tool being assigned as well. However, this requirement is effectively 'hardwired' into the structure of the database and would be difficult to update. Data models tend to be oriented to the storage of a large number of instances of a relatively small number of different object classes with a simple set of relationships between them (such as items stocked and who they are purchased from). These relationships are also assumed to be stable over time.

If we are dealing with a large number of object classes with relatively few instances of each, but with complex and possibly changing relationships between each class (such as the layout of facilities in a factory), this is not the best form of representation. Under these circumstances it is important that the general relationships between different classes of object be represented explicitly. In a **knowledge base**, complex relationships between different classes of object (or collections of facts) are usually represented in the form of explicitly stated general rules about the facts, so that not only can they be readily accessed and updated, but they also can be utilised in reasoning and problem solving. The difference between a database and a knowledge base is that whereas the former consists of large numbers of similar types of fact, and a small number of general rules which are usually represented implicitly in how the facts are organised, a knowledge base usually consists of a relatively small number of facts and a larger number of explicitly stored general rules relating to the facts. The general rules themselves contitute a special type of fact (we may regard them as 'complex' facts).

Explicit representation of general rules about facts can enable new facts to be inferred from those already existing. For example, the general rule 'If job x requires part y and part y is out of stock, then job x is unreleasable' allows a new fact to be deduced about all jobs for which the conditional parts of this rule are true, the new facts being that each of these jobs is unreleasable. Procedural knowledge (in the form of a simple inference procedure) would be required to actually generate these new

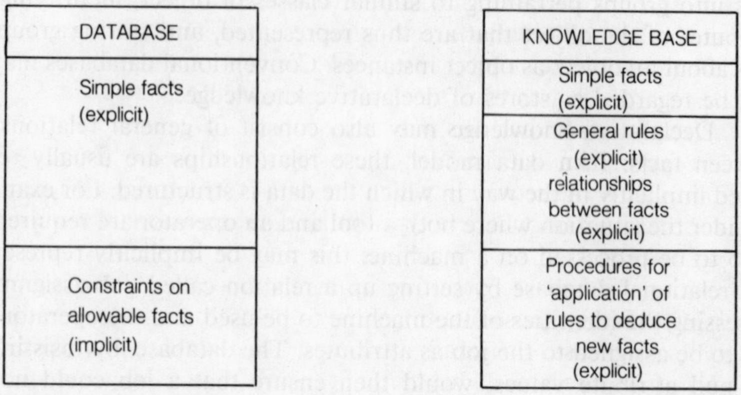

DATABASE	KNOWLEDGE BASE
Simple facts (explicit)	Simple facts (explicit)
	General rules (explicit) relationships between facts (explicit)
Constraints on allowable facts (implicit)	Procedures for 'application' of rules to deduce new facts (explicit)

Figure 6.2 Differences between a database and a knowledge base.

facts for explicit storage in the knowledge base. Without the application of this procedural knowledge, the fact that a particular job (say J56, which satisfies the conditions of the rule) is unreleasable is not represented explicitly but will be *implicit* in the knowledge base (i.e., it can be inferred, when required, from the existing combination of facts and rules by the application of inference procedures). A feature of knowledge bases is that, although they may not store a large number of explicit facts, they do store a sufficient number of general rules to enable large numbers of additional explicit facts to be deduced when required. Knowledge bases thus contain a large number of implicit facts, unlike conventional databases in which all the facts are *explicit*. Another way of expressing this is by saying that knowledge bases store facts at a more abstract and general level.

6.1.2 Procedural knowledge

As we have seen, procedural knowledge is that which enables reasoning and problem solving to occur using the currently existing declarative knowledge. If we have a declarative knowledge base consisting of a collection of a set of facts and a set of general rules, then procedural knowledge (in the form of a set of inference procedures) is required for the deduction of any new explicit facts which are consistent with the existing declarative knowledge. Let us consider that our declarative knowledge base contains the following facts:

Job J56 requires Part P1054
Part P1054 is out of stock
If Job x requires Part y and Part y is out of stock then Job x is unreleasable.

In order to infer that Job J56 was unreleasable, we would need to know about a procedure telling us that, if we could match x and y in conditional part of the general rule with an actual job and actual part for which the condition was true, we could add to the declarative knowledge base the explicit fact that this particular job was unreleasable.

Procedural knowledge can take a variety of forms, and in some cases the distinction between declarative and procedural knowledge can become quite indistinct. Many types of knowledge base contain a set of simple facts, and a set of active 'production' rules consisting of 'condition' parts and an 'action' part which can 'fire' if the condition parts are satisfied by those facts. The executing of the rule then adds new facts to the database. For example, the general rule about unreleasable jobs might be expressed slightly differently as:

> If a job can be found requiring a part that is out of stock then assign the 'status' of the job as 'unreleasable'

This new form of expression makes a production rule subtly different from the rules stored in a declarative knowledge base, since there is an implication that the new rule represents a procedure that is **executed**, involving an active search of the database and the addition of a new fact, whereas the previous form of the rule was merely a passive statement. In a sense the production rule contains a mixture of both procedural and declarative knowledge. These different interpretations of a 'rule' constitute one of the main distinctions between two different types of approach to knowledge representation, the production rule approach and the predicate logic approach; these will be examined later in the book.

The new facts generated by the application of procedural knowledge do not need to pertain to the current state of the world, as represented by the existing declarative knowledge. For example, the action parts of procedural rules might correspond to actions that change the state of the world, and the effect of executing a rule would then be to generate new facts that would represent the state of the world after the action had been taken. Thus, the result of executing a rule of the type:

> If process A has a longer duration that process B then perform process B

might be to update the set of declarative facts to be consistent with the state of the world after process B had been performed (such as updating the facts about current shape, tolerance, surface finish and cumulative cost of a component whose machining is being planned). Such rules might be used to 'simulate' and therefore predict the consequences (in terms of the generated sets of facts) of different actions, and to choose the action (or sequence of actions) most appropriate in a given situation.

In most approaches to knowledge representation, it is convenient to define various levels of procedural knowledge. The lowest level consists of individual modular 'chunks' of procedural knowledge (e.g., in the form of individual procedural rules) each of which is applicable in certain restricted classes of situation defined by the current facts. Rules are usually highly specific to particular classes of problem (e.g., shop floor scheduling) but are not usually sufficient in themselves to solve complete problems. They represent the procedural building blocks of the problem-solving process.

Problems are solved using knowledge of when and how to apply the applicable rules to the declarative fact base in such a way that a new set of facts representing the problem solution can be generated. This type of knowledge could be termed 'control' or 'meta' knowledge since it controls the application of individual chunks of lower level knowledge. A typical piece of control knowledge might be: 'In production scheduling

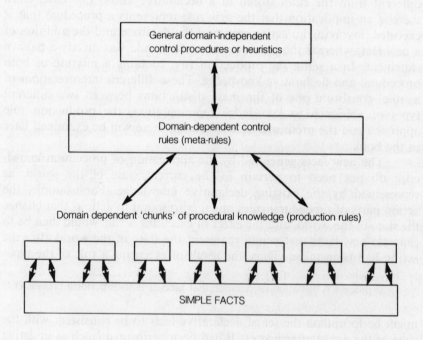

Figure 6.3 Multiple 'levels' of procedural knowledge.

problems, first use rules for sequencing jobs in order of due date, then use rules for loading on work centres, then use rules for resolving precedence conflicts'. This is an example of a domain-dependent piece of control knowledge. Control knowledge may also however be domain indepen- dent, for example: 'Try each procedure in sequence until one is applicable; execute the procedure then try each procedure again; repeat until the goal is reached.' Domain-independent control structures have the advantage that a clear distinction can be made between specific knowledge of the problem domain in terms of facts, rules and procedures, and the control knowledge itself.

Conventional computer programs are one way in which procedural knowledge can be stored. However, these have rather primitive control structures which rely on the sequential processing of a set of symbolic instructions in an order prespecified by the programmer, to represent how new facts derived by the program are connected to the original set of facts. Although conditional branching to different sets of instructions can occur, the whole process must be mapped out and exhaustively defined beforehand. Separate programs must usually be specified for each type of problem that is likely to occur. In environments such as that of manufacturing, where unpredictability and uncertainty are a way of life, it is rarely possible to anticipate in advance more than a few routine problems that can be standardised and pre-programmed in this way. Attempts to program even moderately complex tasks (such as the requirements planning performed by MRP systems) invariably result in the generation of a large number of 'exception' situations for which the designer of the program did not provide procedurally specified solutions. All exceptions require human intervention, and exception messages generated by MRP systems can be so numerous as to threaten the very viability of the system. Although some of these exceptions clearly demand human rather than computer judgement for their resolution, as in the case of MRP, a large proportion of them could be resolved within the MRP system itself if this were based on knowledge structures that afforded a more flexible reasoning capability.

The inflexibility of the conventional approach to representing procedural knowledges with its sequential control structures has been one of the main reasons for the development of alternative types of representation for procedural knowledge that is closer to the structures humans use for knowledge processing. In particular, to achieve more flexible control structures, emphasis has been on representations in which procedures are automatically invoked and interact with each other according to patterns which exist in the factual part of the database, rather than according to a predetermined sequence. This is more analogous to the natural processing that occurs within the human brain, where neurons are fired according to certain stimulii or patterns of stimuli which represent patterns of received data.

6.2   The use of knowledge for problem solving

The main objective of the computerised representation of knowledge is for the eventual utilisation of this knowledge in computer assisted or fully automated problem solving. Problem *solving* requires some adequate means of problem *representation*. It also requires an effective search strategy for finding a problem solution. The representation and storage of knowledge about the problem and of the ways in which it may be solved can be of use in formulating appropriate search strategies, and guiding the search towards a solution.

6.2.1   The key role of representation

Newell and Simon, in their key work on human problem solving published in 1972, introduced the concept of 'problem space', which is the way a decision maker represents a problem in order to work on it. When confronted with a problem, a person formulates a representation of the problem which defines the conceptual space in which problem solving takes place. The nature and the adequacy of the representation will obviously have a strong influence on the quality of the solution and the ease with which it can be found.

Winston (1984) has summarised a set of desiderata for good representations most of which were established as a result of the early work:

- Good representations make the important things explicit.
- They expose natural constraints, making it obvious what is allowable and what is forbidden.
- They are complete: they say all that needs to be said.
- They are concise: things are said efficiently.
- They are transparent: what is said is readily understandable.
- They facilitate computation: information can be stored and retrieved quickly.
- They suppress detail: rarely-used information can be kept out of sight, but retrieved when necessary.
- They are sufficiently rigorously defined so as to be computable by existing procedures.

6.2.2   State space representation

One very common form of problem representation technique is a 'state space' representation, in which the characteristics of the problem domain at a particular point in time are represented by a 'state' defined in terms of the set of facts which are true at that time. The problem itself can be represented by specifying the initial state, defined by the facts that are initially true, and the desired or goal state which is the set of facts that need to be true for the problem to be solved. Facts can be changed, (i.e., new facts added and existing facts deleted) and thus the state of the problem domain altered, by applying operators which correspond to the set of allowable actions or inferences that can occur in the real world for that particular state of the problem, and which convert it to another state. These operators correspond to the procedures for the generation of new facts referred to in the previous section. Thus, starting from the initial state, a large number of different sequences of further states can be generated in so-called state space by a series of applications of permissable operators on successive states.

This situation is shown diagramatically in Figure 6.4 as a network in which the nodes are states, and the arcs between nodes are operators. Different arcs leaving a node represent the different operators that can be

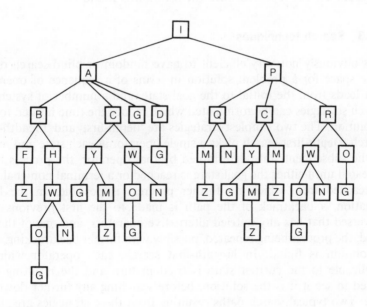

I = Initial state
G = Goal state

Figure 6.4 An example of state space.

applied to the corresponding state. Finding a solution to the problem involves finding a sequence of operators that can convert the initial state to the goal state through a series of intermediate states. Thus, in a process planning problem, the initial state could be specified in terms of a description of the raw materials available, the final state by a description of the end product, and the operators could be the individual process operations (e.g., various types of machining) by which the conversion might take place. In a production scheduling problem, states may represent alternative loadings of jobs on machines, with the initial state being a set of unloaded jobs, the goal state a complete set of job loadings that satisfies various constraints, and the individual operators being the individual assignment of specific jobs to specific machines at specific times.

A sequence of operators that leads to the goal state may be found by a procedure known as **generate and test**. This involves the generation of a new state of the system by applying an operator to the existing state. If the new state is the solution, the process stops. If it is not the solution, another operator can be applied to the new state or an alternative operator to the old state to generate a further state to be tested for the solution. This is repeated until the solution is found.

6.2.3 Search techniques

It is obviously not very efficient to have random or blind search of the state space for a problem solution in terms of a sequence of operators that leads from the initial to the goal state, and a number of systematic search strategies can be formulated which reduce the time needed to find a solution. The two simplest strategies are 'depth-first' and 'breadth-first' search. **Depth-first** search picks a single operator at each state and moves to the subsequent state determined by that operator, the process being repeated until either the goal state is reached or a terminal non-goal state is reached from which no further progress is possible. In the latter situation, a backtrack of the path is made to the first previous state traversed that has any untried alternative operators, and one of these is tried, the process being repeated, possibly with further backtracking, until a solution is found. In **breadth-first** search, each operator which is applicable to the current state is tried in turn and the resulting state tested to see if it is the solution, before searching any further down the tree. Two typical search paths resulting from these strategies are shown in Figure 6.5. In cases where a solution exists near the top of the search tree, breadth-first search will usually discover it first, since depth-first search is likely to have explored in detail a number of wrong paths before the correct one is tried. Depth-first search will also result in difficulties if any part of the search tree is infinitely deep, since search down that path will continue ad infinitum. On the other hand, depth-first search will

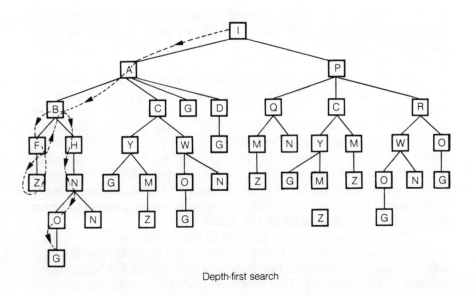

Depth-first search

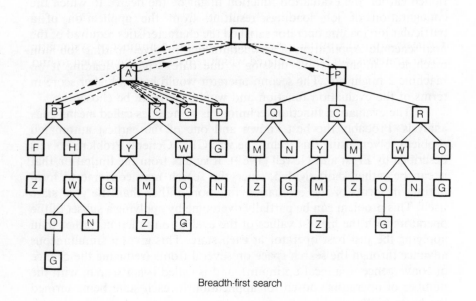

Breadth-first search

Figure 6.5 Depth-first and Breath-first search.

reach a solution more quickly if good decisions can be made about the choice of operator at each node. As will be seen, a good choice of operator to apply at each state is almost essential to make most state-space search problems tractable.

A look at the shape of the typical tree given in Figure 6.4 shows that the number of possible states, and hence possible paths through the tree, increases very rapidly as the depth of the tree increases. We are faced with what is termed a 'combinatorial explosion' of possible paths, which makes any attempt at exhaustive search (i.e., systematic examination of every possible path through the tree) an impracticable proposition. The AI approach to problem solving relies on the use of stored knowledge to reduce the search space by the suggestion of more sophisticated strategies for selecting the appropriate operator (and hence the next state) at each phase of the search process.

One technique to reduce the size of the search space is to make a selective choice of operator based on some type of evaluation function which measures the relative effectiveness of each operator in reducing the distance to the goal state. This is obviously directly applicable to travel problems in which the distance measure can be taken literally. However, it can also be used in any problem in which individual states can be scored in some way that indicates their relative desirability, given the nature of the goal. Thus, in the production scheduling problem mentioned earlier, the evaluation function might be the degree to which the configuration of job loadings resulting from the application of a particular job loading operator satisfied the characteristics required of the final schedule. Application of an operator that involved loading Job 8 on machine 3 might involve missing a due date, whereas loading it on machine 2 might not. The second operator would have a higher score in terms of the evaluation function and would therefore be chosen.

The evaluation function technique is sometimes called **means-ends analysis**. Probably the best known and one of the earliest automated problem solvers using this technique was GPS (General Problem Solver) described by Ernst and Newell (1969). It suffers from the limitation that it can be rather short-sighted, since the search may converge to local optima in terms of the evaluation function, rather than the goal state itself. This problem can be partially overcome by applying a subset of the operators with the highest values of the evaluation function, rather than applying the just best operator at each state. This gives a simultaneous advance through the search space on several fronts (reducing the chance of convergence to a local optimum), and is called **beam search**, with the number of operators chosen for application to each state being termed the **beam width**.

The types of search strategy described above all constitute **domain independent** control knowledge about how to solve problems, since they are applicable over a wide range of different classes of problem. On their own, they are inadequate for many types of problem which humans can solve fairly easily by applying the simple **domain-specific** rules of thumb derived from stored experience of solving similar problems. Study of the problem-solving behaviour of humans, particularly in problem domains such as medicine where there is a considerable amount of specialist knowledge, indicates that they do not use generalised search strategies with complex evaluation algorithms, for the solution of problems. Instead, they tend to narrow down the search space by making use of certain characteristics or patterns inherent in the facts describing the current state, which (they have learnt from experience) indicate that certain choices of next state are good and certain choices are bad. Thus, when planning the machining of a component part, an expert human machinist may utilise the knowledge that for the particular material and the tolerances required, the milling operation should always precede the drilling operation. When the machinist reached the point in the plan where one of these two operations needed to be selected, this knowledge would guide the choice of next state. The many similar types of specialist knowledge employed to reduce the search space would be difficult to incorporate in an evaluation function, which would soon become extremely unwieldy. A more convenient method would be to represent these individual pieces of knowledge explicitly, for example as domain specific production rules. Taking this a step further, we can see that the action part of a production rule is basically equivalent to a state space operator that can change the state of the problem-solving process as defined by the current facts. The conditional parts of the rule specify the characteristics or patterns in the existing set of facts, which if present would indicate this operator to be a good one to use. Search operators in the form of production rules essentially carry their own criteria for selection, and so a significant part of the overall control of the problem solving process becomes embedded in the conditional parts of the production rules, rather than in some overall search strategy imposed from above.

This is not to suggest that all control of the search should be embedded in production rules. In practice, some form of external control strategy is still required, such as determining the order of matching of rules, and the ability to resolve conflicts between several rules which may be applicable at the same time. This external control knowledge may also have domain specific elements, although it is more common for it to be domain independent. The distribution of domain specific knowledge between external control structures and individual rules and procedures is an important topic in knowledge representation and will be a recurrent theme in this book. The term 'inference engine' is usually applied to the control component of a knowledge-based system which governs the order of execution of domain specific rules in such a way as to reach intermediate conclusions about the problem, call in additional groups of rules if necessary, and determine when a solution has been reached. More specific examples of the different functions of an inference engine will be seen in the following chapter.

6.3 Deep and surface knowledge

Problem solving methods which are acquired from experts in the form of rules do not usually contain explicit representations of the basic structural and causal relationships between entities in the problem domain, or of the basic laws, axioms and principles, from which these problem solving methods are derived. Rules are generally articulated in the form of 'compiled' knowledge which constitutes a type of organised and indexed summary of those chains of reasoning derivable from the more basic, or deeper representation or understanding of the problem domain, and which are directly applicable to typical problems requiring solution. Thus, rules tend to represent a few commonly occurring key patterns and relationships which have been compiled by a person over time from his underlying deeper knowledge of the problem domain, and augmented by empirical associations between data and conclusions which are accumulated with experience.

Deeper domain knowledge (in contrast with the rule based problem solving knowledge which is often termed 'surface' or 'shallow' knowledge) includes the ability to reason about a problem from first principles, by having access to some type of model of the basic entities comprising the problem domain, the relationships between these entities, and the constraints (in the form of such things as physical laws and organisational policies) that govern these relationships. It also includes having access to basic inference rules by which reasoning can take place with reference to this model. Efficient rules for solving specific problems are generally *derivable* from this deeper knowledge, and deep knowledge is therefore *implicit* within the rule set. This distinction between deep and shallow knowledge is particularly important for physical systems and processes.

As an example, consider the case of a job shop in which a machine goes down. If an urgent job is waiting to be processed on this machine, the shop foreman may know from experience that an alternative machine using a different cutting tool and a different sequence of cuts may be capable of performing the same job. This would represent surface knowledge (i.e., a direct association between the characteristics describing the job and the alternative process that might be used) and might be represented as a production rule. However, if no previous instance of that type of job had arisen, it would be necessary to perform a deeper level of reasoning to deduce that this particular alternative process could be used. This might involve knowledge of the fact that the material involved

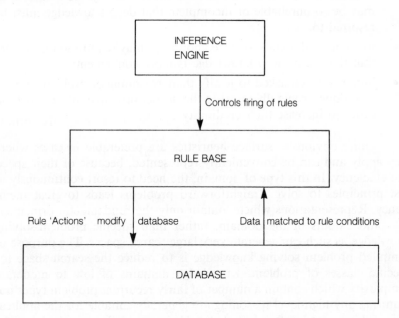

Figure 6.6 'Deep' and 'surface' knowledge.

had a certain set of physical properties, and that certain of these properties indicated that certain types of tool might be permissable and others not. This type of knowledge would be regarded as 'deep knowledge' of the manufacturing technology on which the process was based.

Obviously, the notions of deep and surface knowledge are relative, and what is regarded as deep knowledge will depend on how far back to first principles one chooses to go. What is deep knowledge to a production foreman may be surface knowledge to a manufacturing engineer, and what is deep knowledge to a manufacturing engineer may be surface knowledge to a physicist.

Hart (1982) was the first person to draw the increasingly important distinction between surface and deep knowledge representation, and to indicate the need for deep knowledge representations to complement surface knowledge heuristics, particularly for problem domains in which new classes of problem are continuously emerging. The following observations from Hart's paper capture the essence of this point:

- humans often resort to reasoning from first principles when confronted with non-routine types of problem that cannot be handled by existing sets of compiled rules or empirical associations derived from experience;

- in some fields, surface knowledge either may not be available or may be so unreliable or incomplete that deep knowledge must be resorted to;

- in complex domains, surface knowledge may require so many rules that the use of deep knowledge is more convenient;

- humans, when asked to justify their reasoning or problem solving techniques, generally resort to the deeper principles of their field in order to increase their credibility.

Quite obviously, surface heuristics are preferable in cases where they apply and can be conveniently represented, because of their speed and efficiency. In this type of domain, the need to resort continuously to first principles to solve straightforward problems leads to great inefficiency. Representations which contain only the fundamental principles, laws and axioms of the domain, rather than specific problem-solving knowledge as such can generate very large search spaces. The purpose of compiled problem solving knowledge is to reduce the search space for specific classes of problem. Knowledge domains of low to moderate complexity which contain a number of fairly recurrent problem types not requiring any high level reasoning are generally suitable for the application of this type of surface knowledge. However, as the complexity of the domain increases, it becomes increasingly difficult to anticipate and represent all the different types of problem that might require solution, and the number of rules required can become sufficiently large as to be unmanageable. In this type of situation, it is usually necessary to resort to a deep knowledge representation, even though a considerable amount of search may be required for the solution. Knowledge-based systems which contain a deep knowledge representation are sometimes referred to as **model-based** systems. An increasingly frequent solution is to develop a system that contains surface heuristics for the solution of the more routine types of problem, and also deep background knowledge that can be invoked when surface heuristics are inadequate and which can be used to compile additional surface heuristics as new and unanticipated types of problem start to emerge.

6.4 Knowledge representation paradigms

A variety of representation methods have been developed to store the type of domain-specific problem-solving knowledge we have been discussing above. The most important are respectively the **rule-based** paradigm, the **predicate-logic** paradigm, and the **object-oriented** paradigm. All of these paradigms are based on the concept of 'pattern directed inference', in which certain patterns of basic facts serve to trigger active knowledge components which modify or generate new facts. However, each of these paradigms differs in terms of the structures available for storing declarative facts, the procedures by which new facts are generated from existing facts, and the control mechanism (or inference engine) which directs how this knowledge is used to solve problems. The next three chapters will discuss these three knowledge representation paradigms in more detail.

CHAPTER 7
The Rule-based Paradigm for Knowledge Representation

The rule-based paradigm is the most popular and the easiest to understand paradigm for codifying problem-solving knowledge. The majority of the earlier knowledge-based reasoning systems were based on the representation of knowledge in the form of production rules, including the MYCIN system for diagnosis of blood infections and the XCON system for configuring VAX computers. Many knowledge-based systems being built today continue to use this approach.

7.1 Components of a rule-based system

A rule-based system consists of the following components:

- a database
- a rule base
- an inference engine

The **database** stores the basic facts or declarative knowledge currently known about the problem domain. These may be stored as instances of data objects in the form of object-attribute-value triplets, or as relational tables. The **rule base** stores domain-specific procedural knowledge in the form of situation-action rules of the form:

IF (conditions) THEN (actions)

The left-hand side of each rule is a string of one or more conditions which refer to the existence of certain values or patterns of data in the database (e.g., certain combinations of object-attribute-value triplets). If patterns of data are found which match the conditional elements of the rule, the 'action' part on the right-hand side of the rule may be executed. The action part of the rule may be to modify, insert or delete data, to perform some computation, to request input, or to produce output. The **inference engine** stores generally domain-independent control knowledge about how to apply the rules.

A typical example of a rule expressed in natural language form might be:

If   (Machine 42 is fully loaded)
and   (Machine 43 is down)
then   (process part P2 on machine 50)

This might be more formally expressed in terms of object-attribute values as:

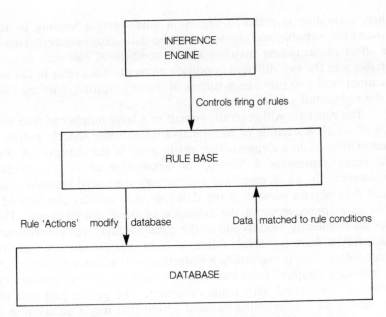

Figure 7.1 Components of a rule-based system.

If   (**Machine** *Number* '42' *Status* 'fully-loaded')
and   (**Machine** *Number* '43' *Status* 'down')
then   (**Part** *Number* 'P2' *process-machine* '50')

In this notation, the object name (bold Type) is followed by the attribute names and the attribute values (in quotes). The action part of the rule is to assign the identity of the machine on which the part is to be processed to the attribute *process-machine*.

The conditional parts of this rule refer to fully instantiated facts within the database. Rules of greater generality may be expressed by using variables in the conditional elements. For example, the more general rule:

If   (a part is normally processed on a preferred machine)
and   (the machine is down)
then   (process the part on the alternative machine)

could be formally expressed as:

If   (**Part** *number* x *preferred-machine* y *alt-machine* z)
and   (**Machine** *number* y *status* 'down')
then   (**Part** *number* x *process-machine* z)

When a variable is matched against a data item, a binding is made between the variable and the value of the data item matched. This has the effect of restricting matches in the conditional elements (e.g., the variable y in the two different condition elements must refer to the same machine), and also provides a means of communicating matched values to the right-hand side of the rule.

The rule base will generally consist of a large number of such rules, each of which is capable of being activated by some specific pattern or combination of data elements that might exist in the database. A single rule really represents a 'chunk' of knowledge about the problem environment, in which empirical associations are stored between instantiated data objects present in the database, and actions that should be taken as a consequence of the existence of these instantiations. These rules are frequently used to add to the database facts (the consequences) which follow from the combination of facts that are already there (the antecedents). This is essentially a **deduction** system. As was indicated in the previous chapter, rules can also be used to express goal-oriented knowledge concerned with plans of action. The action part will then represent some goal-oriented physical action that might be taken in the real world in the situation represented by the activating data pattern; in this case the action part of the rule would update the database in a similar way to that in which the action would be expected to affect the real world.

7.2   Forward and backward chaining

Production rule systems can be run in either forward or backward chaining modes. In the forward chaining, or data driven approach, rules are applicable only if their conditional parts are satisfied and problem solving starts from the initial set of data that describes the problem. When the rule set is executed, each rule in turn has its conditional part matched against the database to see if the conditions are satisfied and the action part can be executed. Those rules that have satisfied conditional parts on a given pass through the rule base are said to be triggered. However only one of these rules will be executed (or fired) on each pass, and conflict resolution determines the choice of rule from the triggered set (known as the conflict set). Execution of the action part will normally change the database in some way. When all the rules have been examined and the database has been updated by the action part of the rule chosen to fire, the cycle through the rule base starts again; but as the data base has been modified, a different set of rules is likely to be activated, and a different one fired. The action part of this rule will again modify the database and the process is repeated until a data configuration is reached that is recognised by one of the rules as a goal state (the solution to the problem) or that does not satisfy the conditional part of any rule (a dead end in the search path, in which case backtracking would have to occur, and a different conflict resolution strategy used). Attainment of the goal state is generally represented by firing a rule that assigns an acceptable value to some **goal variable** stored in the database. For example, a goal variable may be the logical variable *Feasible-Schedule*, and an acceptable value for this variable may be 'True', which would indicate that the goal state had been reached. A rule which assigned the value 'True' to this variable would have conditional parts that represent the properties required by a feasible schedule, and this rule would be triggered if the database contained the representation of a schedule that possessed these properties.

Forward chaining is appropriate for situations where a complete description of the initial facts is available, and it is natural to start from these facts and argue forward. Provided any forward motion in the search space leads towards the goal state, and there are few possibilities for reaching dead-ends requiring backtracking, forward chaining can be an efficient strategy, and may be used in many types of planning problem in which plans are progressively built up by the application of rules in a forward direction. There may however be cases where, given a set of facts which are known to be true, we are interested in discovering whether they are consistent with some hypothesis that can explain them. Most diagnostic problems are of this nature, as, for example, when a machine is continually producing a certain type of defective item and it is necessary to diagnose the cause. In cases like this, it is often more natural to use the goal or hypothesis as the starting point, and work backwards to discover if this is supported by the observed facts, or if a search for any additional facts could be suggested which might confirm or deny the hypothesis. This is termed **backward chaining**. It has the advantage of concentrating attention on the operators most relevant to the problem at hand, avoiding the problem that may occur in forward chaining of considering operators in the early stages of the search that are not relevant to the goal state.

With backward chaining, or the goal-driven approach, problem solving starts with a specification of the goal state (i.e., the goal variable to which an acceptable value must be assigned for the problem to be solved). Rules are selected whose right-hand sides match the goal state, which must usually be representable as a single general fact, completely defined by the right-hand side of the rule (so that attainment of the goal state is recognisable purely by the rule). Generally, none of the rules which match will have a set of conditional parts which are *known* to be true. Therefore, a single rule is selected from those whose right-hand sides match the goal, the conditional parts of this rule are set up as new **subgoals** which are again stored separately from the bulk of the data, and the inference engine attempts to find further rules which have these subgoals as their right-hand sides. Subgoals can be further decomposed into their own subgoals. The problem is solved when a goal is found which can be decomposed in such a way that it can be linked, through successive decomposition into subgoals, to a set of facts which are known to be true, or a set of subgoals known to be attainable.

7.3 Strategies for conflict resolution

In the forward chaining approach, a number of strategies can be used by the inference engine for conflict resolution, i.e. choosing which rule to fire out of the conflict set of rules whose conditions are satisfied by a given set of data values. The type of strategy used can have a major influence on the problem-solving efficiency, and hence cannot be chosen independently of the domain knowledge represented by the rules. Any strategy is a trade-off between sensitivity of the system to changes in the data, and continuity in the line of reasoning. Four typical conflict resolution strategies are:

- **Refractoriness** This derives from the so-called 'refractory' period of neurons in the brain in which neurons are unable to be

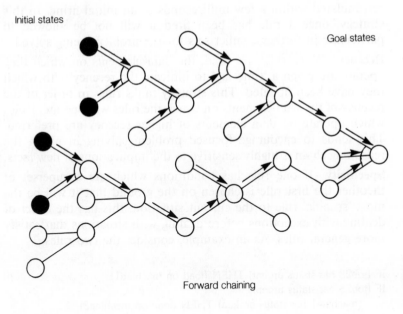

Initial states

Goal states

Forward chaining

● = starting 'facts'

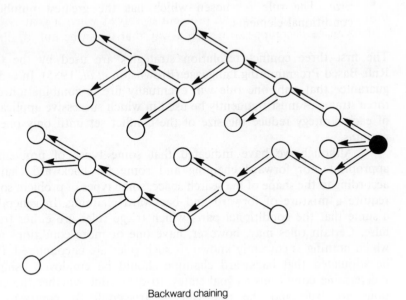

Backward chaining

Figure 7.2 Forward and backward chaining.

restimulated within a few milliseconds of an initial firing. In this strategy, once a rule has been fired it will not be allowed to participate in further conflict sets for the problem being solved.

- **Recency** When rules are fired, the data elements on which they operate are given a 'time tag' to indicate the recency with which they have been updated. This strategy ranks rules in order of the recency of the data elements on which the rules will operate. Rules which operate on data elements of higher recency are preferred. This tends to encourage focused problem solving in which the reasoning chain is highly sensitive to the implications of new facts.

- **Specificity** If one rule has conditions which are a superset of theother the first rule is chosen on the ground that it will be the most 'specific' rule to the current situation; this has the effect of dealing with exceptions before dealing with situations that satisfy more general rules. As an example, consider the two rules:

IF (job23 has-status urgent) THEN (load on machine1)
IF (job23 has-status urgent)
    (machine1 has-status broken) THEN (load on machine2)

Both of these rules may be satisfied by a given set of data, however, only the second rule will fire.

- **Size** The rule is chosen which has the greatest number of conditional elements.

The first three conflict resolution strategies are used by the OPS5 Rule-Based Programming Language (Brownston *et al*, 1985). In order to guarantee that only one rule will eventually fire, a combination of all three strategies must frequently be used in which successive applications of each strategy reduce the size of the conflict set until only one rule remains.

Although we have indicated that some types of problem are appropriate for forward chaining and some for backward chaining, according to the shape of the search space, some types of problem solving require a mixture of forward and backward chaining. In general, we assume that the conditional parts which trigge rules are either true or false. Certain rules may, however, have one or more conditions about which nothing is currently known. If such rules are encountered, it can be stipulated that backward chaining should be employed using the indetermine conditions as goal states, to determine whether the conditions are true and the rule can be triggered. By contrast, in a predominantly backward chaining system, certain groups of rules may always be used in forward chaining mode if they are triggered by known facts which are always relevant to the problem being solved and which can produce higher level facts capable of reducing the backward chaining search required.

It is frequently difficult to match effectively the conflict resolution stategy to the rule set in such a way as to achieve efficient search, and also to predict what the effect of a given strategy will be in terms of the resulting reasoning chain. Rules must always be structured in the light of the particular conflict resolution strategy to be used. It is often useful to augment domain-independent strategies inherent in the method of conflict resolution with a more domain-dependent resolution strategy in the form of meta-rules which can influence which rule out of a particular conflict set should be applied. For example, the rule:

If (machine is L3) and (problem is high rejects) then (apply rules for machine setup diagnosis before rules for tool wear diagnosis)

would indicate that, if both a rule relating to machine setup diagnosis and a rule relating to tool wear diagnosis were applicable at the same time, the rule relating to the former should be selected in preference to the rule relating to the latter.

Another potentially important aspect of the control knowledge contained in the inference engine is concerned with the ability of the system to backtrack. If the remainder of the conflict set is discarded when a rule is fired, or chosen to provide subgoals, then no backtracking is possible if use of this rule leads to a dead-end (i.e., a non-goal state in which no further rules are activated, or a set of facts which are not all true). This can make search more difficult, and only careful structuring of the rule set can reduce the chance of the problem-solving process halting without finding a solution. The ability of an inference engine to support automatic backtracking is therefore a considerable advantage.

7.4 A simple example

The way in which reasoning occurs in a production rule system can be seen more clearly with reference to an AND/OR tree as shown in Figure 7.3. An AND branch emanating from a particular fact indicates that this fact is generated by a rule with a set of conditions corresponding to the facts at the ends of the AND links. An OR branch emanating from a fact indicates that the fact is supported by more than one rule. Facts which are empirical rather than deduced are surrounded by solid lines. Taking the forward chaining mode, in this particular example we might be deciding how to process a particular job, given an existing set of facts in the database. On an initial pass through the rule base, the data might cause only Rule 1 to trigger and fire, creating an instance of a 'past-due

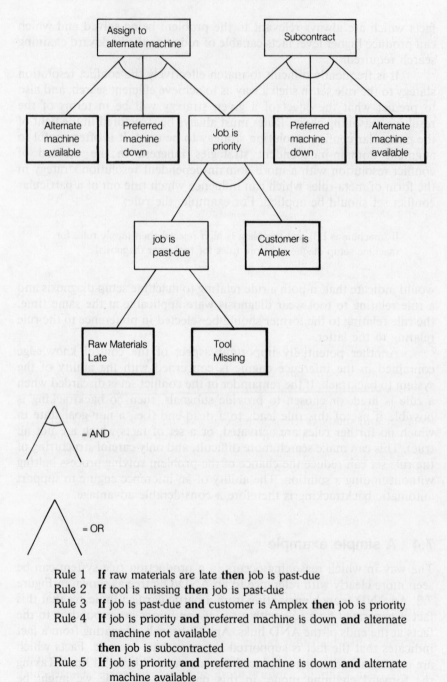

Rule 1   **If** raw materials are late **then** job is past-due
Rule 2   **If** tool is missing **then** job is past-due
Rule 3   **If** job is past-due **and** customer is Amplex **then** job is priority
Rule 4   **If** job is priority **and** preferred machine is down **and** alternate
               machine not available
               then job is subcontracted
Rule 5   **If** job is priority **and** preferred machine is down **and** alternate
               machine available
               then job assigned alternate machine

Figure 7.3 A simple AND/OR representation of a rule-based system.

job'. On the next pass through the rule base, Rules 1 and 3 would trigger if the customer for the job were Amplex. By using either the refractoriness or recency conflict resolution strategy however, only Rule 3 will fire, creating an instance of a 'priority job'. This will then lead to the firing of either of Rules 4 or 5, depending on current status and availablilty of machines on which the job might be processed. The firing of either of these two rules takes us to a goal state.

If we needed to know whether a particular job should be subcontracted, backward chaining would be used. The 'subcontract' state would be the goal, and any rules whose consequents corresponded to this goal (in this case Rule 4) would be selected. The conditional parts of Rule 4 are set up as subgoals. Two of these are observable facts which we shall assume are stored in the database and are true. The third is the consequent of two other rules (Rules 1 and 2) whose conditions must be set up as further subgoals. Both of these conditions are facts stored in the database. They are examined in turn, and if either is true, then all the subgoals represented by the conditional parts of Rule 4 are true. Hence the goal itself is satisfied, and the job should be subcontracted.

7.5 Handling large search spaces

In cases where the rule base is large, and may support knowledge of many different types of problem within a particular domain, the number of rules that may be triggered by any current state of the database may also be large, and many of these rules may not be relevant to the problem being solved. This can result in a search problem of considerable magnitude. The size of the problem is determined by the size of the conflict set on successive passes through the rule base.

7.5.1 Problem reduction and the principle of least commitment

One way of handling this situation is by the process of **problem reduction** in which an attempt is made to break the problem down into a set of weakly- or non-interacting subproblems. This is applicable when, for example, a number of non-interacting subtasks have to be performed to achieve a goal, and may be effected by factoring out the search space into a number of subspaces. Rules can then be grouped in terms of the subproblem to which they relate.

It is usually the case, however, that individual subproblems interact. For example, information required to solve a particular subproblem may only be available after some other subproblem has been solved. One way of handling this is by the **principle of least commitment** in which the problem-solving focus is moved between different subproblems according to the availability of information. This can be achieved by making rules **context sensitive**. One of the conditional parts of each rule refers to the context (i.e., the subproblem which is being solved). The current context is stored in the database. This narrows the conflict set to that set of rules which are actually relevant to the current subproblem. When the subproblem changes, a different set of rules is triggered, and rules themselves can be used to change context. This is eqivalent to embedding further control knowledge explicitly in the rule base rather than entirely relying on a domain-independent conflict resolution strategy. The latter, however, selects which rule to fire *within* the context relevant subset, and may under certain circumstances assist in determining how the reasoning process switches between contexts. Examples of this can be found in the knowledge-based process planning system XCUT (Hummel and Brooks, 1988).

7.5.2 Top-down refinement

Another approach is to structure the search space hierarchically, using the method of so-called **top-down refinement**. This method involves structuring the rulebase in such a way that the initial context is concerned with generating a high-level or rough-cut solution to the problem, at a high level of abstraction. This reduces the size of the initial top-level search space. The high-level solution is then successively refined by breaking it down into subproblems whose solutions are constrained by the solution to the top-level problem. This approach is similar to the top-down refinement method of structured programming described by Wirth (1971). It can again be implemented using context-specific sets of rules.

As an example, Figure 7.4 shows how top-down refinement can be used to store knowledge about the solution of process planning problems.

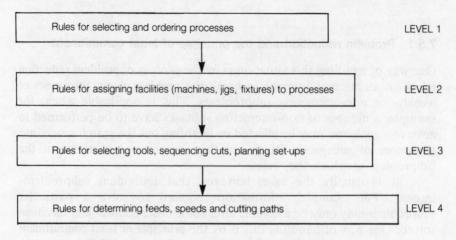

Figure 7.4 Top-down refinement in process planning.

This shows how, at the top level of reasoning about a process planning problem, a group of rules might be activated that decides, from a description of the characteristics and geometry of the starting material and the required part, what individual processes will be required, without specifying the detail of these processes. The next step is to activate rules which assign production facilities to these processes in terms of the machines, jigs, fixtures, etc which are required. Groups of rules operating at lower levels of detail then work out details of the tools, individual cuts, feeds and speeds.

By starting with an aggregate definition and solution of the problem and then refining this solution by conceptually breaking it into components for more detailed analysis, top-down refinement has some similarities with backward chaining in terms of starting with the goal and working backwards. However, the way in which it is implemented is quite different. The method of top-down refinement triggers rules by matching variables in their **conditional** parts to goal variables in the database which indicate the current problem or subproblem under consideration and a rule is fired prior to repeating the matching process. In the latter, rules are triggered whose **action** parts match the goal variables in the database, and depth-first backward search is made to check the conditional parts of these rules, and the conditions of other rules which might satisfy them, before any rules are fired.

7.5.3 Blackboard architecture

It is sometimes convenient to segregate groups of rules which perform separate and well defined functions or lines of reasoning into separate 'knowledge sources'. Each knowledge source then tackles a different aspect of the problem. Communication between knowledge sources can take place through a shared data structure called a **blackboard**. A **scheduler** which might use a number of alternative strategies, such as the least commitment principle, decides which knowledge source to activate-.Knowledge sources can post messages on the blackboard, which can then be accessed and used by other knowledge sources. Blackboard architecture was first used in the HEARSAY2 speech recognition system (see Hayes Roth *et al*, 1983), and has since found numerous other applications including control of flexible manufacturing cells, as will be described in Chapter 12.

7.6 Explanation of reasoning

When rule-based systems are used as a basis for automated problem-solving, it is often not sufficient merely to accept the solution thus derived without checking how it was obtained. The rule-based form of representation allows this to occur very easily by merely arranging that the system maintains a historical record of the path it took from problem description to problem solution, by recording the rules actually fired. The reasoning track can be followed one step at a time by asking the system 'why' or 'how' questions about the application of a given rule. Thus, in the example in Section 7.4, asking the system the question, 'How did you determine job 12 to be of priority' might invoke the reply 'By using rule 3 and knowing the job is past due and the customer is Amplex'. The question, 'Why did you show job 12 to be of priority' might prompt the response, 'In order to use rule 4 to show the job should be subcontracted.'

7.7   Representation of uncertainty in rule-based systems

7.7.1   Components of uncertainty

There are many cases of real-world problem solving, particularly of the type that are frequently represented in the form of backward chaining rule-based systems, where the antecedant (conditional) part of a rule is not certain to be implied from the truth its consequent (conclusion or action part), but only follows with some degree of likelihood. Similarly, observed facts may not be true beyond all doubt, but can only be assigned some likelihood based for example on the conditions under which the observation was made. There are thus two types of uncertainty which typically exist in bodies of knowledge that we might be interested in representing in the form of a rule-oriented knowledge base:

(1)   Uncertainty in the extent to which a conclusion follows from its premises (antecedent-consequent uncertainty).

(2)   Uncertainty in observed facts or facts which been inferred by application of rules (fact uncertainty).

Some method is required for the representation of this uncertainty and its propagation through the reasoning chain. There are four major problems here, namely:

(1)   How do we represent degree of uncertainty in both rules and facts in some consistent way?

(2)   How do we combine the uncertainties of the different facts that make up all the conditional parts of the rule to arrive at an overall uncertainty for the rule's input?

(3)   How do we combine the overall uncertainty of the rule's input with the uncertainty inherent in the rule itself to arrive at the overall uncertainty of the new fact(s) deduced by the rule?

(4)   How do we assess the overall uncertainty of a deduced fact in cases where it is independently supported by more than one rule?

7.7.2 Uncertainty factors

A simple method for representing uncertainty is to associate a numerical measure with each fact or antecedent-consequent relation, for example on a scale between 0 and 1, where 0 indicates that the fact is definitely not true or the consequent definitely does not follow from the antecedent, and 1 indicates the reverse. Varying degrees of uncertainty are represented by numbers between 0 and 1, and we may use the term **uncertainty factor** to refer to these numerical measures.

Depending on how the uncertainty factors are interpreted, they will be combined in a particular manner to represent the way in which uncertainty is propagated through various chains of deduction occurring within the rule base. If we interpret the certainty factors associated with facts as **probabilities** of the facts being true, and if the conditions that trigger a rule are regarded as equivalent to independent events, then the overall uncertainty of a rule's input may be regarded as the product of the uncertainties of the individual contributing conditions. We may similarly associate the uncertainty factor of a rule (i.e., its antecedent-consequent relation) as the probability that the consequent is true given the antecedents, in which case to derive the overall uncertainty of the consequent we may simply multiply the uncertainty (or attenuation) factor of the rule by the overall uncertainty of the rule's input. It may be that the consequent of a rule is also the consequent of several other rules (in other words, a consequent may be simultaneously supported by several pieces of independent evidence from different rules). One method of combining pieces of evidence is to use a Bayesian interpretation of probability to update the probability of the consequent being true as it is supported by an increasing number of rules. But the Bayesian approach demands that we include in the calculation estimates of the truth likelihood of every possible combination of individual pieces of supporting evidence, in cases both of assumed truth and assumed falsehood of the consequent. In practical situations, this not only requires making a number of rather dubious estimates of probabilities which are impossible to measure with any objective accuracy, but also is computationally tedious. An alternative and simpler method of combining certainties of independent pieces of evidence is to use so-called uncertainty ratios first developed for the MYCIN medical expert system (Buchanan and Shortliffe, 1984).

An uncertainty ratio r is defined in terms of an uncertainty factor c (which may be interpreted as a probability) by the formula:

$$r = c/(1 - c); \quad c = r/(1 + r)$$

The uncertainty ratio associated with an uncertainty factor will thus vary between ± 1 as the uncertainty factor varies between 0 and 1. An uncertainty factor of $\cdot 5$ attached to a deduced fact (implying a 'neutral' state of knowledge about the truth of the fact) will give an uncertainity ratio of 0. If the *a priori* uncertainty ratio of a deduced fact is r0, and if the fact is supported by a number of rules with certainty ratios r1, r2, r3, etc, the overall uncertainty ratio of the deduced fact is given by:

$$r0x(r1/r0)x(r2/r0)x(r3/r0)x...$$

This is converted back into an uncertainty factor by applying the second formula given above. This method represents a simplified adaptation of the Bayesian approach which tends to give intuitively reasonable results, but is computationally less tedious and involves fewer estimates of quantities which are inherently unestimatable.

7.7.3 Uncertainty representation based on fuzzy sets

In spite of the fact that the rules for combination and propagation of uncertainty described above have been applied in a number of knowledge-based systems, there are many types of knowledge where a probablistic interpretation of uncertainty is inappropriate. In particular, the assumption of *independence* of the contributing conditions for the firing of a rule (which is required for a probablistic interpretation in which uncertainty factors are multiplied) does not hold in many circumstances. The incorporation of conditional or joint probability distributions to describe probabilities of occurrence of dependent events is usually impossible because the distributions are not known. Probabilistic interpretations are generally associated with randomness in data, in which facts or events are precisely defined, but the degree of certainty of their occurrence is not. However, a great deal of knowledge is imprecise, not because of randomness in the occurrence of precisely defined facts or events, but through vagueness or imprecision in the definitions of the facts or events themselves. Much of human knowledge processing in manufacturing companies (or any other organisation) is based on concepts, ideas and associations which are neither crisply defined nor describable in terms of probability distributions. For example, consider the following piece of procedural knowledge:

If a job is late and of priority then classify job as urgent

Here neither the concept of lateness, priority or urgency are precisely defined in numerical terms. Yet to handle this rule computationally we should need to make the artificially precise division of jobs into the clear-cut classes of late or non-late, priority or non-priority jobs.

The imprecision of statements like this can be represented in a systematic manner using the concept of fuzzy sets, first formulated by Zadeh (1965). Fuzzy sets are sets or classes of object for which the transition from membership to non-membership is gradual rather than being sharply defined. If we consider the set U of all jobs u1, u2, u3, etc. on the shop floor, then the fuzzy subset L of all late jobs can be defined by the membership function $f_L(u)$, which associates with each member u of the set U of jobs a degree of membership in the range [0, 1] of the fuzzy subset of late jobs. Every job on the shop floor thereby has some degree of 'lateness' associated with it, in contrast to normal set theory where a job would have a degree of membership of either 0 or 1 of the subset of late jobs (depending, for example, on whether or not it was past its due date). The degree of membership of the job of the fuzzy subset of late jobs provides a measure of the 'degree of satisfaction' of the conditional part of the rule referring to lateness.

In order to express the degrees of membership of various jobs of the fuzzy subset of late jobs, some mapping of a convenient measure of a job's lateness on to the set membership function is required. Such a mapping is shown in Figure 7.5 in which the number of days past-due is used as the basis for the mapping. The mapping is entirely subjective, and needs to be constructed in such a way that meaningful results can be obtained by combining it with mappings used to assign other membership functions to propagate uncertainty through inference networks.

We may define a job's degree of membership of the set of non-late jobs (denoted by $\overline{L}$) in terms of the complement:

$$f_{\overline{L}} = 1 - f_L$$

If we have no information about the number of days that a particular job is past-due, we cannot give it a precise degree of membership of the fuzzy

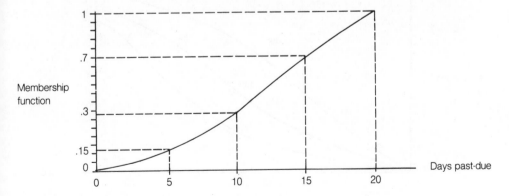

Figure 7.5 Fuzzy set mapping function for late orders.

subset of late jobs. We might, however, wish to describe it merely as 'late' in which case we take the definition of 'late' as being the fuzzy subset itself. Thus, although we do not know the precise number of days the job is past- due, we can say that the possibility of a job described as 'late' being varying numbers of days past-due is given by the membership function in Figure 7.5. The membership function can be said to represent a 'possibility distribution' for the number of days past-due of a job desribed as 'late'. The term late is called a **linguistic variable**.

We can also use the concept of 'intensification' and 'dilation' to define the fuzzy subset of 'very late' and 'quite late' jobs by applying simple arithmetic operations to the fuzzy subset of late jobs:

$$\text{INT } (L) = (f_L)^2 \quad \text{(very late jobs)}$$
$$\text{DIL } (L) = (f_L)^{1/2} \quad \text{(quite late jobs)}$$

As shown in Figure 7.6, a job which is a certain number of days late will have a lower degree of membership of the fuzzy subset of very late jobs than it has of the fuzzy subset of quite late jobs.

Each job can also have a degree of membership of other fuzzy sets, such as the fuzzy subset of priority jobs. These can either be assigned directly, or mapped from some other better defined attribute or combination of attributes (such as dollar value of the job), which give some measure of priority.

The overall degree of satisfaction of the conditional part of the rule that requires a job to be both late *and* of priority would be represented by the degree of membership of the job of the fuzzy subset of late *and* priority jobs. If P represents the fuzzy subset of priority jobs, defined by membership function f_P, then the degree of membership of a job of the fuzzy subset of late *and* priority jobs can be represented by the fuzzy intersection relation $R_{L \cap P}$; this can be represented as a matrix whose

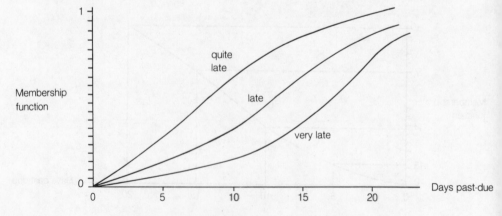

Figure 7.6 Intensification and dilation operators.

elements (u, v) give the degree of membership of a job of the intersection of the two fuzzy sets when the job is u days past due and has a dollar value of v. Each matrix element in the intersection relation is conventionally defined as the minimum of the membership functions of the individual subsets, as shown in Figure 7.7, and defined as:

$$R_{L \cap P}(u, v) = \text{Min } (f_L(u), f_P(v))$$

Interpreted slightly differently, the matrix represents the joint possibility distribution of the days past-due and $ value of a job which is both priority and late. Taking the minimum of the individual membership functions is somewhat arbitrary, but is usually justified on the semantic grounds that when two vague or weak statements are combined, the strength of the composite statement is determined by the weakest of the supporting statements (i.e., a chain is only as strong as its weakest link).

These notions of intersection, intensification and dilation provide a means for expressing and combining measures of uncertainty or vagueness in the antecedants of a rule. Methods can also be formalised for the propagation of uncertainty from a rule's antecedants to its consequents. For example, consider the rule:

If the machine load is high, the job will be late.

This rule denotes a relationship between a fuzzy antecedent (a 'high' machine loading) and a fuzzy consequent (a 'late' job) both of which can

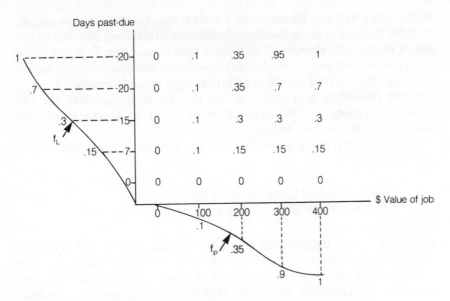

Figure 7.7 Fuzzy set of late *and* priority jobs.

be described in terms of possibility distributions. The rule can be formalised as a fuzzy implication relation R between the antecedant 'high' and the consequent 'late' in which every member of the fuzzy set 'high', defined over the domain W of possible machine loadings, has some degree of association between 0 and 1 with every member of the fuzzy set 'late', defined over the domain U of possible numbers of days past-due of jobs. Again, this is usually described in terms of a matrix whose elements give the degree of association between elements of the two fuzzy sets. There are various ways of computing the elements of the relation $R_{W \rightarrow U}$ such that it provides a good intuitive representation of the association between the antecedant and consequent of the rule. These are beyond the scope of this book, but are comprehensively described by Mizumoto *et al* (1979). The rule (defined by the fuzzy relation $R_{W \rightarrow U}$) can be applied to any fuzzy machine loading described by some arbitrary possibility distribution F (which might for example represent a *very high* machine loading). The resulting possibility distribution C of the days past due of the job can be determined using Zadeh's **compositional rule of inference**, which applies a so-called compositional operator ∘ to F and R:

$$C = F \circ R$$

For the example above, this rule of inference is operationalised as follows:

$$f_C (u) = \max_W (\min (R (w, u), f_F (w)))$$

where w is a machine loading, u is a certain number of days past due, f_C (u) is an element in the possibility distribution of the days past-due of the job, R (w, u) is an element of relation R which associates W and U, and f_F (w) is an element in the (given) possibility distribution of machine loadings. The derived values of f_C (u) for each possible machine loading give the possibility distribution of the number of days late of the job which is implied by the application of the rule to the possibility distribution of machine loadings.

    In the case where a conclusion is independently supported by two rules, such as:

> If the machine load is high, the job is late.
> If raw materials are scarce, the job is late.

there will be two independent possibility distributions C and D for the number of days late, one from each rule. The resulting overall possibility distribution is given by the union of the two fuzzy sets defining the possibility distributions. This which is defined as a relation $R_{C \cup D}$ whose elements are the minima of the two membership functions:

$$R_{C \cup D} = \text{Max} (f_C, f_D)$$

This may be semantically justified by equating it with the saying, 'when several arguments independently support a statement the overall support provided is determined by the strongest of those supporting arguments'.

Fuzzy set theory gives a systematic and consistent way of combining and propagating measures of vagueness or imprecision through a production rule system. However, the particular ways in which the logical connectives such as AND, OR and the implication relation are functionally defined are arbitrary, and have no solid theoretical basis. The justification for use of a particular functional definition lies entirely in whether it produces intuitively meaningful and acceptable results when applied in practice. Nevertheless, in spite of criticism from some quarters, particularly those who are strong advocates of the use of predicate logic to represent knowledge, the use of fuzzy sets continues to grow in all areas of knowledge representation. A review of the use of fuzzy logic in production management research is given by Karwowski and Evans (1986) and further applications are described in Evans, Karwowski and Wilhelm (1989). A good basic introduction to the use of fuzzy sets in decision making is given by Kickert (1978) and Zimmermann et al (1984).

Chapter 8
The Logic-based Paradigm for Knowledge Representation

8.1 The syntax of logic —
    propositions and assertions
8.2 Propositional calculus
8.3 Logical deduction and
    theorem proving

8.4 Predicate calculus
8.5 The automation of logic —
    the PROLOG language
8.6 Non-classical logics

Logic is concerned with the validity of arguments, and with the methods of determining whether given conclusions can be validly drawn from given assumed facts called premises. Systems of logic have been structured to capture notions of truth and inference in human thought processes. Since logic has developed into a rich and highly formulated language with considerable expressive power, it is obviously a strong candidate as a language for the symbolic representation of knowledge. Declarative or factual knowledge can be expressed in terms of logical assertions. The logical rules of inference are a form of procedural knowledge that can be used to deduce new assertions that are logically consistent with the initial set. The automation of the rules of logic is clearly a potentially powerful means of inferring new knowledge from existing knowledge.

8.1 The syntax of logic — propositions and assertions

The precisely defined syntax of logic and its associated syntactical rules of deduction mean that provided the syntactical rules are obeyed, and only legitimate (or what are termed 'well-formed') expressions are used, complex chains of reasoning can be built up which are independent of any semantic attachment to real world entities. The theory of logic has provided a number of efficient computational techniques that guarantee the consistency and soundness of the resulting inferences.

146

In a logic-based representation of the world, simple facts abouts and associations betweens real-world entities can be mapped on to logical **propositions**. Propositions are simple statements of fact, for example:

(Machine 4 is out-of-service)
(Part 21 is-component-of Assembly 3)

Propositions of the above type which represent simple facts are known as **atomic** propositions. Propositions can also be linked together by **connectives** to produce **compound** propositions. Commonly used connectives are:

AND   logical symbol ∩ (disjunction)
OR   logical symbol ∪ (conjunction)
NOT   logical symbol ∩ (negation)
IMPLIES   logical symbol −> (implication)

Examples of compound propositions are:

(Job 423 is late) AND (Machine 42 is out-of-service);

(Machine 42 is out-of-service) OR (Operator 3 is absent)
IMPLIES (Job 423 is late)

The connectives which may be employed to form compound propositions and the rules for their application collectively define the syntax of logic. Atomic propositions which are combined with the permissable set of connectives are termed **well-formed formulas** (wffs). A wff may be regarded as having a 'truth value' of either TRUE or FALSE, and a set of wffs with truth values specified is called a 'truth assignment'. An **assertion** is defined as a wff which has the truth value TRUE.

Propositions which represent facts known or thought to be true about the real world are normally expressed as assertions. If we wish to state explicitly that a proposition is false, its negation is assigned the value TRUE, as in the set of assertions in the following example:

(Job 423 is late)TRUE
(Machine 42 is out-of-service) TRUE
NOT (Operator 3 is present) TRUE

in which a FALSE proposition (Operator 3 is present) is expressed as a negated proposition which is TRUE

8.2 Propositional calculus

Propositional calculus is concerned with determining the truth or falsehood of a **compound** wff from the truth or falsehood of the atomic wffs of which it is composed. Thus, if P and Q (which may for example stand respectively for machine 423 is out-of-service and operator 3 is absent) are atomic propositions which are both TRUE, propositional calculus provides us with rules for determining the truth or falsehood of compound propositions such as:

P AND Q
P OR Q
P IMPLIES Q
NOT P
NOT P AND Q
(etc)

8.2.1   Truth tables

The rules of propositional calculus may be expressed in the form of 'truth tables' which indicate the truth values of a compound proposition for all possible combinations of truth and falsehood of the atomic propositions of which it is composed. A truth table for the compound statement P AND Q is given below:

P	Q	P AND Q
T	T	T
T	F	F
F	T	F
F	F	F

This truth table embodies the fact that for the disjunction of two propositions to be true the propositions must both be individually true and that, if either proposition is false, the disjunction is false. Contrast this with the truth table for P OR Q:

P	Q	P OR Q
T	T	T
T	F	T
F	T	T
F	F	F

This indicates that the conjunction of two propositions is false only if both of the individual propositions are false, otherwise it is true.

Similarly, the truth tables for NOT P and P IMPLIES Q are:

P	NOT P
T	T
F	T

P	Q	P IMPLIES Q
T	F	F
F	T	T
T	T	T
F	F	T

Note that the normal semantic interpretation of implication does not follow from the table defining the IMPLIES connective. The set of assignments in these truth tables may be regarded merely as constituting **definitions** of the corresponding logical connectives.

The truth values of complex combinations of atomic formulae can be derived from these sets of rules. For example, given the truth or falsehood of the atomic propositions of a compound wff such as for example:

NOT (P AND Q) OR (R) -> (NOT R) AND (NOT S OR T)

then the truth value of the compond wff itself can in principle also be derived.

This provides us with a means of deciding whether some complex fact is true given the truth or otherwise of a set of atomic facts which have been explicitly defined. It also enables us to establish whether two compound wffs are 'logically equivalent' ; that is, if they take on the same truth value for every possible combination of truth values of the atomic expressions of which they are composed, giving them identical truth tables.

A set of assertions (atomic or compound wffs all having values TRUE) which correspond to a set of facts in the real world known or thought to be true, is called a **theory**. The individual wffs are the **proper axioms** of the theory. A wff which is not one of the formally stated axioms, but can nevertheless be shown to be TRUE for all cases in which the proper axioms are true, is said to be a **theorem** with respect to the axioms. Thus the set of assertions:

> (Machine 423 is serviceable) OR (Machine 423 is out-of-service)
>
> (Operator 3 is present) OR (Operator 3 is absent)
>
> (Operator 3 is present) AND (Machine 423 is serviceable) IMPLIES (Part409 is producible)

constitute the axioms of a theory which represents a state of the real world in which a particular part is producible only if a certain operator is present and a certain machine is serviceable. The interpretation of this theory in a specific case might involve the addition of the axiom:

(Operator 3 is present) AND (Machine 423 is serviceable)

We might wish to try and show that:

(Part 409 is producible)

is TRUE for all situations in which the set of axioms is true. If it transpires that this can be done, then **(Part 409 is producible)** is a theorem.

8.3   Logical deduction and theorem proving

8.3.1   The rules of inference

Theorem proving is generally performed using so-called inference rules. Given a set of assertions (or axioms) it is possible to generate new assertions which are logically consistent with the original set, by using such inference rules. This is called logical deduction. A method of theorem proving is therefore to attempt to use the inference rules to generate the theorem to be proved, from the axioms. The most commonly used inference rules are:

(1)   **Modus Ponens**   From two axioms of the form P and P IMPLIES Q, it is possible to infer Q.

(2)   **Modus Tollens**   From two axioms of the form NOT Q and P IMPLIES Q, it is possible to infer NOT P.

We can use Modus Ponens to prove the truth of **(Part 409 is producible)** from the set of axioms given above. The expression (Operator 3 is present) AND (Machine 423 is serviceable) IMPLIES (Part 409 is producible) is of the form P IMPLIES Q, where P denotes (Operator 3 is present) AND (Machine 423 is serviceable). We know that (Operator 3 is present) AND (Machine 423 is serviceable) is TRUE since it is one of the axioms. It follows from Modus Ponens that (Part 409 is producible) must be TRUE, and hence it is a theorem.

Although this is rather a trivial example, theorem proving using inference usually entails taking a number of intuitive steps in the choice of *which* inference rules to apply to *which* axioms in order to generate the required expression. It is thus not readily susceptible to automation, since for realistic numbers of axioms the proof procedure becomes a search problem of considerable combinatorial complexity. A more appropriate method of theorem proving, which involves a series of well defined programmable steps, is the method of **resolution refutation**. Since this method is fundamental to the representation of control knowledge using the logic oriented paradigm, a brief description follows.

8.3.2   Resolution-refutation theorem proving

In order to prove that a compound wff is a theorem with respect to a set of axioms, the resolution-refutation method relies on setting up the *negation* of the expression to be proved as one of the axioms, adding it to the original set of axioms, and reducing the resultant set of expressions to what is called **clausal form**. A generalised rule of inference called the **resolution principle** is then used to discover whether the axioms and the negation of the theorem to be proved can be reduced to a set of clauses containing a contradiction, in which case the theorem is proved.

An important element in resolution-refutation theorem proving is the expression of the axioms and the negation of the theorem to be proved in clausal form. This is a form of representation of a wff in which all implications and conjunctions have been removed, and the wff is expressed purely in terms of implicitly conjoined clauses consisting of disjunctions of atomic expressions and negated atomic expressions.

To express a wff in clausal form, we can make use of the equivalences:

$$\sim(\sim P) = P \tag{1}$$
$$\sim(P \text{ OR } Q) = \sim P \text{ AND } \sim Q \tag{2}$$
$$\sim(P \text{ AND } Q) = \sim P \text{ OR } \sim Q \tag{3}$$
$$P \text{ AND } (Q \text{ OR } R) = (P \text{ AND } Q) \text{ OR } (P \text{ AND } R) \tag{4}$$
$$P \text{ OR } (Q \text{ AND } R) = (P \text{ OR } Q) \text{ AND } (P \text{ OR } R) \tag{5}$$
$$P \text{ IMPLIES } Q = \sim P \text{ OR } Q \tag{6}$$

All of the above equivalences can be verified by the truth table comparison and will be found intuitively obvious with the possible exception of the last one, which can perhaps best be illustrated with an example. The statement, 'Machine Down implies Job Late', can be seen to be equivalent to the statement 'Either the machine is not down or the job is late'. In other words the state of affairs in which the machine is not down represents one possibility, and the job being late represents another mutually exclusive possibility. We are here ignoring other reasons for which the job may be late, but this reflects the *logical* rather than the *causal* interpretation of the 'implication' connective.

The above equivalences can be used to reduce any compound wff to a clausal expression of the form:

{P1} {P2} {P3} . . .

where P1, P2, P3, etc are atomic or negated atomic expressions, or disjunctions of such expressions.

As an example of the reduction of a set of axioms to clausal form, consider the following axioms:

P OR Q -> R
R AND S -> T
P
S

The above set of axioms might, for example, stand for the following:

> (Machine unserviceable) OR (Materials unavailable) -> (Job late)
> (Job late) AND (Important customer) -> (Poor service)
> (Machine unserviceable)
> (Important customer)

This set of axioms may be reduced to clausal form in the following stages:

(1)   Eliminate implications using equivalence (6)

> P OR Q -> R is eqivalent to ~(P OR Q) OR R
> R AND S -> T is equivalent to ~(R AND S) OR T

This gives us the set of clauses:

> ~(P OR Q) OR R
> ~(R AND S) OR T
> P
> S

(2)   Move negation inwards to atomic expressions using equivalences (1), (2), (3) and (5). This gives:

> (~P OR R) AND (~Q OR R)
> ~R OR ~S OR T
> P
> S

(3)   Rearrange as a set of conjoined disjunctions using equivalence (4) giving the set of clauses:

> (~P OR R) AND (~Q OR R)
> (~R) OR (~S) OR T
> P
> S

We now drop the AND from the first expression and regard the complete set of axioms as an implicit conjunction of atomic expressions or disjunctions of atomic expressions each within curly brackets, in which the OR connectives are replaced by commas:

> {~P, R} {~Q, R} {~R, ~S, T } {P} {S}

Let us now assume we wish to use this set of axioms to prove the theorem T (poor service). To do this, we add the refutation of T (~T) to the axiom set, and apply our single rule of inference, the resolution principle, to pairs of clauses to attempt to eliminate terms from the axiom set until we have a contradiction.

The resolution principle states that two clauses, one of which contains certain atomic expressions and the other of which contains the negation of one of those expressions, can be replaced with a single clause containing only the remaining expressions. The original atomic expression and its negation have been 'resolved' between the two clauses.

In our example, the clauses:

$\{\sim P, R\}$ and $\{\sim R, \sim S, T\}$

which contain both the atomic expression R and its negation, can be resolved by eliminating R to give the single expression:

$\{\sim P, \sim S, T\}$

We now have the remaining expressions, including negated T:

$\{\sim P, \sim S, T\} \ \{\sim Q, R\} \ \{P\} \ \{S\} \ \{\sim T\}$

The clauses $\{P\}$ and $\{S\}$ can be successfully resolved against $\{\sim P, \sim S, T\}$ to give the single clause $\{T\}$. We now have the two clauses $\{T\}$ and $\{\sim T\}$ coexisting, which is a contradiction. The presence of a contradiction when the negation of the theorem to be proved is added to the list of axioms proves that the theorem itself must be true.

By adding the refutation of what we are trying to prove to the axioms, we are essentially using a backward reasoning approach, starting at the goal state, and this serves to focus the search for a solution. Resolution, since it merely generates new wffs from existing wffs, can also be used in a forward reasoning mode which starts from the axioms and attempts to generate the expression to be proved.

8.4 Predicate calculus

8.4.1 Universal and existential quantification

So far we have been dealing entirely with propositions of the form:

(Machine 3 is unserviceable)
(Machine 3 is unserviceable) -> (Job54 is late)
(*etc*)

The rules of propositional calculus we have described above deal only with the manipulation of specific propositions of this nature which refer to *instances* of objects. Of considerable importance, however, is the ability to deal with more general statements such as assertions that apply to similar sets of cases. An example is the statement:

> **For all** x and y {(Machine x unserviceable)(Part y processed-on machine x) -> (Part y is late)}

The above statement represents the knowledge that for *any* machine (designated by identifier x), if that machine is unserviceable, then *any* part (designated by y) processed on that machine will be late. This type of statement allows more general reasoning to take place since it embodies generalised knowledge about types rather than specific knowledge about instances.

The term **For All** indicates that the statement is true for every instance of machine and part and is known as a **universal quantifier**. The curly brackets indicate the scope of the universal quantification, that is to say the universal quantifier applies to all expressions within the curly brackets.

Some expressions are not true for all possible instances of the generalised objects referred to in the general statements (i.e., are not *universally* quantified), but are only true for some objects. To cater for this, we can introduce the notion of an *existential* quantifier **For Some**. For example, the expression:

> **For Some** y (Part y processed-on Machine5)

indicates that *some* parts in the sense of at least one (though not necessarily all parts) are processed on machine 5.

Universal or existential quantifiers must precede all general propositions in which the identity of the object instance is not explicitly specified. Variables such as x which appear within the scope of a quantifier are said to be 'bound', and variables which are not bound are free. Substitution of values for variables in a quantified expression which make that expression TRUE is called Universal Specialisation. A bound variable which appears more than once in such an expression must have the same value assigned in all its occurrences. For example, the expression:

> **For Some** x {x processed-on machine4) (machine4 unserviceable) -> (x late)}

which is true for substitutions of x which represent the parts made on machine 4 must have the same substitution made for each occurrence of x in the rest of the expression.

Two existentially quantified expressions may be identical for certain substitutions of bound variables. For example, the assignment x = Machine 4 makes the two expressions — unserviceable(machine4) and unserviceable(x) — identical. The process of finding a variable substitution which makes two expressions identical is called **unification**.

8.4.2 Predicate notation

In order to deal with reasoning using universally or existentially quantified propositions, it is more convenient to express propositions as **predicates** with sets of **arguments** in the form P(a, b, c) etc., where P is the name of the predicate and a, b, c, etc. are the arguments. The predicate P can denote a property that an object possesses, or it can denote a relationship between two or more objects. The values given to the arguments are the identities of the objects which are so related or which have this property. Thus the propositions:

> (Machine 42 is unserviceable)
> (Part 53 processed-on Machine 42)
> **For Some** y {(Part y processed-on Machine 5)}

would be expressed as:

> unserviceable(machine-42)
> processed-on(part-53, machine-42)
> **For some** y {processed-on(y, machine5)}

An example of a predicate containing three arguments would be:

> process(part-8, part-53, machine-5)

indicating that part 8 is processed into part 53 using machine 5. The use of predicates will be seen to correspond to the concept of a *relation* introduced in chapter 5. The predicate of a logical expression is equivalent to the relation name in a relational database representation, with arguments equivalent to the attributes of the relation.

8.4.3 Theorem proving in predicate calculus

The rules for manipulating general expressions which contain universally or existentially quantified variables constitute what is known as the **first-order predicate calculus**, as opposed to propositional calculus which allows no variables of any kind. Note that in first-order predicate calculus, we allow variables to stand for objects only. The more advanced **second order** predicate calculus also allows variables to represent predicates but this is beyond the scope of this book.

The rules of the first-order predicate calculus for constructing expressions of logical equivalence, and the rules of inference, are basically the same as for propositional calculus with some slight additions and modifications necessitated by the introduction of universal and existential quantifiers. For example, we have the additional equivalence:

For Some x {A} is equivalent to NOT **For All** x {NOT A}

where A is a general wff containing variable x.

Reduction to clausal form for resolution-refutation theorem proving requires the additional steps of (a) removing existential quantifiers by a process known as 'Skolemisation', and (b) removing universal quantifiers by using distributive equivalences to move them to the outside of the expression and then dropping them, implying that all variables are universally quantified. Once an expression has been reduced to clausal form, resolution-refutation theorem proving can proceed in the same way as for propositional calculus. However, as we now have expressions which contain variables, we need to make appropriate substitutions of terms for variables in order to perform resolutions. More details of reduction to clausal form and the resolution-refutation theorem proving procedure for first-order predicate calculus can be found in for example Winston (1984).

First-order predicate logic provides us with a powerful means of representing quite complex facts about the world in a formal, unified and homogeneous way. We can represent both simple facts and general rules about some problem environment in the same representation, with the facts represented as logical propositions, and the general rules as wffs with variables and quantifiers. New facts can be deduced from the combination of existing facts and general rules by applying the logical rules of inference (e.g., modus ponens) or the resolution principle in a forward chaining manner. The process of discovering whether some hypothesised fact is consistent with the starting set of facts and rules can be performed by a method such as resolution-refutation, which is the equivalent of the backward chaining approach of the production rule paradigm. The logical rules of inference and the particular procedures adopted for their application correspond to the 'inference' engine of the production rule paradigm.

8.5 The automation of logic — the PROLOG language

The PROLOG language (Clocksin and Mellish, 1980; Giannesini *et al*, 1986), which was chosen as one of the bases of the Japanese Fifth Generation Computer Project, provides a means for knowledge representation using the logic-oriented paradigm. PROLOG was originally designed to assist in the analysis and interpretation of natural language. It caters for the expression of logical propositions including universal and existential quantifiers in the form of particular types of clauses called **Horn Clauses**. An existing set of declared propositions represents a set of axioms, and an automated resolution-refutation proof procedure enables the user to enter as a query some statement which is interpreted as the statement to be proved from the axioms. PROLOG adds the refutation of this statement to the axiom set, and automatically applies the resolution principle to attempt to generate a contradiction.

8.5.1 The Horn Clause subset

A set of axioms expressed in terms of the Horn Clause subset takes the form:

G <– A AND B AND C AND . . .

where the IMPLIES connective has been reversed, meaning that G *is implied by* a conjunction of A, B, C, and so on.

To convert a set of axioms in clausal form into a set of Horn Clauses, the following procedure is adopted:

(1)   For each clause, collect the negated expressions on one side; e.g., the expression {A, ~B, C, ~D} is equivalent to {~B, ~D, A, C}

(2)   Use the equivalence (3) of Section 8.3.2 to transform disjunctions to negated conjunctions; the expression {~B, ~D, A, C} becomes {~(B AND D), A, C}

(3)   Reintroduce the implication connective using equivalence (6) of Section 8.3.2; the expression {~(B AND D), A, C} becomes {B AND D –> A, C}

(4)   Restrict each clause to one implication and place the 'implied' part of the clause at the beginning; B AND D –> A OR C becomes:

A <– B AND D
C <– B AND D

Statements in PROLOG thus consist of factual statements of the form:

unserviceable(machine 3)
processed-on(job698 machine3)

and conditional statements of the form:

late(x) <– job(x) AND processed-on(x y) AND unserviceable(y)

These can be arranged in a simple AND/OR tree as shown in Figure 8.1. This is closely analagous to the production rule representation of knowledge in which a series of conditions connected by AND statements give rise, if they are true, to a conclusion. A PROLOG conditional statement is the equivalent of a production rule, and a PROLOG unconditional fact is eqivalent to a data item in the production rule representation. Conclusions supported by several conditions connected by ANDs will be represented by a single Horn Clause and give rise to AND nodes, whereas a conclusion which is supported independently by more than one Horn Clause implication statement will give rise to an OR node.

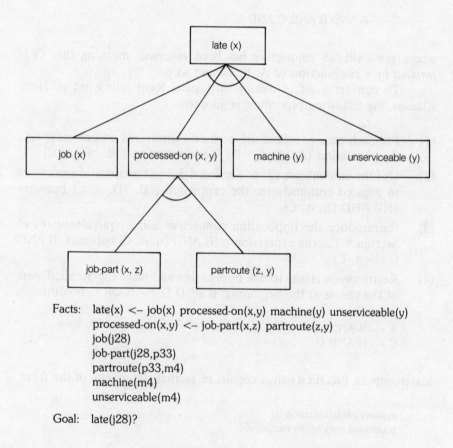

Facts: late(x) <– job(x) processed-on(x,y) machine(y) unserviceable(y)
         processed-on(x,y) <– job-part(x,z) partroute(z,y)
         job(j28)
         job-part(j28,p33)
         partroute(p33,m4)
         machine(m4)
         unserviceable(m4)

Goal: late(j28)?

Figure 8.1 A PROLOG example.

8.5.2 Theorem proving in PROLOG

Given that the set of propositions which comprise our knowledge base is expressed in PROLOG in the form of a set of Horn Clauses, the theorem to be proved (entered by the user) is automatically negated. PROLOG does not, however, merely add this to the existing axiom set and attempt to resolve pairs of clauses at random in an attempt to reach a contradiction. Instead, it regards the negated proposition as a goal to be satisfied, and attempts to match the goal to the conclusions of each of the implication statements by trying legitimate substitutions for any variables present. Thus, assuming that the query entered by the user is the 'theorem' Q, the expression ~Q is automatically set up by PROLOG as a goal state, and is resolved against all expressions which have Q as their conclusions. The terms Q and ~Q are resolved, leaving as new subgoals the conditional parts of the expression containing Q as the conclusion. These subgoals are already implicitly negated by virtue of having been transformed to implications by equivalence (6) of Section 8.3.2.

   PROLOG will then attempt to satisfy these subgoals by trying to resolve them against expressions that have the subgoals as their conclusions, again making consistent substitutions for variables. The strategy used is equivalent to a left to right depth-first search of the AND/OR tree in which PROLOG attempts to resolve all conditional clauses containing variables to leave a set of basic facts corresponding to the starting set.

8.5.3 A Prolog example

To see the process more clearly, consider what happens when we assert the theorem late (j28) to be proved from the set of assertions represented in the AND/OR tree shown in Figure 8.1.

late(x) <− job(x),processed-on(x,y),machine(y),unserviceable(y)	(1)
processed-on(x,y) <− job-part(x,z),partroute(z,y)	(2)
job(j28)	(3)
job-part(j28,p33)	(4)
partroute(p33,m4)	(5)
machine(m4)	(6)
unserviceable(m4)	(7)

PROLOG will first negate the assertion to ~late(j28). The first rule of the set has late(x) as its conclusion and this can be resolved against ~late(j28) by making the substitution x = j28. This leaves as subgoals the negations of the conditions of this rule with j28 substituted for x. These subgoals thus become   ~job(j28),   processed-on(j28,y),   ~machine(y)   and ~unserviceable(y). The first subgoal ~job(j28) can be resolved against the existing axiom (3), job(j28). We can resolve the second subgoal, ~processed–on(j28,y), against the conclusion part of the second rule, leaving again the conditions of the second rule, with j28 substituted for x, as sub-subgoals. The first of these is ~job-part(j28,z), which can be resolved against axiom (4), job-part(j28,P33) by making the substitution z = P33. The second sub-subgoal now becomes ~partroute(P33,y) where we have made the appropriate substitution for z. This can be resolved against axiom (5), partroute(P33,M4), by making the substitution y = M4. We now move to the third subgoal of the first rule, ~machine(y). We have already made the substitution y = M4, so this subgoal becomes ~machine(m4) which is immediately resolvable against axiom (6), machine(M4). Similarly, the subgoal ~unserviceable(y), again with the substitution y = M4, is resolvable against axiom (7), unserviceable(M4). We now have a completely resolved set of clauses leaving us with the null clause, and the theorem is proved.

Had PROLOG not found the axiom unserviceable(M4), it would have backtracked to the point at which the substitution of M4 for y was made, and would have tried another substitution for y (e.g., if an additional axiom had been partroute(P33,M5), M5 would be a possible substitution) to see whether the resulting clause could be resolved against an axiom. In the example, if the axiom unserviceable(M5) had been found, this would have been possible, and again the theorem would have been proved. It is clear that the concept of backtracking is a very important feature of PROLOG.

Using similar techniques, and keeping track of the substitutions made, it is also possible to answer questions about the substitutions that make a particular theorem true. For example, we may wish to ask which jobs are late. This can be done with queries such as ?x late(x). In this case PROLOG will have to make substitutions for x as well as for the other variables and will record and respond with all values of x for which complete resolution can be achieved.

The control strategy used in PROLOG is precisely analagous to the backward chaining strategy used in production rule systems and is hence a subset of the more generalised strategies found in such systems. PROLOG is very well suited for representing knowledge domains in which the majority of problem solving is performed inferentially.

The depth-first search strategy used in PROLOG is conceptually simple, but can be very expensive in computation. It also has the disadvantage that the order in which clauses are entered can affect the efficiency of the search. Considerable research effort is currently underway to develop more effective strategies.

A further disadvantage of a language such as PROLOG is that the emphasis on one particular problem solving strategy (e.g., backward chaining) makes it difficult, though not impossible, to implement other types of strategy such as forward chaining. Although claims have been made (e.g. Kowalski 1979) that all types of problem can be equally well represented, these claims do not take into account the fact that many problems, in order to be cast in terms of a language such as PROLOG, must be viewed from an aspect which is often unfamiliar to those working in the problem domain. The resulting programs are often difficult to read and comprehend for anyone other than the person who wrote them.

The advantage of knowledge representation in a logic-based language such as PROLOG is that logic provides an established formalism which has an accepted natural language interpretation. Strict application of the rules of inference allows conclusions to be guaranteed. PROLOG is particularly suitable for so-called 'truth maintenance' systems which tackle the problem of keeping a database of facts consistent. If a new fact is added to such a database, it may well contradict or be logically inconsistent with the existing facts. If the facts are maintained in a PROLOG database, and the additional fact is entered as a theorem to be proved, PROLOG can indicate whether or not it is inconsistent with the existing facts, and where any inconsistency lies.

In addition, PROLOG is not restricted to theorem proving, but may be regarded as a general purpose logic programming language, in which procedural as well as factual or declarative knowledge may be represented. For example PROLOG may, as has already been pointed out be used to emulate a forward chaining rule-based system with the provision of a suitable interpreter. However, the main strength of the language lies in its emphasis on the correct logical declaration of the problem, while the procedural aspects of problem solution are left in the background to be handled by the reasoning system of the language.

8.6 Non-classical logics

The class of logics we have so far examined in this chapter (propositional and first-order predicate logic) are sometimes called **classical** logics. Because of their assumptions, they are rather restrictive in the types of real-world situation they can represent. However, other logics (in the sense of formal languages for representation and rules of inference) do exist which overcome some of the limitations in expression of classical logic.

Classical logic assumes that the entities which populate the world come from a single domain, and that the formulae of logic apply equally over the whole domain. **Many sorted logic**, on the other hand, regards entities as being of different 'sorts' which can be related to each other in various ways in a relational structure. Using the concept of 'restricted quantification' (cf. universal quantification in classical logic) different logical formulae can be restricted to apply to entities of a particular sort. This makes automated reasoning more efficient, as it can eliminate variable unification substitutions resulting in obviously nonsensical statements such as **(assembled-from(operator-1, customer-25))**, by restricting the domain of applicability of the **assembled-from** predicate to entities of sort 'part'.

Situational logic is another form of logic in which each predicate is associated with the 'situation' in which it is true. Situations are related through temporal events. Thus the occurrence of a particular event (e.g., a machine breakdown) which changes a situation can invalidate a predicate (a particular job completion date) which was true in the original situation but is not explicitly defined to be true in the new situation. (The need to state explicitly all predicates which retain their truth values across events is called the 'frame problem'; it is a problem because there are normally very many of them.) This contrasts with classical logic which is **monotonic** in nature (one assumes that by adding a proposition to a set of existing propositions, the truth values of the latter will not change).

Because monotonic logic can be restrictive, a very important general class of logic called **non-monotonic logic** has been developed for cases where the assumption of monotonicity is inappropriate. Such cases include reasoning requiring temporary assumptions which may later prove to be invalidated, or reasoning about a world which is changing, thus involving assertions that may become out of date. In non-monotonic reasoning, the making of new assertions may require that previous assertions be retracted. This may in turn destroy previous chains of reasoning. So called Truth Maintenance systems have been developed (see for example Doyle, 1982) which check consistency of additional with existing assertions and indicate which assertions, if any, will require retraction. As mentioned in the previous section, PROLOG is itself useful for implementing truth maintenance systems.

Another assumption made by classical logic is that propositions can only be assigned the values TRUE or FALSE. This fails to take into account situations in which varying degrees of evidence exist for and against a proposition, or where no evidence exists to suggest it is either true or false. **Many-valued logics** (of which fuzzy logic mentioned in the previous chapter is an example) remove this restriction by allowing propositions to have values which are intermediate between true and false, with corresponding modification of inference procedures. **Modal logic** is another form of logic which allows reasoning about 'possible' worlds in addition to the one that exists. Modal 'operators' of the type 'it is necessary that', 'it is possible that' are used to qualify propositions as to whether they pertain to the 'actual' or 'possible' world. The notions of modal logic have been extended to so-called **temporal logic** in which the modes of 'necessity' and 'possibility' are augmented by the modes 'past' and 'future'. This can be developed to represent past time as a linear sequence of states, and future time as a branching sequence of states representing different possible future worlds.

All of these types of logic have relevance for automated reasoning in manufacturing environments, particularly when this reasoning is concerned with planning future actions (e.g., how to produce a part, when to start work on an order). Planning obviously involves dealing with future possible worlds about which we must make assertions (e.g., machine availability) whose truth values may not be definite, or which may subsequently be invalidated. It is of course possible to build knowledge- based systems that handle these problems informally. For example, informal knowledge of temporal states and basic temporal reasoning may be wired in to the database schema and rules of a production rule system, insofar as this knowledge is required for the problem being tackled. However, the advantage of abstracting out this knowledge using a formal method of representation and a general set of inference procedures can in many cases greatly increase the power and flexibility of the approach.

CHAPTER 9
The Object-oriented Paradigm for Knowledge Representation

9.1 Semantic nets   9.2 Frames

Both the rule- and logic-based paradigm for knowledge representation tend to ignore the fact that much of human thinking is oriented towards structuring the world in terms of closely related packets of information about objects, entities or concepts of importance to them. People working in a manufacturing environment would tend to think in terms of objects such as products, customers, machines, orders and production jobs, the properties of these objects, and how they interact. This type of thinking is captured to some extent in modern data modelling approaches which focus on objects, attributes and relationships, albeit in a simplistic manner. However, knowledge representation implies the ability to *reason* about objects (or for objects to reason about themselves). The types of information about objects and their relationships that are required for effective reasoning to take place are considerably more complex than can be represented in a standard data model; hence, largely independently of developments in data modelling, a paradigm for the object-oriented representation of *knowledge* has emerged. This originated from the work of Quillian on semantic nets and from Minsky's concept of frames, and has received impetus from the parallel development of object-oriented programming languages such as Xerox's SMALLTALK (which was originally developed as a high-quality human machine graphics interface). This chapter discusses the basic concepts of the object-oriented representation with associated advantages and limitations, using a simple factory example.

9.1 Semantic nets

9.1.1 Representation using semantic nets

In Chapter 5 the concept of an 'entity-relationship' model was introduced as a basis for the initial structuring of a data environment. In this model, entities (distinguishable from each other through being described by different sets of attributes) are represented as the nodes of a graph structure, in which the links represent the relationships between entities (implicitly stored in relational databases in the form of common linking attributes). Whilst this network representation was introduced primarily as an aid to conceptualising the relationships existing between data items in a conventional database, the idea of a network representation of knowledge (as opposed to data) was also developed largely independently of work on data modelling, starting with the work of Quillian (1968) on the representation of knowledge through natural language.

Quillian introduced the idea of a **semantic** or **associative** net in which individual concepts are linked by named associations that exist between pairs of concepts. The links can represent causal or functional relationships, spatial relationships, class membership relationships, and so on. For example, the network shown in Figure 9.1 indicates that machine 46 is a lathe situated in department D3, having a cost per hour of $48, and is operated by employee J. Smith. Here the concept machine 46 is linked to the class concept lathe by the link is-a indicating that machine 46 is a member of the class lathe. It is also linked to the concept department by the link belongs-to, to the monetary quantity $48 by the link cost-per-hour, and to the person J. Smith by the link operator. The class concept lathe is itself linked to other class concepts — owning-department, operator, and cost-per-hour — by has links, indicating that lathes in general have these characteristics; it is also linked to the higher level class concept machine by the link ako (a kind of) indicating that the class lathe is a member of the more general class machine. The concepts owning-department, operator, etc. will be similarly linked to other concepts which describe their identifying properties and their individual instances. Each concept can be regarded as being semantically defined in terms of the concepts to which it is linked, as in a dictionary in which words are defined by other words which are themselves defined in terms of yet further words. Note that the network consists of named associations between pairs, and as such can be represented by a series of two argument predicates of the form P(x,y).

One of the values of the semantic net representation is the way in which hierarchies of concepts can be readily built up and facts about these concepts distributed over the hierarchy at the appropriate level of generality. Thus, rather than associating each individual lathe with the general facts that it will be located in some department and will have an

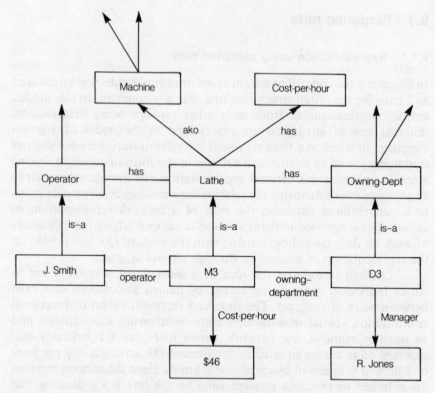

Figure 9.1 A semantic net.

operator and a cost per hour, these facts can be associated with the concept of the class lathe. Individual lathes which are members of this class and which are connected to the lathe concept by is-a links will automatically inherit these properties. Individual property values are directly connected to the concepts (nodes) which represent individual instances of the lathe concept. It should be noticed that the arcs are *directed*. If we wish to represent facts in both directions, this must be done explicitly, using two arcs in opposite directions with separate names.

Note that the concept lathe has been linked to the higher level class machine by an 'a kind of' link (ako), and that the properties that we have associated with the class lathe might also be true of the more general class machine. If this were so, we could link these properties directly to the class machine, and they would be inherited not only by lathes, but all other sub-classes of machine such as drills and presses. Concepts linked directly to lathe would then be those properties or characteristics possessed only by lathes and by no other class of machine.

The use of hierarchical ordering of concepts facilitated by the semantic network representation corresponds to an important aspect of human memory and reasoning which was hypothesised by Quillian. He observed that humans tend to store information at the most abstract level possible and to perform general reasoning in terms of classes rather than specific instances (which he termed 'cognitive economy'). For example, rather than remember that a lathe has a cost-per-hour, a human is liable to remember that a lathe is a machine and that a machine has a cost-per-hour, thus abstracting the cost-per-hour property to the highest level at which it is generally applicable. Only the more specific properties peculiar to, for example, individual lathes, are stored at lower levels of abstraction. This leads to information generally being stored at the node where it is most frequently required. This type of memory storage allows reasoning to take place in terms of higher level concepts (e.g., one can make deductions about lathes in general in terms of their class properties, rather than having to talk about any specific lathe).

9.1.2 Reasoning using semantic nets

A method of reasoning within a semantic net is called **intersection search**. If we wish to establish whether two concepts can be related within a network by some series of links, processing of the network can start independently at each concept. Surrounding concepts, to which these concepts are linked, are progressivley activated until an intersection is achieved between the two spreading areas of activation. The achievement of an intersection indicates that a linking path exists between the two concepts, and the intervening links and concepts through which the path lies define the nature of the association. Thus, to establish whether an association exists between the concepts J. Smith and R. Jones, activation would spread from the two corresponding nodes and would meet through the succesive links operator, owning department and manager. The interpretation of this path would require access to a higher level of the hierarchy which would indicate that J. Smith was an operator of a machine M3 owned by department D3 who had a manager R. Jones.

One of the problems with the above form of reasoning lies in the combinatorial complexity of the search space required, particularly in cases where paths do not in fact exist. In such cases an exhaustive search of the whole network is required before it can be established that two concepts are not linked, either at all or by some hypothesised relation. Modern forms of representation of semantic nets (e.g., using PROLOG) have concentrated on trying to reduce the problem by providing additional heuristic power, such as graph search techniques, to aid in the search process.

Semantic nets can in fact be easily represented in PROLOG as sets of binary propositions using a restricted set of predicates such as 'IS-A', 'SPECIALISATION-OF', 'HAS-PART', etc. Control knowledge must generally be represented outside the network in some external control strategy or inference engine, as in the depth-first search with backtracking used by PROLOG.

9.2 Frames

An additional problem with the representations described so far is that, although facilities have been provided to store information about class properties in addition to individual properties of a particular instance of that class, one important feature of human reasoning is not catered for within these systems, namely reasoning with prototypical objects or objects which are in some sense typical of their class. In addition, factual knowledge tends to be stored separately from procedural knowledge about how to reason with the facts. These problems are rectified with the use of frames.

9.2.1 Frame notation

The concept of **frame** notation was developed originally by Minsky (1968) with the idea of organising the properties of objects in such a way as to form prototypes which enable default reasoning about objects to occur in the absence of any specific instances of such objects. Thus a frame enables the properties which define an object to take on typical values which would be expected to be true for the majority of examples of that object, but which we would expect to have to adjust when dealing with a specific instance. The frame concept also allows explicit procedural information to be stored, together with the object's properties, which indicates how these properties may be obtained or computed and how objects of different types interact.

A frame, which may be regarded as a complex node in a network, consists of a name (which will be the name of the object or object class the frame is intended to represent) and a set of **slots** which identify the basic set of structural elements or properties which define the object. Slots may contain names of, or values for, attributes, pointers to other frames, and '(unlike the relational model or other conventional data models which can merely compute the value of an attribute)' active procedures which can access and modify any attributes within the frame system, pass messages to the user, or perform complex nested computations. When the slots of a frame are filled, the frame is said to be 'instantiated' and represents an instance of the entity represented by the unfilled frame.

Frames can be linked together into class hierarchies, termed **specialisation or generalisation** hierarchies. One frame may represent the class lathe, whilst another frame represents the more general class machine. The class lathe is a **specialisation** of the class machine, while the class machine is a **generalisation** of the class lathe. At the bottom of the hierarchy, an individual lathe is an **instantiation** of the class lathe. When a particular class of object is created which is a specialisation of a more general class, the attributes of the general class are automatically inherited by the rest of the class hierarchy. Thus, a specialised class such as lathe automatically 'knows' about many of the attributes and procedures associated with it as soon as it is created, since these are inherited from the more general class machine. The only details that have to be added are those which make lathes different to other classes of machine.

9.2.2   Example of a frame-based representation

As an example of a frame system, consider the following set of frames and their relationships (as indicated in Figure 9.2) which represent the concept of 'machine' and the particular subclass of machine called 'lathe'.

name:	MACHINE	
	specialisation of:	MANUFACTURING RESOURCE
	identifier:	
	department:	range (P1,P10)
	cost-per-hour:	units $ range (0,1000)
	status:	range (serviceable,unserviceable)
	load:	LOADING PROC
name:	LATHE	
	specialisation of:	MACHINE
	cost-per-hour:	$50
	status:	serviceable
	speeds:	units rpm range (200,10000)
name:	L4	
	instance-of:	LATHE
	identifier:	L4
	department:	P8
	cost-per-hour:	$47
	load:	LOAD-L4
name:	LOADING-PROC	
	load-wk1:	procedural code
	load-wk2:	,,
	load-wk3:	,,
	load-wk4:	,,
name:	LOAD-L4	
	instance-of:	LOADING-PROC
	load-wk1:	38

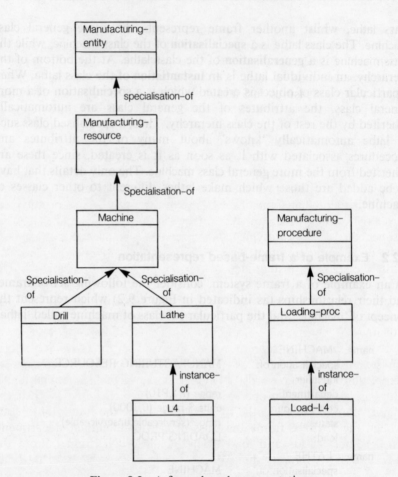

Figure 9.2 A frame-based representation.

```
load-wk2:        43
load-wk3:        27
load-wk4:        48
```

The first frame has the name MACHINE and it indicates that the object machine, which the frame is intended to represent, has the properties of department, cost-per-hour, status and load. It also indicates that a machine is a **specialisation** of the more general class of object Manufacturing Resource. A manufacturing resource is itself represented by a frame which will have a more general set of properties. The properties attached to the Machine frame are those properties which are specific to the Machine subclass of Manufacturing Resource.

The Machine frame is not instantiated (i.e., the properties do not have any values associated with them), since we are describing the general concept machine rather than a specific machine. Each property

method is to use a set of production rules which can themselves be organised in the form of frames, either as an independent hierarchy of procedures or as slots attached to the frame objects with which the reasoning is concerned. Local procedures attached to frames in order to control the flow of computation within a frame system are known as **methods**, and are stored in slots of the frame which have been identified as 'message responders'. Computation is initiated by sending a message to a frame specifying the message responder slot and any arguments that might be required. The message will invoke a series of actions by the procedure in the message responder slot, which may include the passing of messages to other frames, each of which may respond to the message by passing further messages. This will continue until so-called 'primitive methods' are invoked, which will return results to be stored in the appropriate frames and pass no further messages. The primitive messages of a frame system are normally a set of simple computations which result in changing the state of one or more objects, assignments, or input/output procedures.

Control of the flow of computation by message passing between objects is known more generally as **object-oriented programming**. When one object sends a message to another, then provided the message is valid (i.e., understandable by the receiving object) it is not necessary for the transmitting object to know about the details of the computations performed by the receiving object as a result of the message, nor the data that will be used. These are entirely local to the receiving object. The latter can also obtain data, if required, by looking up its class hierarchy. In addition to giving programs a structure which should reflect familiar objects in the real world, this localisation of data and computational procedures to objects can facilitate program construction, since procedures for a particular object can be developed and refined in isolation without requiring any knowledge of the detail of other objects. The first fully-developed, object-oriented programming language was Xerox's SMALLTALK. Other languages such as C++ have since been developed, and there is currently a general convergence between the facilities of commercial object-oriented programming languages, and those of research-based knowledge representation systems using frames.

9.2.4 An example of frame-based reasoning

As an example of frame-based reasoning, assume that we are given an object described in terms of a certain set of properties corresponding to the symptoms of a certain type of machine fault, and we wish to know the cause of the fault. We could send these symptoms in the form of a message to the message responder slot in a general frame named

MACHINE FAULT. The method invoked through this slot would take the symptoms as arguments and use some strategy to select a subclass of machine fault and match the symptoms described against the properties (units, range, etc.) of the subclass (Figure 9.3). If a precise match was obtained in the sense of all properties of the subclass matching the symptoms, but with some additional symptoms not described as properties of the subclass, an instantiation of the subclass would be made, and the method would send a message to a still more detailed subclass. It would then attempt to match the additional symptoms with a more detailed set of properties of the subclass which represented a more specific classification of the fault. A particular subclass might also contain properties not directly observed or input, and would ask whether these existed. If the symptoms did not match, the method might pass a message to another subclass to see if a match could be obtained here. When a sufficient match has been made (normally above the most detailed level of instantiation), the object will be instantiated to represent the inferred existence of this particular entity along with the full range of default and generic properties.

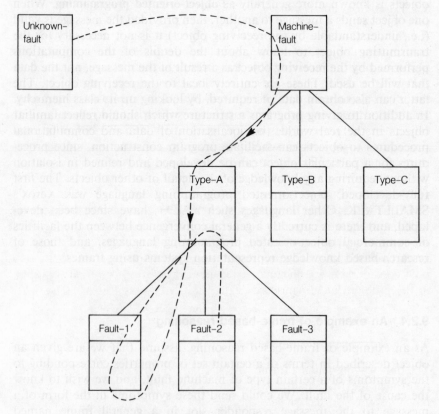

Figure 9.3 Depth-first search of a frame hierarchy.

It will be seen that this particular strategy represents a depth-first search of the hierarchy of classes representing possible machine faults, in which control of the search is exercised by message passing between local procedures. Of course, it may often be impossible to obtain precise matches, in which case a 'match value' could be computed, based in some way on the degree of match. If the match value exceeds some threshold, and the frame is specific enough for the task in hand, search could be terminated. On the other hand, if the match value were below the threshold, or if the frame were not specific enough, the system could move to other frames, again using selection strategies embedded in the frame methods. Depending on the strength of the final match of the observed object to a particular frame, the default properties of the matched frame can be inferred with some degree of certainty as properties of the observed object. Confirmation or otherwise of these default properties by more detailed examination of the observed machine condition might, of course, prompt further search.

9.2.5   Multiple inheritance

Another feature that may be supported by frames is that of multiple inheritance. If we allow a particular class of object, represented by some frame, to be a member of more than one superclass, the membership of the object of different classes can be regarded as equivalent to looking at the object from different 'points of view'. Thus, the subclass **machine** might be a member of the two superclasses manufacturing resources and current assets. Different sets of properties might be inherited from each superclass. For example, when viewed as a manufacturing resource, a machine might inherit generic properties such as cost-per-hour and output. When viewed as a current asset, it would inherit properties such as purchase-price, date-of-purchase and depreciation-rate.

Depending on how the object machine is viewed through its various inheritances, certain aspects are emphasised as important, while the remaining aspects which are not important are suppressed. What is important from one viewpoint may be unimportant from another. This is of considerable significance in terms of presenting potential solutions to the problem of semantic context of data mentioned in Chapter 4.

9.2.6   Messages and message passing

The only way in which a frame can be accessed is by communicating with it through local procedures which restrict the type of interaction we can have; in other words, we can only interact through a 'wall of code'. This makes the objects independent of their environment so that they can be designed and tested without any knowledge of their particular application. Internal representations may be changed without affecting other users, and objects may interact without any excessive syntactical constraints.

The use of methods and message passing as a control mechanism relies on the fact that frames only communicate with each other in terms of the allowed message set and that manipulations of data using the methods of a frame are hidden and not accessible to other frames or to external users of the frame system; in other words, only private and localised procedures of the frame are allowed to manipulate the data. If a message is sent to a frame to produce a certain item of information, the way in which the information is computed will be the concern *entirely* of the methods associated with the frame within which it computed.

9.2.7 Polymorphic programming

We have already mentioned how procedures themselves may be stored as frames with generic procedures at higher levels of the hierarchy being superclasses of more specific procedures. Thus the cost-per-hour of a lathe might be computed by amortising the purchase price of the lathe over its expected lifetime and adding some additional factor depending on the energy consumption rate. For example:

$$\text{cost-per-hour} = \text{price}/(\text{lifetime} \times \text{working hrs per year}) + e$$

However, this procedure is clearly not applicable to lathes alone but to other classes of machine as well. Hence this procedure can be stored as an active value attached to the more general concept 'machine' and will be inherited by frames representing subclasses of machines, including lathes. Adjustments to the procedure in terms of typing the data items referenced to deal with specific classes of machine can be performed by allowing the subclasses of machine to add their own more detailed data typing restrictions to the general procedure. The general procedure attached to the 'machine' class which uses abstract rather than specific data types is an example of polymorphic programming.

9.2.8 Implementation of frame systems

Frame systems are most commonly implemented in the AI programming language LISP. However, as we have already indicated, the frame paradigm is also very similar to that of object-oriented programmimg such as SMALLTALK, and there is a convergence of the facilities offered by frame systems and those offered by object-oriented languages. Frame systems have proved useful in conjunction with the production rule paradigm for organising large systems of production rules into taxonomies with associated inheritance, that correspond to an object-oriented description of the knowledge domain. The slots of a frame can contain production rules which relate to the behaviour of the object that the frame represents, or which can assess the degree of match of a hypothesised object with the object described by the frame. Rules can thus be used in *context* when embedded in frames.

The frame-based representation has proved very appealing from the intuitive and conceptual point of view. Yet its very flexibility in terms of the inheritance and overriding of default properties, and the absence of any formal underlying theory for the mechanisms of inference and consistency checking, mean that it is difficult to use frames in any reliable or predictable way, even though they provide a considerable degree of freedom and latitude of representation.

CHAPTER 10
Domain Knowledge Representation for Manufacturing Decision Making

10.1 Classification of manufacturing tasks

10.2 Characterisation of manufacturing tasks

10.3 Categories of knowledge-based support for manufacturing tasks

This chapter contains a brief overview of the various areas of problem-solving and decision making required in manufacturing organisations, with specific reference to the potential contribution of knowledge-based technologies to make such activities more effective and to achieve their genuine integration. Selected systems will then be examined in more detail in Parts 3 and 4. This discussion will be confined to the manufacturing (as opposed to finance and marketing) operations of a manufacturing company; in other words, the tasks considered will be those directly concerned with the design and physical production of goods to the specifications of time and quantity required by the customer.

10.1 Classification of manufacturing tasks

It is convenient to make the following classifications of tasks required in a manufacturing company (excluding those connected with finance and marketing):

(1) Production management
(2) Production systems design
(3) Manufacturing technology

Production management is concerned with coordinating the flow of material and the use of manufacturing resources in such a way that products can be produced efficiently and delivered on time to the customer. It is primarily concerned with the 'how much' and 'when' aspects of manufacturing. Effective production management aims at achieving an integration of activities along the 'materials flow' axis of Figure 10.1.

Production systems design is concerned with the design of the framework, or production environment within which production management takes place (e.g., factory layout, groupings of products and parts to achieve balanced material flow and establishment of production policies to optimise this flow). These decisions are concerned with the 'what' and 'how' of the systemic and informational aspects of manufacturing, and represent 'meta-level' production management knowledge. They normally come under the general heading of 'industrial engineering', and provide a key integrating link between production management and manufacturing technology.

Manufacturing technology is concerned with the design of products that meet marketing and quality requirements, with planning the best ways of making these products, and with troubleshooting and rectifying the causes of problems and defects in the production process. These decisions are primarily concerned with the 'what', 'how' and 'why' of the physical aspects of manufacturing. Effective management of this aspect of manufacturing requires close integration of all the above activities along the 'design flow' axis of Figure 10.1. Product designs should pay due regard to manufacturability, process plans should be oriented towards achieving simplified work flows, and quality or work-flow

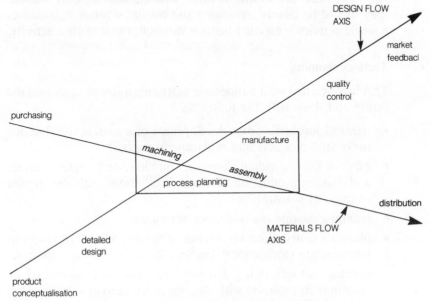

Figure 10.1 Integration axes in manufacturing.

problems should result in rapid feedback to the other activities so they can be cured at source.

10.1.1 Production management

Production management can be classified hierarchically, into strategic planning, tactical planning, and operational control, as described in Chapter 3. The scope and characteristics of these activities are:

(1)   **Strategic planning**

This involves developing plans which extend a year or more into the future, typically covering the following areas:

- forecasting aggregate demand and development of an aggregate production plan for product groups over the planning period;

- setting aggregate production resource capacity levels, target inventory levels and target lead times over the planning period that are consistent with the company's overall strategic business plan;

- negotiating contracts with vendors for the supply of bulk or long lead-time raw materials of appropriate quality and favourable price, at times required by the more detailed tactical plan.

Although these are shown as three separate activities, in practice they should be closely integrated and might be better regarded as a single activity with each being a distinct *output* of that activity.

(2)   **Tactical planning**

This is concerned with a timescale extending a few months into the future and deals with the following:

- demand forecasting and development of a master schedule for individual products and replacement parts;

- establishing individual shop- and purchase-order release dates, and making production resource reservations with due regard to capacity constraints;

- planning routine maintainance activities;

- planning distribution requirements for delivery of products to intermediate storage locations and thence to the customer;

- quoting and estimating delivery times and costs of one-off or custom built products with due regard for current work backlog and capacity limitations;

Again, all of these areas will need to be closely integrated, and should all represent the outputs of a single tactical plan developed for each product group (the product groups themselves being coordinated at the strategic level).

(3) **Operational control decisions**

These are concerned with the detailed implementation of tactical plans and may be broadly classified into:

- shop floor control: this deals with release of orders into the shop at a rate that is consistent with capacity limitations, and the actual dispatch of work to cells and workstations; it ensures that actual conversion of raw materials into finished products takes place in accordance with the plan, and deals with short-term capacity problems as they occur;

- materials and inventory control: this involves physical control of materials such as receiving, shipping, reconciliation of predicted and actual stock, and adjustment of planned replenishment orders to meet actual requirements;

- tools control: this involves assignment and tracking of individual tools, monitoring of tool life, and determining when tools should be replaced;

- purchasing and vendor control: this involves the evaluation and selection of vendors based on past performance and the actual release and follow-up of purchase orders.

Operational control decisions need to be performed using 'high variety' control models of each individual control activity. Integration can be achieved by ensuring that these control models are consistent both with each other and with tactical and strategic plans.

Conventional data-processing techniques applied to individual areas of manufacturing which follow a traditional division by function, result in computer representations which can be of high variety with respect to the well-defined and specialised functional requirements of each area, but are low variety with respect to the less well-defined and predictable interactions between areas. The emphasis is on the independent manipulation of large volumes of data in each area, using standard procedures developed specially for that area. A change from a functional to a product-oriented division, accompanied by integration of different functional areas within product groups will require computer representations which handle lower volumes of data, but which are of high variety with respect to the interactions between functional areas within product groups. Since these interactions are not well defined (in the sense of all possible interactions being predictable), knowledge-based systems (which virtually by definition are intended for high variety, non-predictable manipulation of relatively low volumes of data) appear to offer a potentially very powerful contribution to the achievement of this form of integration. Thus each product group should have its own customised and integrated, high variety representation (or model) of the knowledge required to coordinate the fulfillment of the individual functional requirements of each hierarchical level described above, with each activity being performed with reference to a consistent set of stored knowledge bases.

10.1.2 Production systems design

Production systems design is concerned with the design of both the physical and the informational environment within which production takes place. It may be divided into the following areas:

(1)   Grouping of products and components according to Group Technology considerations, and production flow analysis to identify common routings.

(2)   Design of physical factory layout; this will often involve the reorganisation of existing functional layouts in a more 'product-oriented' form to take advantage of rationalisations achieved by GT analysis to achieve balanced production flow. It will also require decisions about the numbers of production facilities of each type, number of conveyors, the size of buffer storage areas, etc.

(3)   Design of production management policies to coordinate the flow of materials through the factory; this will involve decisions on the extent to which continuous (JIT) manufacturing as opposed to discrete batch manufacturing is possible, policies for evolution towards continuous manufacturing, whether to use centralised or distributed planning and control, the design of planning and control hierarchies, the type of information flow required, and the type of knowledge and information required at various decision levels.

Not only do these types of design decision require a high degree of integration between themselves, but they also need close integration with manufacturing technology on the one hand, and production management on the other. They are an important constituent of the 'glue' that binds production management and manufacturing technology decisions together.

10.1.3   Manufacturing technology decisions

Manufacturing technology decisions are concerned with the design and maintainance of products and the processes by which they are manufactured. They consist of the following tasks:

(1)   Product design: designing products that meet customer requirements, and can be manufactured efficiently at an acceptable cost to the desired quality in the desired timescale.

(2)   Process planning: design and specification of the detailed machining or other processes and their sequence that will be required to produce the product, together with tooling required.

(3)   Maintenance: ensuring the efficient running of all equipment with minimal downtime.

(4)   Quality control: ensuring that the product is made to engineering specifications and troubleshooting possible reasons for poor quality by identifying problems at source, with associated feedback to design or process planning.

A sense of a hierarchy of tasks is not so evident here as in the production management area. Product design and process planning are activities which by tradition are functionally separate, but which in fact require a close degree of integration. Quality control provides feedback to design and process planning from the physical execution of plans on the production management axis. Further connections to production management come from the requirement for close integration of both process planning and maintainance with shop floor scheduling. Again, the integration of these tasks can be performed through restricting product variety by grouping, and providing each product group with knowledge bases which are of high variety with respect to the interactions between these areas of manufacturing technology. This can enable manufacturing technology decisions within each product group to be made coherently with respect to all interacting issues that need to be considered.

10.2.   Characterisation of manufacturing tasks

10.2.1   A state space view of manufacturing problem solving

In order to discuss the nature and type of knowledge-based support that might be appropriate for the integration of the above functional areas, it is convenient to take a state space oriented view of the various problem domains characterising each area. In this view, the starting state is defined in terms of the information available to define the situation at the start of the problem-solving or decision-making process. The goal state represents the characteristics of the desired solution. Problem solving involves searching for a sequence of operators which allows progression from the starting state to the goal state.

The size of the search space is defined by its *breadth* (the number of alternative states that can typically be reached by the application of a single operator — which will, of course, partially depend on the number of decision variables characterising a state), and its *depth* (the number of states that must be traversed before the goal state is reached). For any particular class of problem, the applicability and possible mode of using knowledge-based systems in helping in the problem-solving process, and the type of knowledge representation technique most appropriate, will depend upon the following:

(1)   The size of the search space: Is it a relatively small search space in which the current state is characterised by a well-defined set of state variables (which will generally be current attributes of objects in the problem domain), and do only a small number of intermediate states need to be traversed to reach the solution? Or, is it a large search space with many state variables (i.e., many object attributes of potential relevance) required to define a state, many degrees of freedom for the decision maker as to what to regard as the decision variables, and many possible intermediate states between the initial and goal state?

(2)   To what extent can the task be factored out into non-interacting or weakly interacting subtasks, thus yielding a number of smaller search spaces? Can hierarchical refinement or other similar techniques be used to cut down the search?

(3)   What type of domain-specific knowledge is available to the decision maker for reducing the combinatorial complexity resulting from large search spaces? Is this knowledge encodable in the form of a well-defined set of production or inference rules? Are these simple and deterministic, or is a sophisticated level of reasoning required with conflict resolution and backtracking? Can deep knowledge in terms of model-based causal or structural relationships between objects in the problem environment be used to reduce the search space? Is the knowledge stable or will it be subject to continuous change?

(4)   Is the goal state clearly defined in terms of its characteristics, or could there be many alternative goal states with different sets of characteristics that might be equally acceptable?

(5)   Is all the knowledge ideally required likely to be available and precisely known, or will problem solving have to proceed with uncertain or guessed values for key parameters, necessitating the use of prototypical objects?

Task domains with well-defined starting and goal states, a relatively small search space, and a well-defined set of operators for moving between states might be regarded as analagous to the 'programmed' decision problems of Simon (1960). As the size of the search space increases, and an increasing amount of domain-specific knowledge is required to reduce combinatorial complexity, tasks move from the programmed category towards the category generally regarded as requiring human judgement (Simon's 'unprogrammed' decisions). This human judgement will in many cases correspond to the domain-specific knowledge used to reduce the search space. Further complications arise in situations of uncertainty or ambiguity where knowledge is incomplete and the goal state is underdefined, and at this point we move firmly into the region of unprogrammed decision problems. The harder, or more unstructured, the problem, the more sophisticated will be the required types of knowledge representation and processing techniques for any realistic attempt to emulate the types of decision-making process that can be performed by humans. For many types of problem, automated decision making using current levels of knowledge representation technology is impossible. However, use of such technology in a decision support role can have potential benefits, for example in analysing more structured subsets of the overall decision problem.

10.2.2 Synthetic versus analytic problem solving

Problems in general can be divided into those which primarily require a process of **synthesis** in their solution, and those which primarily require a process of **analysis**. Synthesis can often involve creative problem solving, in situations where the solution is possibly ill-defined and underconstrained, and the search space is large, often requiring a forward chaining approach using human judgement, analogical and lateral reasoning to find a path to a good solution. Creative synthesis is one of the most difficult tasks to automate due to our current lack of full understanding of the human processes of creativity. Analysis, on the other hand, involves reasoning which is more convergent in nature, with better defined goal states. The analytical knowledge used to reduce the search space tends to be more systematic and better defined than the knowledge used in creative synthesis. Problem solving and decision making requiring a high component of analysis are generally those which are most amenable to support by knowledge bases and knowledge-based systems.

Different types of manufacturing task involve varying degrees of the three general activities of design, planning and control (Figure 10.2). Manufacturing tasks involving either **design** or **planning** contain a strong component of synthesis. Design involves searching for an appropriate

	Production Management	Production Systems Design	Manufacturing Technology
design		Facilities layout design; Product and part rationalisation; Information systems design;	Product design
Planning	Strategic planning; Requirements planning; Forecasting; Distribution; Maintenance; Quoting and estimating		Process planning
Control	Shop floor control; Materials and inventory control; Tools control; Vendor control;		Diagnostic maintenance; Quality control;

Figure 10.2 Characterisation of manufacturing tasks.

combination or configuration of individual elements to form a whole that will satisfactorily fulfill a predefined function, with the function itself being generally both ill-defined and under-constrained. Planning involves synthesising a set of individual tasks required to meet some generally well-defined goal, and is frequently a more constrained activity than that of design, with constraints often imposing a **temporal ordering** on individual tasks. Thus planning, unlike design, is generally concerned with the temporal dimension and is basically a **predictive** activity. Although primarily synthetic in nature, both design and planning can also involve components of analysis to establish whether the design or plan meets the detailed functional requirements or constraints.

On the whole, manufacturing tasks involving **control** are primarily analytic rather than synthetic in nature. Control is basically a **reactive** activity involving *monitoring* patterns of data that will indicate whether tasks are being executed according to plan, *interpreting* these patterns to establish whether in fact they indicate a significant deviation, and *diagnosing* the likely causes of the deviation and the ways it might be overcome such that the original plan is recovered.

10.2.3 State space characterisation of manufacturing design tasks

Design is a fundamental activity of manufacturing, not only of products but also of tools, facilities and their layout, and the planning and control procedures to be used for the management of production. The design process may be divided into two stages, the **synthesis** stage and the **analysis** stage (Figure 10.3). The **synthesis** stage is the stage in which, given a partial specification of the functional requirements and desired performance of the design, an overall concept is developed which meets design objectives in a broad sense. Detail is then progressively added to this skeleton design with due regard for the rules and constraints governing good design practice within the particular domain of the design, to the level of a complete specification. In the **analysis** stage, the design is subject to detailed scrutiny and testing to examine its performance over the range of expected operating conditions, and any necessary design modifications are made.

The design process may be regarded as a process of *generate and test*. A conceptual design is first *generated* by a process of conceptual synthesis. Detail is then progressively added to the design by the method of top-down refinement. Since the goal state (a final design which satisfies a number of partially specified functional requirements) is usually not

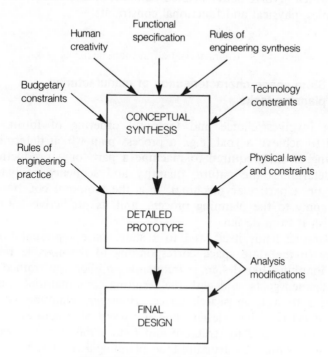

Figure 10.3 The design process.

clearly defined, the search space is usually very large. Many conceptually different designs may be produced which satisfy the initially stated requirements, but only a small number of these will be satisfactory, since a clearer specification of requirements often emerges only as the design progresses; the full nature of the goal state is fleshed out during the search process itself.

The heuristics used by the human designer to reduce the search space during the conceptual phase of design is the complex and little understood mental process of human creativity by which intuitive jumps within the search space are made in the general direction of the goal. Given the vast amount of taken-for-granted factual and practical knowledge that would need to be represented, and the lack of our insight into the processes of human creativity, there seems little prospect, using current knowlege representation techniques, that the generalised conceptual design synthesis process could be captured and represented in a computer, although there are reports of attempts to do this in limited and tightly constrained design problem domains in which the design possibilities are sufficiently restricted as to result in a limited search space (see section 14.1.1). There would, however, appear to be considerably greater potential for the application of knowledge-based technologies to the detailed phase of design synthesis, and the analysis phases of the design, both of which involve better defined domains of knowledge, in terms of design rules, physical and functional constraints.

10.2.4 State space characterisation of manufacturing planning tasks

Planning involves choice and temporal ordering of future actions required to achieve a goal (e.g., a process plan which determines the sequencing of cuts required to machine a part, or a production plan which determines the nature, quantity and sequence of batches to produce on a particular machine). It is the temporal constraints that usually apply to the planning process, and its predictive nature, that distinguish it from design.

Planning lends itself well to a state space representation, with operators in the state space corresponding to permissable real-world actions. Planning, like design, is frequently an underconstrained activity with ill-defined goals, and with the resulting combinatorial complexity giving rise to a large search space. However, planning is a more structured activity than design, and a variety of generalised methods have been developed to structure and reduce the search space, based mostly on how humans structure their planning activities. Most of these methods can be used in conjunction with each other.

Hierarchical planning (Sacerdoti, 1977)

This involves the development of a rough-cut plan in terms of a sequence of aggregate actions (or operators) within a simplified search space. The initial plan is then refined to increasing levels of detail by decomposing the aggregate operations into their constituents (object-oriented representations supporting inheritance are useful in this decomposition process). This has a clear correspondence with methods of hierarchical planning used in production management, in which an aggregate production plan is decomposed into more detailed tactical plans, which are in turn decomposed to individual shop floor actions. It avoids the problem of getting 'bogged down' in unnecessary detail in the early phases of planning.

Refinement of partial plans

Frequently, many or all of the permitted actions or operations of a plan may be prespecified, but their ordering is only partially specified. We may therefore start the planning process with a set of plan fragments (partially ordered collections of operations). In this case we have what is termed a partial plan, which can be represented as series of nodes in the search space, as in Figure 10.4. The planning problem is then reduced to extending the partial plan, typically by ordering the unordered operations, adding additional operations, or specifying operations in greater detail. The starting information for production scheduling and process planning problems is often in the form of partially ordered sets of actions (e.g., certain types of operation must *always* be done in sequence).

Constraint-directed search

This involves the use of domain-specific knowledge to restrict the search space by only considering those sequences of operations that will satisfy

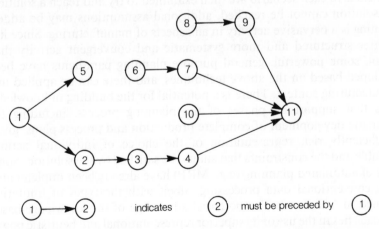

Figure 10.4 Partial plan represented by nodes in the search space.

the constraints imposed by the planning domain on the solution. This approach is directly relevant to manufacturing planning tasks, in which managerial, technological, temporal, capacity and preference constraints on the plan usually abound.

Dependency-directed backtracking

If the planner explores a part of the search space that leads to a dead end, backtracking occurs not to the most **recent** choice point, but to the choice point **responsible** for the dead end. To do this, a record must be kept of choices made so that failures can be analysed. This is a common feature of human problem solving in limited problem domains.

Non-linear planning (Chapman, 1985)

Many types of plan contain operations that can occur in parallel, and hence overlap in time. In non-linear planning, both plans and goals are represented as partial orders, in which ordering constraints resulting from interactions between parallel operations are *only* introduced when necessary to reach a solution. Planning does not have to progress linearly from initial to goal state. Different sections of the plan can be developed in any order consistent with the partial ordering constraints, and the planner can move from one part of the plan to another according to 'focus of attention' heuristics (e.g., the recognition of which planning goals should be satisfied as soon as possible, and which should be postponed as long as possible).

Assumption-based planning (de Kleer, 1986)

This involves generating a collection of partial plans each of which is based on a unique set of assumptions (called a scenario). All possible partial plan extensions in each scenario are then examined to try and reach a solution. If a solution cannot be reached, additional assumptions may be added. Planning is a pervasive activity in all aspects of manufacturing. Since it is a better structured and more systematic and convergent activity than design, some powerful, general purpose planning paradigms have been developed based on the above techniques, and these can be applied in a manufacturing context. There is a potential for the building of knowledge bases that support all phases of the planning process, including the automatic development of complete production and process plans, given a sufficiently rich representation of the choice of individual actions available and the constraints that should be satisfied by the solution. Some types of automated planning (e.g., MRP) have already been implemented using conventional data processing, albeit with the types of limitation outlined in Chapter 2. The potential advantage of the knowledge-based approach lies in the use of its superior representational and heuristic power to overcome these limitations.

10.2.5   State space characterisation of manufacturing control tasks

Control activities are concerned with the actual execution of tasks, rather than their planning. They involve a process of monitoring to ensure that execution is being performed in accordance with the plan, problem solving to establish the probable causes of deviations, and decision making concerning choice of the best possible actions for plan recovery.

The **monitoring** aspects of control involve the establishment of a set of normal or acceptable values, or combinations of values, for chosen operating variables. In state space, the acceptable combinations of values of these variables may be regarded as a goal state (or set of goal states), in which the system is regarded as being in a state of control. Variables are checked at regular intervals, and alerting or diagnostic procedures are triggered when values are outside the acceptable limits, or unacceptable combinations are found. It is then required to search for a set of actions that brings the system back to a goal state (a state of control).

Databases containing components which automatically **monitor** data values and initiate actions when certain conditions are found are called 'active' databases. Monitoring for specific conditions would generally be 'triggered' whenever the database is accessed or updated. Obviously, the monitoring of complex conditions involving multiple objects and views can present a large search problem, which might be reduced by the use of heuristics such as 'lazy' and 'eager' evaluation, or local domain-specific knowledge in the form of production rules designed to optimise the search. Object-oriented representations are generally suitable for use as active databases. The ability to construct hierarchies allows monitoring to take place at different levels, and detailed search triggered by a condition detected at the aggregate level, can be guided down the hierarchy. The ability to manage the time dimension of condition monitoring is also important, not only in terms of detecting trends in historical values, but also in terms of respecting timing and concurrency constraints. Dayal *et al* (1988) describe an object oriented data model which uses knowledge-based techniques to support complex condition monitoring.

Control also involves **diagnosis** of abnormalities and the establishment of the actions required for the recovery of the normal state (which will be a goal state in a state space representation of the problem). Automated problem diagnosis, particularly in well-structured task domains, is an activity that lends itself to the application of knowledge-based systems, with some of the earliest examples of this approach being in the medical diagnosis field (see Buchanan and Shortliffe, 1984). Diagnosis requires domain-specific knowledge of the problem area to be stored in the form of a model of the task environment. This can be stored either implicitly in the form of surface heuristics such as production rules, or explicitly in the form of various structural and causal relationships between objects in the task domain implemented in an object-oriented representation. Diagnosis may proceed by backward chaining from a hypothesis about the nature of the fault, using production rules, or by instantiating a 'best-fit' object as described in Section 9.2.3.

Plan **recovery** involves assessing, from the diagnosis, the cause of the deviation and the appropriate remedial action. This type of knowledge may often be embedded in forward chaining rule-based systems. It is also necessary to determine how far through the original plan the effects of the deviation will propagate, and therefore the extent to which the latter can be localised by appropriate corrective action. Effective incorporation of uncertainty in the representation of the plan is important in this phase, so that a false sense of precision in the plan does not result in frequent, needless small adjustments (which often manifest themselves as 'nervousness', for example, in MRP systems).

In general, all forms of control in manufacturing organisations are potential candidates for knowledge-based support in one or more of their individual aspects. Some simple forms of control (e.g., inventory control) are already commonly supported through conventional data processing. Use of knowledge bases should enable far more complex forms of control to be supported.

10.3 Categories of knowledge-based support for manufacturing tasks

In discussing computer knowledge-based support of manufacturing tasks, we can specify three possible categories:

(1)   Knowledge-based systems that are capable of replacing the human decision maker simply by producing the required decision, or sequence of decisions, which will then be implemented with little if any human intervention. These might be termed **knowledge-based decision systems**.

(2)   Systems that analyse problems and produce recommendations for solution which are then analysed in some depth by the human decision maker. These might be termed **knowledge-based advisory systems**.

(3)   Systems that provide support to the human decision maker by providing chunks of information or knowledge which are relevant to the problem at hand, or are capable of using stored knowledge to analyse some particular aspect of that problem, or can assist the decision maker in constructing and manipulating representations of that problem. These might be termed **knowledge-based decision support systems**.

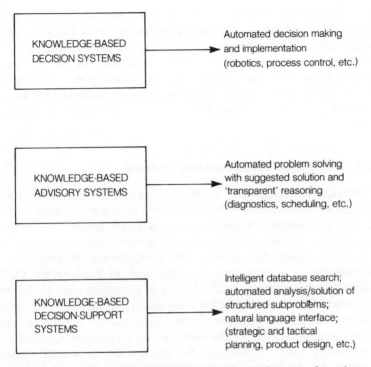

Figure 10.5 Types of knowledge-based system for manufacturing.

10.3.1 Knowledge-based decision systems

Knowledge-based decision systems can obviously only be used for tasks which are relatively well defined, and have a high degree of structure. Such tasks are often amenable to programmimg by conventional algorithmic means, and the choice between an algorithmic and a knowledge-based approach will depend on such factors as the combinatorial complexity of the task, its stability, the type and diversity of the data inputs on which it is dependent, and the extent to which it is decomposable into quasi-autonomous subtasks.

In general, a knowledge-based approach is suitable for tasks of higher complexity which are sensitive to diverse data inputs from the environment, and which may be soluble by decomposition into weakly coupled subtasks which would cause control problems in an algorithmic approach. The relative ease with which a knowledge-based system may be modified or updated also makes this approach more suitable for tasks which are dependent on knowledge that may change over time. In the area of process control, intelligent monitoring systems have been developed which are capable of diagnosing and adjusting the conditions of a complex process without human intervention, learning from the results, and updating their knowledge bases accordingly. Robotics is clearly also an area requiring autonomous knowledge-based decision systems. Knowledge-based process planning systems likewise have the ultimate aim of achieving the completely automatic translation of a design specification to a set of coded instructions for an NC machine. Such systems will obviously require, at least, as complete a representation of the problem environment and as effective problem-solving heuristics as would be available to a human for them to be a viable proposition for routine use.

10.3.2 Knowledge-based advisory systems

A knowledge-based advisory system is a system that applies its knowledge base to the solution of some problem or the performance of some task, and *recommends* a decision or course of action. The individual responsible for the task may then use their own judgement as to whether to accept or reject this advice. The transparency of reasoning of a knowledge-based system, and the provision of explanation facilities, usually make it possible to track the line of reasoning used (which would not be possible with an algorithmic approach). Thus, a knowledge-based diagnostic system for machine faults might use its knowledge base to suggest a possible reason for the fault and, on interrogation, could display the reasoning used. This could be checked by a human trained in diagnostic maintainance, to establish whether the conclusions and reasoning were consistent with the known facts. The system's reasoning might also trigger a set of diagnostic associations in the mind of the human that would otherwise have remained latent. Thus, knowledge-based advisory systems can sometimes produce synergy between human and computer in performance of the task. They are also potentially useful in the training role.

Silverman (1987) has enumerated in more detail the potential benefits of this synergy, some of which are given below:

(1) **Procedural cuing** The user is reminded of the reasoning steps required, and is cued on the most recent techniques or organisational changes.

(2) **Corporate memory** This reminds the user of what has been previously learned about the problem by storing previous sessions in some accessible form.

(3) **Similar results** These recalls results and experiences with similar problems, perhaps with other users.

(4) **Cross-stage advisor** This gives the user easy access to results from earlier stages of the problem-solving process.

(5) **Training** This provides training, tutorials and instructional documentation for those new to the task.

10.3.3 Knowledge-based decision support systems

A common definition of a **Decision Support System** (DSS) is 'an interactive computer-based system that helps decision makers use data and models to solve unstructured problems' (Sprague and Carlson, 1982).

Decision support systems thus do *not* aim to provide solutions to problems, or to enumerate fully all the actions required to perform a task. They merely provide ways of conveniently accessing information relevant to the problem or task through selective data retrieval functions, helpful ways of structuring the available data into abstract representations (or models) of some aspect of the problem or task, and facilities for manipulating these representations. The focus is on ease of use and flexibility and adaptability to user needs. Thus a DSS in a production scheduling environment might allow a human scheduler to interact directly with a graphical Gantt Chart representation of the schedule by moving jobs around on the Gantt Chart using a mouse or cursor keys. Simple background models might then automatically advise of any other jobs affected, and any constraints violated by moving the job, or to automatically reschedule other jobs according to some user-selected scheduling heuristic.

Sprague and Carlson conceptualise a DSS as consisting of a database subsystem, a model base subsystem, and a dialogue subsystem (Figure 10.6). The user interacts with the system via the dialogue subsystem to retrieve relevant data, and models to manipulate this data and to provide information relevant to the solution of the problem. The

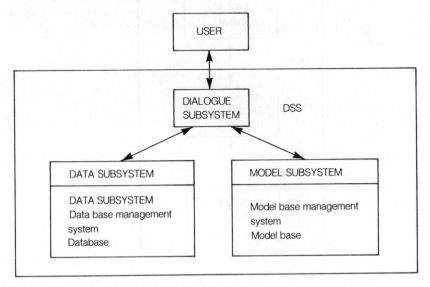

Figure 10.6 Sprague and Carlson's architecture for a DSS.

models may be mathematical programming models for optimisation, statistical models for forecasting or regression analysis, models of cash flow, simulation models, etc.

Bonczek *et al* (1981), on the other hand, conceptualise a DSS as consisting of a language system, a problem-processing system, and a knowledge system (Figure 10.7). Users interact with the DSS by stating their requirements using the language system. The problem processing system then matches user requirements to the available knowledge in the knowledge system to generate the information required to support the human decision-making process.

On the assumption that the functions of the problem processing system are (a) to retrieve relevant information from the knowledge system, and (b) to perform computations using this information to generate useful results using predefined models or other analysis tools provided by the DSS, Bonczek *et al* propose a classification scheme for DSS as shown in Figure 10.8. This allows a DSS to be classified according

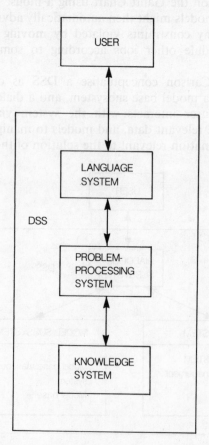

Figure 10.7 Bonczek *et al*'s concept of a DSS.

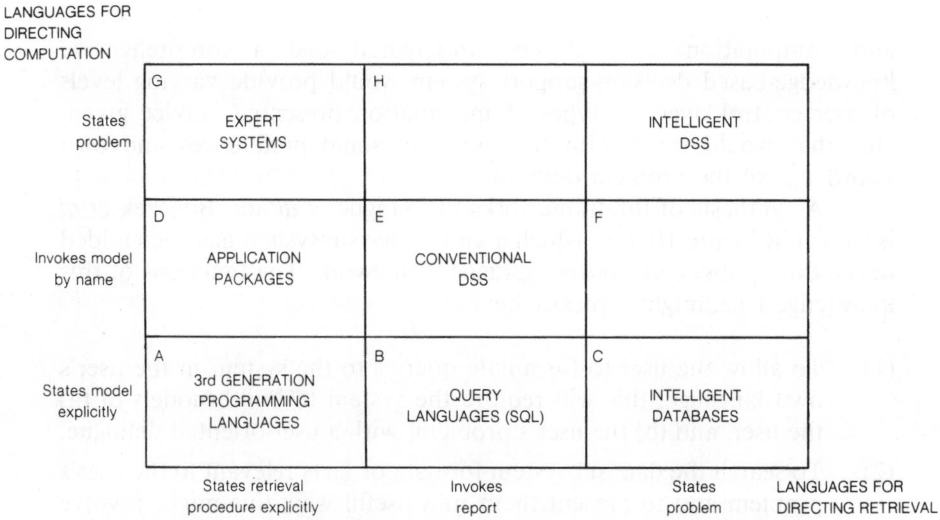

LANGUAGES FOR
DIRECTING
COMPUTATION

	States retrieval procedure explicitly	Invokes report	States problem	
States problem	G EXPERT SYSTEMS	H		INTELLIGENT DSS
Invokes model by name	D APPLICATION PACKAGES	E CONVENTIONAL DSS	F	
States model explicitly	A 3rd GENERATION PROGRAMMING LANGUAGES	B QUERY LANGUAGES (SQL)	C INTELLIGENT DATABASES	

	States retrieval procedure explicitly	Invokes report	States problem	LANGUAGES FOR DIRECTING RETRIEVAL

Figure 10.8   Bonczek *et al*'s classification scheme for DSS.

to its location in a two dimensional space in which one axis represents the division of responsibility between user and system for retrieving information from the knowledge system relevant to the problem in hand, and the other axis represents the similar division of responsibility for executing relevant computational models.

Nine regions of this space are identified. At one extreme (region A in the lower left-hand corner), we have systems in which the user must have a clear idea of the data required and must be able to explicitly specify procedures for its retrieval; similarly, the user must know what computations are required, and must be able to specify them in some appropriate programming language. At the other extreme, systems in the top right-hand region (region I) require the user merely to specify the problem. The problem processing system will then establish what data or models are required to provide relevant support to the solution of the problem, and will automatically retrieve the data, execute models, interpret results, and display reports. This might include the provision of various forms of technical or expert advice about certain aspects of the problem by calling upon specialised knowledge bases. Note that as this classification relates to decision *support* systems for unstructured problems, we assume that systems in region I will stop short of actually making, or advising on, the final decision, but will provide information and analyses on specific aspects of the problem which may be relevant and useful in reducing the problem search space. Systems falling in the upper right region of Figure 10.8 include systems in which so-called 'intelligent front ends' (Bundy, 1985) are provided for analysis tools which are otherwise too complex for unaided use by unskilled users.

Between these two extremes are the types of DSS which place varying degrees of responsibility on the user for directing data retrieval and computation. It might be anticipated that a comprehensive knowledge-based decision-support system would provide varying levels of user control over the types of information presented, advice given, etc., that would mesh with the user's personal preferences and own knowledge of the problem domain.

A synthesis of the frameworks of Sprague *et al* and Bonczek *et al* is shown in Figure 10.9, in which a knowledge subsystem has been added to the three subsystems of the Sprague framework. The functions of this knowledge base might typically be:

(1)   To allow the user to formulate queries to the system in the user's own language; this will require the system to build models of (a) the user, and (b) the user's problem, with a user-oriented dialogue.

(2)   To search the data subsystem for data or facts relevant to the user's problem and to present them in a useful way; this might involve automatic construction of data retrieval statements in languages such as SQL; it might also involve some form of inferential retrieval.

(3)   To determine which models or knowledge subsystems might usefully be applied to the data describing the problem in order to create new information or give new insight; in other words, to

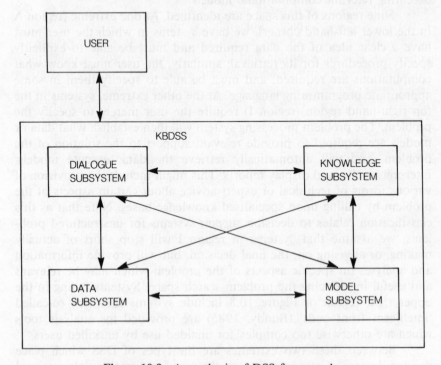

Figure 10.9 A synthesis of DSS frameworks.

extract relevant knowledge from the knowledge base and bring this knowledge to bear on the problem.

(4)   To determine and extract from the data subsystem and/or the user, the input data required for such models, to check for accuracy, consistency and completeness, and to determine a strategy to handle cases of missing, incomplete or inaccurate data.

(5)   To perform parametric and other analyses using these models to examine sensitivity of the results to key assumptions; this might involve performing analyses of solutions generated by the user to examine their performance or the extent to which they satisfy constraints.

(6)   To interpret and analyse the results and to determine the best form of displaying them to the user.

Varying levels of human intervention or overide can be conceived as occurring in the different phases of this process. Obviously, to fulfil all these functions, the knowledge base would need to contain diverse types of knowledge of the task domain, mappings between task-domain characteristics and analysis models, analysis techniques, etc., and would in fact involve replicating the knowledge of a skilled human analyst.

Although the concepts of decision support systems have evolved largely independently of work on Artificial Intelligence and knowledge-based systems, a complementary relationship exists between them, and there is evidence that in several aspects, the two strands of research are converging (see for example Turban, 1988). In production management (in which the majority of decisions particularly at tactical and strategic levels cannot be fully automated) and in those areas of manufacturing technology requiring creative problem solving such as product design, knowledge-based decision *support* systems will be the only effective means through which stored computer knowledge can be utilised.

Part III

APPLICATIONS TO PRODUCTION MANAGEMENT AND

PRODUCTION SYSTEMS DESIGN

The following three chapters review some of the current applications of knowledge-based systems technology to production management and production systems design. The first chapter provides a brief overview of the state of the art in this area. The succeeding two chapters discuss in more detail some selected applications.

Chapter 11
Knowledge-based Production Management and Production Systems Design — a Review

11.1 Knowledge-based systems for strategic production planning	11.3 Knowledge-based systems for operational control
11.2 Knowledge-based systems for tactical planning	11.4 Knowledge-based production systems design

11.1 Knowledge-based systems for strategic production planning

Strategic production planning generally involves the development of an aggregate, rough-cut plan for the projected production of product groups over a relatively extended time horizon, which is roughly within the capacity constraints of the factory. Decisions have to be made on the extent to which demand changes will be absorbed through inventory or through matching production to demand. Choices will often have to be made between varying product mix, additional inventory investment, overtime, subcontracting, working with excess capacity, extending lead times, varying the size of the workforce, and so on. Many alternatives might present themselves, with constraints that must be satisfied, such as trade union work contracts. This is a combinatorially complex problem with a large number of decision variables and many constraints. Conventional tools, such as linear decisions rules (Holt *et al*, 1953), linear programming, heuristic search, and simulation have all been proposed as potential solutions, but none has gained wide acceptance, because of combinations of excessive mathematical complexity and data requirements and unrealistic assumptions. In practice, most companies have developed planning policies specific to their particular operations and sets of circumstances, which are based on experience. A typical example of such a policy is quoted by Duchessi (1987):

'If it becomes clear three months prior to the final month that the target inventory cannot be achieved, then production in the last two months can fall below the lowest allowable limit. However, if production in the last two months of the year is below the lower limit, and stockouts occur in the first three months of the following year as normal increases in production are scheduled, then adjust the target inventory upwards and adjust the last two months of production to ensure that stockouts are avoided and the lower production limit is not exceeded'.

This type of knowledge cannot easily be represented using conventional techniques. It can, however, be quite conveniently represented in a production rule system. Duchessi proposes a conceptual design for an aggregate production planning system, using production rules within a state space representation of the problem, in which individual states represent partial production plans. The initial state is an empty plan. Intermediate states represent a specification of production rates, ending inventories, work force levels, period costs, etc. for a finite number of periods. The goal state is represented by a complete plan (i.e., a specified values of the above decision variables for each period over the entire planning horizon) that satisfies planning constraints (relating for example, to production, overtime and inventory levels) at the lowest possible cost. Production rules are applied to partial plans using forward chaining, thus extending them in a search for a goal state. To reduce the search space, the rules incorporate a combination of company-specific constraint knowledge (e.g., ending inventory for period 1 must be at least 10% of that period's marketing requirements) and heuristic problem-solving knowledge (e.g., if marketing requirements are increasing, only consider production plans for next three periods with rates greater than the current period). This knowledge is elicited from experienced planners. The system described by Duchessi is programmed in the OPS5 production rule language, and only considers two decision variables (production rate and overtime) and ten production rules. It appears, however, that extension of the system would be relatively simple.

A major problem with planning at the strategic level is the need to satisfy multiple conflicting objectives. Bitran and Papageorge (1987) have described a system (the Operations Advisor) which performs reasoning about trade-offs between aggregate capacity, work-in-progress, and lead times. Given basic data on product families and flows, their system represents a manufacturing operation as a network of queues. From this queueing model, automatic inferences are made about the location of optimal trade-off curves between these three strategic parameters. The system provides a route map enabling the company to move from a sub-optimal position, away from the efficient frontier defined by the trade-off curves, to any desired position on the frontier. A similar approach is taken by the strategic planning module of the ISTOP system described in Chapter 14; the IMPS system developed at Boston University (see below) also makes use of knowledge-based systems for this purpose.

Currently, the function least well supported by knowledge-based systems is the strategic planning function. Interestingly enough this is traditionally one of the least structured of manufacturing management tasks and requires a higher proportion of human judgement than decisions taken at lower levels. An invaluable aid would be the provision of decision support in the form of a rapid what-if analysis capability in which the logical consequences of using various production strategies under various alternative qualitative and quantitative assumptions about future markets, actions of competitors, etc., could be rapidly assessed. Knowledge-Based Decision Support Systems with embedded knowledge of constraints and performance criteria might also assist in the aggregate planning task by allowing the rapid evaluation or critiquing of alternative plans developed by human planners in terms of constraints and management objectives. These could evaluate plan feasibility with reference to bottleneck resources, budgetary and other constraints, and score them in terms of their success in meeting explicitly stated business objectives. Such capabilities would require systems with both symbolic reasoning power, and a set of embedded quantitative models allowing cash flows, etc. to be computed from a given set of planning parameter assignments.

A system of this type, which seems to be applicable to strategic production planning, is ROME (Reason Oriented Modelling Environment) developed at Carnegie Mellon University (Kosy and Wise, 1985). This is a knowledge-based decision support system designed to contain declarative knowledge of strategic level variables and relationships, between these variables. It allows business planning models to be built quickly and easily, and automatic inferences and evaluations to be made using these models which are consistent with the explicitly declared assumptions. ROME is built on an object-oriented database

Published reports of any substance on this type of support for strategic production planning are still few and far between. Nevertheless, there is evidence that an increasing number of companies are actively experimenting in this area. The relative sparseness of publications possibly reflect the fact that strategic planning is a commercially more sensitive area than shop floor control.

11.2 Knowledge-based systems for tactical planning

11.2.1 Medium- and short-term forecasting

The medium- and short-term forecasting of end product demand is an important activity from the tactical planning point of view, requiring information from a wide variety of sources, including access to historical sales data, knowledge of market factors that might cause shifts in current patterns of demand, knowledge of activities of competitors, and so on. Forecasting by projecting trends in previous sales data, using such techniques as regression or time series analysis, is a relatively well-developed technique for which a number of standard procedures exist. However, forecasts thus obtained must generally be combined with forecasts obtained from other sources. The knowledge of *which* type of forecasting technique is appropriate and *how* to combine forecasts from different sources is, under certain conditions, the type of knowledge that might be representable in a computer knowledge base. For example, a knowledge base might be incorporated which infers from the properties of the data whether a Box-Jenkins, exponential smoothing, or simple moving average model would be more appropriate. It might also be possible for a knowledge-based forecasting system to monitor certain economic or other indicators known to have a likely effect on sales, and use trends in these indicators together with known relevant facts (e.g., impending launch of new product by competitor) to modify forecasts obtained by time series analysis of historical demand, according to a set of production rules representing Judgemental assessment of the nature and magnitude of the effects. Such rules would take the form of *surface heuristics*. Forecasting based on *deep reasoning* would require causal or associative models of the effect of such external factors on sales (assuming they were known) and would probably become unmanageably complex, requiring the explicit representation of a considerable amount of common-sense knowledge to avoid drawing naive conclusions.

11.2.2 Requirements planning

Requirements planning at the tactical level involves refining aggregate plans over the medium term by establishing material and production requirements, and reserving capacity on production resources such that production requirements can be met. This will generally mean developing a master production schedule for individual end product items, and using this to drive production requirements for components and raw materials, and capacity reservations on resources. Over the short term, the operational control level is concerned with translating the tactical plan into detailed schedules for batch production, or rate and mix adjustment for repetitive production and for monitoring plan execution.

Computerisation of the requirements planning activity has until recently been largely within the province of the MRP approach, which uses conventional procedural data-processing techniques to generate and coordinate plans for different functional areas. The limitations of this approach are well documented and are described in section 2.2.4. MRP does not in general allow any iterative adjustment of plans to ensure they are *feasible*, since infinite capacity is assumed when loading production resources. Decisions taken at one level concerning such parameters as lead times and batch sizes are generally irrevocable, regardless of whether the resulting lower level plan can be executed within capacity constraints. Plans tend to be *made* feasible by building slack into the system in the form of excessive lead times or safety stocks. Although application of the basic MRP algorithm is computationally intensive for a realistic number and complexity of products, it is procedurally straightforward, and does not as such involve any combinatorially complex search problems, due to these simplifications. There is, however, considerable scope for the generation of superior plans to those obtained by MRP, through the iterative adjustment of planned capacities, lead times, lot sizes and end-product master schedules, to create feasible, finite capacity plans that not only satisfy forecast demand, but are also feasible at all planning levels and result in faster throughput times and lower inventory levels.

What is required is a more opportunistic approach to planning based on the representation of search heuristics (using local knowledge) by which good plans and schedules can be constructed. These should be feasible at all levels, and attention should be paid to iterative improvement of the plan by adjustment of lead times, batch sizes, and routings rather than taking these as givens. For companies that make a high variety of complex products involving thousands of components, the resulting degree of combinatorial complexity poses severe problems. A considerable amount of work has been performed in attempting to develop algorithms and heuristics in simplified cases — see for example, Karmarker, 1987. The approach adopted in the OPT system (Section 2.3.4) attempts to reduce the combinatorial complexity by a factoring of the search space through identification of the bottleneck resources and concentrating scheduling activity on these, using a proprietry algorithm. However this suffers from problems resulting from the wandering bottleneck phenomenon in which unexpected contingencies at non-bottleneck resources cause these to become the bottlenecks.

It is likely that future solutions to this problem will use a combination of algorithms and knowledge-based systems, in association with new ways of factoring the search space, hierarchically or otherwise. An integrated manufacturing planning system called IMPS developed at Boston University (Ebner, Lindgren and Vollman, 1986) attempts to simplify the search space by evaluating the extent to which detailed shop floor plans contribute to or block the achievement of strategic company goals, the latter being expressed in terms of the three 'currencies' of revenue, capacity, and materials. IMPS does not implement a closed loop planning philosophy from strategic planning down to the factory floor. It is only interested in detailed activities to the extent that they constrain the achievement of strategic objectives. Resources are assigned or reassigned, using knowledge-based systems operating at the detailed levels of master scheduling, reservation management, and vendor management. These check the implications of a plan and resolve problems so that minimum disruption is experienced. Thus it would appear that the philosophy of IMPS is to use locally embedded knowledge-based systems in an overall flexible supervisory structure which allows considerable local autonomy.

Another integrated manufacturing planning system is ISTOP (Kerr and Walker, 1989); in this system individual workstations have embedded knowledge-based advisory systems for planning and coordinating their own operations by structured negotiation with each other within an overall set of planning parameters set by a supervisory strategic planning module. (See Chapter 13 for more details.)

An effective means of reducing the combinatorial complexity of the search space is by rationalising and simplifying product structures and process plans to form a number of pseudo-autonomous 'factories within factories' that can be planned and scheduled largely independently. To the extent that set-up times and hence batch sizes can be reduced to the point where a continuous flow of mixed components, rather than discrete batches can be produced (i.e., the Just-in-Time ideal), planning can be reduced merely to determining the composition of the *mix* required to meet the end product requirement over some appropriate planning period, rather than planning discrete batches. This will require careful planning at the product design and process and facilities planning level, and provides an additional set of goals and constraints which will apply to those activities. However, given a rationalised set of product, process and facility designs, that enables continuous flow production to take place, the operational problem of planning and updating component flow rates and mixes is an activity that can be performed using relatively straightforward algorithms as described for example by Bitran and Chang (1987). The main support required would be in the form of a knowledge-based system for interfacing the user to these planning algorithms and as a means of checking that planned mixes do not violate constraints that have been declared elsewhere.

In cases where batch sizes are irreducible or where there is so little repeatability of manufacture (as in the case of a job shop) that continuous flow production is impossible, planning on the basis of discrete batches will still be necessary. This will also apply to long lead time raw materials. Product and process rationalisation might nevertheless at least reduce the component variety processed on individual workcentres, even if continuous flow production cannot be achieved. The incorporation of domain specific knowledge-based heuristics into MRP type algorithms might then be used to reduce the remaining combinatorial complexity of the problem of simultaneously optimising batch sizes, lead times, capacity levels and routings, in a form of state space search, which at least finds better solutions than the current MRP approach in an acceptable amount of computer time.

To date, very little work has been reported in this field, with the majority of research-based attempts to improve on MRP still heavily oriented towards conventional algorithms or general heuristic search, rather than towards the explicit use of domain-specific knowledge such as constraint-directed reasoning to reduce the search space. As a result, these approaches have had until now had little practical utility, since they are mathematically over-complex and ignore many of the practical constraints that would apply to the problem in a real rather than a theoretical environment. Constraint-directed reasoning (which will be discussed in more detail in connection with the ISIS scheduling system in Chapter 14) could overcome these limitations, since it requires a much richer representation of the production environment, with guiding heuristics based on the detailed specifics of that environment.

In the shorter term, many companies still employing MRP-type approaches might profitably use knowledge-based advisory systems to interpret MRP output and to suggest suitable courses of action. The number of daily exception messages issued by most MRP systems can present a major problem to operating personnel who must interpret the action implications of each message. Simple reasoning mechanisms (using production rules) might not only filter out many of these messages, but might also analyse the significance of the exception in the light of other relevant data and make specific recommendations in terms of the options available (e.g., increase capacity rather than delay a job finish date). In particular, a knowledge-based decision support system might be employed in the capacity planning phase of MRP to assist in analysis of infinite loading reports and establish whether apparent capacity problems can be solved within a detailed schedule without resorting to a change of MPS. Current problems in this area stem from the difficulty in interfacing knowledge-based systems with existing MRP databases. However, this may be alleviated by a trend towards universal adoption of the relational model for which knowledge-based interfaces have already been developed (see Chapter 17).

11.2.3 Maintenance planning

Maintenance involves ensuring that the production facilities keep operating and that disruptions due to breakdowns are minimised. It may be divided into the **tactical planning** aspects of preventive maintenance, which involves planning for facilities to be regularly taken out of service for routine checking and attention to known potential problems, and the **operational control** or diagnostic and reactive aspects of maintenance in which equipment functions are monitored to detect any signs of malfunction, which is then diagnosed and repaired. A planning strand to reactive maintenance is the decision on how an unplanned breakdown will impact on the preventive maintenance cycle.

Planned preventive maintenance is an activity that needs to be coordinated with the overall capacity planning and scheduling performed as part of the production planning activity. Trade-offs are required between the predictable loss of capacity incurred when a facility is taken out of service for planned maintanance, and the unpredictable loss of capacity that occurs when it breaks down. These trade-offs can only be made if the effect of varying levels of preventive maintenance on appropriate performance criteria such as expected number or orders delayed and mean throughput time can be established and the relative weighting of these criteria agreed upon.

Knowledge-based support for this type of coordinative decision negotiated between maintenance and production planning could be provided by developing and storing models which supply a predictive relationship, and hence a 'what-if' analysis capability between maintenance level and the appropriate performance factors of interest. Levels of preventive maintenance required to achieve a given reduction in unplanned downtime could be assessed from models based on statistical analyses of the previous performance history of the facility. This would require keeping systematic records for each facility of the faults encountered, distribution of times between occurrences, etc. The updating and refinement of models in response to ongoing data acquisition is a task that could perhaps be handled by embedded knowledge-based routines containing a knowledge of basic statistics and probability, which could be implemented in the form of a production rule system. An intelligent interface could be provided to such a suite of models to facilitate user interaction. The relationship between planned and unplanned downtime and the higher level performance factors of job throughput time, proportion of orders late, etc. would require the use of a simulation model in which a representative sample of typical orders flows through the shop under varying maintenance conditions. Again, an intelligent interface in the form of a model manager might be provided to facilitate the choice of model, model updates, experimental design and interpretation of results.

The interaction of planned maintenance with unplanned repairs is another area in which effective decision making depends on the availabilty of a good predictive model to evaluate the effects of alternative policies on the various performance criteria. The effects of opportunistic maintenance strategies can be complex, and responsive analytical tools are essential if good decisions are to be made. Modern philosophies of production management such as JIT embrace the devolution of responsibility for activities, such as planned and preventive maintenance, to the group of production workers responsible for each production cell, rather than centralising it in a separate functional department. It is therefore all the more important that appropriate statistical analysis and other appropriate tools are made available to such groups. Knowledge-based systems provide a means for greatly extending the amount of knowledge that can be applied to these problems by non-specialist groups of workers.

11.2.4 Distribution planning

The logistical aspects of distribution planning entail making decisions concerning the optimal flow of a defined supply of products through a specific distribution network, involving intermediate storage points, to meet a known or projected customer demand. Distribution networks for large companies selling a diversity of products may be very complex, with thousands of intermediate storage locations. A variety of types of computer assistance are generally provided, including network optimisation models (for example Glover, *et al* 1978) and system dynamics models. Again, it is conceivable that AI planning techniques might be employed in this task in cases where the objectives or constraints of the distribution planning exercise cannot be adequately represented using conventional approaches. There will, however, be many problems for which conventional approaches will be useful, hence a tandem architecture would be appropriate in which a knowledge-based system chooses the best type of model (e.g., a network model) for the problem, retrieves the required input data and performs parametric and post-optimality analysis using the model. An approach to distribution planning using this architecture is described by Klingman and Phillips (1987).

11.2.5 Quoting and estimating

In jobs shops making one-off or highly customised products, the ability to provide rapid quotations and estimates is very important. This involves being able to retrieve in real time similar designs to the one requested, to estimate the material quantities, manufacturing resources and processing times required and to simulate the addition of the requisite production jobs to the existing production schedule so that a completion time can be estimated. An integrated product knowledge base (of the type to be described in Chapter 15) would facilitate inferential retrieval of similar designs to assist in cost estimates. Using an object-oriented representation, this knowledge base could also contain flexible, parametric or typical product definitions which could be further instantiated to specific customer requirements, thus decreasing the time and cost of generating proposals. A production planning system in which jobs to be scheduled could be classified as to whether they represented firm or tentative orders could then perform a resource loading for tentative jobs to estimate their completion dates.

11.3 Knowledge-based systems for operational control

11.3.1 Shop floor control

Shop floor control involves the actual execution of tactical plans through the development of detailed short-term shop floor schedules, the release of work on to the shop floor in accordance with those schedules, the monitoring of capacity and work in progress, and reaction to shop floor contingencies as far as possible within the limits of the original schedule.

Predictive shop floor scheduling

Detailed shop floor scheduling involves determining the sequence of loading jobs on individual machines or work centres with due regard for capacity, such that precedence constraints on the ordering of operations are satisfied, and due dates of jobs are as far as possible met. Scheduling for continuous flow production is relatively straightforward, involving the fine tuning of planned flow rates and mixes to actual shop floor conditions. However, detailed scheduling for batch production (particularly in job shops in which each job may need processing in a different sequence on several machines) is not a trivial problem. The number of ways of scheduling of scheduling N jobs through M machines is $(N!)^M$ (10^{32} for ten jobs on five machines), and rises exponentially with the number of jobs. This class of problem has been termed 'NP Hard' since no known algorithm can be guaranteed to converge to an optimal solution.

Conventional approaches to batch scheduling have used network techniques and integer programming formulations, which are soluble in principle by branch and bound heuristics (see for example Baker, 1974), in order to develop predictive schedules but the performance of such approaches has been limited, both in their ability to represent realistic situations, and the time taken to reach a solution. Other approaches have used simple priority rules for sequencing jobs (e.g., 'load the job with the earliest due date', 'load the job with the shortest processing time') whose performance in different situations can be investigated using simulation. The problem with this type of approach is that lack of foresight can result in poor scheduling decisions in many circumstances.

The combinatorial complexity of the scheduling problem, and the observation that human schedulers use large quantities of domain-specific knowledge about local scheduling constraints in order to reduce the search space, has resulted in the problem becoming a major focus for the application of AI and knowledge-based techniques. Whereas in 1985 only a handful of knowledge-based scheduling systems had been reported, the number has been approximately doubling each year since then, and scheduling is currently the area of manufacturing management that is being most actively researched from a knowledge-based perspective.

Most knowledge-based scheduling systems may be divided into those that use a pure production-rule-based representation of scheduling knowledge, and those that use rules embedded in a frame-based representation. As examples, the systems reported by Erschler and Esquirol (1986), Subramanyam and Askin (1986), and Kerr and Ebsary (1988) for job shop scheduling, and by Shaw and Whinston (1986), and Bruno *et al* (1986) for FMS scheduling use production rule approaches with a relatively unsophisticated representation of jobs and production resources. A high proportion of the knowledge about the environment, including constraints, is implicitly embedded in the rules that manipulate these objects. The ISIS system (Fox and Smith, 1984) developed at Carnegie Mellon University uses a frame-based representation of jobs, production resources and constraints. The domain knowledge here is represented in the frames, with the embedded rules and procedures that manipulate the assignments of jobs to machines being more domain independent in nature. The OPAL system of Bensana *et al* (1988) also uses a hybrid approach of an object-oriented and rule-based representation, whilst the PLATO-Z FMS scheduling system (described in more detail in Chapter 13) uses a blackboard architecture. Scheduling clearly involves aspects of **temporal reasoning** (section 8.6), but in the majority of systems this is embedded informally in the rules that manipulate the schedule rather than being generalised in terms of formal temporal logic.

Various combinations of the AI planning techniques mentioned in Section 10.2.4 may be used to reduce the search space. The most commonly used of these is probably constraint-directed state space search. The fact that a realistic schedule will have to satisfy a large number of constraints such as due date constraints, work-in-progress constraints, cost objectives, machine utilisation goals, operation precedence constraints, preference for specific alternatives in terms of operations, machines, tools, etc. means that the knowledge and explicit representation of such constraints could be used to direct and bound the search for a feasible solution. Constraint-directed beam search is used by ISIS progressively to add jobs to an existing, partially ordered schedule whereby each alternative decision is evaluated on the extent to which various scheduling constraints are satisfied.

ISIS (and a number of other systems) also use hierarchical resolution of the search space, starting with the construction of a broad, incompletely defined schedule, to which detail is progressively added at a number of hierarchical levels. ISIS uses a three level hierarchy.

Constraints of varying degrees of detail are successively introduced at different hierarchical levels: a schedule determined at one level generates constraints on the lower level. Resulting schedules are subject to analysis and possible constraint relaxation in order to resolve conflicts and determine the best schedule; this involves an important concept whereby some constraints, such as preference constraints, are 'soft' and can be relaxed if necessary.

The FMS scheduling system of Shaw and Whinston uses techniques of non-linear planning in which the satisfaction of each order is regarded as a subgoal for which a linearly sequenced, partially ordered plan is developed. Interactions between parallel plans are then identified and conflicts resolved by the sparing application of operation precedence constraints based on a least commitment strategy to maximise the degree of parallelism between subplans. A scheduling system for wafer fabrication reported by Elleby *et al* (1988) uses assumption-based reasoning allowing the systematic retraction of 'soft' constraints as additional 'hard' constraints are added to the schedule. The FMS scheduling system of Bruno uses a combination of production rule and algorithmic reasoning in which each scheduling lot is examined in turn and added to the schedule if its associated constraints are satisfied. Capacity constraints are checked by running the schedule through a closed queueing network algorithm, and if they are not satisfied, another lot is introduced. A hybrid algorithmic/knowledge-based approach using tandem architecture is also proposed by Kusiak (1988a) in which production rules are used to select appropriate scheduling algorithms.

Reactive shop floor scheduling

A very important element of shop floor control is the activity of monitoring the actual shop floor situation in terms of current status and assignments of jobs, machines, tools, materials, operators and setters to ensure that production proceeds on schedule, and making schedule revisions when deviations occur. It may also involve the monitoring of selected aggregate control parameters such as the quantity of work waiting to be processed, number of jobs past-due, etc. in order to establish the extent of any deviation, and take appropriate corrective action.

Probably the most significant and the most difficult factor in shop floor control is the inescapable element of randomness as evinced by the pervasiveness of Murphy's Law. Decisions continually have to be made on how to cope with unexpected contingencies such as breakdowns and missing tools and whether these contingencies can be contained in such a way that the original schedule need not be modified. In other words, some degree of **fault tolerance** needs to be built into the system. Although the traditional way of doing this is by placing safety stocks at all points in the system at which contingencies could occur, modern trends to reduce stock levels will require that other methods be introduced.

Shop floor controllers usually accumulate a store of knowledge concerning how best to overcome contingencies, for example in terms of rerouting work from a broken machine to an alternative machine, or using alternative materials, and may also be able to assess how far forward into a plan the effects of a particular problem are likely to propagate before being swamped by other uncertainties. The size of the problem space will depend on the complexity of the shop floor. Job shops present the most complex environment, in which the status of a large number of dissimilar jobs requiring different types of process must be tracked, and the number of alternative ways of overcoming a contingency may be large. The frequent production of non-standard items means it is unlikely that the full range of processes used for a particular part will be formally specified, and the shop foreman will have to use his experience to choose an alternative methods if, for example, the specified processes are causing a severe bottleneck on a particular workstation. This type of reasoning would be more likely to be based on such things as the materials involved, the process required, and the processing capability of other machines available, rather than an explicit association of a particular part with the full range of alternative processes possible (a display of 'cognitive economics' in which reasoning takes place at the highest possible level of abstraction). In other words, the shop foreman would be applying informal knowledge of process design in order to solve a local contingency.

For real-time control, automated shop floor data acquisition systems would be required to ensure that the status of all shop floor entities was updated continuously. With current technology, conventional databases are more suitable for the concurrent, multi-user access required by this type of task, therefore a means of interfacing conventional databases to the knowledge-based scheduling system would be necessary. To be useful in support of contingency-driven reactive decision making, efficient rescheduling capability would be essential. This includes such facilities as the suggestion of alternative routings, materials or tools in cases of machine breakdowns, or resource shortages. Local knowledge about overcoming contingencies might be implemented in the form of production rules, or alternatively, the scheduling system might be directly linked to an object-oriented, integrated product/process knowledge base from which the information could be inferred. However, the requirement for rapid response would normally favour the use of production-rule-type surface heuristics, at least for the more common alternatives, with a deeper level of reasoning using the product/process knowledge base for exceptional situations. In support of this type of task, a language called CML (Cell Management Language) has been developed at Carnegie Mellon University for interfacing and scheduling complex systems of multi-vendor manufacturing equipment. CML is a rule-based language that can be used to operate on a dynamic model of a manufacturing cell and react to contingencies on the basis of current, real-time data from machines and their sensors (Bourne, 1986).

The importance of this area is demonstrated by the major current research focus on *reactive* (as opposed to purely predictive) scheduling, in which rather than relying purely on local problem solving to try and recover a fixed schedule, the schedule itself is constructed dynamically and is continually being adapted in the light of contingencies. The frequency of occurrence of such contingencies, and the need to avoid nervousness in the system still implies that schedules must be developed which are relatively robust against unexpected events, and in which the effects of significant events on the schedule can be rapidly assessed. One approach to this problem is to use a least commitment strategy in which particular parts of the schedule are refined only when it appears that the assumptions on which they are based will remain valid during execution (i.e., the schedule must extend no further into the future than the reliability of the data). An experimental system which develops schedules in terms of fuzzy numbers has been developed by Kerr and Walker (1989). This associates increasing imprecision in the schedule with increasing temporal distance from 'fixed' events, and results in the effects of contingencies being localised within the schedule to a particular 'circle of precision', outside which they may be assumed to be swamped by the cumulative uncertainty coming from other sources.

Reactive scheduling has been the object of focus in further developments of the ISIS system. OPIS (Smith, 1987) takes an opportunistic approach to scheduling, in which changes to the schedule (e.g., addition of an order or breakdown of a machine) are regarded as a source not only of scheduling conflicts but of scheduling opportunities. Schedule revision can take place by allowing the focus of attention to vary between an order-oriented and a resource-oriented view according to the criticality of the various constraints operating. Thus OPIS would take a resource- rather than an order-oriented view for the rescheduling of bottleneck resources. The idea of reactive scheduling according to multiple perspectives has been extended in the development of a cooperative scheduling system (Ow *et al*, 1988) which uses the idea of multiple problem-solving agents with different perspectives on the scheduling problem, integrated through a system of contract negotiation. These ideas are examined in more detail in Chapters 12 and 17.

In reactive scheduling, issues of non-monotonic reasoning will arise, since the initial assumptions made in order to develop a schedule may prove to be faulty as the schedule unfolds and is revised. While many existing reactive systems treat this at an informal level, it is more explicitly represented in the Assumption-Based Reasoning scheduler of Elleby *et al* which uses a Truth Maintenance system, combined with temporal reasoning to manage the retraction of previous assumptions and constraints.

Obviously, good diagnostic systems for machine faults will facilitate shop floor control. Diagnosis is also required of reasons for problems whose existence is manifest through values or trends displayed by aggregate shop floor parameters. For example, the reasons for a steady increase in work-in-progress may be attributable to a single cause such as an excessive amount of rework required on a bottleneck work centre. Diagnostic systems using the same principles as those employed for diagnostic maintenance or quality control might be employed in this role.

Although most of the knowledge-based scheduling systems described are oriented towards detailed operational control at shop floor level, the knowledge representation structures and AI planning techniques employed would make this type of system useable in the role currently filled by tactical planning systems such as MRP or OPT, to develop feasible production plans by iterative adjustment of batch sizes and lead times. Much of the domain knowledge required for scheduling (e.g., operation and job precedence constraints, and resources required) corresponds to data stored in the bill of materials and routing files of MRP systems. Thus it is likely in the future that the traditional network database architecture of MRP will be replaced by architectures supporting data representations in which parts and their relationships within products, processes, and manufacturing resources all form part of an integrated conceptual factory model, used as a basis for requirements planning and scheduling at all levels from aggregate planning of product families to detailed scheduling of individual operations on the shop floor (Figure 11.1). At higher levels of the planning hierarchy, one would expect to see a prevalence of knowledge-based decision support systems with the user primarily in control of the planning process (e.g., the type of system described by Bitran and Papageorge could be used to examine trade-offs between aggregate inventory investment, throughput time and extra capacity) while at more detailed levels, decisions would become increasingly automated, with FMS scheduling being performed entirely automatically. However, knowledge-based decision support will still be appropriate for scheduling of non-automated job shops. Given a good representation of the requisite objects, it would be possible to provide varying levels of scheduling decision support, from interactive scheduling in which a human manipulates the properties of the job entities in terms of their start and finishing times and resulting schedules are displayed on an 'electronic' Gantt Chart with automatic background checks on whether any constraints are violated, to full automatic scheduling in which the manipulation of start and finish times is performed automatically.

11.3.2 Materials and inventory control

In a manufacturing company with a centralised production planning system, instructions for the release of production and purchase orders for

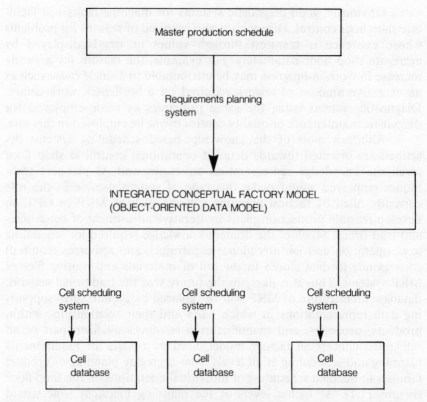

Figure 11.1 Integration of requirements planning and detailed scheduling through an integrated conceptual factory model.

the replenishment of inventory items will normally come directly from production planning. In a more decentralised system in which a continuous flow of materials through the shop has been achieved, manufactured components would generally flow through to the assembly process without going into store. The only items actually stocked would be long lead-time raw materials and items with irreducible set-up times which required manufacture in discrete batches.

The main tasks of the materials and inventory control function are the physical reconciliation of actual and computed stock with feedback of any discrepancies to production planning, and the design and execution of storage and retrieval procedures.

Physical reconciliation of stock against records requires the systematic manual counting of selected items on a regular basis, and is referred to as 'cycle counting'. Items can be automatically selected for counting based on their required frequency of count (a function of their importance) and their current recorded inventory level, with items generally being selected when they are at their minimum level. Procedures to perform this selection can be programmed in a straightforward, conventional manner and will simply need to access the database in which current inventory levels are stored.

Storage and retrieval procedures will require regular decisions on the physical location in the stockroom used to store a particular item when it comes in, and the sequences and locations from which withdrawals should be made to satisfy the material requirements of a given production order. These decisions are generally made by humans on the basis of information such as pallet or container capacities, distances between storage locations, order urgency and anticipated future demand. There is considerable combinatorial complexity in this type of problem, which humans reduce by the use of simple, practical heuristics and by the acceptance of a satisficing rather than an optimising solution. With the advent of the automated warehouse, it will clearly be necesary to represent a reasonable set of heuristics for automated materials handling. A method of simplifying the problem is to restrict the size of the search space by tightly defining in advance fixed storage locations for specific items, fixed tracks for Automatically Guided Vehicles, and so on. A number of such automated systems have already been implemented, using algorithmic approaches, but many research projects are currently investigating the use of knowledge-based systems in this area.

11.3.3 Purchasing and vendor control

Given that timings and quantities of orders for raw materials are generated either by a centralised planning system (as in MRP) or by local requirements (as in continuous flow JIT type systems), the task of purchasing is to select and negotiate contracts with a vendor, monitor vendor performance, and evaluate when a change of vendor is necessary.

There will usually be a number of features that must be considered simultaneously, such as length of delivery time, ability to adhere to the due date, price and quality, and different weights may pertain to these criteria at different times. In addition, the effect of rebates on the quantities ordered must be considered. For example, checks must be made to see whether a rebate might be obtained by ordering slightly more than current requirements, or by placing a blanket order for a complete year's supply, in which case the implications of being tied to that particular vendor would need to be evaluated.

The ability to maintain records of previous vendor performance and to extract information rapidly in the form of various types of summary is an essential form of support to this task. The heuristics required to make good decisions are not, in general, complex. However, determining which variables to include and ensuring consistency of the analysis can be difficult. We should again expect to see knowledge-based decision support as opposed to decision-making systems for negotiating vendor contracts, which enable the purchasing department to call up and have automatic analyses performed on past vendor performance, current terms offered, etc. The actual placing of specific purchase orders within a blanket contract is something which could then be performed automatically in response to needs generated by inventory management or by a centralised planning system. This would be unlikely to require any sophisticated reasoning or problem-solving capability.

Helferich *et al* (1988) describe two knowledge-based systems (Price Quotation Evaluation and Cost Price Evaluation) for vendor analysis on factors such as unit cost, unit price, transportation charges, on-time delivery and performance to specification. They also describe a Merchandise Mix system which uses production rules to recommend a best buying strategy from an analysis of vendor performance using factors determined to be important by experienced buying personnel.

11.4   Knowledge-based Production Systems Design

Production systems design is concerned with the planning of facilities layout using the application of Group Technology principles to the identification of groups of products and components suitable for production on appropriate groupings of production resources, the design of work practices, and the design of planning and control systems suitable for the management of the manufacturing process.

11.4.1   Facilities layout and Group Technology

With the current trend towards product rather than process-oriented layout to achieve a balanced and continuous flow of work through the shop, facilities layout design is becoming increasingly important. Facilities design based on grouping facilities by function is relatively straightforward, the major decisions being the number of machines of a particular type to purchase, the location on the shop floor of each group, and the number of transporters (e.g., fork lift trucks) to procure. The former requires an estimate of the total volume of flow through each group of machines so that the total processing capacity of the group can be matched appropriately. Locational decisions can be made on the basis of human judgement, or using a layout optimisation algorithm such as CRAFT (Buffa *et al*, 1964) which computes the relative positions of groups that would minimise the total distance travelled by parts during their journey through the shop. The number of transporters would be estimated based on the expected frequency of part movements and the distance to be travelled.

The move to a process-oriented layout means that the facilities planner has the data-intensive task of identifying families of parts with similar process paths with a view to assigning a group of machines to each family in a 'cell'-oriented layout, such that parts flow from one machine to the next in sequence of operation. The capacity of the cell (generally measured by the capacity of the most expensive or important machine within the cell) must then be matched to the anticipated workflow. Another important consideration is the size of buffer storage areas between machines. The relative physical location of machine cells is generally less important than the relative positioning within a cell, and the latter is generally restricted by practical considerations to few possible alternatives.

For this knowledge-based activity, the facilities planner will require access to a Group Technology database, or integrated product knowledge base which either contains embedded knowledge of the process paths or routings of each part, or has pointers to a separate routing datafile, a database of existing or planned production facilities and their capacities, and a breakdown of the estimated gross requirements for each part (e.g., from the aggregate planning module of an MRP system) from which the volume of flow of each family could be identified. The algorithms adopted for the grouping of parts and the identification of machine cells are generally quite well defined and procedural in nature and include such techniques as production flow or cluster analysis in which a part-machine 'incidence' matrix is set up, in which the rows are rearranged in an attempt to form separable submatrices corresponding to machine cells (see for example, Gallagher and Knight, 1986). There are, however, a number of areas requiring human judgement and interpretation. For example, it is often impossible to decompose the machine-part incidence matrix into fully separable submatrices. Alternative process paths can exist, and various constraints exist on the configuration of machine cells, connected with considerations such as technology, space, budget, safety or worker convenience (e.g., heat treating furnaces must be situated greater than some minimum distance from the paint facility). The required problem-solving approach therefore needs a mixture of algorithms, for performing such things as basic cluster analysis, and heuristics which determine which algorithms should be employed at what stage of the analysis. Checks are required to ensure that none of the constraints are violated, and if necessary the algorithmic solutions must be modified.

To the extent that general rules can be identified for algorithm selection based on a well definable set of problem characteristics, and provided that general parameterisable constraints of the type that might apply over a range of problem domains can be abstracted, it might be feasible to embody much of the judgemental and heuristic knowledge associated with facilities planning in the form of a production rule-based system. Kusiak (1988b) describes such a system based explicitly on

Group Technology considerations, and this is examined in more detail in Chapter 13. Kumara *et al* (1988) report on a facilities layout system in which facilities and their relationships are represented in a semantic net, and production rules are used to produce alternative configurations consistent with current goals and constraints. A similar system (FACSIM) which also contains a simulation capability is examined in more detail in Chapter 13. However, because of the relatively infrequent occurrence of the facilities design process, and the probable changes in the dimensions of the problem between occurrences, the amount of such knowledge that could justifiably be formalised and stored is probably somewhat limited.

Facilities planning is also a problem that requires a 'generate and test' solution procedure. Given the application of algorithms and heuristics to generate a solution, testing to examine the dynamic behaviour of the solution in terms of bottlenecks, adequacy of buffer storage areas, etc. can be performed by means of discrete event computer simulation. This task requires knowledge of an appropriate simulation language by which a model of the proposed layout can be constructed, and also requires the skills to construct an appropriate model, design experiments and interpret the results. There is growing interest in trying to structure and abstract the knowledge involved in developing and using simulation models (see for example, Flitman and Hurrion, 1987) for use within a knowledge-based DSS framework. A point worth noting is that discrete event simulation involves the explicit representation of objects and relationships such as machines, parts and part-routings. Hence, a natural extension for frame or object-oriented knowledge representations of the factory is to use them as a basis for a discrete event simulation by some form of dynamic execution of the knowledge structures representing the objects in the factory.

Intellicorp's SIMKIT system (Stelzner *et al*, 1987) and SIMULATION CRAFT of the Carnegie Group (Reddy *et al*, 1986) both provide facilities for discrete event simulation overlayed on object-oriented knowledge representation systems. The possibility arises of using object-oriented knowledge in an overall real-time factory data/knowledge representation as a basis for semi-automated discrete event simulation, with the user merely specifying which objects are to be involved, the rules for their interaction, and a statistical distribution of event occurrences to drive the simulation. Some assistance in interpreting the results (e.g., in automatic selection and application of statistical analysis techniques) might also be provided by encoding the appropriate knowledge, although the ultimate responsibilty for this would have to rest with the user.

11.4.2 Design of planning and control systems

In addition to structuring the production environment in terms of rational groupings of products, parts and facilities, the production systems designer is also concerned with the design of techniques and procedures for the planning and control of production. This cannot be divorced from the facilities layout planning task, since the latter should be oriented towards layouts which simplify the planning and control task (as should product design and process planning). The nature of the production planning and control system designed will be constrained by the variety of the operation (the number of subparts involved), the degree of repetitiveness of production, and management policy in relation to factors such as product cost, quality, delivery time, inventory investment and capacity utilisation. The design of a particular production planning and control process will first involve the conceptual process of establishing which type of philosophy (e.g., MRP, JIT) is most likely to meet management's strategic business objectives for the particular type of operation concerned. Once this has been established, detail can then be added in terms of designing detailed procedures and setting values for parameters such as sizes of buffer stocks and minimum batch sizes.

Decisions as to what type of manufacturing philosophy to employ will be intimately bound up with the strategic business objectives of the firm. It is conceivable that the knowledge required to choose a particular production planning and control philosophy given a set of strategic objectives, and a set of descriptive operational parameters, could be structured in the form of a knowledge-based system. The system described by Bitran and Pappageorge (1987) referred to earlier in this chapter, although not explicitly recommending particular planning and control philosophies as such, does appear to contain much of the necessary knowledge and reasoning capability for this to occur. There have however been some problems reported with practical implementations of this system (Reilman 1989).

At the more detailed level, control stategies for individual work-cells can be investigated using simulation. The use of Petri nets has been found advantageous in this area since Petri net representations are particularly suitable for modelling the flow of information and control within complex systems (unlike conventional factory simulation systems and languages which generally provide only limited facilities for the explicit modelling of different information transfer and control strategies). Browne *et al* (1988) report the development of a design tool for so-called 'production activity control systems', which has facilities both for investigating alternative ways of structuring the production environment with regard to Group Technology considerations, and for examining alternative detailed scheduling strategies at the plant and individual cell level. The design tool consists of a number of interlinked modules controlled by a knowledge-based systems approach, and using a shop floor emulator based on Petri net modelling for the investigation of alternative scheduling strategies. This system is examined in Chapter 13.

As in the case of production planning systems, much of the current research emphasis on the application of knowledge-based systems has been at the operational control level, rather than at the strategic or tactical levels. The problems at this level tend to be well defined and bounded, with knowledge-based approaches mostly offering an alternative to existing conventional methods of computational solution of traditionally defined problems. The current challenge however is the application of knowledge-based systems to less well defined problems in the strategic and tactical planning area, and in the development of knowledge-based systems at the operational control level that transcend the traditional functional boundaries and make a more positive contribution to functional integration.

11.4.3 Knowledge-based integration of production tasks

The majority of existing knowledge-based systems which have been designed to provide support in the production tasks described above, exist as localised implementations with their own specialised data and knowledge representation schemas. They are rarely integrated with company-wide databases or information systems, and may therefore duplicate some of the factual knowledge already stored in such systems. This has partly arisen because of inconsistency in the types of knowledge representation paradigm used for different manufacturing tasks, and the lack of suitable interface technology between knowledge-based systems and conventional databases, although progress is being made in this area in the form of such products as KEE Connection (Intellicorp, 1987), and in the increasing trend of knowledge system building tools to be programmed in conventional rather than AI programming languages. However, at present, these isolated implementations contribute more to the 'islands of automation syndrome' than to the achievement of task integration.

One conceptual form of integration, discussed by Davis and Oliff (1988), which lends itself primarily to the integration of knowledge-based systems using the rule-based paradigm, is to store all factual information in a centralised database. Procedural knowledge connected with individual manufacturing tasks could then be stored in localised rule bases (each having an inference engine and a dynamic database section for temporary storage of facts inferred during the task or reasoning process), and these would access the central database for the initial factual data required (Figure 11.2). A 'knowledge manager' could be given responsibility for consistency of the rules in the individual rule bases, similar to the way in which a data manager has responsibility for the consistency of data in a database.

Problems with this form of integration arise from the questionable feasibility of the single centralised database concept. Different types of

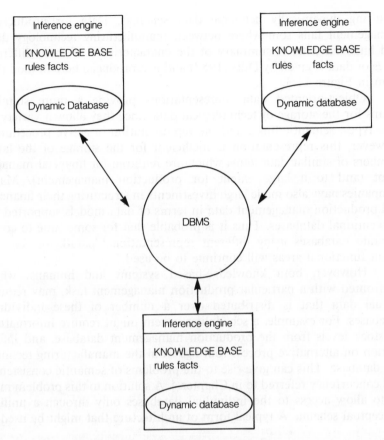

Figure 11.2 Integration of knowledge-based production management systems using centralised database.

factual knowledge are suited to different types of representation. Financial tasks, which largely motivated the development of existing database technology, involve the storage of large quantities of similar data in a homogeneous form. A simple set of relationships usually exists between data items, which are numerical or textual in nature, and lend themselves to storage in stable data structures which support routine structured queries and simple transaction processing. Conventional database technology has been directed primarily towards the efficient processing of this type of data, with its emphasis on integrity enforcement, efficiency of retrieval, concurrency of access, etc. On the other hand, tasks concerned with manufacturing technology such as CAD and process planning involve storage of heterogeneous data such as geometric shapes, procedural and mathematical data, generally using special formats. A large number of complex and sometimes unique relationships and integrity constraints exist between a relatively small number of data items, requiring dynamically definable data schemas. Data for production management falls somewhere between manufacturing technology data and financial data. A summary of the characteristics of these different types of data is given by Dilts (1988) and is reproduced here in modified form in Figure 11.3.

Object-oriented data representations provide a more suitable means for the storage of technological data since they allow a variety of data types, semantic links, and the representation of active procedures. However, this representation is inefficient for the storage of the large numbers of similar data items which are required for financial management (and to a large extent for production management). Many companies have also made large investments in structuring their financial and production management data in terms of data models supported by conventional databases. Thus it is probable that for some time to come separate databases using different representational paradigms for different functional areas will continue to be used.

However, both knowledge-based systems and humans, when confronted with a particular production management task, may require factual data that is distributed over a number of these individual databases. For example, a scheduling system might require information on stock levels from the production management database, and information on alternative process routings from the manufacturing technology database. This can give rise to the problems of semantic consistency and concurrency referred to in Chapter 4. A solution to this problem may be to allow access to the individual databases only through a unified conceptual schema. A typical form of architecture that might be used is

	CAD/CAM	Production management	Business management
Data	Heterogeneous	Mixed	Homogeneous
Data types	Complex	Mixed	Simple
Transactions	Mixed	Mixed	Simple
Relationships	Object-specific	General	General
Application	Dependent	Independent	Independent
Data access	Local	Mixed	Global
Types	Many	Many	Few
Instances	Few	Many	Many
Timing	Real-time	Mixed	Historical
Schemata	Dynamic	Static	Static
Semantic-consistency	Inconsistent	Mixed	Consistent

Figure 11.3 Characteristics of different types of manufacturing database.

shown in Figure 11.4. This shows an object-oriented engineering database, and relational production management and financial databases whose structures are described in terms of a common schema, with which both humans and local knowledge bases interact as though they were all one database. The schema represents a 'semantic interface' between the user and the database, and allows the efficiency of conventional data representation and the expressive power of the object-oriented representation to be utilised in the areas for which each is appropriate. It would also contain rules to enforce data integrity across the whole unified database by automatically propagating the effects of updates in one area to the other areas affected. The representation used for the conceptual schema would need to match the expressive power of the object-oriented representation used for the more complex manufacturing database in order to ensure that the desired information can be extracted, and hence would itself likely to be object oriented. Entity-relationship modelling might be used here as a representational technique that maps equally well on to both relational- and object-oriented logical schema (Dilts, 1988). Retrievals from the production management and financial databases expressed in terms of this unified conceptual schema would be automat-

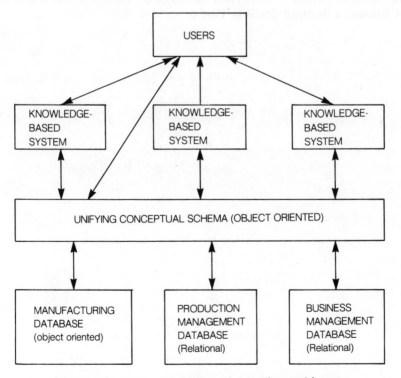

Figure 11.4 A possible database integration architecture.

ically translated into the appropriate embedded database query language such as SQL.

Varying degrees of coupling could exist between local knowledge bases and the unified database. Tightly coupled knowledge systems would perform reasoning, through the semantic interface, directly on the database, with the latter being updated during the course of the reasoning process. Loosely coupled systems may operate by retrievals from the database giving rise to separately stored knowledge objects within each local knowledge base, with subsequent reasoning taking place entirely within the local knowledge-based system. Further access to the database would be as required. The type of coupling used would depend on the specific application area, with performance considerations being important factors in the choice.

The architecture shown in Figure 11.4 is of the 'blackboard' type in that local, client-centred knowledge bases interact asynchronously via a central blackboard (the unified database) which stores not only commonly used data but can also be used as a repository of messages. Another alternative is to allow direct communication between individual knowledge bases by networking them together. Again, the solution is situation dependent, with the state of advance of various interfacing technologies having an important influence on choice. These issues will be discussed in more detail in Part 5.

Figure 11.4 A possible database integration architecture.

CHAPTER 12
Knowledge-based Applications for Production Management — examples

This chapter examines in detail some existing prototype knowledge-based systems for production management tasks. ISTOP is a system under development which has the objective of integrating strategic planning at the factory level with tactical planning at the cell or work centre level using localised knowledge-based systems operating within an overall set of strategic constraints. The ISIS/OPIS development at Carnegie Mellon University represents a major and important evolutionary development of real-time, knowledge-based scheduling systems for job shops. This work is somewhat of a landmark in the application of knowledge-based systems to manufacturing control and so it will be examined in some depth. Following this is a description of a knowledge-based control system for a flexible manufacturing cell. Since the ultimate objective of introducing such cells into a factory is generally to achieve total automation, their control is obviously a strong potential area for the application of knowledge-based systems.

12.1 ISTOP — an intelligent strategic and operational planning system

12.1.1 Introduction

This section gives a general specification of a system that is capable of assisting in the manufacturing resources planning process at both strategic and operational levels. Unlike MRP, which relies on highly centralised planning, with the generation of a master production schedule whose implications for lower levels are propagated downwards in a deterministic fashion in the form of planned order releases and due dates, ISTOP is more decentralised, allowing much greater freedom and flexibility of action to lower planning levels within a set of broad constraints at the strategic level. This is consistent with the notions of decentralised planning and control outlined in Chapter 3.

ISTOP (Kerr and Walker, 1989) contains a number of components, which act as knowledge-based decision-support systems at the strategic planning and operational levels. At the operational level, individual local knowledge-based systems operate within an overall planning framework to perform analyses, generate pieces of advice or recommended detailed local plans of action based on integration of knowledge from a variety of sources, obtained both laterally and from above. Since many of the constraints are soft, a feature of this decentralised approach is that of negotiation of constraint relaxations between local knowledge-based systems, rather than the imposition of hard constraints from higher levels, as occurs in MRP.

An important feature of ISTOP is that of **minimal intervention** by the strategic plan on the detailed operations of the factory. The strategic plan is sufficiently loosely constraining to allow individual operational areas to react to problems in the most appropriate way, using local knowledge of the current situation and local problem-solving heuristics which can be 'tuned' to the major strategic objectives currently in force.

12.1.2 The components of ISTOP

ISTOP is designed for use as a planning system from the factory level down (although it could easily be extended to handle multi-plant organisations) and consists of the following major components:

(1)   An integrated database of forecast orders, product bills of materials with alternative process plans for each part, sales forecasts, planned and released production orders with due and scheduled completion dates, current work-in-progress and stock levels, the manufacturing resources available and their current reservations by different production orders.

(2)   A strategic planning module containing a knowledge-based, decision-support system which allows the user to conduct trade-off analyses between different policies in relation to aggregate levels of production capacity and inventory, and average lead times, and to examine the implications of different policies for strategic business objectives.

(3)   A master planning module containing a knowledge-based, decision-support system to assist in the development of an end product build schedule to meet customer demand, which is consistent both with what is feasible at the factory level, and with the policies set at the strategic level.

(4)   A set of tactical planning modules at the individual cell or workstation level, containing knowledge-based advisory systems responsible for planning and scheduling work through each cell in a manner consistent with the policies set by the strategic planning module, the delivery dates for end products requested by the master planning module and the plans developed by neighbouring cells.

The relationships between these components are shown in Figure 12.1.

12.1.3   The ISTOP database

The ISTOP database is organised in an object-oriented manner. The basic manufacturing entities form both a specialisation/generalisation hierarchy and an aggregation hierarchy, as shown in Figure 12.2. The main classes of entity are **resources**, **processes** and **orders**. Resources are subdivided into material resources (raw materials, components, subassemblies, finished products, etc.), and production resources (machines, tools, operators, setters, etc.). These in turn are divided into subclasses. Processes consist of the various types of machining, assembly, and inspection operations by which the conversion of raw materials to

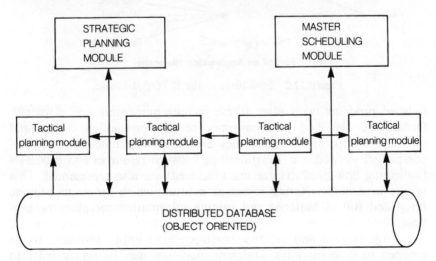

Figure 12.1 Block diagram of ISTOP.

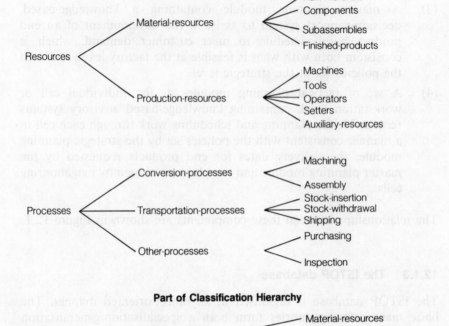

Part of Classification Hierarchy

Part of a Manufacturing Resources Network

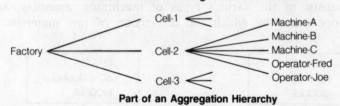

Part of an Aggregation Hierarchy

Figure 12.2 Structures in the ISTOP database.

finished products takes place (these include purchasing and dispatch). Orders are classified into customer orders, production orders and purchase orders, and whether they are forecast, planned, in progress, completed, stocked, etc. Relationships between resources and processes (indicating how products are manufactured) are also represented. This results in a **manufacturing resources network** which serves to provide integrated Bill of Material and routing information for planning purposes.

Aggregation and set membership allows entity instances to be grouped in different ways. Different machines may be aggregated into cells, cells into shops, parts and products into families, and so on. This type of description facilitates planning at various hierarchical levels as it introduces the ability to reason with and about these aggregate objects. The manufacturing resources network is, in fact, repeated at a more aggregate level to indicate how product **families** are manufactured using aggregate resource groupings such as machine cells. Each machine cell has varying levels of capacity associated with it, as well as the cost of providing that level of capacity. (This may reflect the cost of additional shifts, or providing extra machines.) In addition, the object-oriented representation allows reasoning using prototypical objects with default values, which is useful when working with cases such as forecast orders for which the specific details are not yet known. For example, prototypical products can be defined for each family.

The object-oriented database is implemented in a distributed fashion with the data relating to individual manufacturing cells, and the associated knowledge-based cell planning systems stored locally at each cell. The knowledge systems at each cell can exchange messages with each other, and with the strategic planning module.

12.1.4 The strategic planning module

The competitive posture of a manufacturing company can be regarded as depending on its policies in relation to desired values of three interrelated strategic manufacturing parameters: total capacity, total work-in-progress and average product lead time. For example, a company concerned with cost minimisation will operate with lower capacity investment, but this will result in longer lead times and higher work-in-progress. On the other hand, a company concerned with responsiveness (i.e., minimal lead time) as its main competitive thrust will need higher investment in capacity. A company will have to make trade-offs between the target operating values of these aggregate parameters to achieve its desired competitive position in the market place.

The strategic planning decision support system commences by performing an automated analysis using a state space heuristic search technique to produce aggregate trade-off curves for capacity, work-in-progress and lead time. This is performed by the following steps which are very similar to those used in a system known as the Operations Advisor (Bitran and Papageorge, 1987):

(1)   For each product family, the monthly production requirements are decided over a one year timescale.

(2)   Each production family has a 'prototypical' product defined for it in the database, and each is associated with the machine cells involved in producing a unit of product (along with alternatives) and the process and set-up time required in each cell. Using this

information and an assumed batch-sizing policy, the loading profile for each cell resulting from the monthly product family requirement is computed on a weekly time bucket basis for a particular set of assumed routings.

(3)   A simple heuristic is used to analyse this profile in relation to cell capacity and batch sizes to estimate the average queue length and work-in-progress at each cell.

(4)   A constraint-directed, beam search with additional knowledge-based guiding heuristics is performed with alternative batch-sizing policies, routings and cell capacity levels to determine the policy which, for a given expenditure on capacity, gives the minimum aggregate lead time (measured by average total time in queue for each prototypical product), and minimum aggregate work-in-progress (average queue length at each production cell).

(5)   This is repeated for varying levels of total expenditure on capacity to give a set of trade-off curves representing the relationship between total capacity expenditure and the related aggregate parameters of lead time and work-in-progress for the most efficient batch-sizing and capacity allocation policies.

A typical set of trade-off curves obtained from this analysis is shown in Figure 12.3. These curves represent the aggregate relationships between capacity, work-in-progress and lead times for efficient or non-dominated manufacturing policies which are using given levels of capacity (within a set of user-defined constraints) to best effect. Capacity and work-in-progress are both represented in monetary units. The system also makes an assessment of the current actual position of the company with respect

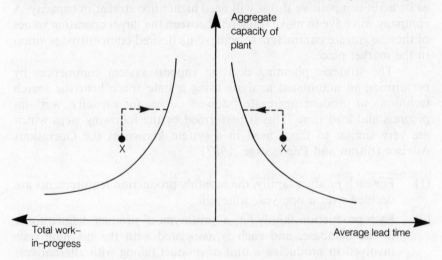

Figure 12.3 Trade-off curves in ISTOP.

to these variables. If the actual position lies outside the trade-off curves then possible room for improvement is indicated.

Strategic planning using this module can involve the following:

- determining the current posture of the company in relation to the postures theoretically achievable with the most efficient set of capacity allocations and batch-sizing policies, using existing types of resource;

- deciding on the required competitive posture of the company and developing strategies for moving to this posture from the existing position using alternative forms of batch sizing or capacity allocation;

- generation of alternative trade-off curves for different types of product mix, aggregate build schedules or alternative types of capacity investment in order to evaluate alternative mix, build or investment policies.

For example, consider the company who is assessed by the system to lie at position X in relation to the normative trade-off curves computed for its current operation. The first decision will be for management to decide where on the trade-off curves their desirable posture lies. For example, they may decide they wish to increase their competitivness in terms of response to market needs by reducing lead time. This will require a further investment in capacity, along with the most effective use of that capacity. The amount of investment in extra capacity required is immediately apparent from the trade-off curves. Furthermore, by performing a set of inferences using backward chaining, the system can recommend a strategy for increasing and allocating capacity to achieve this objective, within any constraints that might apply concerning the ways in which capacity can be added.

Another company may be planning to invest in set-up time reduction coupled with a change in product mix to move towards Just-in-Time production. If it is assumed that the change in product mix is such as to reduce the variability in the total demand for each product family, thus levelling the required factory output, and also that set-up time reduction reduces typical batch sizes, then this information can easily be used in an analysis to produce a new set of trade-off curves shown by the dotted lines in Figure 12.4. This indicates the area of competitive posture in which the JIT stategy dominates the existing strategy and hence the desirability of the former can be evaluated.

The main output of the strategic planning module to lower levels is in the form of a set of cost functions passed to individual cells, which are used by the cells' local knowledge-based planning systems to compute cost penalties for the number of days by which due dates are missed, for the quantity of work-in-progress carried, and for capacity cost as a

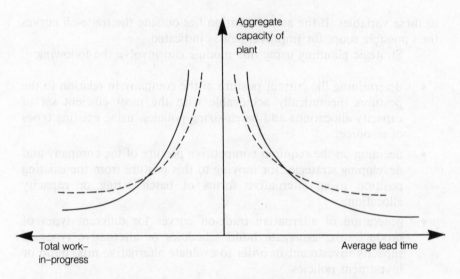

Figure 12.4 Alternative investment analysis using ISTOP.

function of utilisation. The values to which these are set are dependent on the particular competitive posture adopted by the company and are automatically computed within the strategic planning module. This enables individual cells to develop their own plans and schedules to minimise their costs in a way which is consistent with overall company strategy. For example, a low cost, low service strategy would place a low cost penalty on missing due dates and a high cost penalty on capacity non-utilisation, encouraging volume production in large batch sizes. A higher cost, high service strategy would encourage the reverse type of production at cell level in which missed due dates would be given a high cost penalty and capacity non-utilisation a lower cost penalty.

12.1.5 The Master Planning module

The Master Planning module maintains the final build schedule for individual finished products, and manages the release of orders for these finished products to the shop floor. These orders relate only to the final product assembly process. The Master Planning module is thus concerned with the development of a build schedule in response to customer demand which is consistent with the level of service required by the company's strategic posture.

Given a combination of actual and forecast customer orders, and a set of planning time zones which approximate to the length of the established product lead times, the Master Planning module performs a rough-cut capacity check on whether the demand in each zone can be met with existing capacity. This is performed in a rather similar way to existing MRP systems, although the object-oriented representation makes analysis easier by automatically aggregating existing forecasts into product groups and performing the check against cell capacity. Decisions to increase capacity in certain zones may be made if necessary, and the costs of so doing will be apparent from the trade-off curves provided by the strategic planning module. For any overloaded time zones, a set of inference procedures checks whether the problem can be solved by shifting work to an earlier time zone, and the additional cost this would incur in work-in-progress, for comparison with the cost of providing extra capacity. A further alternative is to shift work to a later time zone and to negotiate late deliveries with the customers involved. To assist in this, customer orders are given a measure of importance when they are entered, and the system will automatically suggest which orders should be delayed, based on the amount of overload, size of order, and customer importance. The output of this process is a capacity-tested build schedule distributed over time zones, in some of which capacity may or may not be increased. It should be noted that all the decisions in this process are made by the user on the basis of the various analyses or recommendations performed automatically by the system.

12.1.7 The tactical planning modules

All production cells, including final assembly stations, are associated with a local tactical planning module containing a knowledge-based system which develops a production plan for that cell, based on the requirements of immediate downstream cells and the cost functions provided by the strategic plan. Individual cells act as 'suppliers' and 'customers' of each other, and part of the responsibility of a cell is to provide all of its 'suppliers' with an indication of its requirements over the timescale of the cell production plan (which is normally one planning period of the Master Plan). In addition to planning production, individual cells are responsible for their own buffer stocks. The cell planning system must thus develop a local plan which determines projected stocklevels and plans and schedules lot sizes to meet due dates of its 'customer-cell' orders in such a way as to minimise the cost of the schedule as computed from the internal cost functions provided by the strategic plan.

The only interactions between cells are between those which are the immediate customers or suppliers of each other. The final assembly and inspection cell will communicate its requirements only to the cells which immediately supply it with subassemblies or components. If two alternative 'supplier' cells are capable of fulfilling an order, the 'customer' cell can take bids from each and can assign the order to the bidder whose promise date best fulfils its own requirements. It should be noted that the work-in-progress cost function can result in penalisation of early deliveries, if these are merely stocked until they are required. Thus, each cell is effectively acting as an 'entrepreneur' with complete local autonomy in its response to the demands placed on it, its reaction to problems, and its negotiated contracts with neighbouring cells. The purchasing activity is regarded as being equivalent to a production cell, since all the functions of its planning system in terms of contract negotiation with suppliers will be almost identical.

The planning system provided for each cell uses a simple Gantt chart representation of the cell's production schedule, in which the human user has a choice of directly manipulating jobs (represented as coloured bars on the chart) using a cursor, or requesting a schedule to be derived automatically using a simple set of heuristic scheduling rules. Both human- and computer-generated schedules are checked for constraint satisfaction and automatically scored in terms of their cost. An important set of constraints on a cell's operations are the promised delivery dates of materials from supplier cells to meet that cell's schedule. These are generally negotiable, and several planning iterations may be required, in which an unconstrained schedule is initially generated, and the set of resulting requirement dates broadcast to supplier cells, who respond with feasible dates that may impose additional constraints on the schedule.

This electronic communication between the planning systems of individual cells means that the master planning module will be rapidly informed of any impending serious capacity problems from the final assembly cell. A problem in any cell's production plan that seriously affects downstream cells will be rapidly propagated by communication between respective planning systems. This also gives the problem a chance of being resolved at intermediate cells by virtue of any excess capacity or stock that may exist, or by the use of alternative suppliers. Only problems that propagate right through the system to threaten the integrity of the final build schedule are reported to the Master Planning module, which can respond by allocating extra capacity, or modifying the build schedule.

ISTOP currently exists as a conceptual design which is in the process of being implemented and tested in a medium-sized manufacturing company. It is representative of a trend towards the development of more decentralised planning systems capable of fostering flexible evolution of manufacturing planning and control in line with changing manufacturing strategies. There are reports of other systems, in various stages of development, which follow a similar type of approach. For example, the IMPS system (Ebner et al, 1986) uses the notion of embedded local expert systems in an overall, flexible planning supervisory structure. The SCHED-STAR system (Morton et al, 1987) is oriented toward a similar decentralised approach to planning at cell level in which each cell performs a cost benefit analysis with externally given cost functions for tardiness and internally derived prices for work centre capacity. SCHED-STAR is implemented within a general hierarchical Framework For production planning and scheduling called PATRIARCH (Mortan and Smunt, 1986).

The commonality of these approaches is a recognition of the limitations of current MRP-like systems which result from their over-centralised style of decision making, and the massive information processing burden this places on the decision logic. In the cybernetic framework, control in the systems quoted above is taking place at the level where the variety of the controller is capable of matching the variety of the system being controlled.

12.2   The ISIS system for job shop scheduling

12.2.1   Introduction

ISIS is a knowledge-based job shop scheduling system developed at Carnegie-Mellon University, and is comprehensively described in Fox (1983), with overviews in Fox and Smith (1984), and Smith, Fox and Ow (1986). Its rationale is based on the observation that in job shops most of a human scheduler's time is taken up with searching for schedules that satisfy the many types of constraint that exist. ISIS uses a strategy of **constraint-directed search** to find satisfactory (i.e., constraint satisfying) rather than optimal schedules.

ISIS uses an object-oriented description language, SRL, for the representation of production orders, processing operations, machines, tools, and operators, in the form of a type of semantic net. This language has subsequently been used as a basis for the AI programming environment marketed by the Carnegie Group under the name of 'Knowledge Craft'. The use of SRL to represent the required level of knowledge of factory floor operations to produce realistic and detailed factory schedules is a good example both of the representational power of object-oriented description languages, and of the complexity of the knowledge that needs to be represented. We shall therefore look more closely at the ISIS representation of the shop floor.

12.2.2   Shop floor representation in ISIS

The ISIS representation uses a variety of different types of entity to capture the important concepts and relationships of the shop floor knowledge domain. Consider the following description of a small fragment of that domain:

Order #3146 for assembly A involves production of parts P90 and P107. P90 requires a milling and a drilling operation. The milling operation precedes the drilling operation and consists of two steps, set-up and run. Set-up takes one hour and run time is ten minutes. The milling operation may use machines MM-56 or MM-67. Two resources are required, a five pound wrench and an operator. Machine MM-56 has no available capacity until 10/3/88.

The description first refers to different types of *object* such as order, part, machine, milling machine, wrench, and operator, and these may be arranged in classification hierarchies such as that shown in Figure 12.5 using is-a and instance-of relations.

This is a specialisation/generalisation hierarchy of the type described in Chapter 9, and would obviously support inheritance of attributes from superclasses to subclasses. However, in addition to class relationships, the description contains information about structural relationships of objects, for example that subassembly A consists of P90 and P106. These relationships may be displayed by has-part or part-of links in Figure 12.6.

In addition to objects, the description also refers to activities which transform objects into other objects. The production of P90 is an activity, as are the two operations milling and drilling of which it is composed, and the individual components of the milling operation, milling set-up and milling-run. In addition to classes of activity such as operations and milling-operation, another concept is implicit here,

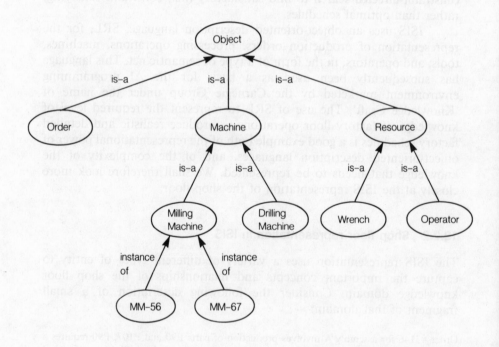

Figure 12.5 Specialisation and generalisation hierarchies in ISIS.

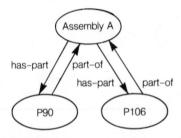

Figure 12.6 Structural relationships in ISIS.

namely refinement. Production of P50 may be refined into the individual production operations of milling and drilling. Milling may in turn be refined into set-up and run. A new relation denoted by refined-by (inverse refines) displays these relationships as shown in Figure 12.7 with class relationships between activities.

We have indicated that an activity transforms objects into other objects. More generally, we can define a **state** as a compound description of objects or object instatiations which is true at a particular point or over a particular period of time. Thus during the milling set-up, the milling machine must be in possession of a wrench. This concept may be defined as a *state*, as shown in Figure 12.8.

The state in which MM-56 is reserved from now to 10/3/88 is represented as a manifestation of the machine MM-56, as in Figure 12.9.

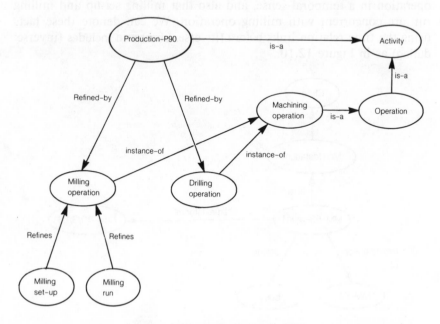

Figure 12.7 Refinement in ISIS.

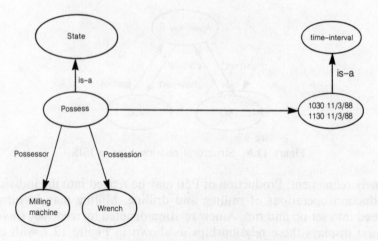

Figure 12.8   States in ISIS.

A manifestation is, in a way, a more particular description of an object than an instantiation in that it tells us the time period over which the object exists in some particular state.

Through the concept of state we have introduced the notion of the time interval over which the state exists. There are also some other aspects of the representation of time to be considered. The fragmental job shop description tells us that the milling operation precedes the drilling operation in a temporal sense, and also that milling set-up and milling run are concurrent with milling operation. We can denote these facts using the time relation links before (inverse: after) and includes (inverse: during) as in Figure 12.10.

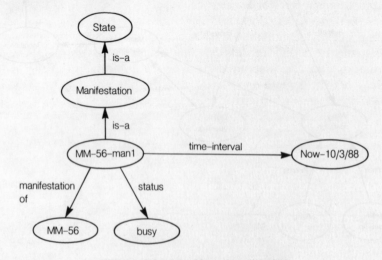

Figure 12.9   Manifestations in ISIS.

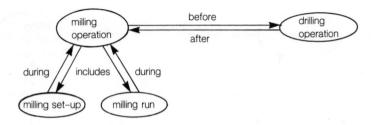

Figure 12.10 Time relations in ISIS.

Also implicit in the time precedence orderings of individual operations is the notion of **causality**. A causal relation links an activity to a state in the sense that it indicates the state that follows a particular activity. Thus the activity transport-wrench could cause the state of possession of the wrench by MM-56, as in Figure 12.11.

The reverse relation of **cause** is the **enable** relation which links a state to an act, that is to say it specifies the state that must exist before an act can occur. Thus, before the milling operation can occur, the milling machine must be in possession of both a wrench and an operator, as in Figure 12.12.

Both nodes and links of this semantic network are formally defined in SRL in terms of schemata. A schema is basically a description of a particular entity using a frame-based notation. A schema will have a number of slots which can contain information concerning attributes of the entity and its relationship with other entities. Attributes and relations are themselves defined in terms of schemata which contain further information about the attribute or relation. Each slot can also have a number of facets associated with it of the type demon (a procedure that is executed when the slot is accessed), domain, range (which restrict the values that may fill a slot), and cardinality (restricting the number of values a slot may contain). A schema may also contain meta-information associated with itself, its slots, or the values in the slots. This meta-information may be used to document the information given in the schema and to elaborate on its semantics. Simple examples of schemata in SRL are shown in Figure 12.13.

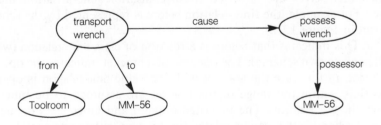

Figure 12.11 Causality in ISIS.

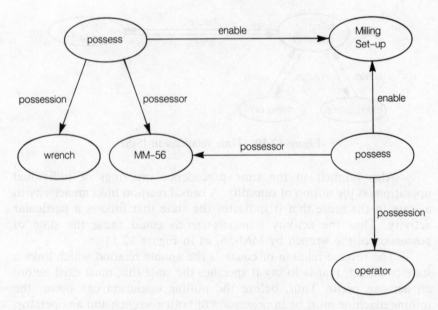

Figure 12.12 Enablement in ISIS.

Here we have an entity called operation which is a prototype (defined by the meta-information *type* attached to the schema), is a specialisation of the more general entity act, and has attributes next operation, previous-operation, work-centre, operator, and duration. A further specialisation of operation is defined by the schema machining-operation which is a specialisation of operation, thereby inheriting its attributes with the additional attribute machine. The schema milling-operation is an instance of machining-operation defined by values in the attribute slots as shown. Milling-operation has an attribute duration which is an instance of the entity time-interval, itself defined by a schema.

The relations is-a and instance-of are relations which are defined as part of the SRL language for supporting specialisation/generalisation hierarchies. Other types of relation such as refines, part-of, before and enables are user-defined relations and must possess associated schemata, which themselves are arranged in specialisation/generalisation hierarchies. For example, the time-relation before is represented by the schema shown in Figure 12.14.

This indicates that before is a relation of class time relation (which will have its own schema). The opening of a bracket indicates the opening of a slot, in this case the is-a slot with the value time-relation is opened, and slots within the range of the bracket are assumed to be inherited down the is-a relation. The inherited domain and range slots define the type of schemata that can be related (in this case, either acts or states, but not objects, can be related by before).

{{**operation**
  type prototype
  is–a: act
  next operation:
  previous operation:
  work centre:
  operator:
  duration: }}
{{**machining-operation**
  type prototype
  is–a: operation
  machine: }}
{{**milling-operation**
  type instance
  instance: machining-operation
  next-operation: drilling-operation
  work-centre: milling-centre
  machine: mill–1 }}
  duration: {{instance time-interval
  duration: 5}]
{{**time-interval**
  begin-time:
  end-time:
  duration:
  dated-by: }}

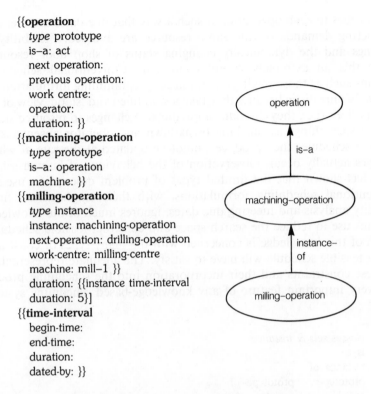

Figure 12.13   Example of ISIS schemata.

A summary of the important user-defined relations employed in ISIS is shown in Figure 12.15, grouped according to which aspect of the representation they refer. Each relation has its inverse (e.g., the inverse of has-part is part-of), and inheritance properties of relations may be separately defined for each relation.

12.2.3   Constraint representation in ISIS

Shop floor scheduling involves selecting a process routing for a particular order, and assigning the necessary resources with associated start and

{{**before**
  {is–a: time–relation
    domain:
      range (or (type is–a act) (type is–a state))
    range:
      range (or (type is–a act) (type is–a state))
    inverse: after}
  time: before }}

Figure 12.14   The user–defined 'before' relation.

finish times to each operation, in such a way that due dates are met and conflicting demands on the same resource are avoided. Flexibility of routings and the dynamically changing status of shop floor resources make this an extremely complex problem. Conventional scheduling systems such as those relying on an integer programming formulation are generally unrealistic because they take a simplified and 'static' view of the factory floor (i.e., they discount unpredictable changes to resource status due to such things as machine breakdown and operator absenteeism), and the schedules they produce cannot be updated at the rate at which changes actually occur. Observation of the behaviour of human schedulers has shown that the limited types of problem description used in conventional scheduling formulations, with their emphasis on finite capacity analysis and meeting due dates, ignores much of the knowledge humans use to reduce the search space and construct feasible schedules. Much of this knowledge is concerned with the many types of constraint that a feasible schedule will have to satisfy. The adequate representation of these constraints and their incorporation into the scheduling process is a very important feature of any knowledge-based scheduling system,

```
classes sets & instances
is–a
instance–of
prototype      prototype–of
member         member–of

physical–structure
attribute      attribute–of
has–part       part–of
structure      sub–structure–of

hierarchical decomposition
refined–by     refines

temporal–relations
before         after
during         includes
meet           met–by
overlap        overlapped–by
time–equal     time–equal

causal relationships
cause      caused–by    (links act to state)
enable     enabled–by   (links state to act)
state–couple
cause–couple
act–couple
```

Figure 12.15 Summary of standard and user-defined relations in ISIS.

and in fact ISIS provides quite a sophisticated means of constraint specification.

In ISIS, constraints are divided into the following categories:

(1) Organisational goals

These are measures of how the organisation is required to perform and will constrain the values of various organisational variables. These include due dates, work-in-process, levels of resources maintained, production costs, production levels, and shop stability (measured by the frequency with which the schedule is changed). Schedules should generally be found which result in the values of these organisational variables lying within acceptable ranges (e.g., as might be defined in the ISTOP strategic planning model described in Section 12).

(2) Physical constraints

These define the physical limitations of individual production resources and processes. For example, there may be a physical limit to the length of time a drill can run in a particular material at a particular speed, or there may be a constraint on the time allowed between two consecutive processes.

(3) Causal restrictions

These define the conditions that must be satisfied before an operation can be started. For example, precedence constraints on operations indicate that one operation must occur before another: a certain combination of available resources and materials must be present before a job can be started, and so on.

(4) Availability constraints

As resources are assigned to the operations of a job, they will become unavailable over this time period for other operations or jobs. When a resource is allocated, these constraints must be generated and enforced.

(5) Preference constraints

For certain types of operation, even though alternative machines may exist, one particular machine may be preferred (e.g., due to cost or quality). Preferences may also exist for particular sequences of jobs which minimise set-ups. These are examples of preference constraints which are not rigid, but which should be satisfied if possible.

Constraints will need to have a variety of different types of information associated with them. For example, in the case of a due-date constraint, it may be that the due date cannot be met. Under these circumstances, there may be other dates that are acceptable. Constraint **relaxations** may allow a constraint to be satisfied by alternative values, which will require specifying, as will relative preferences between these values. Constraints may also be of varying importance. For example, meeting the due date of a high priority order will be more important than satisfying an operation preference constraint, and it should be possible to attach the importance measure to the constraint. Constraints will also interact with each other, in the sense that the satisfaction of one constraint may have a positive or negative effect on the ability to satisfy another. For example, reducing overtime to satisfy a cost constraint may cause a due date to be missed. Again, these interactions must be represented. The conditions under which a given constraint applies must also be specified. A constraint may only apply over a specified time period (e.g., during an operation). Finally, many constraints will not be givens but will be generated dynamically during construction of the schedule. This must be capable of being performed automatically using constraint **generators** which are activated whenever a scheduling decision is made and which results in a constraint becoming effective.

In ISIS, constraints and the information associated with them are represented as explicit entities in the form of SRL schemata, which can be arranged in a specialisation/generalisation hierarchy. The general constraint schema is as shown in Figure 12.16, whilst a due-date constraint may be specified as in the schemata shown in Figure 12.17.

The due-date schema, which is a specialisation of range-constraint, constrains the values that may be taken by the **due date** slot of the lot schema. The constraint actually imposed is specified in the due-date-constraint schema which is a specialisation of continuous-constraint. The choice of due date has a utility specified by the piecewise-linear-utility. This utility is specified as a set of (due-date, utility) pairs. The tester for due-date constraints takes the candidate due-date and the constraint as parameters and applies the value of the utility function slot to the due date to return a utility. The due date has an importance taking the form of a weighting which may be dynamically determined according to

```
{{constraint
   value:
   utility:
   context:
   importance:
   interaction:
   duration:
   consistency:
   generator:
   tester: }}
```

Figure 12.16 The general constraint schema in ISIS.

```
{{due–date
  {is–a range–constraint
    importance:
    context:
    domain:
      range: (type is–a lot)
    relation: due–date
    constraint:
      range: (type is–a due–date–constraint)
    priority–class }}
{{due–date–constraint
  {is–a continuous–constraint
    consistency: exclusive
    domain: dates
    piecewise–linear–utility}  }}
```

Figure 12.17   A due-date constraint in ISIS.

prespecified scheduling goals (which are themselves defined as schemata).

Similar types of schemata are defined for the specification of other constraint characteristics. Schemata exist for specifying the alternatives to (or relaxations of) given constraints and for assigning utilities to alternatives. Interactions between constraints are handled by specification of a constrains schema, which indicates the constraints that interact and the direction (positive or negative) and strength of the interaction. This allows the definition of a network of interacting constraints, which can be hierarchical in nature (e.g., organisational goals at the top of the constraint hierarchy influence other constraints at lower levels). Separate schemata indicate the time period over which a constraint applies, and constraint generation is handled by active procedures attached to the relations linking acts to their post-states.

12.24   Schedule construction in ISIS

Schedule contruction in ISIS takes place hierarchically at four different levels, as shown in Figure 12.18. The top level is concerned with the selection of orders for scheduling. The second level is concerned with performing a capacity analysis to detect bottlenecks. The third level is concerned with the detailed allocation of resources to the order, and the lowest level makes the detailed individual resource reservations for the blocks of time for which they are required. The hierarchical approach provides a way of keeping the search space manageable. Scheduling is an incremental activity with orders being progressively added to the existing schedule in such a way that as many constraints as possible are satisfied. Each level consists of a pre-search analysis phase which constructs the seach space and selects applicable search operators, a search phase which

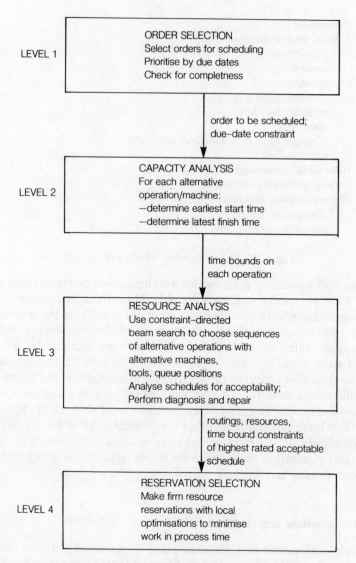

Figure 12.18   The ISIS scheduling hierarchy.

attempts to find a solution to the problem at that level, and a post-search analysis phase which determines the acceptablilty of the solution and tries to improve it. The solution at a given level generates a set of constraints on the solution at the next lower level.

Level 1: Order selection

The top level of scheduling is concerned with order or lot selection. An order may become a candidate for scheduling if it is a new order which has just been received at the plant, or if it is an existing order whose schedule has been invalidated by, for example, machine breakdown. Orders are prioritised according to their due dates, and are checked to ensure that they are complete for scheduling. Due-date constraints are chosen by matching the order's priority class to a corresponding class in the set of alternative due date constraints. The output from level 1 to the next level is the highest priority order to be scheduled next.

Level 2: Capacity analysis

This level performs a capacity analysis of the shop to determine the earliest start and latest finish times for each operation of the order on each alternative routing consistent with existing machine loadings. Presearch analysis supplies forward and backward scheduling operators. The function of the forward scheduling operators is for each alternative operation of the order, taken in sequence, to look forward from the order start date to find the earliest contiguous block of time available on each machine capable of performing the operation. The backward scheduling operator starts from the due date and schedules backward from the final operation (assumed to complete on the due date) to find the latest possible finishing date of each alternative operation on the alternative machines that may perform it. The search phase performs a breadth-first search in which earliest start and latest finish times for operations on each alternative routing are set. The time bounds on each operation are then passed to level 3.

This phase is similar to the Critical Path Method of Project Scheduling, and its purpose is to give early visibility to potential bottlenecks in performing the order.

Level 3: Resource analysis

The resource analysis phase performs a detailed search using all required resources and applying all the relevant constraints. A 'machine centred' search is employed within the space of alternative operations, machines and positions, to generate reservation time bounds for the machines and resources required for each operation. This search space is shown diagrammatically in Figure 12.19. The different paths through this search space represent the different ways in which an order may be scheduled, and a path from beginning state to end state represents a completely scheduled order. The search operators, established during presearch analysis, are typically 'choose operation', 'choose machine' 'choose queue position' 'choose shift' or 'choose tool' — and are represented as schema containing if–then production rules, of which an example is given in Figure 12.20.

Search operators may be regarded as generating **constraint relaxation** (i.e., alternative permissable values) for operations, machines,

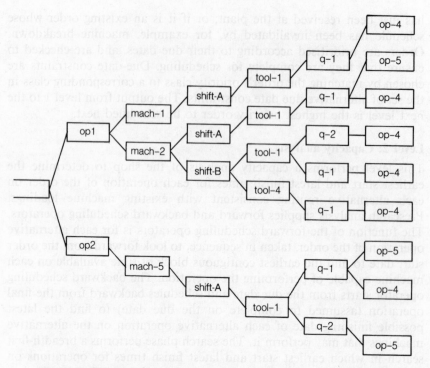

Figure 12.19 The ISIS search space in the resource analysis phase.

{{**choose–operation**
    {instance: search–operator
    IF 'a state has its operation machine and reservation
    bound
    THEN 'create a state binding the operation for each
    operation that follows in the proper direction, the
    current state's operation'

Figure 12.20 An ISIS search operator.

queue positions, etc. Two types of operators may be used for reserving
queue positions. The 'eager reserver' operator jumps to reserve a
machine and ancillary resources at the earliest possible time in the queue.
The 'wait and see' operator 'tentatively' reserves the entire time block,
but delays firm reservations of resources in terms of precise start and
finish times to the next level. Search takes place in either a forward or a
backward direction and is established using a set of rules during the
presearch analysis phase. For example, if the due-date constraint is
important, it provides the major anchor in the search space, and
scheduling takes place in a backward direction from the due date.

A 'beam' search strategy is used. At any given search depth, each state in the search space is given a rating according to the extent to which it satisfies any constraints that are relevant, and only the states with the best ratings are further expanded. In order to determine the rating of a state, it is necessary to resolve which constraints apply to the state. A state is defined here not just as the current node in the search space representing the most recent scheduling decision, but by the path (i.e., the chosen sequence of operations, machines, etc.) taken to reach that node. Thus the applicable constraints are not just those local constraints that apply to the current node, but also the constraints applicable to all nodes on the search path leading to the current node.

To resolve constraint applicability, constraints are divided into **invariant** constraints such as operation precedence, which will apply locally to a node and will not change as the path is expanded, and **transient** constraints such as due-date or work-in-process estimators, whose degree of satisfaction will be continuously updated as the search space is traversed. The rating of a state is obtained by collecting all the invariant contraints that apply along the path, and the latest instantiations of the transient constraints to form the **constraint set** applicable to the state. This is effected by examining the constraint slots of all the schemata which define the current state. Each constraint is weighted according to its importance (which may be either fixed or dynamically determined). Constraints then assign utilities to the state. The utility is a form of relaxation preference measure (defined in the constraint schema), taking a value between zero and two. A value zero indicates the state is inadmissable and can be deleted from further consideration, while a value of two indicates maximum preference. The rating of a given state is taken as the sum of the utilities of the individual applicable constraints, weighted by their importance.

It should be remembered that the applicable constraints at the resource level include the operation earliest start and latest finish time constraints generated at the capacity level. These can have the effect of generating due-date constraints for operations at the resource level which are derived from a global capacity analysis and hence anticipate the existence of bottlenecks.

When a set of candidate schedules have been generated, a post-search analysis is performed to examine their acceptability. Any schedule with a rating greater than one is accepted. If no acceptable schedule has been generated, a **diagnosis** is performed. For example, if scheduling has been performed in a backward direction, the required start date for all scheduling alternatives may have already been exceeded, resulting in an inadmissable set of schedules. In this case, the scheduling direction would be changed to forwards. If on the other hand no schedule is rated sufficiently highly to be considered, the presearch analysis phase would be re-entered, and additional search operators (which might, for example, generate extra shifts) might be selected. Facilities are also provided to determine the point of the search at which a poor decision was made and to backtrack only to that point. Analysis of the 'indirect utility' of a constraint, in which the constraints with which it interacts (defined by the **constraints** relation) also contribute to its utility, allows the selection of alternative constraint relaxations giving better results.

Level 4: Reservation selection

Process routings, resources and their time-bound constraints established at level 3 are passed to level 4 for the generation of firm reservations for each resource required in the schedule, and local optimisations are performed to minimise the order's work-in-process time. The resulting resource reservations are added to the shop schedule to act as constraints on the scheduling of further orders.

12.2.5   Implementation of ISIS

The initial version of ISIS was tested in 1984 in the Westinghouse Turbine Components Plant in Winston-Salem, North Carolina. Although valuable performance data was provided (e.g., schedules as good or superior to those produced by human schedulers were obtained, taking one to 20 minutes per order), the system was not fully installed because the underlying software architecture was not sufficiently robust, and did not interface satisfactorily with the existing order entry system of the factory. Implementation was postponed until a more robust, commercially-supported version of the system was available. In the meantime, however, some of the limitations of the predominantly **order-based**, problem-decomposition strategy of ISIS were becoming apparent. The investigation of alternative strategies, coupled with the perceived need to focus on **reactive** scheduling, lead to the OPIS project.

12.3   Reactive scheduling — the OPIS system

12.3.1   Reactive scheduling and multiple-problem decomposition

Much of the scheduling performed in a factory is of a **reactive** nature. Unplanned shop floor contingencies such as machine breakdowns, missing tools, late deliveries and rework mean that any predictive schedule will require continuous update in the light of these contingencies. OPIS (Opportunistic Intelligent Scheduler) is a system developed at Carnegie Mellon University (Smith, 1987) to exploit the notion of reactive scheduling.

OPIS uses the same form of factory representation model as ISIS, based on definition of orders, operations, resources, constraints, etc. in terms of SRL schemata. However, it differs from ISIS in that different forms of top-level problem decomposition are possible depending on the criticality of the various constraints that apply to the problem. The ISIS scheduling architecture takes an 'order-oriented' perspective by assuming the scheduling problem is decomposable into the subproblems of sequentially scheduling individual orders to best satisfy due dates subject to constraints imposed by existing resource reservations. An alternative form of problem decomposition would be to focus on the scheduling of resources rather than orders, such that the scheduling of each resource with operations from different orders was regarded as a separable subproblem subject to operation precedence constraints and due dates. This would allow better use of resources, for example by giving greater visibility to operation sequences that minimised machine set-ups.

OPIS takes the view that when some unexpected shop floor event occurs which causes the existing schedule to become invalidated, then in addition to the inconsistencies in the previous schedule that must be resolved, there may also be opportunities for improving the schedule, due to the removal of constraints that previously existed. In order to take advantage of these opportunities, it is necessary to focus the reactive scheduling effort on the set of constraints that will be most affected by the change. The position taken by OPIS is that the scheduling perpective adopted should be chosen according to the set of constraints that is most important for the particular aspect of the schedule under consideration. This will allow the most effective assessment of the effects of shop floor status changes both from a conflict resolution and an opportunistic point of view, by focusing on the component (order or resource) of the schedule that best surrounds the problem at hand.

When scheduling operations on bottleneck resources, a resource-based scheduling perspective would be used to make optimum use of the resource. The timings of operations on the bottleneck resource then serve as constraints on order-oriented scheduling of the remainder of the operations.

When a contingency occurs, reactive scheduling takes place according to the perspective that gives most prominence to the constraint conflicts introduced as a result of the change. Thus if a bottleneck resource unexpectedly goes down for a period of time, the schedule will focus on resolving the capacity conflicts generated by all the orders requiring that particular resource. If a change in a due date results in an operation needing to start before the completion date of the previous operation, this conflict would be resolved using an order-based scheduling perspective, in which the individual operations of the order would require rescheduling. On the other hand, an extra shift put on a bottleneck resource to solve capacity conflicts might create opportunities that could be exploited using an order-based perspective.

12.3.2 The OPIS architecture

OPIS uses a blackboard architecture using a number of different Knowledge Sources, as shown in Figure 12.21. Factory status updates are communicated to the system through the **external interface**. The effects of the change will be propagated in an object-oriented fashion, and the change will introduce a set of conflicts or opportunities into the existing schedule which are computed by the **constraint propagator** and **consistency checker** and posted to the **search manager** as 'control events'. The Search Manager analyses these control events using a set of rules, and invokes the appropriate strategic scheduling perspective according to event type. Each perspective uses a different set of methods for schedule revision. The **order scheduler** provides a set of methods for revising the scheduled operations, machines and queue positions of an individual order, using the same techniques as ISIS. The **resource scheduler** provides methods for revising the schedule of a designated resource, and assumes that competition for the resource is high, thereby eliminating the need to introduce slack times between operations. The **schedule shifter** implements a less sophisticated means of reaction by moving scheduled times of individual operations forward by a designated amount. The **demand swapper** implements another relatively simple reactive method by exchanging the affected portion of an orders schedule with another order of the same type that may not be so urgently required, thus exploiting any

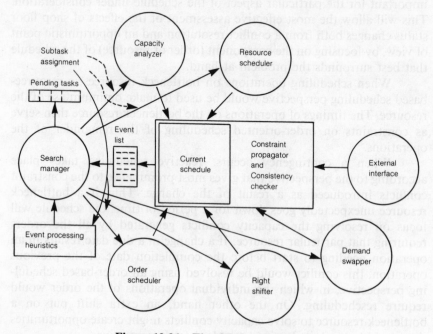

Figure 12.21 The OPIS architecture.

flexibility that may exist in the schedules of existing orders. The **capacity analyser** performs an aggregate analysis to identify bottlenecks and thereby to indicate when the resource scheduler, rather than the order scheduler, should be invoked. This provides a means of structuring the overall scheduling problem (in addition to reactive problems), by focusing on resource-oriented scheduling of bottleneck resources as a highest priority.

12.3.3 Observations on the ISIS/OPIS development

The ISIS/OPIS development work is concerned with using a rich problem description language to capture in full all the many complexities of the shop floor. As such this implies an attempt to match the variety of the control model with the variety of the system being controlled. Inevitably, however, this leads to a proliferation of complexity in the control model itself. Both the representation and control strategies in ISIS and OPIS are undoubtedly somewhat complex and this can lead to problems in troubleshooting and system maintenance. In addition, the complexity of the schema representation means that much time has to be spent during model execution merely in manipulatng schemata to obtain the necessary information. Although rich in expressive power, object-oriented data bases are not yet noted for their performance. In the dynamic environment of the shop floor, the ability for the system to respond rapidly to contingencies is obviously essential, and in this regard the OPIS approach, with multiple-problem decompositions being driven opportunistically from the bottom rather than hierarchically from the top, has a clear advantage over ISIS. The predominance of uncertainty on the shop floor also gives few realistic points at which a schedulue can be anchored. Whereas ISIS uses start or due dates of orders as the anchor point, OPIS uses islands of certainty surrounding a whole variety of shop floor events, such as machine breakdowns, from which to spread the schedule in an opportunistic fashion. These ideas are being extended further in the Cooperative Scheduling System (Ow, 1988).

12.4 PLATO-Z — a knowledge-based control system for a flexible manufacturing cell

12.4.1 Introduction

Increasing interest is being taken in knowledge-based approaches to the automated control of flexible manufacturing cells. The environment in which a flexible manufacturing cell operates is typically highly dynamic, with the machines being capable of performing a wide variety of operations with different set-ups. Using extensive computer control, a flexible manufacturing cell is in principle capable of achieving the efficiency of a well-balanced transfer line whilst at the same time retaining a job-shop level of flexibility for machining multiple types of parts.

A typical flexible manufacturing cell consists of a number of computer-controlled machines, an automated materials handling system which transports parts between machines, and a supervisory computer. This arrangement is shown in Figure 12.22.

This shows a cell consisting of three machines, each with its own tool magazine and with either a CNC computer containing stored sets of instructions for part-machining operations or a DNC microprocessor with a paper tape backup. The materials handling system comprises automated storage and retrieval facility and automated guided vehicles for transporting parts to and from the cell, and between individual machines. These are controlled by their own CNC computer. Loading and unloading at the machines can be performed by a shuttle system or by robot. The overall operations of the cell are controlled by a supervisory computer.

Because the 'flexibility' of a flexible manufacturing cell implies that a given operation can be performed on several alternative machines, the control of the cell can be very complex, with a large number of interrelationships between machines, tools, parts, raw materials and AGVs. The control problem is made even more difficult by the requirement for a high flow velocity of parts through the cell, making on-line, real-time automated decision an absolute necessity. The assignment of parts to machines will depend on the actual state of system at the time, defined by such factors as which machines are up, which parts are

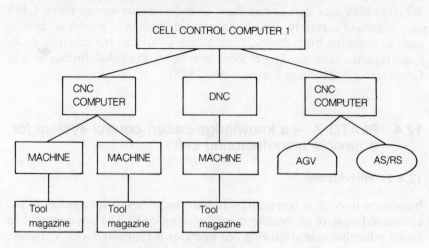

Figure 12.22 Architecture of a flexible manufacturing cell.

currently waiting for which machines, and relative priorities. Machine breakdowns may necessitate the re-routing of parts. The control system must therefore be capable of monitoring operations from feedback on the status of machines, tools, and individual part lots, recognise when an error occurs in the system and take corrective action.

The planning and control of flexible manufacturing cells is usually addressed within a hierarchical structure (e.g., Stecke, 1984; De, Nof and Whinston, 1985; Kusiak, 1986; O'Grady, 1987). A typical hierarchical structure consists of four levels: factory, shop, cell and equipment. The factory level deals with the relatively long-term strategy of the plant and passes goals to the shop level; the shop level interprets subgoals set by the factory and passes goals to individual cells, which in turn interpret these goals and pass commands to individual pieces of equipment which carry out the operations. The tactical planning level determines the job mix to be manufactured within each cell and any constraints on sequencing, with due regard for short-term customer demand in relation to shop capacity (a form of Master Production Schedule for the cell). It can also determine, at a more detailed level, the sequence and timing of release of individual jobs to each cell. This would be an intermittent planning activity that would be performed off-line on a weekly or even daily basis according to the type of environment in which the shop operates. Systems such as ISTOP would be suitable for planning at this level. The **input** to the flexible manufacturing cell is a production mix of jobs with a known entry sequence and a set of requirement dates or priorities. The task of the cell control system is to allocate these jobs to machines dynamically and in real time, and to monitor continuously the status of all operations to react to errors. It should also be capable of monitoring machine performance and tool life, scheduling preventive maintainance as appropriate, and controlling automatic inspection procedures.

Much has been written about control systems for flexible manufacturing cells (see Buzacott and Yao, 1986 and O'Grady, 1987 for reviews). A variety of control techniques have been proposed. Analytical models for machining and tool assignment have been developed, but these require computer processing times which are too long for a real-time environment (Stecke, 1984). Another technique which has been examined is the use of Petri nets (Dubois and Stecke, 1983), which model the static properties of a discrete event system using a network in which the nodes stand for transitions and the required conditions for those transitions (an example of such a representation is given in Section 14.2.4). Although these techniques have proved useful in planning cell configurations through the modelling of cell operations, once again they have not been very effective in real-time control. The requirement for the control system to be dynamically adaptive in a stimulus-response fashion to a variety of real-time changes in status, and to be capable of estimating whether unexpected problems will have any effect on the system's goals as set at the tactical level, is something that lends itself to a knowledge-based approach, as pointed out by Stecke (1984); a number of such systems have been described (Shaw, 1988; Subramanyam and Askin, 1986; Bu-Hulaiga and Chakravarty, 1988; LeCocq *et al*, 1988) which are mostly oriented towards detailed real-time scheduling of the cell. These systems employ a variety of different methods including constrain-directed search for a predictive schedule (as performed by ISIS), heuristic rules for machine and tool assignment based on current queue lengths and cell status, and a heuristic search for feasible tool loading configurations that minimise the remaining marginal cost of achieving the Master Production Schedule given current cell status.

The approach which is outlined here is due to O'Grady and Lee (1988) and uses a blackboard architecture that performs the functions of scheduling, error handling and monitoring. The system has been named PLATO-Z (Production, Logistics and Timings Organizer).

12.4.2 Architecture of PLATO-Z

A knowledge-based system using blackboard architecture contains several independent knowledge bases called **knowledge sources**, each designed to tackle a specific aspect of the problem, and exchange information via a blackboard, regarded as a common working memory to which all have access. Overall control of problem solving is effected through message passing between knowledge sources via the blackboard, and through a blackboard controller which generates and maintains the current list of blackboard events.

PLATO-Z contains four blackboard subsystems through which different tasks are coordinated, and to which different types of message can be posted. Each blackboard is surrounded by the knowledge sources which are relevant to the performance of the overall task being coordinated through the blackboard. The four blackboards are:

(1)   A **scheduling blackboard** which schedules individual resources within the cell to achieve the goals established at the shop level.

(2)   An **operation dispatching blackboard** which is responsible for generating requests for detailed operations to be performed at the equipment level.

(3)   A **monitoring blackboard** which filters and classifies the information from the equipment level.

(4)   An **error-handling blackboard** which detects and analyses errors and unexpected contingencies occurring in the cell and deduces possible courses of corrective action.

Three other support functions are also provided:

(1) **Initialisation and termination** which initialises or terminates cell activities at start-up or finish.

(2) **Communication and networking** which handles the communications and networking interface between the cell and the outside world.

(3) **User interface** through which the user communicates with the system.

Dataflows occur between these four blackboards as indicated in Figure 12.23.

PLATO-Z uses three different knowledge representation formalisms: structured objects, production rules and procedures. Structured objects are used as the basic representational building block of the

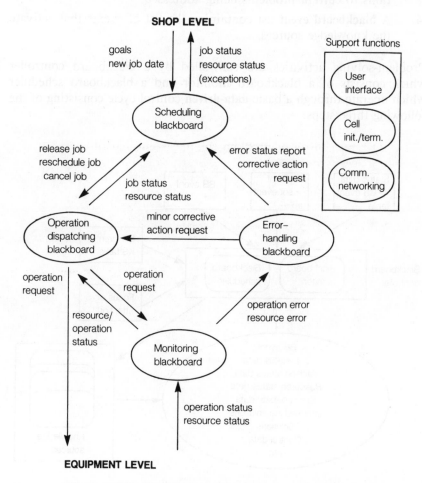

Figure 12.23   The PLATO-Z blackboard architecture.

system. Production rules are used for blackboard control and to represent rule-based knowledge present in the different knowledge sources. Procedures are used for certain types of algorithmic and heuristic knowledge (such as optimisation techniques) which are better represented in procedural than rule-based form.

The operation of a blackboard is shown schematically in Figure 12.24. Each blackboard in PLATO-Z consists of four components:

(1)   A **static** database of data which is stable over time, such as the cell configuration, the attributes of the various machines, tools, etc.

(2)   A **status** database which stores the current status of the cell, and the individual jobs and machines in the cell.

(3)   A **solution** database containing either intermediate or final solutions to current problems being addressed.

(4)   A **blackboard event** list containing the list of events that activate the knowledge sources.

Problem-solving activities are controlled by a blackboard controller which consists of a blackboard monitor and a blackboard scheduler which operate through a basic **data-driven** control cycle consisting of the following three steps:

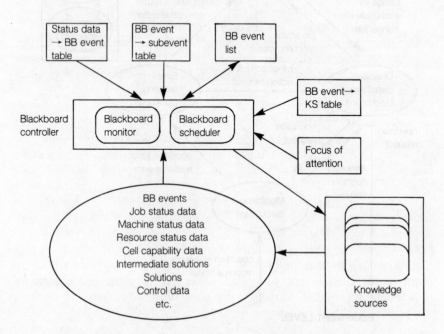

Figure 12.24 Schematic operation of a PLATO-Z blackboard.

(1)   Generate any new blackboard events triggered by current status data.

(2)   Select the highest priority event from the event list and identify and select the appropriate knowledge source required for handling the event.

(3)   Execute the selected knowledge source.

The first of these steps (generate blackboard events) is handled by a set of production rules in the form of status data/blackboard event pairs in the local database of the blackboard monitor. These allow certain status data configurations to trigger the generation of blackboard events. If an event has a series of subevents associated with it, the blackboard monitor will also generate these subevents.

The next step is performed by the blackboard scheduler, and involves selecting the most urgent event, which may be determined by a set of 'focus of attention' rules in a separate knowledge base. The knowledge sources which are relevant to the processing of that event are stored in a blackboard event/knowledge source table. If more than one knowledge source is relevant, then a single one is selected by a bidding method (which may effectively be thought of as a conflict resolution strategy for knowledge sources). Each knowledge source contains rules which evaluate the event and make a bid to be considered in the form of some parameter value. The scheduler then selects the knowledge source returning the most appropriate value of that parameter.

The third step, which involves executing the appropriate knowledge source, results in status changes or solutions being written to the blackboard. Control is then passed back to the first step, with the updated status data generating new blackboard events, thus repeating the cycle.

Each of the three blackboard systems operates in parallel, on its own particular problem-solving activity, and overall coordination is achieved through message passing between blackboards. Thus the execution of a knowledge source may involve passing a message to another blackboard, which is processed by a message handler and becomes a blackboard event on that blackboard.

The individual **knowledge sources** which surround each blackboard consist of a mixture of rule-based systems, heuristic algorithms, and optimisation procedures (which may themselves be selected by rules). Each knowledge source contains a precondition part, which is the blackboard event that invokes it. In general, one knowledge source is required for each (event generated) task, but in some tasks, such as sequencing, knowledge sources containing alternative methods may be invoked, and their solutions compared. Tasks include classification of data input, reporting status changes and error conditions, analysis to determine preferred actions (including simulation of different scenarios), generation of events for passing to other blackboards, and optimisation procedures.

12.4.3 Blackboard operation

The scheduling blackboard

The operation of the scheduling blackboard is shown in Figure 12.25. The scheduling blackboard receives as input from the shop level a list of the jobs to be processed and their required completion dates. The control functions of the scheduling blackboard are responsible for the perfor-

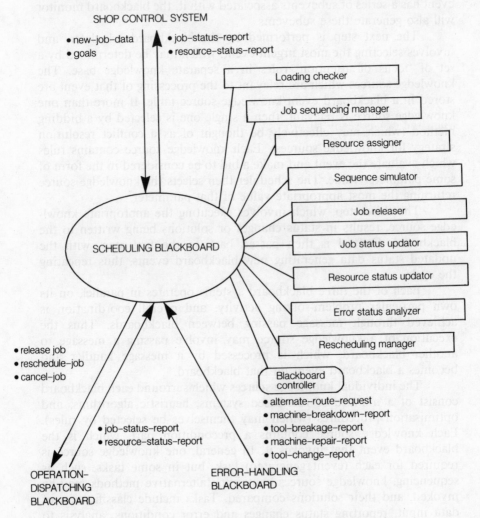

Figure 12.25 The PLATO-Z scheduling blackboard.

mance of two types of scheduling: **regular scheduling** and **rescheduling**.

Regular scheduling requires the application of knowledge sources concerned with *preliminary loading check, sequencing, routing,* and *job release and feedback handling.* The **preliminary loading check** has its own knowledge source which is concerned with ensuring that sufficient capacity currently exists to process a job by its due date, and may reject jobs in inadequate capacity situations. **Sequencing** is performed by the job sequencing manager knowledge source, which contains rules for the selection of the best sequencing method, based on job and resource characteristics. Alternative sequencing rules may be applied (such as scheduling the shortest processing time job first and sequencing by due date) and the sequence simulator knowledge source then evaluates the sequences resulting and chooses the best. **Routing** is performed by the resource-assigner knowledge source which dynamically assigns the required machines to the job based on current machine status. Routing allows the sequence simulator to calculate the start and finish times of each job, and to report back to the shop level if due date constraints are violated. In **job release and feedback handling**, the job-releaser knowledge source releases jobs one by one to the operation dispatching blackboard when the cell is ready to process another job, having checked that the parts, machines, tools, jigs and fixtures are available. Job status data are updated for each job released. Information on the status of all jobs and resources are maintained by the job and resource status updator knowledge sources, which are informed of status changes by the operation dispatching blackboard.

Rescheduling is concerned with reacting to error conditions or contingencies in the cell environment. The ability to react effectively to problems depends on effectively identifying and classifying the problems as they arise, and assigning the appropriate knowledge source to deal with them. Another desirable feature of an error-reaction ability stems from Ashby's law of requisite variety, one of whose implications is that the larger the number of control or reaction options that exist, the less will be the effect of disturbances on system performance. Since all possible types of error cannot be anticipated and catered for in advance, the incorporation of a learning ability in which new knowledge can be added to enable the system to react to a wider variety of errors is also important.

All blackboard systems are involved in the error-handling process. The scheduling blackboard is concerned with the task of rescheduling jobs and resources related to errors of which it is informed by the error-handling blackboard. The error status analyser knowledge source identifies and classifies the messages from the error-handling blackboard, and the rescheduling manager determines the rescheduling to be performed and the knowledge sources to be used. The results of the rescheduling action are recorded by the job and resource status updators.

The operation dispatching blackboard

The main functions of the operation dispatching blackboard are as follows:

- the generation and dispatch of detailed operations to production resources within limited time windows;
- response to corrective action requests from the error-handling blackboard;
- updating of the status of parts, machines, auxiliary resources, and buffers;
- reporting of major changes of status of jobs and machines to the scheduling blackboard.

The major function of the operation dispatching blackboard is the generation and dispatch of operations to individual machines. This is performed by the operation scheduler knowledge source, which determines the schedule of operations required for the job. This knowledge source is rule based and contains three groups of rules: **before-operation rules** which check the preconditions of operations before they start; **after-operation rules** which update part and cell status after the operation has finished; and a **clock-advance rule** which advances the current time to the closest time at which a particular resource is no longer required. Before the operation commences, the relevant parts and resources may be assumed to be in the idle or waiting state (since these are the preconditions for the operation to commence). When one of the before-operation rules is fired, an operation request is issued and the status of the related parts and resources are changed to an in-process or busy state. After the operation, an after-operation rule changes part and resource status back to waiting or idle.

The monitoring blackboard

This blackboard uses feedback information from the equipment level to maintain a record of the current status of all production resources. An important function of this blackboard is to classify and filter this feedback information, and to actively report major status changes of parts and resources to the other blackboards. It also maintains various cell statistics such as machine utilisation, down-times and set-up times.

The error-handling blackboard

This blackboard is responsible for the recognition and analysis of errors or contingencies occuring in the operation of the cell, and for developing possible corrective actions. Corrective actions requiring major changes are passed to the scheduling blackboard, whereas corrective actions involving only small deviations from the original schedule are passed to the operation dispatching blackboard. Major failures which are beyond the control of the system are reported to the shop level of control. Rule-based knowledge sources are used to develop corrective actions, with each class of error having its associated error-handling policy stored as a set of rules.

PLATO-Z is representative of the type of detailed control system that might be used at the back-end of slightly higher level systems such as ISTOP, which would basically provide the list of jobs to be produced together with a set of priorities, leaving the detailed control of order processing to the cell control system. To date there have been few reports of implemented systems showing this degree of hierarchical integration. Yet in the fully automated factory, this is an area where progress must be made. The difficulties appear to lie more in the interface of the cell to its environment and in the development of systems that give the cell a set of goals which reflect the dynamic nature of that environment and the manufacturing strategy being used to respond to it, rather than in the control of the cell itself. The latter, although complex, is fairly well defined and structured. The current challenges in knowledge-based manufacturing control are perhaps more at the strategic than at the operational levels, and in this sense are so inextricably interwoven with the planning function as to be non-separable.

Chapter 13
Knowledge-based Applications to Production Systems Design — Examples

13.1 Knowledge-based design of factory layout — the FACSIM system

13.2 EXGT — a knowledge-based system for group technology

13.3 A tool for the design of production activity control systems

---

This chapter examines some knowledge-based tools that assist in the design of production systems. The FACSIM system is a tool that can both generate factory layouts consistent with a defined set of constraints, and perform simulations to examine the performance of these layouts with an 'intelligent front end' presented to the user. As such, it represents a knowledge-based decision-support system. This is followed by a brief description of a knowledge-based system for detailed Group Technology analysis, and a description of a design tool used for the development and analysis of systems for production activity control in cellular manufacturing environments.

13.1 Knowledge-based design of factory layout — the FACSIM system

13.1.1 General

Design activities associated with manufacturing are concerned not only with products, but also with the best layout of the factory which will be concerned with the manufacture of these products. This design process, if performed properly, is similar in its overall nature to product design, with a synthesis phase concerned with developing a trial factory layout, and an analysis phase which involves simulating the behaviour of this layout under the full range of expected operating conditions. FACSIM (Kerr and Walker, 1988) is an intelligent design tool used to assist in both the synthesis and the analysis phase of factory layout design.

13.1.2 Factory Representation in FACSIM

FACSIM is based on an object-oriented representation of the important characteristic features of the factory that are both static and dynamic. The representation contains predefined 'libraries' of different types of entities. These may be divided into permanent entities which represent permanent factory resources such as machines, transporters, storage areas and the physical connections or paths between them, constraint entities which define constraints on the relative locations of the static factory resource entities, transient entities which are the material items flowing through the factory, along with the queues they form, and process entities which represent the conversion processes undergone by the material items, both in terms of identity and location.

The specific entity classes in FACSIM are:

(1) **Manufacturing resource** entities required for manufacturing conversion process. These include machines, tools, operators, setters, transporters, general purpose auxiliary resources, and aggregations or collections of these resources, which can be defined through the aggregate-of or consists-of links, and can be used to define work centres, machine cells, pools of operators, etc.

(2) **Storage** entities where materials, tools or auxiliary resources may be stored. These include both permanent and temporary (work-in-progress) storage areas.

(3) **Connection** entities which represent different forms of connection between permanent and immovable factory entities. These are such things as transporter or AGV paths, water and power connections.

(4) **Constraint** entities which can associate scores between 0 and 10 for various distance intervals, either measured directly or along transporter or AGV paths, which separate static permament factory entities or groupings of entities.

(5) **Material** entities representing the material items that flow through the various processes in the factory, changing identity en-route. These include both parts and assemblies. They may be aggregated into lots whose relationship to the individual part is defined with the aggregation link.

(6) **Queue** entities representing collections of material items waiting to be processed by a particular manufacturing resource.

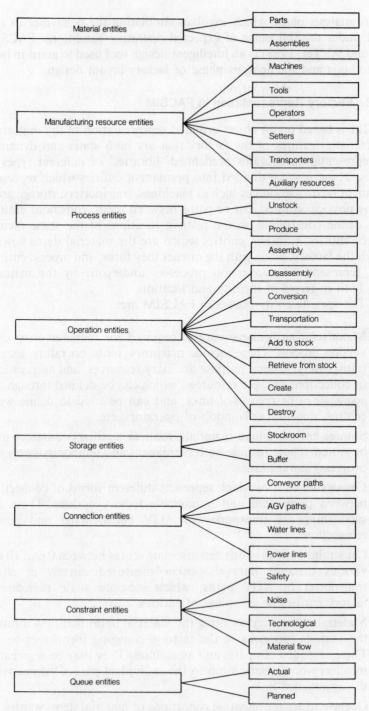

Figure 13.1 Classification of entities in FACSIM.

(7)   **Operation** entities which are acts of changing the characteristics of a material item. These are classified into conversion operations which change the identity of the material item concerned, transportation operations which change the location of the item, and operations which introduce items into the system or remove them from it.

13.1.3   The design synthesis phase in FACSIM

The design synthesis phase of a factory layout design consists of establishing a locational configuration of permament factory entities such that the constraints on relative locations are satisfied to the greatest possible extent. The constraints, which are user specified, can be used to represent what is a desirable configuration from the point of view of considerations such as material flow, safety, noise and technological factors. The problem of arriving at a factory layout that satisfies these constraints can be regarded effectively as a multiple criteria decision analysis problem in which an attempt is made to reach a physical configuration which represents an acceptable trade-off in terms of satisfying different types of constraint.

Trade-offs are made explicit in FACSIM through examining the relative constraint scores of a particular factory configuration. This is performed by collecting all the constraints that apply to the relative locations of all possible pairs of fixed entities in a given configuration, working out how much the configuration 'scores' on each constraint based on the distance separating the entities, and then estimating the average constraint score, weighted by the importance of each constraint, along the four dimensions of material-flow, safety, noise and technology. A constraint score of 10 for a particular distance interval between two entities means that separation distances within that interval are absolutely forbidden. Non-zero constraint scores are undesirable. For example, a constraint may exist on the distance between the heat treating department and the LP Gas store as follows:

Constraint
    type: safety
    between: heat-treat, LP-gas-store
    connection: direct
    distance-interval-scores: ((0,20),10), ((20,30),6)
    importance 5

This indicates that, for safety reasons, the LP Gas store must definitely not be located closer than a direct distance of 20 units from the heat-treating department (score 10 for this distance interval) and it is undesirable (score 6) that it should be located closer than 30 units. Since no other intervals are specified, distances greater than 30 are all equally acceptable. The importance rating of 5 gives the weighting (range 0–10) with which this score will be combined with other constraint scores relating to safety factors.

Material flow constraint scores are based on relative expected volumes of direct flow between departments. These are converted into a 0–10 scale by a mapping function which transforms high material flow combined with low separation values to low constraint scores on a ratio interval basis, and associates a score of zero with a pair of departments with high inter-departamental flow if they are located adjacent to each other.

13.1.4 Setting up a factory layout in FACSIM

There are two methods of setting up a factory layout in FACSIM. The first method involves the user-driven insertion and connection of all relevant entities on a two-dimentional grid representation of the factory, with or without the prior specification within the knowledge base of the constraints that should be satisfied. If constraints have been specified, the system advises the user of the constraint score of each insertion, and the cumulative weighted constraint score of the emerging configuration.

The second method involves the specification in the knowledge base of the numbers and types of permament entity required, *without* giving any locational information other than a set of 'anchor-points' (see below), together with the constraints that affect their relative locations. The system then searches for a configuration of these entities in locational space which has an acceptable total weighted constraint score. The level of 'acceptability' may be defined in various ways, for example by giving maximum allowable scores on individual criteria such as safety, noise and material flow.

13.1.5 User-generated factory layout

An example of a user-driven layout screen is shown in Figure 13.2. The user is initially confronted with a two dimensional grid on which to place, using a cursor, various predefined icons representing the static entities of the factory. A choice of different icons is available to represent different types of machine, storage area, etc. The grid is divided into rectangles which are used for locating departments consisting of groups or aggregations of permanent resources. The size of a rectangle represents a basic unit of area required for the department of smallest physical size. The area required for a department not defined in terms of subentities takes a default user-supplied value, otherwise it is calculated automati-

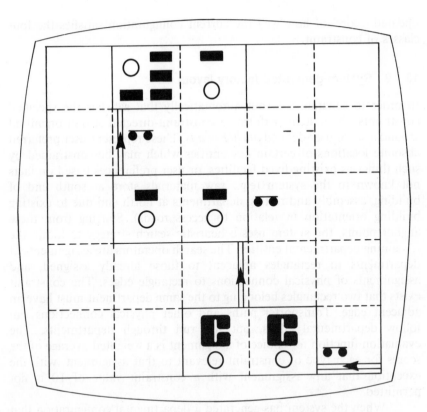

Figure 13.2 Basic layout screen in FACSIM.

cally from the number of individual resource entities it contains, the area specified for each, and the constraints specified for their separation. Most departments will cover several adjacent rectangles, and constraints can be specified on the ratio of width to length. The positioning of an icon representing an entity at a particular point on the screen results in the automatic instantiation of the corresponding entity in the knowledge base, with positional coordinates defined by the location of the icon on the grid. The attributes of the entity to which the cursor is currently pointing appear in an on-screen window, and their values can be edited. Editing the positional coordinates would change the location of the icon on the screen. Using the cursor, icons representing non-moveable factory resources can be connected together by *paths* along which transporters such as AGVs or fork-lift trucks can move.

As entity instances are added, automatic constraint checks occur, with the current cumulative constraint scores being displayed in the constraint window. The user is prevented from placing any entity in a position which results in a constraint score of 10. This enables the factory layout to be developed interactively with the user having a continuously updated 'score' of how well the current configuration satisfies the four classes of constraint.

13.1.6 System-generated factory layout

In order to generate a layout automatically that satisfies the specified constraints, the system performs a constraint-directed search organised around a set of user-defined *anchor points*. These represent user preferred absolute locations of certain key entities which may be constrained by such things as existing fixed facilities, or user preferences based on facts not known to the system (e.g., raw materials store at south end of building, assembly and testing departments at north end due to existing building orientation in relation to access roads). Starting from these anchor points, the system uses a heuristic search strategy to locate the remaining departmental entities. The search operators are assignments of departments to rectangles adjacent to those already assigned, and assignments of physical connections to rectangle edges. The constraint exists that two rectangles belonging to the same department must have an adjacent edge. Transporter paths and other physical connections can follow departmental edges, but not run through departments. The evaluation function for choice of assignment is a weighted average of the scores for each type of constraint relevant to that assignment, with the exception that any assignment with a constraint value of 10 is not permitted.

When the system has generated a departmental configuration that is acceptable in terms of minimal constraint scores, the user can make any required modifications, and the process can be repeated for layouts within individual departments, in which relative positions of such entities as individual machines and buffer storages areas can be assigned within the bounds of constraints specified at this level.

In practice, use of FACSIM in the automated mode produces reasonable layouts with acceptable material flow characteristics in which forbidden configurations in terms of safety, noise and technology are avoided, for factories with as many as 20 departments. However, the most effective use of the FACSIM for synthesizing factory layouts comes from use in a mixed mode, in which a relatively large number of anchor points are specified, the system is run for a time in autonomous mode and then halted for the evolving layout to be subjected to human review and possible modification by establishing additional anchor points. This is evident from the limitations of the heuristic used for assignment of adjacent departments. The best-first strategy, in which adjacent assignments are made based on the lowest value of the constraint evaluation function, represents a rather 'short-sighted' strategy, which in addition is sensitive to the choice of anchor points. The level of spatial reasoning is also rather primitive. Nonetheless, this system does demonstrate how stored constraint knowledge coupled with automatic constraint scoring can be used effectively in the iterative search for configurations that are acceptable with respect to several incommensurate criteria. This is a characteristic that more conventionally based factory layout systems, such as CRAFT and CORELAP, do not possess.

13.1.6 Dynamic analysis of factory layout

Having chosen a set of permanent manufacturing resource entities and configured them in locational space, FACSIM allows the performance of a dynamic analysis of how this set of resources and their configuration will respond to the workloads imposed by various levels of customer demand. This is performed by simulating the material flow through the plant to expose potential bottlenecks and their causes, to examine the adequacy of storage areas to cope with peak expected work-in-progress inventories, to establish whether an adequate number of transport vehicles has been allowed, and to examine the performance of different types of planning and scheduling strategy.

The manner in which material items flow through the factory and are converted to other material items is described in terms of a 'manufacturing resources network' similar to that described for the ISTOP system in section 12.1.3. An example of this network is shown in Figure 13.3, in which the nodes are objects in an object- oriented database. Each material item is linked to the alternative processes by which it can be produced through an intermediate node (i.e., an object) labelled OR which means that the processes are to be interpreted as *alternatives*. Each process node is linked to the individual operations of which it consists through a node labelled either ORDERED–SEQ (meaning the operations are sequential and ordered as indicated), UNORDERED–SEQ (meaning the operations are sequential but have no implied ordering) and CONCURRENT (meaning the operations may be performed in parallel). Each process is also linked to the input materials required (OR nodes may be used to indicate alternative materials), and operations are linked to the manufacturing resources required. Thus in Figure 13.3, process 106-Pa for making part P106 requires either Part 99a or 99b, and consists of three ordered sequential operations, of type Mill–Part , Inspect and Transport. The production resources required by each operation are linked to the operation, with OR nodes indicating substitutable resources. Thus operation **Mill–Part** requires an operator and either of machines MM21 or MM27. Processes can include withdrawal from stock, as well as manufacturing processes, so one of the alternative processes for producing P106 is an **Unstock** process. Transport is regarded as an operation that changes the location attribute of a material item, and the sequence of operations involved in each process must include the

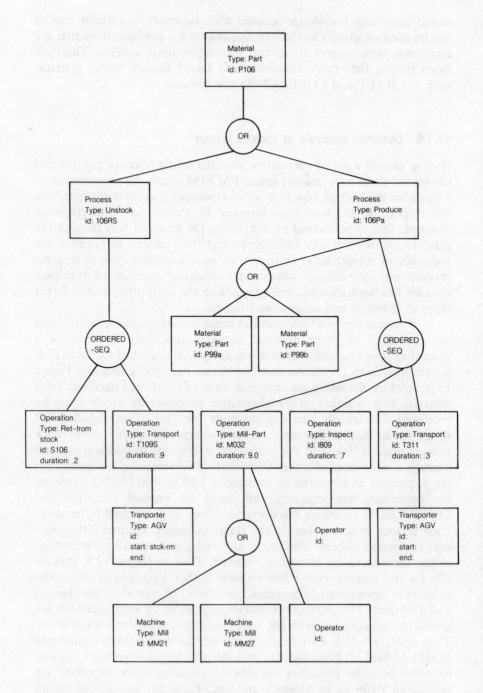

Figure 13.3 Section of a manufacturing resource network representation in FACSIM.

transport operations and associated resources (e.g., AGVs) required to move the item from one point to another in the factory. Varying degrees of instantiation of these entities correspond to plans specified at various levels of detail.

Simulation of the flow of transient material entities through the factory involves the superposition of dynamic 'behaviour patterns' on the knowledge structures representing the permanent factory entities. Specifying system behaviour involves introducing the notion of *time* into the representation in the form of a simulated clock, a calendar, a time-line, time intervals, entity instantiations that have a **temporal** element in that they have scheduled times at which they are due to be created, deleted or modified, and a *simulation manager* that schedules events on an event stack.

FACSIM has a simulated clock which can be set to varying time units, and is advanced automatically on a 'next-event' basis where 'events' occur at the times when various entity instantiations are scheduled to be created, deleted or modified. For example, in Figure 13.4 the end-time in the instantiation of an **operation** entity, representing a particular part being processed on a particular machine, represents the time at which the operation is due to end and the entity deleted. This is scheduled as an event by the simulation manager and placed on an event stack. Events on the stack are processed in order of their scheduled times, with each event possibly involving the creation, modification, or deletion of several other entity instantiations. For example, the deletion of the above operation instance would result in the passing of a message to the instantiation of the appropriate machine entity to change its status to available, and this in turn would send a message to the appropriate queue entity to select, from current members of the queue, the batch of materials with the highest priority to be instantiated as being 'in-process'. These activities are initiated and propagated by rules attached to the slots of individual entities which define their behaviour and can pass messages to other entities.

In order to initiate a simulation, the user must activate appropriate sections of the manufacturing resources network for the item(s) whose production is to be simulated. This is achieved by displaying the network for a particular product on screen and indicating with the cursor the

Mill–Part

      is–a: operation
        id: M032
      Part: P99b
  Start-Time: 342
   End-Time: 351

Figure 13.4   Time instantiation of an 'operation' entity in FACSIM.

top-level part for which production is required (this can be the end product, or one of its sub-assemblies or components) and the 'bottom-level' part which is an input to the simulation. This specifies the simulation boundaries and allows simulation of anything from the complete factory operation to operations on a single part using a single machine. It is also possible to specify a single or a set of alternative process paths for each part (including a withdrawal from stock process) and rules for the determination of which process plan to select, batch sizes for each process, and statistical generation of random events such as machine breakdowns according to user-chosen statistical distributions. The rules determining the way in which material items are generated into the system, and the order in which a queue is processed, can be arranged in the form of hierarchical rule bases which can include algorithmic computations and perform quite complex inferences. The system is thus capable of evaluating alternative production scheduling strategies in addition to alternative production resource configurations.

The system has animated output which allows the user to see the progress of the simulation on screen. The factory layout display is based on that developed during the layout planning stage. Comprehensive statistical output on machine utilisatations, average queue waiting times, etc. are also presented.

As described, the simulation component of FACSIM requires the user to design the types of simulation experiment required to analyse comprehensively a given factory layout, and to interpret the results. A natural extension to FACSIM is the introduction of intelligent front and back ends to perform this automatically. It is possible that sets of rules could be developed which, for example, would allow the user to specify the desired value of some criterion of performance which would then automatically drive the model towards goal achievment by performing experiments coupled with the iterative adjustment of a set of control parameters or strategies. The criteria might be such things as the average time taken by jobs to move through the system, machine utilisation, or average number of jobs late. Decision variables might be batch size, machine capacity, size of storage buffers or sets of alternative machine loading rules. Automation of this type of analysis would require stored inferencing rules to deduce the best parameters to vary at any stage, based on an interpretation of the results of the previous simulation run. Thus a typical rule which might operate in a a goal-seeking simulation might be:

> If goal is maximise utilisation of work centre x
> and mean queue length at work centre y < mean queue length at
> work centre x
> and work centre y is sole feeder of work centre x
> and capacity can be added to work centre y
> then activate rule to increase capacity of work centre y.

This rule stores the piece of knowledge that if the capacity utilisation of some work centre is to be maximised and if this is fed by another work centre which is causing a bottleneck in the system, then the utilisation of the first work centre can be augmented by increasing the capacity of the feeding work centre. The action part of the rule might be to activate a set of rules for increasing this capacity subject to the constraints on how this might be achieved.

Although knowledge of this nature is not currently implemented in FACSIM, a number of systems do exist in which the design and analysis of simulation experiments is at least partially automated, although according to Reddy (1987) this is likely to present challenging problems. Both SIMULATION CRAFT (since renamed 'simpak') of the Carnegie Group (Reddy et al, 1986) and SIMKIT of Intellicorp (Stelzner et al, 1987) allow goals defining performance criteria of model components to be attached to the associated objects, and the user is informed of whether goals are met or not. A research group at the Hungarian Institute for Coordination of Computer Techniques in Budapest have added a set of time-handling primitives to PROLOG to produce a simulation system that allows the user to specify the model in statements of first-order predicate calculus, and to specify the goals to be achieved. The run time interpreter then attempts to find a parameter set that meets the goals (Futo, 1984). Yet in spite of these developments, it appears that a viable knowledge-based simulation system that effectively captures simultaneously the knowledge of a simulation expert and the required knowledge of the problem domain is still some distance away.

13.2   EXGT: A knowledge-based system for Group Technology

13.2.1   Limitations of conventional GT algorithms

One of the goals of Group Technology is the grouping of parts and machines in such a way that individual groups of machines can be identified which can be dedicated to specific families of similar parts. One way of identifying such machine groups and part families is by Production Flow Analysis in which a part/machine 'incidence matrix' is set up. Positive values for elements of this matrix indicate that the corresponding part is processed on the corresponding machine (the value of the element can represent a property of the process, such as its duration). The objective is then to try and decompose this matrix into separable submatrices which represent non-overlapping groups of parts and machines.

Although conventional algorithms for doing this exist, problems arise in their application to realistic GT problems for the following reasons:

(1)   Most part/machine matrices are not completely separable: the presence of a small number of 'overlapping' parts requiring processing on otherwise independent machine groups can cause the algorithm to fail.

(2)   Constraints may exist on the size and composition of machine groups which are difficult to represent algorithmically.

(3)   The large size of the matrix for realistic industrial situations (potentially of the order of 2000 parts and 200 machines) causes problems of massive combinatorial complexity for a conventional algorithm when the previous two factors are taken into account.

13.2.2   The basis of EXGT

Kusiak (1988) has developed a method for solving this problem which combines the algorithmic approach with the reasoning capability of a knowledge based system. The resulting system (which he names EXGT) uses an easily extendable set of production rules containing both knowledge of procedures for handling situations in which constraints on machine groupings are violated, and knowledge of strategies for dealing with overlapping parts which would prevent the algorithm from identifying part families that could otherwise be processed on independent machine groups. These productiom rules interact with the algorithm in a so-called 'tandem' architecture (Figure 13.5) which achieves a synergy between the pure knowledge-based approach and the pure algorithmic approach.

The system makes use of an algorithm originally due to Iri (1968) and extended by Kusiak and Chow (1987). Examples of how this algorithm works using (a) a separable incidence matrix and (b) a non-separable incidence matrix, are shown in Figure 13.6. In these diagrams, the column indices correspond to parts and the row indices correspond to machines. A 1 entry in the matrix indicates the corresponding part is processed on the corresponding machine.

The first step is to draw a horizontal line through any row of the matrix containing non-zero elements. The line corresponds to a machine and the columns containing the non-zero elements represent the family of parts processed on this machine. A set of vertical lines is then drawn through all the non-zero elements crossed by the first horizontal line. The non-zero elements on these vertical lines will now correspond to the other machines on which the parts of the initial family are processed. A further horizontal line drawn through each of these elements will identify other parts involved due to their also being processed on these other machines. This procedure is repeated until either all rows and columns have been crossed with lines, in which case the matrix is non-separable (Figure

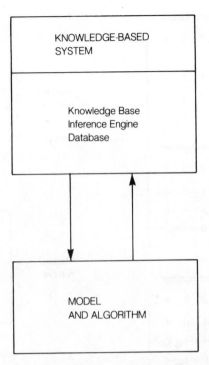

Figure 13.5 The 'tandem' architecture of EXGT.

13.6a), or a subset of non-zero elements is identified in which every element is crossed by one vertical and one horizontal line (Figure 13.6b). In the latter case, a separable family of parts (indicated by the vertical lines) exists which are processed on a separable group of machines (indicated by the horizontal lines). These machines and parts are removed from the matrix, and the same procedure is repeated for the remaining matrix to see if further separable groups exist.

The tandem architecture of EXGT uses a modified version of this algorithm and allows it to interact with a knowledge-based system to handle situations in which constraints are violated. The application of these constraints also enables the knowledge-based system to handle the problem of overlapping parts.

Typical generalised constraints on machine groupings are as follows:

C1 The size of the part family should be such that total available processing time on each machine in the group is not exceeded.

C2 The number of machines in each group should not exceed some upper limit.

C3 Certain machines must always be included in the same group due to technological considerations.

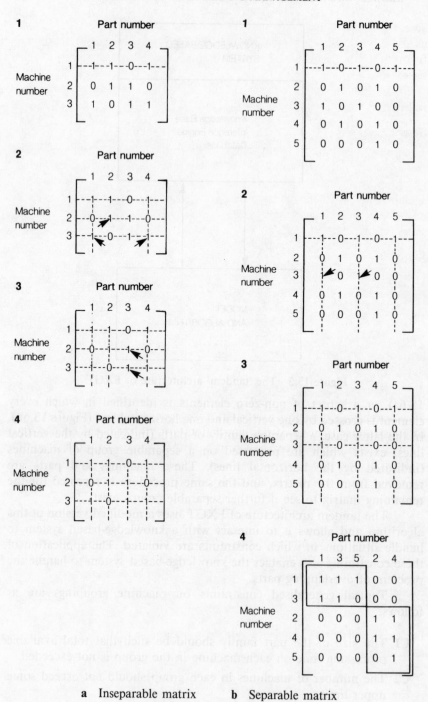

a   Inseparable matrix   b   Separable matrix

Figure 13.6 The basic EXGT 'crossing' algorithm.

These constraints are obviously not exhaustive, and as many constraints as are required in a particular production environment can be handled by further modifications to the algorithm, and increasing the size of the rule base.

In the modified version of the algorithm, the steps proceed as follows:

Step 1

The knowledge-based system selects a minimal set of machines such that constraint C3 is satisfied (in the absence of this constraint a single machine is selected either at random or according to an environment specific rule which incorporates the knowledge that some machines make more logical starting points than others). The selected machines are potential candidates for a machine group.

Step 2

Horizontal lines are drawn through the row corresponding to each of the machines selected in step 1.

Step 3

Vertical lines are drawn through each non-zero element crossed by a horizontal line. Parts corresponding to these lines are potential candidates for a part family.

Step 4

The current machine group and part family are evaluated for satisfaction of constraints. If none of the constraints are violated and all non-zero elements are crossed by one vertical and one horizontal line, the algorithm proceeds to step 7. If at least one constraint is violated, the knowledge-based system is invoked. Otherwise the algorithm proceeds to step 5.

Step 5

For each non-zero entry crossed only by a vertical line, a horizontal line is drawn. If there are no more non-zero elements crossed only by the horizontal lines, the algorithm proceeds to step 4, otherwise it proceeds to step 6.

Step 6

For each entry crossed only by a horizontal line, a vertical line is drawn, and the algorithm proceeds to step 3.

Step 7

A machine group and a part family are formed from the current set of horizontal and vertical lines. These are removed from the matrix and the algorithm proceeds to step 1.

The critical intervention of the knowledge-based system in this procedure is at the point where one of the constraints is found to be violated. Depending on the conditions, a number of actions may be implemented automatically. Some of these actions may involve determining alternative routings for parts, or elimination of parts from the incidence matrix and assigning them to a functional routing. It is by this means that 'overlapping' parts become eliminated.

Some typical rules that might be invoked by the knowledge-based system to handle constraint violations are given below.

> IF Constraint C1 is violated for machine i
> THEN Attempt to satisfy constraint by either:
>   (1) adding an additional identical machine to the group
> OR   (2) considering alternative process plans for parts
> OR   (3) using procedure P1 to eliminate parts from the matrix and
>   assign them to functional routings
> IF Constraint C2 is violated for machine group k
> THEN Randomly remove machines from this cell until constraint C2
>   is satisfied.
> IF Constraint C3 is violated for machine group k
> THEN Add requisite machines to group k in such a way that
>   constraints C2 and C3 are satisfied.

The procedure P1 for selecting parts for elimination from a potential family due to the machine capacity constraint can take various forms. In the example given by Kusiak, a knapsack algorithm is used in which a subset of parts is chosen for inclusion in the family which results in a maximisation of the total production costs of producing the family on the group of machines. This has the effect of including in the family those parts which make heavy use of machines in the group, and eliminates those which make only peripheral utilisation (such as only using one machine). The overlapping parts whose processing is distributed over several potential groups thus tend to be removed first. Note that it is because of the capacity constraint C1 that the overlapping parts are actually removed, resulting in the convergence of the algorithm to the identification of a set of separable submatrices, and preventing it merely from forming one large machine group and one large part family. For example, in the situation shown in Figure 13.7, a capacity check on constraint C1 might indicate that the constraint is violated. Assuming the only way to satisfy this constraint is to remove a part from the family, application of the knapsack algorithm would suggest removal of part 2 since it is only processed on one machine in the group. This part would be assigned to be produced using a functional routing and would be removed from the incidence matrix, resulting in the formation of the groups and families shown.

Naturally, the example rules given are more formally and concisely expressed in EXGT. The knowledge base is reported to contain about 25

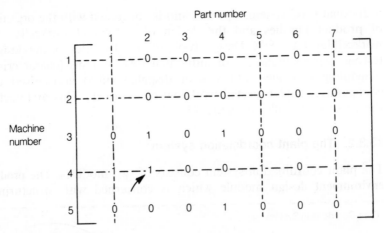

Addition of part 2 to current part group 1,5,7 (processed on machine group 1,2,4) exceeds capacity constraint C1. Part 2 is excluded from group and assigned functional routing, since it only uses one machine in group.

Figure 13.7 Use of constraint violation to eliminate 'overlapping' parts.

rules and meta-rules, handling additional constraints relating to such things as material handling requirements and machine closeness, with an anticipated expansion of up to 50 rules.

13.3 A tool for the design of production activity control systems

The CIM Research Unit at University College, Galway in Ireland are developing a set of artificial intelligence based tools for the design of systems for Production Activity Control (PAC) and the testing of strategies in discrete parts manufacturing environments (Duggan and Browne, 1988). The objective of this work is to develop an 'application generator' which acts as a knowledge-based decision-support system for the generation of PAC systems customised to specific production environments. The term PAC is here understood to mean the detailed planning and control of shop floor operations in the short term (allocation of jobs to work centres, deployment of operators, material handling systems to be used to transport batches, etc.). It corresponds to the operational control level of the production management hierarchy, and is specifically concerned with shop floor production.

13.3.1 The overall design approach

The overall design approach is to examine the problem of PAC design at two levels: the plant coordination level, and the individual cell level. The Plant Coordination System serves to structure the environment in which individual PAC systems operate, and is concerned with the organisation of product families and the design of individual workcells. At the workcell level, the PAC Design Tool provides facilities for the design and testing, using simulation, of individual PAC systems (characterised by scheduling strategies and sets of dispatch rules) customised to the configuration and expected workflow of each cell. This architecture is shown schematically in Figure 13.8.

13.3.2 The plant coordination system

The plant coordination system consists of two modules. The **production environment design** module which is concerned with structuring the

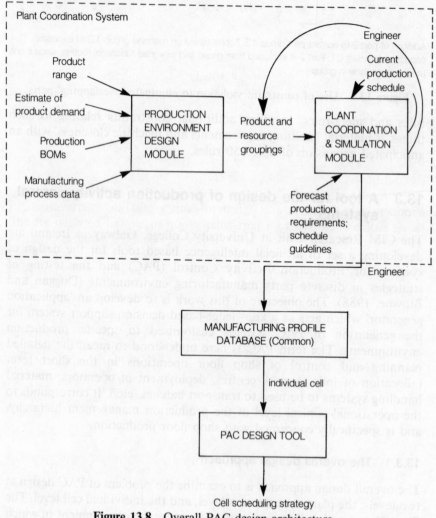

Figure 13.8 Overall PAC design architecture.

manufacturing environment in terms of product groups and categorised resources, and the **plant coordination and simulation** module which simulates various schedules at the plant level using alternative sets of product groupings and resource categorisations so that the relative effectiveness of different alternatives can be examined.

Production environment design module

The inputs to this module are:

- a list of the products being produced;
- manufacturing process data, the resources, equipment and operators required, failure rates, repair times and capacities;
- product bills of materials;
- forecast demand for each product;

The module itself uses a rule-based system which organises products into groups based on the criteria of commonality of components, common process requirements, and common set-ups. Each product has a weighting factor with respect to a particular group which is determined from the differences between the product and the group, measured in terms of these three criteria. The value of the weighting factor determines whether to add a product to a group or to consider the next product on the list. The procedure is repeated until all products are assigned to groups. Production resources are assigned to groups and are characterised as being either dedicated to a particular group or shared between groups. The process is iterative, in that when a new product is added to a group, a capacity check is performed to establish whether the new production requirements of the group will exceed the capacity of production resources assigned to the group, otherwise new assignments must be made.

The outputs from the module are a list of product groupings with their member products, and a list of resources categorised as shared or dedicated, the dedicated resources being assigned to specific product groupings.

Plant coordination and simulation module

The inputs to this module are:

- a list of product groupings with their member products and associated bills of materials;
- a list of resources dedicated to each group and resources shared between groups;

- a production schedule for the current month giving the production requirements for each product;
- a forecast of monthly production requirements for the following month.

The functions of the module are as follows. First, production requirements for each product are smoothed over the number of working days in the month. Second, using bill of materials information, quantities of components required to meet this schedule are generated. Third, product groupings, component requirements and resource assignments are used to compute the bottleneck resources. Fourth, a plant scheduling policy is developed, defined by a set of rules which determine the order in which batches are processed at individual workcells (these may allow process of batches in order of earliest due date, shortest processing time, or more specific rules designed to minimise the effect of potential bottlenecks). Finally, the proposed product groupings, resource categorisations and plant scheduling policy are tested using a **simulator** which consists of a **dispatcher** (which controls the flow of batches according to either a 'push' or 'pull' principle and allows the user to experiment with the scheduling policy), a shop floor **emulator** which simulates the flow of work through the shop floor including machine breakdowns using a Petri Net representation (described in more detail in the next section), and a **monitor** which collects statistics on cell utilisation, work-in-progress, and throughput time.

The overall plant coordination task is intended to take the form of a series of iterations between the Production Environment Design module and the Plant Coordination and Simulation module, in which experimentation takes place with alternative product groupings, resource categorisations and scheduling policies to find the most effective combination. This is followed by application of the **PAC design tool** which is concerned with the examination of detailed scheduling policies at the individual cell, rather than the plant level, after the product groupings and resource categorisations have been established.

13.3.3 The PAC design tool

The architecture of the PAC design tool is shown in Figure 13.9. The individual modules interact with each other through an **application network** which is a distributed software bus enabling the building blocks to communicate with each other in a controlled environment.

The **manufacturing profile database** allows the user to specify in detail the manufacturing data for each cell in terms of:

- resource data: details of individual workstations, buffers and moving devices, in terms of capacities, breakdown rates, etc.

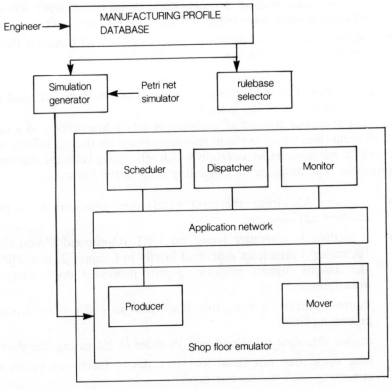

Figure 13.9   PAC Design Tool Architecture.

- stock data: data on all the materials used such as buffers where stored, maximum and current quantities, reorder points and lead times.

- product/process data: details on operations required to convert raw materials into products; operations are classified as combinative, disjunctive, sequential and inspection (Figure 13.10), and details

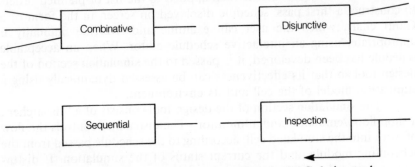

Figure 13.10   Types of process recognised by PAC design tool.

comprise data such as process times, set-up times, work stations where processes takes place and input and output buffers.

- planned order data: details of planned orders with release dates, due dates, and batch sizes.

The data is stored in a relational database which may be accessed by other building blocks of the system.

The **scheduler** consists of a library of scheduling rules, and a rule base of meta-rules which perform reasoning based on the manufacturing profile of a cell in order to ascertain which scheduling rules are the most appropriate. The basic set of scheduling rules in the library are:

- Johnsons Algorithm, the most widely used algorithm for a two machine environment;
- a bottleneck scheduler based on OPT (Optimised Production Technology) principles described briefly in Chapter 2; this scheduler assigns highest priority to jobs processed on bottleneck workstations;
- shortest processing time rule (load jobs in order of increasing processing time);
- earliest due date rule (load jobs in order of increasing due date);
- least slack time rule (load jobs in order of increasing values of remaining slack before due date).

The meta rulebase contains heuristic knowledge about which rules are best matched to specific manufacturing situations. This set of rules therefore analyses the situation as described in the manufacturing profile database, in order to make a recommendation. For example, if a potential bottleneck is noted, the bottleneck scheduler will be recommended. If no bottleneck is found, one of the other schedulers will be recommended according to the user's current criteria.

The chosen scheduler is then applied to the list of planned orders to construct a 'first pass' schedule displayed on screen in the form of a Gantt chart, which the user can examine and override manually if appropriate, using an interactive schedule editor. When an acceptable schedule has been developed, it is passed to the **simulation** section of the design tool so that its effectiveness can be assessed dynamically using a simulation model of the cell and its environment.

The **simulation** section of the design tool consists of a 'dispatcher', a shop floor 'emulator' and a 'monitor'. The dispatcher controls the flow of work into the simulated cell, according to the schedule passed from the scheduling module, and the current status of the simulation. If disturbances occur, the dispatcher attempts to resequence jobs in such a way that the original schedule will be recovered. The shop floor emulator simulates the processing of jobs on individual resources, including breakdowns. The monitor keeps track of stock levels in buffers, production resource status (busy, available or down) and job status, and acts as a real-time feedback mechanism, sending messages to the dispatcher on the status of the simulation, and on disturbances (such as machine breakdowns) which occur. The dispatcher uses this information in deciding which job should be dispatched next and when, using a number of alternative dispatch strategies. The monitor also collects statistics on buffer stock levels, work station utilisation, and so on.

The PAC design tool allows detailed testing of a variety of detailed scheduling and dispatch strategies for the control of individual workcells within a particular plant environment which has been developed through the iterative application of the modules of the plant coordination system. When an appropriate plant environment and set of detailed control strategies for the individual workcells within the plant environment have been developed, the move to **implementation** essentially involves the replacement of the shop floor emulator with the shop floor reality (as shown in Figure 13.11), since the detailed production control functions developed and tested using the emulator are precisely those which would be used in a real situation.

13.3.4 Shop floor emulation using Petri nets

The shop floor emulator section uses a Petri net representation to simulate operations on the shop floor. A Petri net (of which an example is shown in Figure 13.12) is basically a directed graph structure with two types of node called 'places' (represented by circles) and 'transitions' (represented by bars). Places are states of the system being represented by the net, in this case the shop floor. Places may be 'marked' by the assignment of 'tokens', and the set of places with one or more tokens assigned, collectively represents the current state of the system. 'Transitions' are the actions that can occur and that change the state of the system (such as the loading of a job on a resource and the breakdown of a machine). Each transition has a set of 'input' places representing the conditions for that transition to occur, and 'output' places which collectively represent the state of the system after the transition. If all the places linked to a transition are marked, the conditions for the transition are satisfied and the transition can occur. A Petri net executes by firing transitions which have all their input places marked. This results in the removal of one token from each of the input places, and the deposit of one token in each of the output places, which can fire further transitions.

A 'timed' Petri net associates times with transitions which may now represent the start and finish of activities such as job processing,

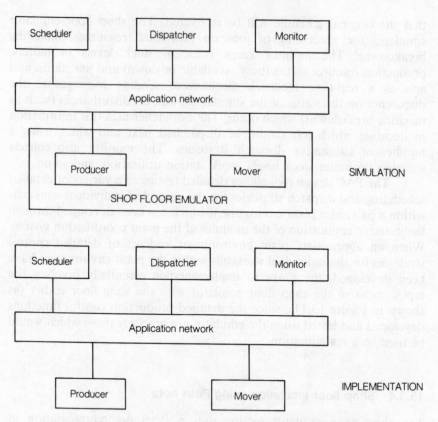

Figure 13.11 From PAC design to PAC implementation.

with one transition (e.g., start processing job) scheduling the time of another transition (e.g., end processing job). Another condition for a transition to fire is that the scheduled time of a transition must equal the 'current clock time', which is advanced to the next scheduled transition when all transitions scheduled for the current clock time have fired. The sequential firing of transitions and reassignment of tokens to places can thus be used as a convenient way to represent the dynamic evolution of events on the shop floor.

It will also be observed that there is a strong similarity between a Petri net representation of the dynamic evolution of a system over time, and a production rule representation of knowledge. Petri net input places correspond to the conditional parts of production rules, marked places correspond to satisfied conditions, the firing of a transition corresponds to the firing of a rule, and the marking of a transition's output places (and removal of markers from input places) corresponds to the action part of the rule. This similarity has been exploited in the shop floor emulator, which uses a production rule type inference engine in a forward chaining

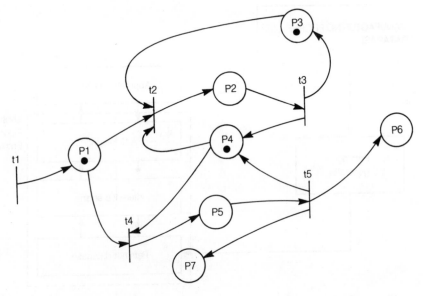

t1:   order arrives
t2:   operator 1 starts on machine 1
t3:   operator 1 finishes on machine 1
t4:   operator 2 starts on machine 1
t5:   operator 2 finishes on machine 1

P1:   order waiting for machine 1
P2:   operator 1 working with machine 1
P3:   operator 1 idle
P4:   machine 1 idle
P5:   operator 2 working with machine 1
P6:   order waiting to be processed on machine 2
P7:   operator 2 idle

Figure 13.12   Example of a Petri net.

mode to control the execution of the Petri net. The system actually contains a Petri net generator which automatically constructs appropriate Petri net data structures from the detailed description of the manufacturing environment contained in the manufacturing profile database, as shown in Figure 13.13. The resulting data structures are stored in a Petri net database which is read by the inference engine to select the next event to be executed. When this has occurred, it constructs appropriate messages about the current shop floor status to send, via the application network, to the monitor and dispatcher.

A significant feature of this system is the **separation** of the control modules from the shop floor emulator. In most manufacturing-oriented simulation tools, the control strategy is embedded in the simulation

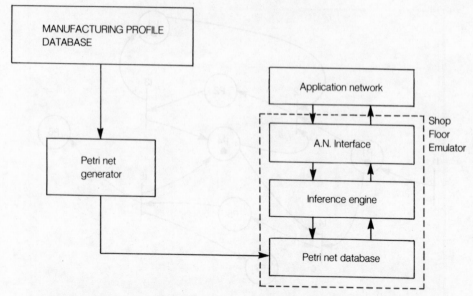

Figure 13.13 Automatic Petri net generation in the PAC design tool.

model itself, and only limited types of control strategy can be modelled. In this system, the modular separation of control from the simulation allows control strategies of virtually any degree of sophistication to be developed, either independently or by arranging the predefined scheduling building blocks, and then tested on the shop floor emulator. In addition, it allows the control system developed for the emulator to become the control system for the production cell itself, since implementation simply involves replacement of the emulator with the actual system. In this sense the system becomes a true 'application generator', avoiding the additional task of having to redevelop the system for the actual rather than the simulated environment.

Part IV

APPLICATIONS TO MANUFACTURING TECHNOLOGY

The next two chapters review some applications of knowledge-based systems to areas of manufacturing technology, including product design, process planning, diagnostic maintenance and quality control. The first chapter examines the potential of each area for knowledge-based systems support, with a brief state of the art review. The second chapter discusses some applications in more detail.

CHAPTER 14
Knowledge-based Systems for Manufacturing Technology — a Review

14.1 Knowledge-based systems in product design

Product design starts with the development of an overall product concept which satisfies functional and performance requirements and is manufacturable within existing or obtainable technology within a specified budget. This phase is performed according to the somewhat ill-defined rules of good engineering synthesis. Detail is then progressively added to this concept down to the level of a complete set of drawings, specifications of materials, hardness, finish information, tolerances, etc. The knowledge constraining the search space in this phase comprises factual knowledge of the full range of different types of material from which the product may be constructed, laws governing spatial relationships, the laws of physics including many common sense laws of cause and effect, and the laws of good engineering practice. In the analysis stage, the design is subject to detailed scrutiny in the context of the range of operating conditions that may be encountered, it is tested in detail for a variety of these operating conditions, the manufacturability is analysed, a prototype is constructed, and a search is made for existing components that might be used in the product thereby avoiding the design of new components.

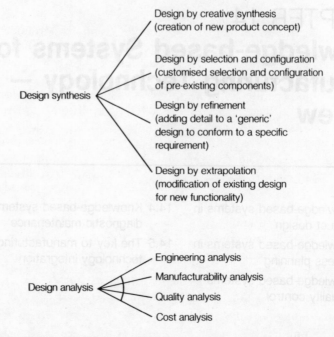

Design synthesis
- Design by creative synthesis (creation of new product concept)
- Design by selection and configuration (customised selection and configuration of pre-existing components)
- Design by refinement (adding detail to a 'generic' design to conform to a specific requirement)
- Design by extrapolation (modification of existing design for new functionality)

Design analysis
- Engineering analysis
- Manufacturability analysis
- Quality analysis
- Cost analysis

Figure 14.1 Classification of design tasks for knowledge-based support.

14.1.1 Design synthesis systems

Knowledge-based systems for product design synthesis have so far been limited to narrow domains. For example, Brown and Chandrasekaran (1986) report an automated design system for the design of air cylinders. This system is based on top-down refinement in which a number of specialist knowledge sources are brought in to the design process at various levels of conceptual detail. Other automated design systems have been reported in equally narrow and structured product domains, with automated VLSI design being a major area of research.

When a basic product or a set of predefined basic product modules already exist, and these can be customised or combined in various ways to meet customer requirements, the design synthesis task becomes restricted to that of *selection* (mapping functional requirements on to attributes of an existing product line) and *configuration* (combining basic components or modules to make a finished product). The type of knowledge required for these tasks is often sufficiently structured and bounded that it can be represented in a knowledge-based system. Both tasks are in fact supported by knowledge-based systems in DEC where the XSEL system (McDermott, 1982a) is used by salespersons in the field to analyse customer requirements for computer systems and produce a comprehensive specification (containing typically 30-40 different items), whilst the XCCON/R1 system (McDermott, 1982b) is used for the detailed configuration of VAX and PDP11 computers to meet this specification. Both systems are production rule based and XSEL has a natural language interface. XCON/R1 was one of the first knowledge-based systems in operational use, and currently has over 4000 rules partitioned into separate configuration steps, which it uses in a forward chaining mode. It has been demonstrated that XCON consistently outperforms human configurers both in speed and accuracy. There are many other examples in manufacturing industry of complex products which need to be specially configured to customer requirements, and hence the scope for the use of knowledge-based systems in this field is wide.

There would seem to be considerable potential for capturing some of the more structured knowledge relating to the rules of good engineering practice that impose constraints, and thus reduce the search space associated with the detailed phases of more basic product design. For example, the knowledge that is called into play when deciding whether to join two pieces of metal by welding, gluing, rivetting, etc. is relatively well structured and could be represented in a knowledge-based system as a series of production rules. Another type of approach is reported by Dixon and Simmons (1983) and uses the concept of 'design by redesign' in which an initial design is input to the system and this is then automatically refined through a series of evaluation and redesign steps. Knowledge-based systems have also been applied to the task of *extrapolating* existing designs for other purposes. The EDISON system developed at UCLA (Dyer and Flowers, 1986) is capable of modifying current designs to meet new sets of functional requirements by setting up and pursuing subgoals relating to the new requirements. This system is exceptional in that it also has a reported brainstorming capability of generalising existing designs to create completely new types of device. The ALADIN system (Farinacci *et al*, 1986) takes the specification of the properties of an aluminium alloy, and alters the alloy's composition and thermo-mechanical processing to produce a new alloy which meets the customer's requirements.

The storage of knowledge about product designs (rather than simply product data) can facilitate the retrieval of previous designs which might enable components designed for other purposes to be used in the current design rather than redesigning the component from scratch. This knowledge is often not readily available and hence an important application of knowledge-based technology is in the intelligent retrieval of similar designs from the knowledge base. Fuzzy set approaches are potentially applicable as measures of similarity. Naturally, a major issue is how to represent the characteristics of the design. Conventional databases usually store characteristics in terms of a set of attributes or code by which the product or part can be retrieved when required. A typical classification system is DCLASS (Allen, 1986). However knowledge-based approaches in which products and parts are represented as collections of primitive features using frames or semantic networks, can allow inferential retrieval-based on complex stored relationships and class hierarchies from a semantic description of the characteristics of the part.

14.1.2 CAD databases and intelligent CAD systems

Conventional computer-aided design systems are predominantly *drafting* systems. The functionality they provide is oriented towards the creation, modification and deletion of graphic elements or primitives and the transformation of these elements and combinations of them in two and three dimensions by scaling and rotation. The graphic elements are stored in the form of *numerical arrays*, which allow a purely *geometric* representation of product and part features and relationships. No explicit semantic meaning is attached to the combination of geometric primitives that comprise the design. The semantic *interpretation* of the significance and *design intent* of the structures formed by combinations of geometric primitives such as faces, edges and vertices is an act of human mental processing which occurs when viewing the pictorial display of the representation on a screen. Computer stored 'libraries' of previous designs which are generated by these types of CAD system are confined to libraries of geometric data only. Other more semantically explicit information about the design must either be stored in a separate database, or must be must be input separately as a set of 'attributes' associated with the geometric data arrays defining the design shape.

If we consider briefly the functions that a design specification should fulfil, we immediately see that purely geometric characteristics represent only a small proportion of the information that is required from a fully specified design. Geometric information alone is insufficient to represent the mathematical and logical reasoning used by the engineer in synthesising the design.

The generally accepted functions of a manufacturing design specification may be summarised as follows:

(1)   To provide a *visual simulation* of ideas to assist in the creative process of design synthesis.

(2)   To communicate ideas between designers and manufacturing. personnel.

(3)   To archive the design in such a way that it can be retrieved on an appropriate set of identifying attributes.

(4)   To detail the logical relationships between the individual components of the design, and between components of different designs,

to allow for example, the sequence of assembly to be deduced, or components belonging to the same class to be identified.

(5)   To specify the *functionality* of each component of the design.

(6)   To specify engineering constraints on the design such as the material characteristics and tolerances of each component.

(7)   To allow verification of design functionality by providing sufficient information to simulate its performance.

(8)   To detail the individual manufacturing features of the design to drive a process plan generator.

(9)   To provide inputs to a generator for NC code for machining the part.

(10)   To provide inputs for an assessment of the *cost* and *manufacturability* of the design.

The conventional computer-aided design system with its predominantly drafting-oriented facilities clearly only fulfils the first two of these functions. To fulfil the remaining functions requires the storing of a large variety of different types of information about the design as a whole, and about the individual components or elements of which it is comprised, and the relationships between them. The complexity of these relationships necessitates a representation containing a rich variety of different data types and explicit semantic links. Although relational representations have been extended for use as CAD databases (see for example, Rasdorf, 1987) the only primitive supported by the relational representation is the simple relation, and data types are generally restricted to integer, string, Boolean, and real. Although these may be well suited to the representation of entities with a fixed set of simple attributes and a stable set of relationships, problems arise, for example, in the representation of geometric models of mechanical parts. When represented in the form of numerical arrays, these require a large number of different relations, giving long execution times for model manipulation and display. Another problem is that as designs evolve and new designs are produced, new interrelationships between the basic primitives are continually being defined. This implies that the database schema must undergo continuous dynamic modification, with each design potentially requiring a different data schema which will evolve during the design and only be complete when the design is fully specified.

In order to overcome the limitations inherent in the relational approach as a means of integrating geometric and other types of design information, increasing interest is being taken in the use of object-oriented representations for storing design specifications. These can contain both a wider variety of different data types, and an explicit user definable and extensible set of semantic relationships between data entities. Thus, not only can an object-oriented database store geometric information about a design and its individual components; it can also store their associated attributes, both single and multi-valued, the semantic relationships between components in terms of function, structure, and class hierarchy, constraints on values and relationships, and sets of rules which automatically infer the extent to which the design satisfies various engineering, cost and manufacturability criteria. The ability to represent class hierarchies with inheritance and default values would allow the storage of 'generic' designs which could be specialised to suit current precise needs.

The ability of an object-oriented database to contain active rules embodying various forms of *design knowledge* allows the possibility of automatic inferences being performed about the current state of the design, and thus gives rise to the possibility of the evolution of a new generation of **intelligent CAD** systems. These types of system would be classified as knowledge-based decision **support** systems in that their intent is not to fully automate the design process, but to provide intelligent assistance to the human designer at a much higher level than is provided by purely geometric modelling systems. Typical of such systems are WRIGHT (Fox and Baykan, 1985), the commercially available system ICAD, and IMDA (described in detail in the next chapter). An increasing number of these systems are moving from the R and D phase to commercial availability. The typical additional functionality of an intelligent CAD system, as compared to a normal CAD system, is shown in Figure 14.2.

However, a number of problematic areas still exist. Currently, one of the major areas of research is that of developing better techniques for representing design features and for automatically mapping them to manufacturing features for use in process planning systems. Conventional CAD systems generally produce two-dimensional drawings. Three-dimensional CAD databases tend to use Boundary Representation models in which objects are described in terms of faces, edges and vertices, since these do not impose the restrictions on the designer that can result from Constructive Solid Geometry representations in which features are modelled explicitly. Automatic recognition of manufacturing features from geometrically-oriented design databases is an approach being investigated (Woo, 1983, Henderson, 1986; Yoshiura *et al*, 1984; Golbogen *et al*, 1988). The representation of the topological relationships of the components in an assembly, and the making of inferences about the characteristics of the assembly processes required is another area receiving attention (Lee *et al*, 1985; Gairola, 1987). Another somewhat problematic area lies in the size and complexity of the resulting databases. Specification of a design to the level of detail described above will generate large requirements on memory, since each design will need a different combination of semantic links to express the relationships

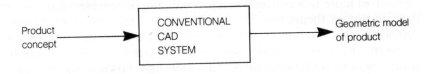

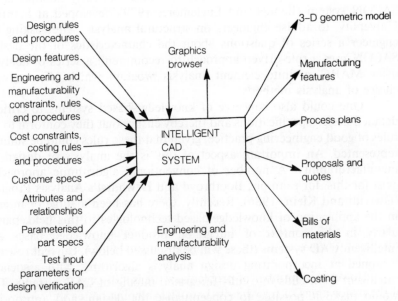

Figure 14.2   From CAD to intelligent CAD.

between its parts, and hence no two designs will be stored in the same form. From the conventional database point of view, this is equivalent to needing to specify a different conceptual data schema for every different design that is represented. This can result in problems if retrieval and manipulation of designs is to occur with acceptable response times. Increasingly rapid developments in computer hardware are, however, likely to result in implementations in which the physical and logical structures of the data are more closely matched, and these problems are greatly reduced.

14.1.3   Design analysis systems

Moving to the analysis phase of the design, much of the knowledge concerned with engineering analysis is concerned with relatively complex but well structured algorithms (e.g., finite element analysis) which lend themselves more to a conventional procedural-type representation, since they do not in themselves involve the type of massive combinatorial complexity that requires knowledge-based search. However, the decision of when and how to apply such analysis techniques is a symbolic reasoning process that does involve a search, and the knowledge required to reduce this search by matching analysis techniques to design specification and choice of analysis parameters could lend itself to representation in the form of production rules or frames. An early example is the SACON system (Bennet and Englemore, 1979) developed at Stanford University, to advise engineers on structural analysis. After asking the engineer a series of questions about the characteristics of the design, SACON uses a rule-driven approach to recommend a series of analyses using MARC, a finite element analysis program which offers a wide choice of analysis methods.

One could also conceive of knowledge-based systems to critique detailed design specifications and thereby ensure that they conform to the rules of good engineering practice, given that these rules could be suitably represented. An important aspect of this is the analysis of design for manufacturability. A number of conventional algorithmic approaches exist for this, for example, Boothroyd and Dewhurst's Analysis Program (Dwividi and Klein, 1986). Recently, there has been a surge of interest in the application of knowledge-based technologies to this field, particularly in the context of integrated product knowledge bases and intelligent CAD systems (these will be discussed below). Current research is aimed at incorporating design analysis algorithms with associated intelligent front ends into fully integrated intelligent CAD systems. This would make it possible to conceptualise the design, add appropriate detail using advice from the system about the various engineering constraints that must be satisfied, then have a detailed analysis of the design performed automatically.

In summary, it can be stated that except for the case of very limited problem domains, use of knowledge-based systems for product design will be confined to the decision-support role by handling some of the more structured subsets of the design problem such as checking designs conform to rules of engineering practice, searching for similar reusable designs already produced, working out cost and manufacturability implications and so on.

14.2 Knowledge-based systems in process planning

14.2.1 Characteristics of the problem

Process planning is concerned with the selection and specification of machines, tools and processes by which the product design can be realised, and with the temporal ordering of these processes. The constraints which operate on this activity come from the detailed product specification developed during the design phase, the production facilities and tools already available, along with information about their operating ranges, processing accuracies, etc. and time and cost budgets imposed by management. In addition to the factual knowledge of these constraints, the process planner will also require knowledge of the technological characteristics of a large number of production processes and the rules by which a particular process is chosen for a component of given specification.

As in product design, many alternative process plans may be feasible, and the process planner will be faced with a choice between alternatives, including such things as make or buy, whether to use a generative approach in which a process is designed from scratch, or a variant approach in which an existing process for a similar part is appropriately modified, whether or not special tools must be designed, which of the many plausible cut sequences to use, etc. The approach to this problem used by human process planners is basically one of **hierarchical** planning in which detail is progressively added to a rough-cut conceptual plan, with occasional backtracking until a completely specified and parameterised process plan is obtained (Figure 14.4). The first stage of the process plan is to select and sequence the basic processes involved and to assign each process to a facility. Having chosen the basic processes and their sequence, the detailed part of the plan must include such considerations as selecting tool slide arrangements, machine feeds and speeds in such a way that initial tool costs and set-up times are given due consideration, and choosing cutting paths and their sequences.

Clearly, the combinatorial problems of process planning result in a search space which could be comparable in its size to that for product design. However, the constraints imposed by a complete and detailed product design specification on the process plan are likely to limit the search more effectively than in the product design case where the constraints imposed by design requirements are in general underspecified.

Many existing attempts to computerise the actual planning process have concentrated on either the **variant** approach or the **generative**

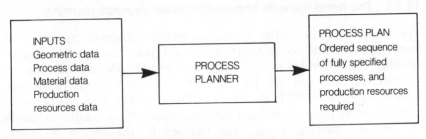

Figure 14.3 Process planning — inputs and outputs.

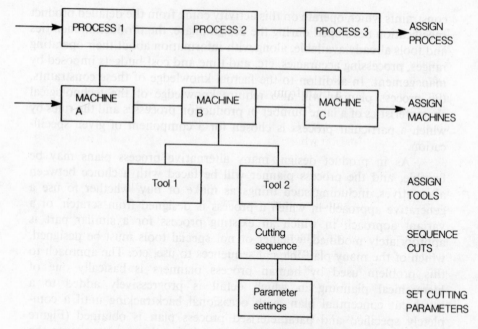

Figure 14.4   Hierarchical process planning.

approach. In the **variant** approach, compiled knowledge of the process plans for all parts previously designed is stored in a database referenced by the code to that part. If a new part is required the process plan of an existing part whose code indicates it has the closest similarity to the required part is retrieved from the database and is modified to make it suitable for the new part. The limitations of this approach stem from the difficulty of finding a coding system that guarantees that a small variation in the classification of a part will result in only a small variation in its processing. This has lead to increased interest in computerising the **generative** approach in which the process is designed from scratch.

14.2.2   The trend towards knowledge-based process planning

The majority of the earlier automated process planning systems have knowledge of how to generate a process plan from a given part specification embedded in the form of procedural code (e.g., Lockheed's GENPLAN described by Tulkoff, 1981, or the United Technology Research Centre's CMPP, described by Dunn, 1982). This places severe restrictions on their reasoning ability and makes them unable to search for solutions that have not been foreseen by the system designers. Obviously such systems are very limited in their knowledge domains.

A more promising approach, which would appear to have the potential of expanding the domain of parts for which process plans could be automatically designed, is the use of hierarchically-oriented, knowledge-based systems, supporting the method of successive refinement that appears to be used by human planners. These systems have the potential to refine a plan from any level of detail, regardless of whether the plan was generated by its own earlier activity or by a human. They could be used in a variety of modes, from totally automated process planning to a situation where a human defined a conceptual plan in terms of choice and sequence of process, and the system refined this plan to a complete specification. Again, the feasibilty of such an approach depends on the size of the knowledge base that would be required, with existing examples being limited to fairly narrow domains.

The majority of research work on knowledge-based, process-planning systems to date has been concentrated on the machining of mechanical parts. Most existing planners are also restricted to considering a limited range of parts and/or manufacturing features (e.g., rotational parts, prismatic parts with pocket features) and many address only a particular level of planning (generally either the 'machine-centred' level at which the individual processes required are identified and each process assigned to a machine with the appropriate capabilities, or the 'tool centred' level at which, given a process and a machine, the individual cuts are planned, together with tools, feeds and speeds, and cutting paths).

The computer representation of this type of process-planning knowledge requires some method of storing specifications of the target part and initial workpiece in a consistent and unambiguous way, the operations that can be performed, and the current inventory of all the production facilities available, with their detailed capabilities. Knowledge of how to select appropriate processes, machines, cuts and their sequence, tools, and cutting parameters from a description of the initial and required part characteristics, physical constraints, and measures of plan effectiveness with regard to minimisation of set-ups, etc. are generally represented using production rules. A summary of the required basic knowledge (in terms of facts and production rules) is shown in Figure 14.5.

One of the first knowledge-based process-planning systems was GARI (Descotte and Latombe, 1985) which was used for machine-centred planning of the milling of parts having faces meeting at 90 degrees. From a specialised user-provided description of the starting and required parts in terms of features and their geometric relationships, it applies a set of weighted production rules for the selection of machines and cuts using the method of successive refinement. Conflict resolution occurs by selecting the rule with the highest weight. It is also possible to generate multiple plans by backtracking to points of conflict and

Declarative knowledge

Geometric facts about workpiece

Qualification facts about workpiece (surface finish, tolerances)

Technological facts about workpiece (material hardness etc.)

Facts about machining operation characteristics

Facts about machine performance

Facts about tools

Facts about holding devices

Procedural knowledge

Rules for extraction of manufacturing features

Rules for operation selection

Rules for operation sequence

Rules for machine selection

Rules for tool selection

Rules for jig and fixture selection

Rules for machine and cutting parameter selection

Figure 14.5 Knowledge requirements for process planning.

reintroducing rules of lower weight. GARI has been further developed by the CAM-I consortium under the name XPS-E (Meyer, 1987), and is described in some detail in the next chapter.

Although the production rules in GARI are organised to use the representation of successive refinement, knowledge representation as such is not hierarchical. HI-MAPP (Hierachical and Intelligent Manufacturing Automated Process Planner, Berenji *et al*, 1986) uses a more explicitly hierarchical organisation of production rules for top-down planning of machines, processes and cuts, at several levels of abstraction. SIPP (Nau and Chang, 1985) uses frame-based knowledge representation and a best-first search strategy to produce least cost process plans according to user-defined cost objectives. XCUT (Hummel and Brooks, 1988) is a hierarchically-oriented rule-based system for planning production of machined parts using single set-up processing on a vertical milling machine. It uses a feature-based part description in which the manufacturing features of a part are represented in an object-oriented database and are hierarchically ordered in terms of their accessibility. An object-oriented system at the machine level described by Young *et al* (1987) uses hierachical representations of operations, machining centres and parts to generate part routings. There have recently been reports of many other process-planning systems, and like production scheduling, this is now a major area for the application of knowledge-based systems.

14.2.3 Feature recognition in process-planning systems

As we have seen, both GARI and XCUT use representation schema to describe parts based on the specification of the part's manufacturing features, and this is in fact a characteristic of the majority of automated process-planning systems currently in existence. A problem in this area is that no formal, generally accepted language for describing features currently exists (although the CAM-I consortium are working actively in this direction), and this has impeded the full integration of process planning with computer-aided design. Existing CAD systems often represent parts only in terms of two-dimensional drawings. Three-dimensional CAD systems either use a boundary representation (BREP) in which parts are specified in terms of faces, vertices and edges, or a volume representation based on constructive solid geometry (CSG) in which a part is defined in terms of a 'tree' structure of primitive volumes using the Boolean operations of union, intersection and difference. However, the feature representation schemata used by current process planning systems tend to be special purpose schemata developed specifically for the application. It is thus necessary to translate the design specification (in whatever form it exists) into the appropriate feature description language to drive the automated process-planning system. This is a procedure that in current systems requires human interpretation of the design specification to identify and specify the features in the form required by the process-planning system. Computer assistance can, of course, be provided for this task (for example, XCUT has a user interface in which the user manually identifies features from a solid model of the part using an electronic pointing device).

Currently, a major area of research is that of 'feature technology' (see Brimson and Downey, 1986), in which systems are being developed to identify automatically and extract the specifications of manufacturing features directly from a CAD representation. A typical system is reported by Goldbogen and Hoernes (1988). This uses a CAD file 'filter' which processes files produced by the CADAM system (a CAD system producing two-dimensional drawings) to produce a file of geometric primitives from which features are extracted using a rule base written in PROLOG. Another system reported by Henderson (1986) also uses PROLOG to recognise features from a boundary representation of volume of the part to be removed, described in terms of faces, edges and vertices. Features are face sets that satisfy relationships defined by production rules. Both of these systems appear relatively effective for recognising simple features, but tend to become inefficient for parts with a large number of complex features.

Another problem arises due to the fact that existing process-planning systems do not contain a complete geometric representation of the part in relation to its machining environment, and this can result in plans failing due to global geometric isses such as collisions between tools and fixtures. The problem of the *accessibility* of surfaces to tools at various stages of the plan also remains. Currently the only way of avoiding such problems is to build implicit surface knowledge of such issues into the production rules that develop the plan, or the rules that extract the features, rather than reasoning about them in terms of an explicit representation. Issues of non-monotonic reasoning require to be addressed in order to make progress in this area.

One possible method of eliminating the necessity for feature recognition systems is to conceptualise the design in terms of features in the first place. New generations of 'intelligent' CAD systems of the type described in Section 14.12 allow the designer to specify feature entities and associate them with combinations of geometric primitives in an object-oriented representation. A potential problem here, however, is that design features do not necessarily correspond to manufacturing features, and having to think in terms of manufacturing features can impose unnecessary constraints on the designer. A possible line of approach to this problem is the addition of rules to an intelligent CAD system to perform manufacturing feature recognition and an ongoing analysis of manufacturability, so that the designer is continuously made aware of the manufacturing implications of design features. This would represent a step in the direction of an integrated 'product knowledge base' in which a single unified and consistent description of the product is maintained, and can be examined, analysed and manipulated from a number of alterative 'views' or perspectives, depending on the phase of manufacturing which is the current focus of attention. Such a knowledge base would open up new possibilities for variant process planning, since more sophisticated reasoning methods for the retrieval of 'similar' products and parts could be used than can be implemented in a simple coding system.

Another required area of integration is between the process planner and the machines that execute the plan. Many existing prototype planning systems (GARI for example) do not plan to the level of detail required to generate NC code describing cutter trajectories, and produce *human* rather than *machine* readable output. Planning to the NC code level requires complete geometric specification of the work piece, its environment and feature accessibility so that such things as collisions between tools and fixtures can be avoided. However the conceptual problems of interfacing with part programming systems are not as great as those of interfacing with CAD systems, and considerable progress is being made in this area.

14.2.4 Model-based reasoning in process-planning systems

The majority of planning systems developed to date are restrictive in their domain of operation both in terms of the type of parts planned, and the level of planning addressed (i.e., machine centred or tool centred). It is difficult to predict the feasibility of developing a general purpose process-planner because of the vast amount of informal domain-dependent knowledge that would need to be captured. There could be major problems in organising and storing this knowledge, and in accessing it for individual applications. However, the majority of the knowledge that has currently been captured has been done so in the form of surface knowledge (i.e., rules and heuristics developed by human planners from their experience). A possible approach is to attempt to specify and encode the deeper knowledge on which these heuristics may be based, in terms of explicit predictive **models** of the different processes available. A system, currently oriented towards the metal cutting domain, which appears to be taking this line of approach, is reported by Kempf (1987). By including explicit models of the physical processes involved, and clearly separating these from a set of fairly general planning heuristics, it is anticipated that this system will be extendable from the metal cutting domain to domains such as metal joining, including welding, rivetting and bonding. Progress is also being made in the development of automatic planners within limited part type domains, that cover the complete spectrum of planning activities from selecting machines to the generation of cutting trajectories in NC code. Since this is conceptually fairly straightforward, it is likely that extensions in this direction will precede generalisations in the types of part or process considered.

14.2.5 Integration of process planning and production scheduling

A final important area of development is the integration of process planning with real-time scheduling systems. If the range of parts manufactured by a company is fairly stable, it may be reasonable to generate and store all the alternative feasible process plans regardless of current machine capacity constraints, and to select one of these plans at execution time according to the current machine loadings. In cases where the ordering of operations is not significant, it would be important in the initial plan to leave the ordering unspecified (i.e., to leave the plan as a **partial** ordering of operations). A complete ordering could then be performed opportunistically at the time of plan execution, according to availability of resources, and would become part of the production scheduling task (an example of the 'goal postponement' heuristic referred to in the paragraph on non-linear planning in section 10.2.4. However in a job shop, in which a larger proportion of parts may be one-off, complete process-plannning 'on the run' may be more appropriate. Real-time information on current machine loadings, material and tool availability would be included as additional constraints on the set of plans developed, which in turn would mean full integration of automated process planning and automated scheduling, either as a single system, or as a set of very closely communicating knowledge bases. This is particularly important for flexible manufacturing cells, and is in fact an essential prerequisite for full computer integration of manufacturing. As yet, the only reported systems of this nature operate in fairly restricted domains, but we can expect to see significant further developments in this area.

14.3 Knowledge-based systems in quality control

With the introduction of Total Quality Control (TQC), concepts of quality control are changing from the traditional technique of testing small samples from large batches towards programs for the systematic improvement of quality at source. Designing the process to stay within tolerance is better than accurate screening of the process output. This represents a change in emphasis from on-line quality control in which defects are detected *after* the fault has occurred, to off-line quality control in which the requisite quality is designed into the product and process, thus concentrating on defect prevention rather than defect detection.

Traditional quality control relies on the application of standard statistical quality control techniques, based on control charts, to indicate whether a batch should be accepted or rejected, based on the number of defectives found in a given sized sample. Modern QC concepts, however, advocate such techniques as 100% inspection, which may be achievable with small batch sizes and automatic inspection techniques, and the stopping of the production line when an unacceptable defect is discovered in order to analyse and correct the cause. Continuous monitoring and analysis of quality variables also facilitates the detection of possible problems *before* they occur. Non-contact methods of continuous inspection can involve the use of computer vision in which knowledge-based systems are used to recognise and analyse features which are indicative of quality problems. A typical such system for visual solder joint inspection is described by Bartlett et al (1987).

The responsibility for total quality control is pushed to individual production workers rather than being concentrated in a separate Quality Control department. An important part of the activity of determining the causes of defects is to have a good, and commonly available and accepted model of the production process in which the possible causes of poor quality are explicitly represented through a series of cause/effect relationships represented diagramatically (Ishikawa, 1976). This model can then be used as an analysis tool to assist in the diagnosis of the process problems that might be responsible for the defects.

Knowledge-based techniques have two potential roles to play in this process. First, stored knowledge of basic statistical analysis techniques coupled with automatic monitoring of quality variables can be used to analyse trends in these variables and provide warning signals when control limits are exceeded. The statistical techniques themselves would be represented in conventional algorithmic fashion, whereas the overall management of the analysis including choice of statistical model could be represented as a set of production rules or in a frame-based system. For example, a knowledge-based system for selecting control charts is desribed by Dagli and Stacey (1988). This selects the type of chart (P chart, NP chart, X-bar chart, etc.) and determines the best values of control limits and sampling interval using information on process mean and variability, number of defective items, and number of defects in each item produced,

Secondly, the cause/effect models of the production process used in pinpointing the possible causes of defectives could be represented in an object-oriented system in the form of semantic networks, in which the various causal relationships are represented by links. Models of each process could be stored and progressively elaborated by members of the workforce organised into 'quality circles', as more information came to light about the potential problems of the process, derived from defect occurrences and statistical analysis of quality variables. Depending on the degree of sophistication of the process model and the amount of deep knowledge represented, it might be possible to provide systems for the automatic diagnosis of cause given a particular set of symptoms using similar principles to those used by diagnostic systems employed for maintenance. In the initial stages of an implementation, however, it is more likely that such models would be used in an interactive support role, for which a good user interface would be required. This would be particularly important in encouraging members of the workforce actually to use and develop the model themselves in a participatory problem-solving mode. Greene (1989) has advocated the introduction of 'AI circles' (see Chapter 16) in which groups of workers are given the responsibility for developing their own knowledge-based systems using simple, low-cost tools for use on the shop floor. Diagnosis of quality problems would be an important application for this approach.

14.4 Knowledge-based systems in diagnostic maintenance

Diagnosis of impending or actual faults through the interpretation of patterns in operating data or observed characteristics of a current malfunction are generally performed by specialists who are trained in the interpretation of such patterns. Diagnostic knowledge may well involve several stages of reasoning and contain a mixture of knowledge gained by training, from maintenance and repair manuals, and through accumulated experience. After diagnosis, a number of decisions must be made, such as whether the facility should be taken out of production immediately or whether it could be kept running until the next planned maintenance period; to what extent should the rhythm of planned maintenance be changed after an unplanned repair? Which of the parts not yet worn out should be replaced during an unplanned repair?, and so on.

It is possible that a certain amount of this activity might be automated. In particular, the automatic monitoring of patterns in the operating data provided to a database by a shop floor data collection system could be effected by comparing them with patterns stored in a knowledge base using standard pattern-matching techniques. Such systems, an example of which is described by Cahill and Demers (1987), could be used in 'predictive control' in which conditions that warn of impending malfunction can be detected before the malfunction occurs. The process of diagnosis, although often requiring experienced human judgement, is nevertheless a relatively well defined and convergent task which embodies problem-solving heuristics that might be extracted from the human specialist. These might be represented in the form of a backward chaining production rule-based diagnostic system, which might perform such tasks as requesting for additional tests to be made in order to gain more evidence for or against a hypothesis. Issues of non-monotonic reasoning emerge here, and the use of Assumption Based Truth Maintenance systems is being investigated as a means of keeping track of possibly conflicting hypotheses and their modification in the light of accumulating evidence (see for example, de Kleer and Williams, 1987). More advanced representations can involve deep knowledge of the functional and structural relationships between different components of the facility (expressed in semantic network form containing qualitative and quantitative information) and these might be used for diagnosis of more problematic faults. Much of the early research on this form of representation was directed towards the diagnosis of faults in electronic circuits (e.g., Davis, 1984) where problems tend to be better defined, although it is now being used increasingly in other areas.

A very large number of diagnostic systems have been reported, mostly for use as knowledge-based advisory systems (implying they can suggest various types of further test to assist the diagnosis, and they contain good explanation facilities). For example, Hakami and Newborne (1983) describe a very successful system using Bayesian reasoning to diagnose equipment faults in a steel rolling mill. UMXD (Mina, 1987) is a system for diagnosing machine faults using model-based reasoning. FF (Savory, 1985) uses a predicate logic representation implemented in PROLOG to diagnose faults in the Nixdorf 8832 computer in an online environment. TURBOMAC (Stuart and Vinson, 1985) is a rule-based system containing 4000 rules for the diagnosis of the cause of vibrations in large turbomachinery. ET (Herrod, 1987) uses a rule-based representation to assist technicians in troubleshooting electronic devices. General reviews of knowledge-based systems for fault diagnosis are given by O'Connel (1987) and Hardy (1987), whilst Goldbogen *et al* (1988) compares the rule- and object-oriented paradigms for representing diagnostic knowledge.

14.5   The key to manufacturing technology integration

From the design phase to the delivery phase, a product undergoes a number of different conceptual and physical processes from initial specification to conceptual design, to detailed design, to process-planning, to production and to testing. These processes are sequentially organised, with a certain amount of knowledge being generated about the product at each phase, some of which is passed on to the next phase. As observed by Smithers (1987), the sequential nature of these steps and the knowledge 'loss' between each step is a major cause of the current lack of integration of such activities. Smithers gives an example of the design of a round shaft element subject to a torsional load, with a change of diameter at some part of its length from d1 to d2, and a shoulder fillet radius of r. This knowledge of the dimensions of the part will be passed from the designer to the process planner. What will not be passed on, however, is the fact that a possibly critical constraint relationship exists between these three variables. In the absence of knowledge of this relationship, the process planner may well slightly modify one or more of the parameters to be more convenient to the production plan (e.g., to minimise tool changes), resulting in problems further down the line. This type of knowledge loss tends to occur between each phase of manufacturing, as shown in Figure 14.6, with complete knowledge of the product thus becoming scattered over different parts of the organisation. Sections of this knowledge are having to be recreated continually, at different times and in different forms, leading to knowledge inconsistencies. These are a direct result of the inability to transfer knowledge by other than the sequential organisation of individual knowledge-generation activities.

Conventional computerisation of the different phases of manufacturing, even when using a common database and computer-controlled data flow, has not changed the basically sequential nature of the knowledge-generation process, and the inefficiencies and feedback and feedforward control problems remain, leading to the 'islands of automation' syndrome.

The solution to this problem, which has been investigated in the UK as a large scale demonstration project under the Alvey program, is to develop an integrated and unified product description whose consistency is maintained and managed by a so-called 'Design to Product' system

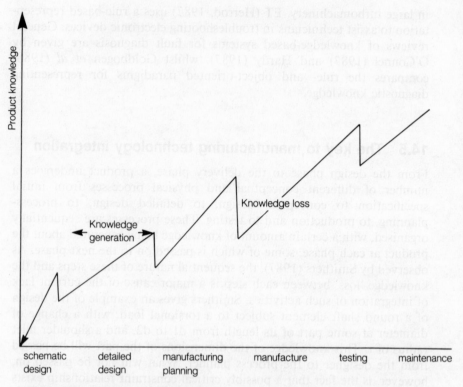

Figure 14.6   Knowledge generation and loss in the manufacturing cycle.

which will contain *all* the knowledge generated about a product at any particular time. The integrating factor in this approach is thus the commonality of this knowledge rather than the automation of individual phases. Thus the Design to Product system is regarded as being central to the whole cycle of conceptualising and manufacturing the product rather than being a tool to assist only at the design end of the cycle. The system consists of a number of modules containing design knowledge, a state space for design description and representation, inference engines, and a number of 'specialists' consisting of rule-based systems which examine the design in terms of various Design for ... aspects such as Design for Assembly, Design for Machining and Design for Cost. A feature of the system is an Assumption-Based Truth Maintenance system allowing tentative, exploratory designs to be conceptualised, and early designs to be modified in the light of their potential implications for manufacturing. The rejection of the strictly sequential organisation of the various knowledge-generation activities makes this a critically important aspect of the system.

In this context, design becomes a central activity, subsuming other normally functionally separate activities, such as process planning and quality control. The 'requisite variety' control model referred to in Chapter 10 is provided by the unified product knowledge base. However, breaking down the manufacturing problem using division by function can only be eliminated if alternative forms of problem breakdown are introduced, otherwise an uncontrollable proliferation of variety will still result. Again, the most rational alternative is likely to be a product-oriented division of the organisation with separately managed product knowledge bases for different groupings of similar products.

CHAPTER 15
Knowledge-based Manufacturing Technology Systems — Examples

This chapter presents in detail some specific examples of knowledge-based systems for manufacturing technology that have been reported or are under development. IMDA (Intelligent Manufacturing Design Assistant) is an integrated intelligent CAD system currently under development for use by Australian manufacturing industry. It is partly based on the CASPER system described by Luby *et al* (1986) with considerably extended functionality in the form of user interface and design detailing and analysis modules, and is a move in the direction of developing an integrated product knowledge base of the type described in chapter 14. The SACON system, although developed a number of years ago, is presented as a good example of a detailed design analysis system with an 'intelligent front end' and displays how such systems can be developed using general purpose knowledge based system 'shells'. Finally, GARI, one of the better documented knowledge-based process planning systems, is described. Although this too was developed a number of years ago, it still represents a good illustration of the main issues that a knowledge-based process planner must address, and an attempt is made to discuss its limitations in the context of more recent but less well documented work.

15.1 IMDA — An intelligent CAD system

IMDA is a CAD system that contains an object-oriented representation of products and parts, and various forms of design constraint and analysis knowledge, so that designs can be analysed in relation to sets of manufacturing and cost objectives. The concept of the system has been freely adapted from a similar system described by Luby et al (1986) and some of the following description uses examples based on their original paper.

15.1.1 Design Representation in IMDA Representation

IMDA uses an object-oriented representation of assemblies, parts, features and geometric primitives. The representation supports a number of complex data types, as shown in Figure 15.1.The structured data types vector and matrix allow the representation and manipulation of geometric information, and the construction of geometric primitives. For example, position has the data type Vector(3) of Integer, defining a domain of vectors each specifying the x, y and z coordinates of a position in three-dimensional space. The identities of components that make up a product would be of the data type set. A sequence of operations required to produce a part may be represented as a data item of the type Ordered-Set of Integer (e.g., the set of integers (1,4,6,7) where the integers stand for operations). However, the individual components of a structured data element are not regarded as having independent meaning and cannot be retrieved individually. A duplicate set is a set in which duplicate elements are allowed. For example, a product may consist of a number of duplicated components which would be represented as a duplicate-set. The data-type compute is associated with a domain whose values can be computational formulae drawing on other attributes of an object type as parameters. The data type Rule allows the representation of production rules which can be associated with objects and are fired when certain conditions are satisfied, resulting in the modification of attribute values or the passing of messages to other objects.

The fundamental semantic links or relationships used in IMDA are the links is-a (inverse: specialisation-of, and part-of (inverse: has-part). These links are used to form:

Basic Data Types	Structured Data Types	Temporal Data Types	Other Data Types
Integer Real Double-Precision Character Boolean	Set Ordered-set Duplicate-set Vector Matrix Time Series String	Time Date	Compute Rule

Figure 15.1 Data types in IMDA.

(a)   classification hierarchies of geometric primitives, features, parts, etc.

(b)   structural relationships between an assembly and its components, a component and its features, or between features and geometric primitives.

A component or 'part' is described in terms of a set of 'macro-features', and a set of 'detail-features'. A macro-feature is a standard geometric form such as a cylinder, L-bracket, U-channel or box. These macro features are themselves described in terms of primitive features such as slabs, 2-D corners, 3-D corners or joints, which are defined in turn in terms of the geometric primitives such as faces, edges, curves and points, represented by the structured data types mentioned above. For example, the open box shown in Figure 15.2 would consist of five slabs, eight 2-D corners, and four 3-D corners. Each slab has six faces, each face has four edges, and each edge has two points. Detail features consist of holes, grooves, notches, bosses, pockets or ribs, and correspond to the features described by CAM-I (CAM-I, 1985). These too can be described in terms of geometric primitives such as edges, faces, etc.

In the IMDA representation, these various types of feature and primitive are arranged in a classification hierarchy, as shown in Figure 15.3. The main classes of entity shown in this hierarchy are features, faces, edges, curves and points. Features are classified as either primitive features, macro-features, or detail features, each of which has some examples given of its type. Faces can be classified as 'rectangular' or 'circular', and curves as 'line' or 'arc'. The basic attributes of each entity class are shown, with inheritance taking place down the hierarchy. For example, 'Boss' would inherit all the attribute types of 'Feature'.

IMDA will normally be set up to contain a basic set of entity classes for the features most commonly encountered in the design

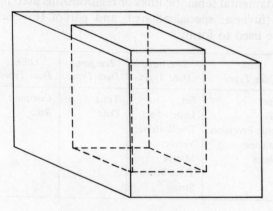

Figure 15.2 Simple open box.

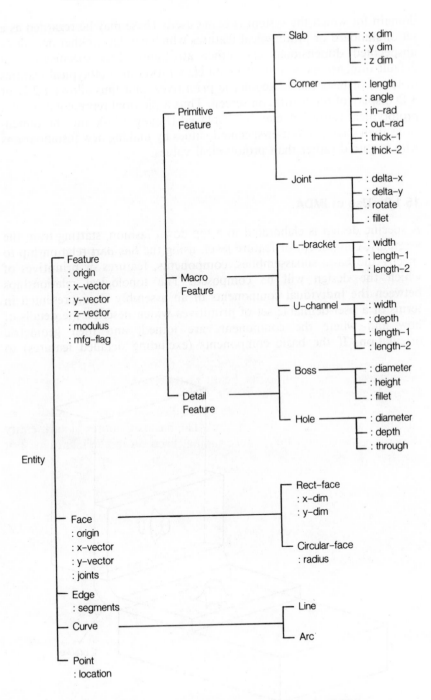

Figure 15.3 Feature classification hierarchy in IMDA.

domain for which the system is being used. These may be regarded as a set of standard or prototypical features which can have either default or unspecified dimensional and other attributes. This specification of default dimensions permits detailed elaboration of prototypical features in terms of instantiated geometric primitives, and thus allows a 2-D or 3-D display of the feature on screen. Thus a pictorial representation of a prototypical L-bracket may be displayed (Figure 15.4), and the dimensions then changed to user-specified values by making new instantiations with required rather than prototypical values.

15.1.2 Use of IMDA

A specific design is elaborated in a top-down fashion, starting from the assembly, component or feature level, using the **has-part** relationship to specify the basic subassemblies, components, features or primitives of which the design will be composed. The topological relationships between the individual components of an assembly are represented in terms of a user-definable set of primitives which describe the details of how and where the components are joined, and their geometric orientation. If the basic components (excluding detailed features) to

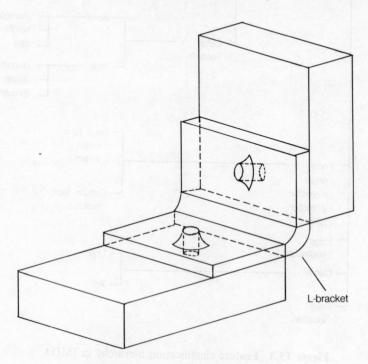

L-bracket

Figure 15.4 A simple assembly.

which the design is decomposed correspond to prototypical macro-features, and their topological relationships are specified using the JOINT entity (which is essentially a complex entity detailing the attributes of the topological links between features, such as a common face on which they are joined), a rough-cut 2 or 3-D graphical representation can be obtained immediately. The prototypical components are then specialised by replacing default with actual attribute values, adding any further attributes required, and fully specifying detail features. By using a system of windows and a 'browser', the designer can view simultaneously the evolving structure of the design in terms of the hierarchical tree representing the level by level breakdown of the design into its components, and a 2- or 3-D display of the current geometry of any specified part, simply by indicating that part with the cursor.

An example of the 'knowledge' structure that might be built up to describe the simple assembly of Figure 15.4 is shown in Figure 15.5. This shows a substructure consisting of two bars joined by an L-Bracket with a boss and hole. The L-Bracket is detailed in terms of the primitive features Slab-1, Slab-2, and Corner-1. Slab-1 consists of six faces

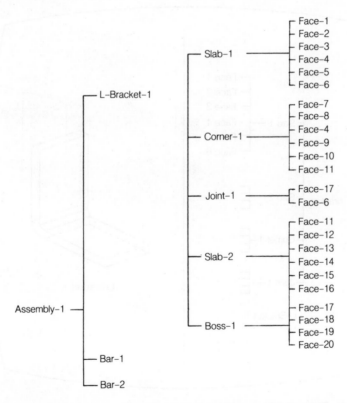

Figure 15.5 Part of the representation of the design in Figure 15.4.

which are not detailed. The detail feature **Boss-1** is specified as being attached to **Slab-1**, the faces of attachment being **Face-6** of **Slab-1** and **Face 17** of **Boss-1** . Positional and dimensional information are specified for each feature. The screen giving the simultaneous view of hierarchical structure and geometry (in this case of the L-Bracket) is shown in Figure 15.6.

Additional user-definable semantic links can be used to describe other types of relationship between the parts in an assembly. For example, the piston arrangement shown in Figure 15.7 consisting of a cylinder and a cylindrical-hole would have the semantic relationship engages linking the cylinder feature and the cylindrical-hole feature. These user-definable links are themselves entities (similar to the JOINT entity) with their own attributes and classification hierarchies. For example, the link engages might be specialised into several different subclasses depending on the function being performed, each of which has a different tolerance.

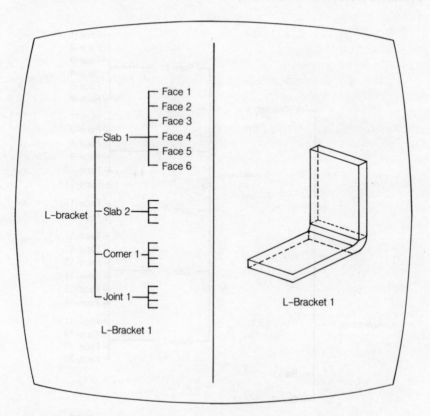

Figure 15.6 A typical design screen layout in IMDA.

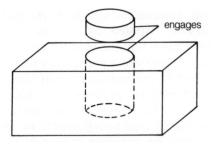

Figure 15.7 A simple piston assembly.

15.1.3 Representation of design rules

The attributes, in terms of which the features in Figure 15.5 have been specified, are entirely positional in nature. The representation so far differs from more conventional CAD representations in the explicit association of named features with certain combinations of geometric primitives, and in the way in which a complete product can be defined in a hierarchical fashion (similar to the multi-level bill of materials in MRP) through its subassemblies, components, macro-features, and primitive features, down to the level of the geometric primitives required to construct a graphics model of the product.

Naturally, the association of attributes with each level of description, which can take on a wide range of data types, allows many items of information other than purely geometric data to be associated with each entity participating in the representation. A fully instantiated feature description can contain attributes specifying such things as the material of the feature, the tolerances of its dimensions, the machine to be used in its production and the standard cost. However, what is more interesting from the point of view of the 'intelligence' in an intelligent CAD system is that the entities in an object-oriented database can have rules or procedures attached to them which allows the possibility of complementing the essentially *factual* knowledge stored in conventional design databases with procedural or 'how-to' knowledge of basic design rules. These can indicate how dimensions, tolerances, relative locations and materials are constrained by each other and by the required functionality of the design.

Some of these rules will be stored in IMDA as general domain-independent rules representing general engineering constraints, of which the following are simple examples:

If surface is 'bearing-surface' **and** material is y **then**
tolerance is x

If feature is 'through-hole' **and** material is y **then** minimum
face clearance is z

Many of the rules will, however, be specific to the particular design and can represent constraints imposed by its function. For example, a particular design may require that the positioning of a through hole in a slab never be less than 5mm from a particular edge. This is represented as a constraint attached to the instantiation of the Joint entity which specifies the topological relationship between the hole and the slab. The rule will indicate that if the hole has been specified to be less than 5mm from the edge, the location should be adjusted to the minimum of 5mm. Constraints such as these are specified as part of the knowledge base associated with a particular design.

Other procedures can indicate how changes to dimensions and tolerances associated with a particular feature will propagate to other connected features. For example, if the thickness of a slab with a cylindrical-hole detail feature is increased, a procedure attached to the relevant instantiation of the cylindrical hole entity can compute the new depth required for the hole. This is implemented by giving the data-type compute to the attribute depth of the cylindrical hole feature, and specifying it as a computational formula with the slab thickness as a parameter.

In specifying the design, the designer is continually on the lookout for chains of deterministic consequences that particular design decisions at a given level can cause for detailed feature dimensions, positions and tolerances at a lower level. Rather than specifying the dependent design variables in terms of their numerical values, they are specified parametrically in terms of other independent variables set by the designer. This is analogous to the way in which spreadsheet models are constructed to allow, for example, the effects change of a product price to propagate through to future cash flows. If the values of these dependent design variables for some particular instantiation as computed by the system violate predefined constraints, rules can be incorporated and associated with the appropriate entities to specify the changes that must be made in order for the constraints to be satisfied.

For example, in a particular application, the maximum depth of a cylindrical-hole detail feature of a given radius to be bored in a slab may be specified. Increase of the design thickness of the slab containing the hole would lead to an automatic increase in the depth of the hole. For slabs greater than a certain thickness, the resulting automatically computed hole depth might violate this constraint. This could activate a rule attached to the instantiation of cylindrical-hole that might reduce its depth and increase its diameter.

The *creation* of particular instances of detail-features can also be effected by rules whose firing is dependent on the specification of design parameters which determine the type of detail-feature required. In the previous example, a slab whose thickness is greater than a certain limit may require two cylindrical holes rather than one. This can be stored as a rule attached to the slab instantiation which automatically creates instances of the appropriate cylindrical-hole entities according to the thickness of the slab. Rules can also be specified which determine the materials that can be used in particular circumstances, or the tolerances required.

These facilities allow the designer to define a 'generic' product design (i.e., a design for a whole class of products) which is specified in terms of a knowledge base containing the basic high level entities and a set of design rules for instantiation of lower level entities which detail the design. These rules are fired by the input specification of the particular version of the product required.

15.1.4   Representation of cost and manufacturability knowledge

A design specification in IMDA can also contain embedded cost and manufacturability rules which determine the types of undesirable or costly requirements or operations a given design or feature may have. For example, the combination of an instance of a cylindrical-hole feature of a certain depth and diameter defined in a slab of a given material may activate a rule attached to the cylindrical-hole instantiation to inform the designer that this particular combination is inadvisable from a manu-facturing point of view. The rule may also be defined to suggest improved configurations. Similar rules can be defined and associated with each type of feature entity to make an estimate of the likely cost contribution of that entity to the total.

The feature-oriented design description used in IMDA also contains sufficient information for direct input to finite element analysis models and automated process-planning systems. IMDA is intended to contain its own finite element analysis package with a user interface similar to the SACON system described later in this chapter. However, having deduced an appropriate analysis strategy, the analysis will be performed automatically using as input the object-oriented feature description of the design. The ability of the object-oriented representa-tion to associate separate hierarchies of rules with individual features also opens the possibility of using IMDA to represent process-planning knowledge and to *integrate* this with the design knowledge. Thus the prototypical feature descriptions in IMDA can be arranged to link into a hierarchically organised set of rules which generate the machines, tools and cuts and their sequences required to produce each feature. Specific rules could be activated by the fully specified instances of these features to generate a process plan consisting of the alternative operations, machines and tools required to machine each feature. To implement this successfully, however, would require a module for the mapping of design features to manufacturing features, since the two will not always correspond.

Cost, manufacturability, materials and process information can all be displayed on screen simultaneously with the geometric and feature information of a design. For example, Figure 15.8 shows the relevant display relating to the L-Bracket. In the top left window, the part's feature description is displayed, with the geometry simultaneously appearing in the top right. In the lower left window, the material is specified. In the example shown, constraints elsewhere in the design have left options of three alternative materials, the final choice being left to the user. Density and unit cost are computed by the system, and attributes such as temper, surface finish and carbon content can also be specified or left at default values. The processes required and the associated cost summary are given in the middle right window, and a manufacturability summary obtained by activation of the manufacturability rules is given in the lower right window.

The hierarchical description of a product in terms of levels, and specification within IMDA of alternative operations that may be used and the manufacturing resources required allows the representation to be used as a source of composite Bill-of-Materials and Routing data for the

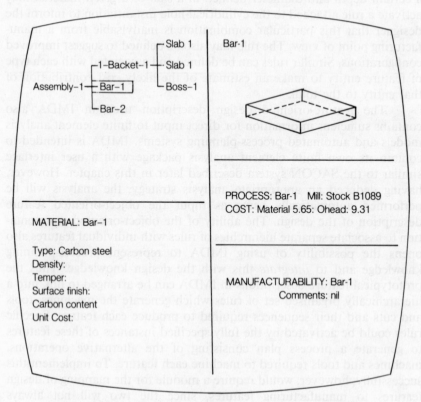

Figure 15.8 Cost and manufacturability screen in IMDA.

performance of requirements planning and scheduling. IMDA allows the abstraction of a **manufacturing resources network** as a particular high level 'view' of the product design representation at an appropriate level of detail for this task. This is similar in concept to the network representations desribed in relation to the ISTOP system (Chapter 12) and the FACSIM system (Chapter 13). Indeed, it is ultimately intended that these representations will be merged in an environment in which the three systems are used concurrently in an integrated manner. An example of the representation as used in IMDA is shown in Figure 15.9. The notion

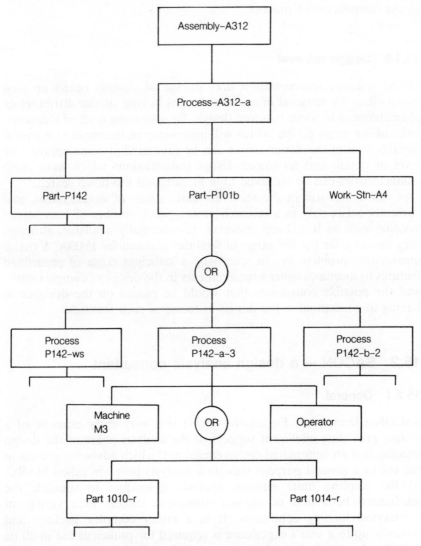

Figure 15.9 Part of a manufacturing resources network representation in IMDA.

of 'levels' is used as in a conventional bill-of-materials structure. However, this network representation shows not only the material components of the product but also, at each level, the processes and manufacturing resources required to produce the material components represented at that level. As in the versions of the representation described previously, an explicit distinction has been made here between conjunctive combinations of materials and resources required, and the *alternative* materials or resources that may be used at a given stage of manufacture. The latter are represented by 'OR' nodes in the network. This allows the specification of any number of alternatives at any stage of the manufacturing process.

15.1.5 Design retrieval

Object-oriented representation and storage of designs opens up new possibilities for retrieval of existing designs having similar attributes or characteristics to some required design. By specifying a set of characteristics of the target design (which will necessarily be incomplete), a partial instantiation of the design object can be generated at some appropriate level of detail, and all stored design instantiations which have these characteristics can be retrieved by a hierarchical top-down search.

IMDA is still in the relatively early stages of development, and currently exists only as a research prototype. A number of commercial systems such as ICAD are, however, commercially available, although they do not offer the full range of facilities planned for IMDA. A major outstanding problem lies in specifying a sufficient range of predefined features to meet a designer's requirements in the design of complex parts, and the possible constraints that would be placed on the designer in having to conceptualise the design in terms of such features.

15.2 SACON — a design analysis consultant

15.2.1 General

SACON (Bennet and Englemore, 1979) is a very early example of a system providing intelligent support to the analysis phase of the design process. It is an 'automated design consultant' which advises engineers in the use of a general purpose structural analysis program called MARC. MARC employs finite element analysis techniques to simulate the mechanical behaviour of physical structures subject to a variety of mechanical loading conditions. It is a rather complex package and typically up to a year's experience is required for proficient use in all its features, because of the large variety of analysis methods, material properties and geometries that can be used. SACON is designed to accept as input a description of the analysis problem, posed in a language familiar to the engineer, and to recommend, as output, an analysis strategy for the problem using the MARC package.

15.2.2   The SACON shell — EMYCIN

SACON was developed using a system called EMYCIN (van Melle *et al*, 1984) which is the domain-independent core of the medical consultation expert system MYCIN. MYCIN was developed at Stanford University in the mid 1970s as an expert system to advise physicians in the diagnosis and treatment of infectious blood disorders. It uses a production rule form of knowledge representation, with a backward chaining strategy in which a top-level goal rule defines the objective of the consultation, and further rules are then sought whose right-hand sides match one or more of the conditional elements of the goal rule. The left-hand sides, or conditional elements of these rules will either correspond to the right-hand sides of other rules which are then regaded as subgoals, or are questions that must be asked directly of the user. The MYCIN development involved a considerable amount of work in refining the inference engine and the user interface, with the inclusion of facilities for the easy entering and checking of rules, and provision of explanation facilities. To take maximum advantage of the development effort, this structure was generalised by removing the domain-specific medical knowledge of MYCIN and just retaining the 'shell' (which basically consists of a language for defining the domain knowledge base, the inference engine and the user interface) with EMYCIN standing for 'empty' MYCIN. The basic shell consists of the facilities shown in Figure 15.10.

The idea of EMYCIN was to put it to work in a variety of knowledge contexts to construct *consultation programs*. These simulate the problem-solving behaviour of human consultants or domain experts by eliciting this knowledge from the expert and representing it in the form of production rules. The consultation program itself elicits from the user information relevant to the problem or case about which advice is required by asking a series of questions which define the basic set of facts specific to the case. The production rules are then applied using backward chaining to attempt to establish a hypothesis that is consistent with the set of facts known about the case. Additional facts may be asked of the user during the reasoning process. EMYCIN provides a variety of built-in facilities including explanations of current, past and likely future lines of reasoning. For example, if it is not clear why the program is asking for information, the user may enquire why this information is needed. The system will respond by explicitly displaying the rules which it is

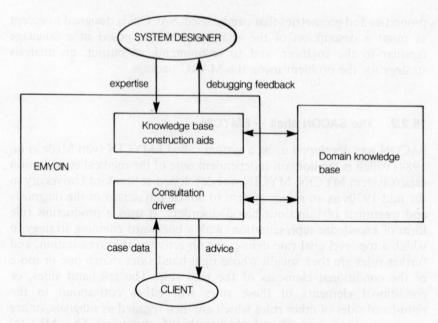

Figure 15.10 The EMYCIN shell.

attempting to satisfy. It can also explain the reasoning that lead to the current point and the use that might later be made of the information being requested. Another feature of EMYCIN is a simple natural language interface which can accept English language queries about the conclusions reached and about the domain in general. The returned explanations are presented in terms of relevant rules which are matched on keywords and a data dictionary to an automatically parsed version of the user's query.

Facts in EMYCIN are stored in the form of object-attribute-value triplets. A structured language (Abbreviated Rule Language — ARL) is provided for writing rules, and an editor is provided for changing the knowledge base. This enables syntactic checks to be made to ensure that valid parameters with allowed values have been entered. It also allows limited semantic checks in which new rules are compared with existing ones having conclusions about the same parameter, to check for any contradictions or subsumptions.

An example of a SACON rule written in ARL is as follows:

```
IF Composition = (List of Metals) and
      Error < 5 and
      Nd-stress > .5 and
      Cycles > 1000
   THEN: Ss-stress = Fatigue
```

Written in normal English, this rule is interpreted as:

IF (1) The material composing the substructure is one of the metals and

(2) The tolerable analysis error (in %) is between 5 and 30 and

(3) The substructure's non dimensional stress is greater than .9 and

(4) The number of loading cycles to be applied is between 1000 and 10000

THEN it is definite (1.0) that fatigue is one of the stress behaviour phenomena in the substructure.

15.2.3 Use of SACON

A general overview of the structure of the inferences performed by SACON is shown in Figure 15.11. To use SACON, each structure to be analysed must be decomposed into one or more substructures, where a substructure is defined as geometrically contiguous regions composed of single materials, and with a specified sets of kinematic boundary conditions. Each substructure must have specified the materials, general geometries and boundary conditions that are associated with it. There

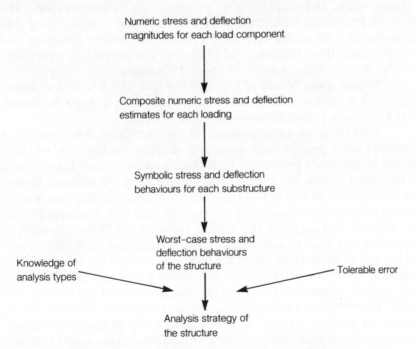

Figure 15.11 The inferences performed by SACON.

will obviously be several different ways in which a structure can be divided into substructures, and the one chosen will normally be that which most effectively illuminates the worst case behaviour of the structure.

Once the user has specified the substructures, he must now specify a set of loadings in the form of point and distributed load components, to be applied to each substructure. These represent the mechanical forces the substructure will experience during its working life (e.g., the loadings experienced by various substructures of an aircraft during braking, banking, etc.). From the user-supplied specification of the loading, SACON uses a set of simple mathematical models to estimate stresses and deflections for each substructure. SACON then estimates the behaviour of the complete structure from the sum of the peak relative stress and deflection behaviours of all the substructures which represent the worst case behaviours of the structure. From these peak responses, together with the tolerable analysis error (specified by the user), SACON finally uses its knowledge of the available analysis techniques to recommend an analysis strategy.

The reported version of SACON is able to select from among 36 non-linear analysis strategies, with linear analysis being recommended in cases where non-linear analysis is not indicated by the response estimates. The system may also indicate that no analysis is required, if relative stress and displacement estimates are sufficiently low. The SACON knowledge base consists of 170 rules and approximately 140 consultation parameters. A typical consultation session involving two substructures, three loadings, and three load components, is reported to involve an interactive session of about 25 minutes.

To give some flavour of a typical dialogue with SACON, a sample consultation session with SACON reproduced from a paper by Bennet and Englemore (1984) is shown in Figure 15.12.

SACON is an early example of an 'intelligent front end' to a conventionally programmed computer analysis package, in which a model of the user's problem is built from a user-oriented dialogue, and is then used to generate a set of strategies for using the package. Ideally, an intelligent front end should translate the analysis strategy into a set of inputs in the format required by the package, and then automatically run the package and interpret the results. However, SACON falls short of providing this level of automation. This is partly due to the limitations of the EMYCIN shell on which the system is based. This has no explicit mechanism for translating between representations, nor does it contain any explicit, semantically meaningful representation of the analysis task itself. The production rules are used merely to represent the reasoning by which an analysis strategy is *inferred* from the problem description. Intelligent front ends which overcome these limitations would require a more sophisticated form of knowledge representation, including a deeper

July 26, 1978 10:54AM in <SACON>MARC.SAV;80709 by SACON>

Hello Dr. Melosh,

This consultation concerns the 747 wing. The purpose of the consultation is to demonstrate the general features of a structural analysis consultation on a simple problem. Thus the consultation involves only one substructure: The total wing.

26-Jul-78 10:54:44
[consultation of 13-Jul-78 1:55PM].
------STRUCTURE-28------
1) What is the name of STRUCTURE-28?
** BOEING 747 WING
2) Assuming that your characterization of the boeing 747 wing in terms of its geometry, material characteristics, and boundary conditions are accurate, how much error (in percent) is tolerable for the analysis?
** 10
3) Do you want to examine the responses of the boeing 747 wing, to evaluate its instability, or both?
** EXAMINE-RESPONSES
4) Does the boeing 747 wing have any time dependent terms in its equations of equilibrium?
** NO
5) Is heating or cooling of interest in determining structure responses?
** NO
6) Have you decomposed the boeing 747 wing into a number of potential sub-structures which are relevant to this analysis?
** YES

------SUB-STRUCTURE-1------
7) What is the name of SUB-STRUCTURE-1?
** TOTAL WING
8) What is the material composing most of the total wing (SUB-STRUCTURE-1)?
** HIGH-STRENGTH-ALUMINUM
9) Enter the average longest dimension of the total wing (SUB-STRUCTURE-1) in inches (or <number> CMS):
** 1420
10) Enter the weight of the total wing (SUB-STRUCTURE-1) in pounds (or <number> KGS):
** 4600
11) Is the total wing (SUB-STRUCTURE-1) thin-walled or solid?
** THIN-WALLED
12) What is the configuration of support for the total wing (SUB-STRUCTURE-1)?
** ONE-SIDE
13) Is the total wing (SUB-STRUCTURE-1) to be modelled as a 1, 2, or 3 dimensional system?
** 2
14) Would you describe the construction of the total wing (SUB-STRUCTURE-1) to be truss and/or frame elements (NETWORK), sheets and/or blocks of material (CONTINUUM), or a combination of both?
** CONTINUUM
15) Is the overall geometry of the total wing (SUB-STRUCTURE-1) curved or planar?
** PLANAR

The first loading applied to the total wing (SUB-STRUCTURE-1) will be called:

------LOADING-1------
16) What is the name of LOADING-1?
** FLIGHT
17) Enter the number of loading cycles to be applied:
** 20000
The first load component associated with LOADING-1 will be called:

------LOAD-COMPONENT-1------
18) Would you describe LOAD-COMPONENT-1 as being DISTRIBUTED over most of the sub-structure or as acting at a POINT of the sub-structure?
** DISTRIBUTED
19) Which surface of the sub-structure does LOAD-COMPONENT-1 act NORMAL to? (If more than one surface, you should consider the loading as two or more component loadings)
** WIDTH-LENGTH
20) Enter the average wall thickness of the total wing (SUB-STRUCTURE-1) in inches (or <number> CMS):
** .31
21) Enter the average depth of the total wing (SUB-STRUCTURE-1) in inches (or <number> CMS):
** 41
22) Enter the magnitude of the distributed load (in psi):
** 1

23) Are there any other load components associated with LOADING-1?
** NO
24) Are there any other loading conditions associated with the total wing (SUB-STRUCTURE-1)?
** NO
25) Are there any other sub-structures of the boeing 747 wing relevant to this analysis?
** NO
26) Do the supports of the boeing 747 wing involve Coulomb friction, nonlinear springs, and/or gapping?
** NO

The following analysis classes are relevant to the analysis of your structure:
  1) general-inelastic

The following recommendations apply to this case:

Activate incremental stress—incremental strain analysis.

Model nonlinear stress-strain relation of the material.

Solution will be based on a mix of gradient and Newton methods.

Logic to scan peak stress at each step and evaluate fatigue integrity should be used.

Logic to scan stresses, smooth, and compare with allowable stresses (with appropriate safety factors) should be used.

Logic to scan deflections, calculate relative values, and compare with code limits, should be called upon.

Cumulative strain damage should be calculated.

Analysis should include two or more load cycles (if cyclic) with extrapolation for strain accumulation.

Shakedown extrapolation logic should be used.

A single cycle of loading is sufficient for the analysis.

Do you wish advice on another structure?
** NO

Figure 15.12 A sample consultation session with SACON

level of knowledge of the structure of the task, as might be provided by an object-oriented task description. Thus, systems such as SACON might be interfaced as separate design analysis subsystems to an object-oriented design system such as IMDA, using object level descriptions of both the design to be analysed and the analysis task itself.

15.3   GARI — a knowledge-based-process planning system for mechanical parts

15.3.1   Introduction

GARI (Descotte and Latombe, 1981, 1985) is a knowledge-based, process-planning system developed to perform generative process planning for machined parts. It consists of three components:

- a *feature-oriented description language* allowing specification of the part to be manufactured in terms of its geometric features;
- an *expert knowledge base*; this contains a set of production rules (called 'manufacturing rules') whose left-hand sides contain sets of conditions about the part to be manufactured and whose right-hand sides contain weighted pieces of advice concerning technical and economic preferences concerning choice of process;
- a *planner* consisting of an inference engine which supervises the implementation of pieces of advice embedded in the production rule base.

The basic function of GARI is to take an initial description of the part to be manufactured, to extract the set of potential actions (cuts) to be executed given the part description, and to constrain the ordering of these actions and how they should be executed.

15.3.2   Part and resource description

GARI uses a *feature-oriented* representation to describe the geometric characteristics of the part to be machined, based on sets of predicate calculus formulas which describe the part's features and the dimensional and geometric relationships between them. A feature in process-planning terms is a region of the part that has some manufacturing significance. Feature-oriented part descriptions are used by the majority of existing automated process-planning systems, not only because the features themselves determine the cuts that need to be executed, but also the feature descriptions and relationships provide information that can constrain the direction and ordering of cuts. The different types of feature that can be specified include holes, grooves, notches, bores and faces. Each type of feature has attributes specifying its type, relation to other features, dimensions, and any 'child' features needed to describe it. For example, Figure 15.12 shows an engineering drawing of a simple part with a notch and a countersunk hole, together with the associated feature description.

In this description, the notch N1 is described in terms of the faces into which it is cut (which are specified as separate features), its dimensions and the child features (the new faces created by the notch). H1, the countersunk hole, is described in terms of dimensions, surface quality, and the faces between which it is drilled. N1 and H1 are top-level features (as opposed to child features) in this description since they have no parent 'features' in whose description they are used.

Dimensional and geometric *relationships* between features can be specified by a predefined set of predicates, for example:

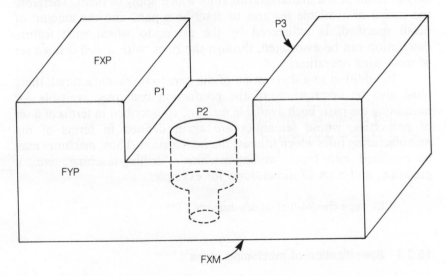

```
(N1 (type notch) (width 20)
    (starting-from FXP) (opening-into FYM FYP)
    (children (P1 (type face) (direction zm)
              (P2 (type face) (direction xp)
              (P3 (type face) (direction zp))

(H1 (type countersunk-hole)
    (diameter 6)
    (countersink-diameter 12)
    (surface-quality 7)
    (starting-from P2)
    (opening-into FXM)
```

Figure 15.13 A simple part feature description in GARI.

(distance FXM FXP 20±50)
(countersink-depth H1 P1 3±80)
(perpendicularity H1 FXM ±50)

Finally, global pieces of information about the part as a whole are represented:

(matter XC38)
(quality 6.3)
(tolerance ±100)

There is no explicit classifaction hierarchy of features (in the object-oriented sense) in GARI, so inheritance of characteristics is not supported. This can make feature descriptions rather tedious to specify. It also implies that features are entities which have semantic meaning only in terms of the manufacturing rules which apply to them. Therefore the choice of available features to describe a part, and the amount of detail specified, is influenced by the extent to which each feature description can be associated, through the rules, with a well-defined set of machining operations.

In addition to a description of the part to be manufactured, there must also be descriptions of the production resources available for machining the part. Each available machine is described in terms of a set of properties, whose semantics are again defined in terms of the manufacturing rules which utilisise the information. Thus, machines may be classified into types 'milling-machine', 'drilling-machine', etc., a precision, and a set of dimensions, for example:

(CL1 (type chuck-lathe) (chuck-diameter 2.0))

15.3.3 Specification of machining plans

A machining plan is specified in terms of a set of **phases**. A **phase** is a seqence of operations performed on the same machine with the same setting. Thus a phase will be specified in terms of the machine used, the face on which the part rests, and the sequence of operations of which the phase consists. Each operation involves a set of simultaneously performed cuts using the same or different tools.

A typical process plan might thus be specified as follows:

PHASE 1 Machine: FU203 Resting Face:
    Operation 1.1–Roughing Cut of FPX
    Operation 1.2–Finishing Cut of N1
    PHASE 2 Machine: FU203 resting face:
    Operation 2.1 Finishing Cut of FZP

PHASE 3 Machine: GSP205 Resting Face FZP
Operation 4.1 Finishing Cut of H2

Detailed process parameters such as the tool to be used and the cutting speed are not generated by current implementations of the system.

15.3.4 Manufacturing knowledge

Manufacturing knowledge is represented in GARI in the form of production rules whose left-hand sides contain a conjunctive set of conditions relating to the part to be manufactured, and whose right-hand sides are weighted conjunctions of constraints which must apply to the plan when the conditions of the rule are satisfied. The weights of the right-hand sides can take values between 0 and 10. These weights are used to make compromises amongst conflicting constraints. A weighting of 10 indicates that the constraints expressed on the right-hand side of the rule *must* be satisfied.

Typical production rules (expressed in structured English) might be as follows:

If the finishing cuts for two features x and y which are linked by an input geometric constraint are not executed in the same operation **then** it is advised (weight 4) that roughing cuts for both x and y be executed.

If a finishing cut x is executed on a grinding machine **and if** a cut y is executed on another type of machine **then** it is required (weight 10) that y be executed before x.

If the surface quality of feature x is to be better than Ra3.2 (technical standard) **and if** the extra thickness of a feature y is greater than 3.0mm **and if** the part rests on x during the first cut of y **then** it is advised (weight 8) to execute the first cut of y before the finishing cut of x.

The second of these rules defines a constraint that the final plan *must* obey (i.e., the first cut of y must occur before the finishing cut of x). The other two rules embody constraints that are advised but are not essential to the plan (i.e., they can be relaxed).

15.3.5 Generation of machining plans

GARI works from the initial feature description of the part, and starts by generating the set of potential cuts required to produce the features described. This is a simple *a priori* procedure based on the premise that each feature will require at most two cuts, a roughing cut and a finishing cut. These cuts are described merely as 'roughing cut of feature x', 'finishing cut of feature y', etc. Using the part description to activate the manufacturing rules results in the application of the 'pieces of advice' on the right-hand side of the rules. These cause the assignment of cuts to machines, their groupings into operations and phases involving the same setting, and their sequencing.

Progressive application of the manufacturing rulebase to the current production plan has the effect of iteratively constraining the 'current solution'. The initial current solution is loosely constrained and consists merely of the set of roughing and finishing cuts for each feature. Each cut forms a single operation and each operation forms a single phase. The only constraints which apply at this stage are that the roughing cut must either be prior to, or merged with, the finishing cut (the latter implying that a finising cut only is required), and that the resting face cannot be that containing the feature to be cut. Every machine/resting-face combination (other than those including the feature face) is regarded as a candidate for each cut, and all sequences of cuts, subject to the constraint on roughing/finishing-cut sequence for a given feature, are regarded as possible. The initial solution will therefore form a set of plans corresponding to all these possible combinations. As the constraints corresponding to the 'pieces of advice' forming the right-hand sides of the rules are progressively incorporated (in the form of specifying machines, grouping operations into phases, specifying orderings, etc.), the new current solution will contain a progressively smaller subset of the original set of plans forming the initial loosely constrained solution.

More particularly, pieces of advice constrain the solution in the following ways:

(1)   Constrain an operation to be performed prior to or simultaneously with another operation.

(2)   Merge two operations or phases, or constrain them not to be merged.

(3)   Restrict the allowable machines or resting faces for a phase to a subset.

At any given stage in the generation of the plan, rules are divided into those which have their conditional elements satisfied (termed 'active' rules), those which have their conditional elements contradicted (termed 'inactive' rules), and those which have their conditional elements neither satisfied nor contradicted (termed 'pending' rules). Rules are applied according to the following procedure (which in fact constitutes a set of implicit metarules):

If there exists at least one available piece of advice (i.e., for which the conditional elements are satisfied)
Then apply the piece of advice with the highest weight

If there are no currently applicable pieces of advice
And a pending rule exists (whose conditional elements are neither satisfied nor contradicted
Then construct a new piece of advice with the goal of making the pending rule inactive, and apply it

The first of these metarules implements a forward-chaining strategy using conflict resolution based on rule weight. The application of a piece of advice is implemented by the generation of *assertions* about the current solution which constrain it in the way indicated by the advice. GARI contains the ability to make simple deductions from a given set of assertions about the current solution, which allows a form of constraint propagation. For example, merging two operations into one implies merging the phases to which they belong, which in turn implies restricting the set of machines attached to the merged phase to the intersection of the sets of machines attached to the individual phases. Generation of the set of assertions consistent with the current piece of advice results in new rules becoming active, and the process is repeated until no more rules are activated.

The second metarule is concerned with the handling of pieces of advice containing conditional parts which are neither satisfied nor contradicted by the current solution. If such a rule exists, it would be conceivable that some additional constraint imposed on the current solution (which is still underconstrained at this stage of the plan) might create a more specialised plan subset for which the rule became active and with which the resultant piece of advice conflicted. GARI makes an attempt to remove this possibility by taking the conditions of the pending rule, and looking for an assertion that negates at least one of these conditions, but is still consistent with the current plan. Such an assertion would ensure that the pending rule was inactivated (i.e., it would not become activated by further constraints on the plan because at least one of its conditions would remain definitely violated). If such an assertion is found, it is applied as a piece of advice with weight zero (implying there is no technological reason for its existence). It can then be subsequently retracted at no cost.

15.3.6 Handling conflicting pieces of advice

As pieces of advice are applied to the current solution and propagated in the form of assertions, it is possible that a given piece of advice results in assertions that conflict with those already generated. For example, the current piece of advice might suggest two operations be merged, whereas an already existing assertion resulting from a previous piece of advice states they should not be merged. The reasoning process is basically non-monotonic and 'truth-maintainance' problems exist. Under these circumstances it is necessary to *backtrack*, and to reject one of the conflicting pieces of advice (this can occur provided the conflicting pieces of advice are not all of weight 10, indicating they are mandatory: mandatory conflicting pieces of advice cause the current solution to be invalidated). The procedure for doing this is to reject the most recently applied previous piece of advice of the lowest weight. For example, if the most recently applied pieces of advice were as shown below:

Advice	A1	A2	A3	A4	A5	A6	A7
Weight	2	5	3	7	3	9	5

and if the conflict were introduced by the application of A7, the piece of advice rejected would be A5. However, the introduction of A5 must have contributed to the assertions about the current solution that lead to the generation of A6 and A7, since if this were not the case, A6 and A7 being of higher weight than A5, would have been applied before it. Removal of A5 therefore involves removing all the assertions made as a result of the application of A5, A6 *and* A7. Thus a complete backtrack takes place to the point at which A5 was applied.

A rejected piece of advice is not completely deleted from further consideration. If a conflict occurs later, it may be necessary to reintroduce a previously rejected piece of advice, and if this occurs, the conflict must be resolved in a different manner to avoid an infinite loop. This is achieved by generating, for every piece of advice A rejected, a set of assertions corresponding to the **negation** (~A) of the piece of advice rejected. This has the effect of making the rejection of A explicit rather than implicit. ~A is regarded as a real piece of advice, and is given a weight W equal to the lowest weight of all the pieces of advice that was originally applied subsequently to A. This ensures that when the process resumes from the point of backtrack, the advice ~A has sufficiently high weight that it will be applied. Assume now that a fresh conflict amongst constraints occurs after ~A has been applied. If an attempt is made to recover from this conflict by rejecting ~A, this would simply imply the reintroduction of A which would regenerate the original conflict. However, this will cost at least the contradiction of a piece of advice of weight W, and hence backtracking will occur to pieces of advice applied before ~A with lower weight. If no piece of advice was applied before ~A with lower weight, the same conflict as before will appear. However, each time this loop occurs, it can be shown quite simply that the weight of the reintroduced piece of advice ~A will increase, and hence eventually a piece of advice applied before ~A must have lower weight. This ensures that having backtracked to the conflict, the process then takes a different path and does not loop forever, successively applying and rejecting the advice A.

15.3.7 Application and limitations of GARI

The version of GARI reported in 1985 contained approximately 50 rules mostly containing multiple pieces of advice, and implemented in the MACLISP language. The system has been used for 25 parts of varying degrees of complexity, containing up to 100 features. Some output plans were constrained by of the order of 1000 pieces of advice generated after recovering from approximately 250 conflicts.

Subsequent development work on GARI, to eliminate some of the disadvantages of the original system, is continuing under the new name XPS-E with partial sponsorship from the CAM-I consortium (Meyer, 1987). One of the disadvantages of the original version is that all the planning process takes place at a single level of abstraction. There is no attempt to factor the search space, hierarchically or otherwise. GARI basically performs a depth-first search which involves a considerable amount of backtracking. Suggestions have been made that problem solving could be improved by managing the search in such a way that the most difficult features are planned first, and that this would reduce the requirements for backtracking. Another reported problem with GARI is the difficulty in deciding the magnitude of the weights to apply to individual pieces of advice. The final solution has been found to be sensitive to the individual weights assigned (unlike results obtained from consultation-based Expert Systems using uncertainty factors, where results are usually insensitive the precise magnitudes assigned to these factors). This problem has been partly identified as being due to the fact that the advice weightings are used by experts as an implicit way of expressing the frequency of occurrence of *exceptions* to the piece of advice. A method of coping with this problem is to introduce rules in which the exceptions can be explicitly declared.

The feature-oriented description language of the original version of GARI was somewhat primitive in relation to that of more recent systems. The way in which features are represented in XCUT (Hummel and Brooks, 1987) provides an interesting contrast to GARI. XCUT uses an object-oriented representation of features (which are regarded as volumes of solid to be removed from the initial workpiece). They are specified structurally in terms of primitive entities which describe the topology, geometry, and tolerance of each feature. Primitive topological entities include vertices, edges and faces. Primitive geometric entities include points, vectors, lines, circles, planes and cylinders. Primitive tolerance entities include location, size and angle tolerance, roundness, straightness, flatness and cylindricity. In the same way that individual features are specified in terms of primitive entities, the total volume of material to be removed from the part is described in terms of its individual features through a *feature access* hierarchy. The *access face* of a feature is a face through which the cutting tool must pass to machine the feature. The parent features in the feature access hierarchy block one or more access faces of the child features. This is seen in Figure 15.13 in which the notch feature N1 blocks the access face of countersunk hole H1. Since each of the cuts of a parent feature must precede each of the cuts of its child features, this hierarchy contains valuable embedded process-planning knowledge as it constrains the possible ordering of cuts.

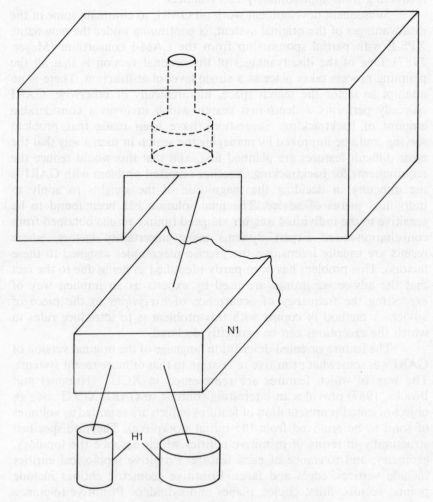

Figure 15.14 Access hierarchy in XCUT.

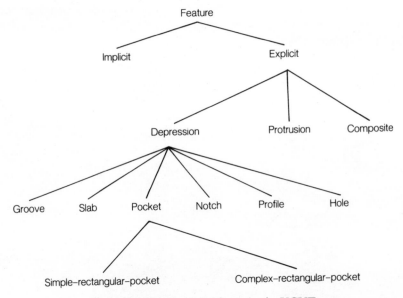

Figure 15.15 Feature hierarchy in XCUT.

Features in XCUT are also arranged in a taxonomic class hierarchy which clusters similar feature types into generalised object classes and supports inheritance. An example of a typical class hierarchy is shown in Figure 15.14. In addition to allowing reasoning to occur at several different levels of abstraction, this type of generic representation can also facilitate adding, deleting and changing feature definitions with a minimum of effort. This is very important in a dynamic manufacturing environment. XCUT, like GARI, is in a state of ongoing development.

Part V

IMPLEMENTATION CONSIDERATIONS

CHAPTER 16
Implementing Knowledge-based Systems

16.1 General considerations

Implementation of a knowledge-based system in a manufacturing context implies the commitment of the manufacturing organisation to the routine use of the system as a normal part of its operational activities. The *process* of implementation is concerned with ensuring the system is designed and installed in such a way that it *will* be used by those for whom it was intended. For this to occur, the eventual users and their needs, the prevailing organisational environment and the various interfaces (both conceptual and physical) to other functions, should be considered at all stages of the development project, from original conceptualisation through to final installation and testing. This is a fact which is generally true of the implementation of any type of computer-based information or decision-support system. The pragmatic aspects of implementation, particularly the human issues concerned with user and organisational interfaces, are at least as important as the technical issues concerned with the design of the system itself.

From the point of view of implementation, knowledge-based systems are still in their infancy compared to more conventional data-processing systems. Typical implementation cycles of the latter have received fairly intensive study, and are relatively well documented, resulting in the emergence of standardised implementation methodologies. Typically, the 'life cycle' approach is used in which development is divided into a sequence of distinct *phases* (e.g., requirements analysis, specification, design, implementation, usage and maintainance). By contrast, implementation methodologies for knowledge-based systems are still in an evolutionary state; a variety of 'success recipes' are promulgated based on practical experience, but still lacking any fully coherent and tested philosophy.

There is some contention about the extent to which the implementation cycle for a knowledge-based system will differ from that for a conventional data-processing system. It has been suggested in some quarters that the problems confronted by the builders of knowledge-based systems are not only substantially different to, but also substantially more complex than, the problems faced by the builders of conventional systems, and the standardised and disciplined approaches developed for the latter are simply not appropriate. On the other hand, this view has been challenged by those who maintain that the disciplined approach associated with the development of conventional data-processing systems must become a more or less essential feature of the development of knowledge-based systems if timely delivery, quality assurance, system maintenance, and system credibility are to be effectively achieved. Teknowledge, a company concerned with the development of AI products, were in the habit of using the following as a closing slide in their presentations:

'Knowledge engineering is more than software engineering'

To this, a further line has now been added:

'(but not much more)'

which indicates a possible trend of convergence of knowledge and software engineering paradigms. On the one hand it seems that 'knowledge engineering' may indeed require new sets of skills and sensitivities that are not generally displayed by conventionally trained software engineers. On the other hand, it also appears that knowledge engineering itself requires to be subject to much more disciplined development and maintenance standards at least as rigorous as those that currently apply to existing conventional software development projects. The decision by Westinghouse in 1984 not to go ahead with the implementation of ISIS until better standards of software support and maintainance were available (Smith, Fox and Ow, 1986) is an example of the degree of importance that needs to be placed on this aspect of KBS implementation.

A further important point stressed by Lu (1986) is that much of the current 'wisdom' associated with the construction of knowledge-based systems has evolved from early applications in fields such as medicine and geophysical prospection, which are the province of professional experts who have received formal training in their fields, and are accustomed to thinking in terms of the types of abstraction that can relatively easily map on to available knowledge representation schemata. Acquisition of knowledge from these human experts has traditionally placed heavy reliance on person-to-person interviews and on the ability of the expert to articulate clearly his or her knowledge. The development of knowledge-based systems for the factory floor depends, however, on the acquisition of knowledge that resides in the minds of human operators, schedulers, process planners, maintainance technicians, etc. who have developed what might be termed 'craft' rather than 'professional' knowledge, accumulated through many years of experience, but rarely or never explicitly articulated. The knowledge acquisition problem is discussed in more detail later in this chapter, but it would appear that it is likely to be a more acute problem in manufacturing than in other fields, in which the knowledge may be more formalised.

A number of other important differences between the manufacturing/engineering knowledge domain and knowledge domains such as medicine from which standard KBS development paradigms have evolved are also given by Lu in his 1986 paper. Some of these points are examined in greater depth later in this chapter. However, it is important to note that most of the early knowledge-based systems developed to date have been stand-alone prototype systems. As should be clear from the earlier chapters of this book, one of the principle motivations for applying knowledge-based systems technology in a manufacturing environment lies in their potential for contributing to manufacturing integration. This means that individual knowledge-based systems will require real-time access to factual knowledge (data) that may exist in a variety of forms in a variety of different places in the organisation. An inescapable element of the implementation of knowledge-based systems in a manufacturing environment is thus concerned with such things as the organisation and storage of data in commonly accessible databases, and the interfacing of individual knowledge-based systems to these databases and to each other. These integration aspects are examined in more detail in Chapter 17. For the present we will explore the issues connected with the implementation of stand-alone knowledge-based systems, on which much of current implementation experience is based.

16.2 Development strategies for knowledge-based systems

16.2.1 The development cycle

Despite the differences between knowledge engineering and software engineering, the development of a knowledge-based system will still need to follow, in a broad sense, the standard phases of any major software development effort. These have been varyingly expressed, but for the purpose of adaptation to include knowledge-based systems development, we shall express them here as follows:

(1)   Requirements analysis
(2)   Feasibility analysis.
(3)   Conceptual systems analysis and design
(4)   System development
(5)   System installation
(6)   Post-installation review
(7)   System maintenance

These standard phases of a software design are normally applied to conventional software design projects through the so-called **life-cycle** approach in which the system requirements and specifications are exhaustively documented and signed off before any coding takes place. Thus the system development phase might be subdivided into the further sequential phases of logical design, physical design and coding, each of which is completed before the next is commenced. The main way in which development of both knowledge-based and decision-support systems differ from a conventional system is that the life cycle approach is replaced by the **prototyping** approach. In this approach, a simplified prototype of the system is built as early as possible in the development cycle and used as a test bed for the exploration and elaboration, in conjunction with the end user, of the full potential of the system for providing knowledge-based decision support. This prototype provides insights into the nature of the final system which can then, depending on the size of the project, be employed in a more conventional and disciplined life cycle approach which formally commences after lessons from the prototype development phase have been fully absorbed.

    The prototyping approach has evolved in response to a recognition of the difficulty that end users experience in specifying their needs precisely, without the ability to react to and actively experiment with a *specific example* of the type of system the systems analyst or knowledge engineer has in mind. The prototyping approach is possible because most existing knowledge-based and decision-support systems are generally of considerable smaller scale than, for example, the large company-wide information systems for which the life cycle approach was developed. An analogy can be made here between the life cycle approach to software engineering, and the design and implementation associated with major civil engineering construction projects in which each phase must be complete before the next commences. Here prototyping is unfeasible

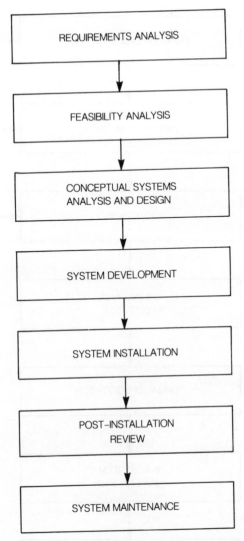

Figure 16.1   The life cycle approach to system design.

because of the scale of the project. The design and production of smaller scale mechanical devices, on the other hand, is invariably associated with the development of a prototype for experimentation and is analagous to the process of small scale DSS or knowledge systems design.

A modified version of the development phases tailored to the special characteristics of knowledge-based systems design is shown schematically in Figure 16.2, and is detailed below. This is an adaptation of what appears to have become a fairly standard approach to knowledge-based systems development.

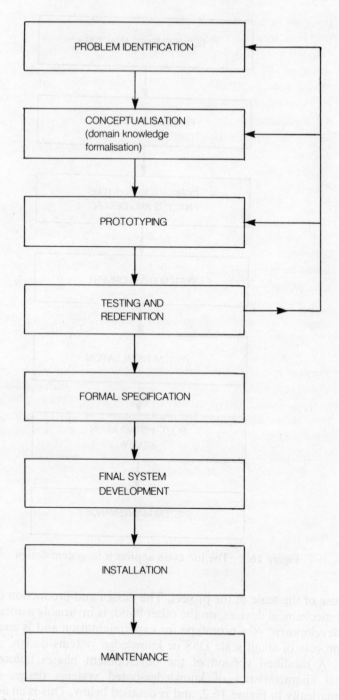

Figure 16.2 Life cycle approach modified for knowledge-based system development.

(1) **Problem identification** This includes the choice of a suitable problem area, an analysis of feasibility and appropriateness of the knowledge-based systems approach, a preliminary justification in terms of the potential benefits that would accrue, and a selection of the sources (human experts, documented rules or procedures) from which the knowledge to be encoded will be obtained.

(2) **Conceptualisation** This phase involves the initial conceptualisation and formalisation of the domain knowledge that will be encoded in the system, a preliminary requirements analysis of the functions that the knowledge-based system will perform, and selection of a programming environment or shell within which to develop a prototype.

(3) **Prototyping** The prototype should be developed to embody some core aspect of the problem, focusing on some fairly detailed example, with experimentation with various types of user interface; an intensive period of knowledge acquisition from the knowledge sources identified in step 1 will occur during this phase.

(4) **Testing and redefinition** The prototype is tested with a variety of users on a range of different representative test problems (historical or sample cases); this may be followed by a redefinition of the system and the development of a new prototype.

(5) **Formal specification** When experimentation with the prototype has given a sufficient indication of the probable nature of the final system, formal specifications may be developed as the initial phase of a more disciplined life cycle approach to development of the final system.

(6) **Development of final system** This development may involve redesigning of the architecture of the system and recoding it in such a way as to improve performance and maintainability; it also will involve attention to user access and security considerations, since much of the encoded knowledge may be of a confidential nature.

(7) **Installation** Installation may involve running the system in parallel with existing procedures for a period of perhaps several months until the user is assured that it will perform adequately.

(8) **Maintenance** The system should be designed and coded in such a way that new knowledge can be added easily and its functional specifications can be changed as experience is gained with its use; constant monitoring of usage patterns should occur, and comprehensive maintenance plans should be in place.

The extent to which the formal life cycle approach is employed after the prototype has been developed depends to some extent on the type and stability of the knowledge domain that is encoded. The development of systems that aim to encapsulate the heuristic problem-solving knowledge of human experts in fields such as process planning, is generally a more open-ended activity than the development of systems containing deep knowledge or well-documented knowledge from a stable knowledge domain (e.g., trouble shooting faulty production machinery). Most systems that aim to mimic 'human expert' heuristics never leave the prototype stage, and are in a state of continuous development.

16.2.2 Choice of problem area

In the initial stages of introducing knowledge systems technology into a manufacturing company, decisions must be made concerning which task areas in the company to tackle first in terms of provision of knowledge-based support. Conventional wisdom here suggests that the most effective strategy is to focus initial development on a relatively simple and straightforward area which has a high probability of success, and in which potential pay-offs are high. This strategy can help to establish credibility, and to build organisational confidence in the approach. As confidence and credibility increase, more difficult or problematical areas can be tackled.

Guidelines on the types of problem or task that best lend themselves to a knowledge systems approach have been given by a number of authors, in the context of expert systems development (evolving, as we have observed, mainly out of experiences in developing knowledge-based systems in domains of professional expertise such as medicine). For example, Waterman (1986) lists the following seven characteristics of a task area that would make it a suitable candidate for knowledge systems development:

(1)   The task does not require common sense.
(2)   The task requires only cognitive, not physical skills.
(3)   At least one genuine expert, who is willing to cooperate, exists.
(4)   The experts involved can articulate their methods of problem solving.
(5)   The experts involved must agree on the knowledge and the solution approach to the problem.
(6)   The task is not too difficult.
(7)   The task is well understood, and is defined clearly.

To these seven characteristics, other authors have added further characteristics:

(8)   The task definition is relatively stable.

(9)   Conventional algorithmic approaches are not satisfactory.

(10)   Incorrect or non-optimal results can be tolerated.

(11)   The domain must be well bounded and narrow.

(12)   Data and test cases are available.

(13)   The vocabulary has no more than a couple of thousand concepts.

The above criteria relate to the context of 'expert' systems in which the knowledge to be represented consists of informal knowledge residing in the minds of human experts. However, as has been noted in Chapter 8, knowledge-based systems can be built based on various types of formalised, structured and documented knowledge that could not really be regarded as embodying 'expertise' but nevertheless lends itself to being encoded using the types of knowledge representation paradigm we have described in this book. In these cases, the criteria concerning the availability of experts are obviously less significant.

In addition to criteria that should exist to make a knowledge-based systems approach *feasible*, additional criteria have been identified to determine whether a knowledge-based systems approach is *appropriate* (i.e., better than other forms of approach such as an algorithmic approach). These are listed below:

(1)   The task has a structure that involves symbolic rather than numerical information processing.

(2)   The task involves informal heuristics or chains of reasoning, rather than well defined algorithms.

(3)   The task is decomposable into a number of relatively independent, loosely coupled subtasks which may be performed in parallel.

(4)   The task involves reasoning with possibly erroneous or incomplete data.

(5)   The task is sensitive to a variety of environmental inputs which can change the problem-solving focus.

(6)   The task is neither too easy nor too difficult, and is of manageable size.

In terms of choosing tasks for which the use of a knowledge systems approach would be expected to generate high potential pay-offs, the following factors have been proposed which, if present, can be used to *justify* the development of a knowledge-based system:

(1)   The task is important.

(2)   A knowledge-based approach improves task performance, either in

terms of speed or quality, or both.

(3)   The task involves human expertise that is likely to be lost on resignation or retirement of the person possessing it, unless it is permanently encoded in some form.

(4)   Critical areas of knowledge possessed by relatively few people need to be more widely distributed in the organisation (elimination of knowledge 'bottlenecks').

(5)   Consistency in performing the task is desirable.

(6)   The knowledge is needed in hazardous environments.

(7)   The system can be used for training purposes.

It is worth stressing again that the above criteria have mostly been distilled from experience with building knowledge-based systems in environments in which 'professional' expertise is applied to stand-alone problems which do not demand a very close degree of integration, in areas where little previous computerisation may have taken place. It is assumed that the resultant system will be employed in the consultant or advisor role in which the user has little control over the way in which the system goes about solving the problem. They have also been mostly based on assumptions that the knowledge to be encoded is 'surface' or heuristic knowledge rather than deep knowledge based on well-defined causal models of the problem domain, and that this surface knowledge can be captured in the form of rules appropriate for direct representation in a rule-based shell similar to the EMYCIN system described in Chapter 15. The next section examines the peculiarities of the manufacturing domain to establish whether these principles are transferable.

16.2.3 Peculiarities of manufacturing domain problems

In the manufacturing domain, not all of these assumptions are necessarily valid. We have already referred to the fact that many shop floor personnel may find their informal heuristics difficult to articulate explicitly. Another problem is that the knowledge involved in manufacturing comprises a mixture of well-defined algorithms, and deep knowledge of engineering and manufacturing principles (including principles of manufacturing planning and control) embedded in causal and structural models, in addition to rules or heuristics based on experience of how algorithmic or model-based knowledge should be applied in practical situations. In other words, tasks in manufacturing tend to be of a hybrid nature, with many potential applications in which a knowledge-based system might appropriately be used as an adjunct to more conventional problem-solving tools or techniques. As pointed out by Lu (1986), the consultant/advisor paradigm for expert systems development, in which it is assumed that a rule-based approach is to be used to simulate diagnostic or classification heuristics used by human experts, is not really appropriate for a large class of manufacturing problems in which support is required not for solving stand-alone problems in a simulated consultant role, but for providing task assistance in the form of the following type of activities:(a) using embedded deep knowledge to check the quality or feasibility of human-generated solutions (e.g., whether a human generated product design satisfies certain engineering constraints); (b) the automatic performance of certain subtasks within a broader, human-controlled problem-solving activity (e.g., selecting an initial feasible machine loading plan as part of the activity of generating a weekly schedule for a production cell); or (c) in the role of intelligent front ends for systems using complex algorithms such as finite element analysis or mathematical optimisation. Clearly, many potential applications for knowledge-based systems lie in the **decision support** rather than the consultant/advisory role, and this requires effective integration of the system with other decision aids. In an automated factory environment, knowledge-based systems will of course play an important role in fully automated decision-making tasks such as FMS scheduling and dispatching. However, this type of development will require at least an equally high degree of integration with existing computerised systems. This produces complications for the application of the criteria we have been discussing for problem selection within the conventional KBS development paradigm.

The role played by purely descriptive factual knowledge of the manufacturing organisation, and the dependence of different manufacturing tasks on common access to this knowledge creates further special

'Professional' tasks	Manufacturing tasks
Mostly surface heuristics	Mixture of surface heuristics, algorithms and deep knowledge of underlying principles
Suitable for systems acting in consultant/ advisory role	Require systems acting in decision support role
Do not require access to large volumes of data	Often have voluminous data requirements
Problem domains relatively bounded	Integration requirements result in unbounded problems with proliferating complexity
Professionals trained in articulation	Manufacturing personnel rarely articulate their knowledge

Figure 16.3 Differences between 'professional' and manufacturing tasks.

problems not fully addressed by the conventional KBS development paradigm. For example, many different potential KBS applications such as scheduling, process and layout planning, and simulation require access to information on manufacturing entities such as parts, assemblies, machines, tools and transporters, and their various relationships to each other (such as the alternative machines and tools that can be used to convert one part into another). This is the type of knowledge that can be effectively encoded at multiple levels of abstraction using an object-oriented description. However, the complete specification of the factory by the encoding, within the object-oriented paradigm, of all the instances of these entities,with the specific and generalised relationships between them, would be a major undertaking. The fact that this knowledge of structure and function would need to be in place before individual task-specific heuristic knowledge modules (e.g., a scheduling KBS) accessing the knowledge could be implemented implies that KBS development in manufacturing environments may require a substantial commitment by management. There will also need to be a major investment to elicit and encode a large and complex volume of basic descriptive knowledge for access by individual applications before any system demonstrating a worthwhile return can be successfully implemented.

Problem complexity is, in fact, an almost inescapable feature of most realistic manufacturing environments. Although the conventional KBS development paradigm suggests that problems chosen for pilot development projects should be of an 'appropriate' level of complexity (not too complex and not too simple), many manufacturing tasks that from other viewpoints would appear to be suitable candidates for KBS application prove in practice to be so highly complex that the approach has to be abandoned; this is often because the knowledge base becomes unmanageably large, leading to unacceptably long response times, problems of knowledge-base maintainance, and so on.

From the preceding discussion, we might conclude that typical current manufacturing environments possibly contain relatively few problems or tasks which satisfy conventional criteria for pilot knowledge-based system development in terms of appropriate level of complexity, availability of experts who can readily articulate their knowledge, suitability of knowledge for encoding in a single representation paradigm, and potential for rapid return on investment. It may therefore be legitimately asked whether this implies that manufacturing environments in general are unsuitable areas for the application of knowledge-based systems. The answer to this is that the current state of knowledge-based systems technology is such that relatively little success is likely to result, particularly in terms of increased integration, from its application in manufacturing organisations who have not first committed themselves to an intensive program of rationalisation and simplification, and have achieved significant tangible progress in these areas. The application of current knowledge systems approaches per se is not likely to prove a panacea to the problems of complexity discussed in Chapters 2 and 3. Knowledge-based systems of requisite variety for highly complex manufacturing environments will of necessity be highly complex. However, the use of the philosophies of Just-in-Time production and the techniques of Group Technology to achieve simplification by, for example, movement from functional to product-oriented layout with rationalised and simplified production flows, can result in environments in which complexity and hence requisite variety of associated knowledge-based systems are reduced to a level that is viable using current knowledge-based system technologies. This is corroborated by experiences in companies such as 3M (Butcher, 1987). Simplification prior to the introduction of knowledge-based systems technology implies de facto that a commitment has been made to change which itself is likely to create a more favourable climate for KBS introduction. A model of organisational change due to Lewin (1947) suggests that the change process involves first 'unfreezing' the present organisational behaviour patterns, second changing or developing new behaviour patterns, and finally 'refreezing' or reinforcing the new behaviour patterns (Figure 16.4).

The unfrozen organisational state that will be necessary for the implementation of rationalisation and simplification programs can be used as an opportunity for the initiation of KBS development programs that can amplify the productivity improvements that accrue from the former. Since the change process will itself be associated with a period of organisational learning, much of the knowledge to be captured and encoded will be new knowledge that evolves as experience is gained in

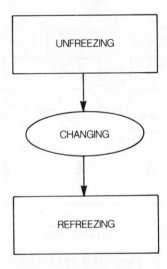

Figure 16.4 Lewin's model of organisational change.

running the reorganised factory. This provides a unique opportunity for the employment of knowledge acquisition systems which can assist in structurimg and encoding this knowledge *as it evolves* and which can also provide leverage on the process of restructuring itself.

The above factors tend to suggest that, although the conventional KBS development paradigms for initial choice of problem based on the 'start small to gain credibility' approach may work well in some types of manufacturing organisation as a means of stimulating or inititiating the process of change, for the majority of companies, in order to reap the major benefits of KBS technology, its introduction must be accompanied or preceded by a major commitment to change. The opportunities to use KBS technology in an integrative role (discussed in Chapter 17) and the associated requirements to build up a consistent and commonly accesible 'deep' knowledge base will be a major project that must be managed by techniques similar to any other large software project. Small application knowledge-based systems which access the common knowledge base can then be developed using the prototyping approach.

16.2.4 AI Circles

In a recent book based on seven years' experience of implementing AI systems in Japan, Greene (1990) introduced the notion of using 'AI circles' as an implementation strategy for getting knowledge-based systems onto the factory floor. Rather than having a centralised AI group employing specialised knowledge engineers to elicit and encode knowledge from shop floor personnel (the domain experts), Greene advocates

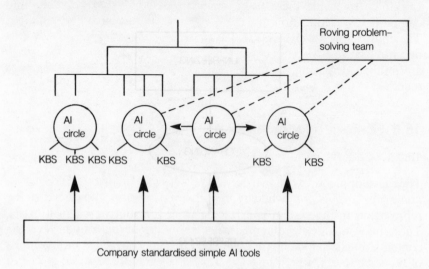

Figure 16.5 AI circles.

encouraging shop floor personnel to develop their own knowledge-based systems using personal computers, and simple, cheap company-standardised software tools. The idea is to form groups of between four and six people (AI circles) who receive basic training in knowledge repesentation techniques and in the use of the relevant software tools, and are then responsible for developing at least one major knowledge-based system over timescales of about eighteen months, spending a maximum of half a day per week on the project. By this means, a large number of distributed knowledge-based systems could be built in parallel. Thus several circles may be developing individual knowledge-based systems for materials control, purchasing, design, process control, diagnostic maintainance, etc. Other circles may be involved with developing a shared implementation platform, whilst others simulta-neously may be developing or refining knowledge representation and elicitation tools and techniques. The individual systems are eventually integrated, and replaced by shared knowledge-based networks. The AI circles are supplemented by a full- time roving problem-solving team, and by regular conferences and informal meetings at which common problems are discussed.

This approach, which is essentially characterised as a decentra-lised, incremental approach to knowledge-based systems implementa-tion, has much in common with programmes for implementing Just-in-Time production and Total Quality Control, which have a similar emphasis on worker participation, and the use of informal problem-solving groups, rather than the use of full-time specialists. The knowledge engineer becomes largely redundant, with individual domain specialists performing their own knowledge engineering. The degree of reskilling the workforce to tackle these tasks would obviously be considerable, and comprehensive education and training programmes would be required. The approach is nevertheless fully consistent with current trends towards decentralisation, workforce participation and group motivation which are finding increasing favour as general principles of effective manage-ment.

16.3 Knowledge acquisition

16.3.1 General

The development of knowledge-based systems involves a process of *knowledge acquisition* whereby the domain-specific knowledge to be represented in the system is extracted from the sources where it exists. These may include documented rules and procedures, written text, the contents of existing database or undocumented knowledge in the minds of human experts. Knowledge acquisition is generally regarded as one of the most problematic activities in the development and implementation of knowledge-based systems, and is currently attracting a great deal of research effort. This section gives an overview of the main issues and trends in the acquisition of manufacturing domain knowledge.

16.3.2 Types of knowledge

For the purposes of knowledge acquisition in the manufacturing management domain, knowledge may be divided into three types:

(1)   Knowledge of well-established facts about the organisation, its structure and resources, and of standard, well-documented organisational procedures and practices.

(2)   Knowledge of the basic underlying principles of the technologies on which the operations of the company are based (e.g., design and manufacturing technology, production planning and control techniques).

(3)   Knowledge of informal heuristics used to solve operational, tactical or strategic problems.

The first type of knowledge may be regarded as constituting knowledge of the *operational structure* of the manufacturing domain. It comprises a specification of the different entities, attributes and relationships between entities which collectively comprise the domain of the manufacturing operation. Entities would include the products manufactured, the component and purchased items involved, processes by which the conversion takes place, the manufacturing resources available and their characteristics, together with significant aggregate groupings of these entities, such as groups of similar components, parts or products, and the concepts of 'customer order', 'production order', 'purchase order' and 'cost'. Domain relationships would include the ways in which purchased items and components may be combined to form products, the relationships between manufacturing resources and conversion processes, and the way in which costs are related to products, components, processes and resources. This type of knowledge is commonly represented in an *implicit* sense (to the extent that the semantic relationships are implicit rather than explicit) in company databases or information systems containing bill of materials, routing and manufacturing resource data, and cost and accounting data. Information systems also contain representations of the standard procedures for creating, deleting and modifying entities and for ensuring data consistency and integrity.

The second type of knowledge consists of knowledge of underlying structural and causal relationships between entities embodying technological aspects of the organisation. Entities might include the different

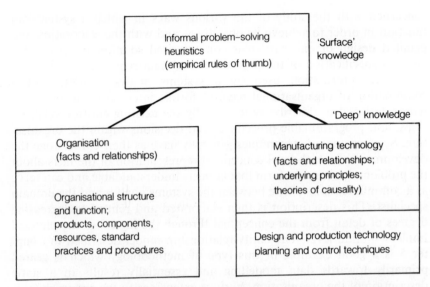

Figure 16.6 Structure of manufacturing management knowledge.

types of materials used and their physical characteristics, and cutting characteristics of individual tools concepts such as 'lead time', 'work-in-process' and 'machine utilisation'. Relationships might, for example, include causal relationships between lead times, machine utilisation, and work-in-progress. This knowledge would not generally exist in a computerised database, but would nevertheless be relatively well structured and documented in handbooks and reference manuals.

The third type of knowledge includes rules of thumb used for activities such as scheduling, process planning or fault diagnosis which have evolved from accumulated empirical evidence that they appear to 'work' in practice, rather than being derived from basic underlying principles. This knowledge would be unlikely to be documented and would be very loosely structured.

We shall now examine the types of technique that may be used for the acquisition of these different types of knowledge.

16.3.3 Acquisition of organisational domain knowledge — systems analysis

Methodologies for capturing knowledge about an organisation in terms of systematic descriptions of entities, relationships, the various integrity constraints and existential dependencies between entities, and procedures for their update have been developed over several years within the discipline of **systems analysis**. In its broader sense, systems analysis is concerned with the study of the various ways in which a system can function in order to achieve its objectives, and with the elaboration and detailed design of one particular computerised solution in terms of a detailed specification of the procedures and data required.

The information used by a systems analyst comes from a combination of organisational records, forms, interviews and question-naires designed to describe systematically the existing entities, relation-ships, and programmable procedures and decisions within the organisa-tion. Systems analysis techniques generally have as their cornerstone the development of a high-level conceptual representation of the facts about the problem domain in a form that is easily understandable and can serve as a communication vehicle between the systems analyst and the domain specialist. This description is then elaborated and refined to increasing degrees of detail from the conceptual through the logical to the physical implementation level. The entity-relationship model described in Chap-ter 5 is a good example of this type of methodology which is geared primarily towards data modelling and essentially results in a static description of the organisation. Various extensions to the approach (e.g., Petri net modelling of discrete events) allow existential and temporal dependencies between entities to be represented in order to model the functional aspects of the various components of the organisation that the entities stand for and the data flows between entities.

In organisations which handle a high volume of routine transac-tions whose processing involves programmed decision making, (which occurs in various functional areas of manufacturing — for example, at the level of planning handled by an MRP system) a natural extension to the representation of the entities which are created, destroyed or otherwise involved in transactions is to also develop explicit representations of the processes themselves. This results in the development of not merely a data model, but an automatic transaction processing system which performs such functions as automatic report generation, or the automatic update of all the entities and attributes necessitated by a particular event, such as the completion of a particular customer order.

In the attempt to lay down formal guidelines for Systems Analysis so as to establish it as an Engineering-type discipline, a variety of structured design methodologies have been developed for integrated representations of both data objects and the processes by which objects are created or destroyed, usually involving some type of **diagramming technique.**

Some systems analysis and design techniques are based on the premise that the structure embodied in the overall system should correspond to the structure of the data being processed. The initial emphasis is therefore on defining and elaborating the hierarchical input and output structures of the various processes by which transactions are created, and then defining a structure of procedures which are a composite of the hierarchical structures of the input and output data streams. In other words, processes themselves are initially regarded as being black boxes which serve to *define* the data streams, which are then structured, with the processes being defined at a later stage. The Jackson methodology for structured program design (Jackson, 1975) is the best known example of this technique (Figure 16.7).

Another class of technique is based on the analysis of *data flows* rather than data structures. Typical of the data flow approaches is the **Structured Design** technique described by Yourdon and Constantine (1979) which concentrates on developing the best partitioning of the system into relatively autonomous loosely coupled modules as the initial stage of the design, and then developing data structures that preserve this low degree of coupling. Each individual module is then expanded in further detail, perhaps involving decomposition into another set of submodules. Further developments along these lines are the 'Structured Analysis and System Specification technique' of de Marco (1980) and the 'Structured Analysis and Design Technique' (SADT) of Ross (1977). The latter is supported by commercial computer packages, and uses activity and data flow diagrams consisting of activity boxes and data boxes (Figure 16.8) to encode an initial top level description of a system. This is subject to discussion and criticism prior to decomposition into more detailed subdiagrams. An interesting point is the correspondence that

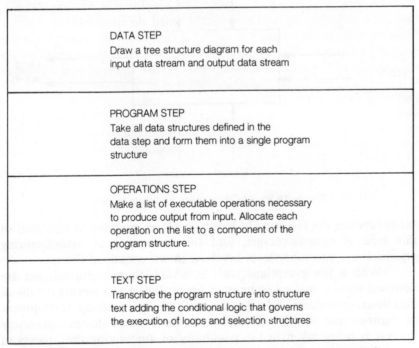

DATA STEP
Draw a tree structure diagram for each
input data stream and output data stream

PROGRAM STEP
Take all data structures defined in the
data step and form them into a single program
structure

OPERATIONS STEP
Make a list of executable operations necessary
to produce output from input. Allocate each
operation on the list to a component of the
program structure.

TEXT STEP
Transcribe the program structure into structure
text adding the conditional logic that governs
the execution of loops and selection structures

Figure 16.7 The Jackson methodology for structured program design.

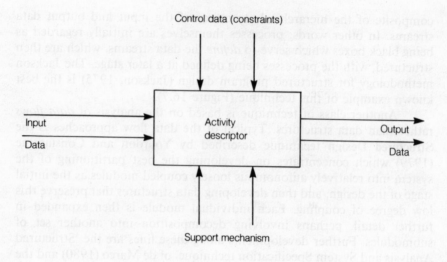

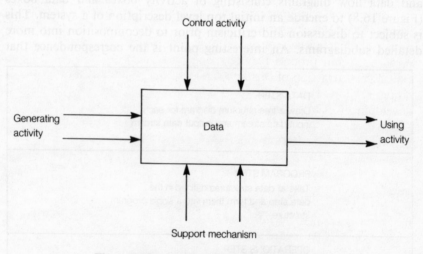

Figure 16.8 SADT activity and data boxes.

exists between the factoring of loosely coupled modules, as practised in this type of systems design, and the structuring of manufacturing organisations into subsystems involved in self-contained tasks.

With a few exceptions such as SADT, these methodologies are designed around manual techniques for analysing and storing details of data flows, procedures and data objects. With the increasing development of rigorous and formalised techniques for systems design, increasing interest is being taken in the possibility of automating the process of systems analysis and design. The term 'Computer-Aided Software

Engineering' (CASE) has been coined to describe the development of tools to assist in the formal structuring (usually by some form of top-down decomposition) of data, data flow and data transformation processes, and in the automatic translation of specifications to executable computer code (for a review see Martin, 1988). A number of systems have been developed, varying from automatic maintainance of a data dictionary to systems which extract from the user in a series of structured question and answer sessions, the entities, attributes and relationships in the domain of interest and checks the resulting database schema for consistency (for example, Hawryszkiewycz, 1985), and systems such as HOS (see Martin, 1988) which assist in top-down process decomposition and automatically translate the result into computer code. The full encoding of structured design knowledge could lead potentially to the almost complete automation of the task currently performed by the systems analyst.

16.3.4   Capturing heuristic problem-solving knowledge

Heuristic knowledge concerned with operational problem solving within the manufacturing organisation often resides in some implicit and not obviously structured form in the mind of human domain experts such as production and process planners, schedulers and maintainance technicians. The extraction of this knowledge into a systematic and formalised representation is one of the most difficult and challenging aspects in the development of any computer knowledge-based system. It is impossible to divorce the process of knowledge acquisition from the issue of knowledge representation since any process of knowledge acquisition must utilise some prior organising framework within which to make sense of the utterances and descriptions, and to guide the asking of questions of the individual who is providing the knowledge. The reduction of a large body of knowledge to a precise set of facts and rules has been described by Feigenbaum (1979) as 'knowledge engineering'. This is generally regarded as the 'bottleneck' in the process of the development of knowledge-based systems, as shown in Figure 16.9, and has become informally known as the Feigenbaum bottleneck.

Whereas capturing the knowledge of the more routine aspects of an organisation's activities in the form of the entities and attributes required to describe them and the structured and routine processes by which entities and attributes are updated, is a relatively straightforward and structured task in itself, the capture of heuristic problem-solving knowledge is associated with the high variety tasks of regulating and controlling the various subsystems of the manufacturing organisation. The effective performance of these tasks generally result from extensive experience of the task, backed up by requisite variety models of the subsystem's

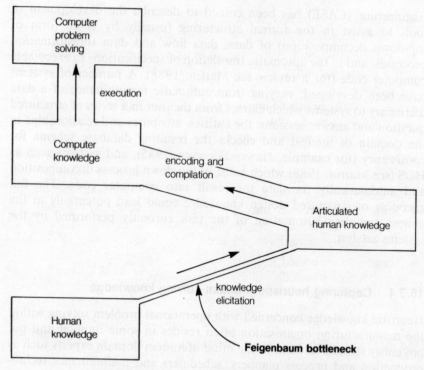

Figure 16.9 The Feigenbaum 'bottleneck'.

operation, and the ability to reason with such models. In contrast to the relatively well established techniques of systems analysis, there has been little formal development of processes for acquiring this type of procedural knowledge. This partly stems from our present lack of fundamental understanding of the nature of expertise, either technical or managerial, the way in which humans use knowledge in problem solving, and the process of knowledge acquisition and transfer in general.

Operational problem-solving knowledge is inherently less easily definable than the essentially factual or *simple* procedural knowledge of organisational structure and dynamics captured by the standard techniques of systems analysis. It includes such things as the ability to perceive meaningful relationships amongst facts, the weighing up of the potential outcomes of various problem-solving paths, knowing what to do in the face of conflicting or incomplete data, and recognising complex patterns in data that might suggest certain interpretations or courses of action.

The problem of eliciting problem-solving expertise from a skilled person has been recognised in psychological literature for several years. Some of the problems that have been documented can be summarised as follows (Gaines, 1987):

- expertise may be fortuitous; results obtained may be dependent on features of the situation the expert is not controlling.

- expertise may not be expressible in language; an expert may not be able to transmit expertise explicitly because of an inability to express it.

- expertise may not be applicable even when expressed in language; it may not be possible to convert verbal comprehension of a skill into a skilled performance.

- expertise expressed may be irrelevant; much so-called expertise is superstitious behaviour that neither contributes nor detracts from performance.

- expertise expressed may be incomplete; there will usually be implicit situational dependencies that make explicit expertise inadequate for performance.

- expertise expressed may be incorrect; experts may make explicit statements which do not correspond to their actual behaviour and lead to incorrect performance.

16.4   Capturing heuristic problem-solving knowledge

16.4.1   Linguistic transmission of knowledge

The techniques for overcoming the problems of 'expert' knowledge elicitation are still themselves very much in the domain of unstructured expertise and are regarded by many as belonging to the realm of art rather than science. Most of the techniques of knowledge elicitation used so far have an emphasis on the linguistic transmission of expertise, using a human knowledge engineer to extract or 'mine' the knowledge from the expert. The literature on the process of knowledge acquisition places considerable importance on the skills required by the knowledge engineer such as those listed by Hart (1986):

- communication skills
- ability to learn about the problem domain
- tact and diplomacy
- empathy and patience
- persistence
- logicality
- inventiveness and versatility
- self confidence

Hints abound as to how the knowledge engineer can most effectively extract knowledge from the expert (Hart, 1986). In the context of the interview, for example, a number of strategies may be used such as:

- interesting cases: the expert is asked to recall a number of specific 'interesting' problems and describe how they were tackled. This is sometimes termed the 'critical incidence technique'.

- characteristics and decisions: the expert is given a number of alternative sets of problem symptoms and characteristics and asked to match sets of characteristics to decisions.

- distinguishing goals: the expert is given a specific reasoning goal and asked to distinguish what set of facts are necessary and sufficient for this to be true. If this is performed for both final goals and intermediate goals used during the reasoning process, a model of the expert's knowledge structures can be built up.

- reclassification: the expert works backwards from a set of goals, and classifies pieces of evidence for and against each goal. These pieces of evidence are regarded as subgoals, and the process repeated until the evidence has been broken down to observable facts.

- dividing the domain: the expert starts with a focus on facts and successively classifies them in a hierarchical manner until the final goal is reached.

- talk through: the expert is asked to think aloud whilst at work, by talking through a specific case.

An intensive analysis and feedback phase is required after a knowledge elicitation session, in which the information obtained is refined, edited and reorganised, and the knowledge engineer attempts to deduce any implicit knowledge that the expert is using (such as backgound or common sense knowledge). It is also important at this stage to analyse the order in which the knowledge is applied. When analysis has been completed and the elicited knowledge represented in the form of some conceptual schema that will bear some resemblance to the final repre-sentation but which is intelligible to the expert, a feedback session occurs in which the expert critiques the schema and is asked to fill in gaps, look for inconsistencies, correct misinterpretations, and attempt to remove irrelevant details.

Obviously, this process can be very time consuming; in situations where the knowledge of the domain expert is changing, leading to frequent updates of the elicited knowledge base, or where the domain expert cannot spare the time for lengthy interview sessions, it can turn out to be impracticable. Another problem connected with the manufac-turing domain is that many shop floor experts simply may not be accustomed to thinking about the nature of their expertise in abstract terms, and hence may have difficulty in articulating it. Since the use of human intensive effort for the knowledge engineering process is counter to the trends towards automatic programmimg and automated systems design, alternative methods of knowledge elicitation are being actively sought. Two methods which are being investigated, repertory grid analysis and machine induction will be briefly described.

16.4.2 Repertory Grid analysis

Repertory Grid analysis is based on the theory of personal constructs developed by George Kelly (Kelly, 1955). Kelly maintained that each person is in a sense a 'scientist' with his own model of the world around him based on the categorisations he makes and the theories he develops. Using these theories he is able to anticipate the possible consequences of his actions, and to act based on these anticipations.

The set of categorisations used to make sense of and therefore predict the world is, according to Kelly, hierarchical in nature and is called the 'construct system' of the individual. The process of knowledge engineering is therefore mainly concerned with eliciting the construct systems of domain experts. Important aspects of a person's construct system are the concepts and vocabulary used by the expert to talk about the domain. The repertory grid is a formal and readily computerisable system for the elicitation of domain concepts by focusing on the similarities and differences, as perceived by the expert, between various individual entities or entity instances within the problem domain.

The technique is based on the method of 'triads' in which the expert is confronted by three specific entities or types of entity from the problem domain (e.g., three machines or three production processes) and asked to think of a way in which two are alike and differ from the third. For example, a production scheduler might be confronted with three specific machines and might nominate 'reliability' as the way in which two were similar but differed from the third. This would indicate that reliability is a construct of possible importance in the production scheduler's mind. If a computerised knowledge elicitation system is given a set of basic entities (e.g., production processes) which give a first-level description of the problem domain, then it can be programmed to automatically present randomly chosen triads to the expert in order to elicit factors that in the mind of the expert, are significant. As each factor (which is basically an attribute of the triad entity used to elicit it) emerges, the expert is asked to indicate the opposite (or **negative**) 'pole' of the attribute (e.g., the negative pole of costly might be cheap). He is then asked to score each entity on a continuous scale ranging from definite possession of the attribute to the definite possession of its opposite pole. The repertory grid itself is built up in the form of a cluster diagram with entities on one axis, attributes on the other, and the individual scores at the grid intersection.

Figure 16.10a shows an example in which constructs (attributes) C1, C2, etc. of different types of production process (labelled P1, P2, etc.) have been elicited using the method of triads. The negative 'pole' of each attribute is also shown. The expert has given each process a ranking between 1 and 3 on each attribute, with 1 indicating definite possession of the positive pole of the attribute, and 3 indicating definite possession of the negative pole. Cluster analysis can be used to establish a 'measure of similarity' between either entities or attributes, and can be used to group them into similar clusters. This has been done for attributes in Figure 16.10b, where the measure of similarity between two attributes has been computed from the sum of the absolute values of the differences in scores of each machine on these two attributes (including negative poles) and then scaled to a range of zero to 100. The diagram shows the attributes (only one pole of each attribute being chosen) connected in a tree structure with the point of connection of any pair of attributes corresponding to the computed degree of similarity between those two attributes. Thus the attributes Flexible and Unfocused have the highest similarity rating (a similarity score of 85), with substitutability and controlability belonging to the same cluster. In this way, patterns and associations between entities and attributes can be detected and a concept hierarchy progressively built up.

The earlier types of automated repertory grid technique were not intended to replace the knowledge engineer, since a considerable amount of further knowledge structuring and elicitation was required to develop the knowledge base to the point where it could actually simulate the problem-solving behaviour of the expert. The main advantage of a grid

		P1	P2	P3	P$	P5	P6	P7	
C1	High Yield	3	1	3	1	1	1	1	Low yield
C2	Complex	1	2	1	2	3	2	2	Simple
C3	Focused	1	3	2	1	1	3	1	General purpose
C4	Substitutable	1	3	3	2	2	3	1	Non substitutable
C5	Reliable	1	3	2	2	1	3	2	Unreliable
C6	Controllable	3	1	1	2	3	2	1	Uncontrollable
C7	Flexible	1	3	3	1	2	2	3	Inflexible
C8	Costly	3	1	1	2	3	1	3	Economic

1 = positive pole of construct
3 = negative pole of construct

Figure 16.10a

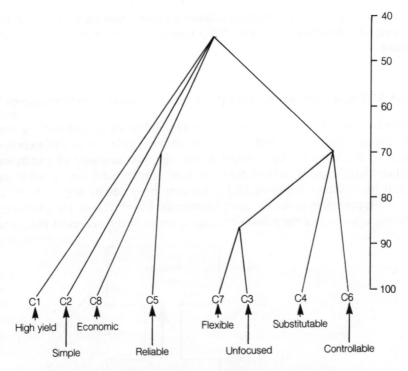

Figure 16.10b Example of repertory grid analysis.

elicitation process was claimed to be that it made the expert think carefully about his own knowledge in a structured way and focused his thoughts on key issues. Relationships between entities could be clearly seen, and the exercise could help break down a complex body of knowledge into smaller subsets. A number of automated repertory grid systems of this type have been described in the literature including PEGASUS, PLANET, KITTEN, AQUINAS and KSS0, some of which automatically generalise grids into rules (see Gaines 1988 for a review, also Boose and Gaines, 1988). For example, the AQUINAS system developed by Boeing (Boose and Bradshaw, 1987) is claimed to have a capability not only of generating hierarchies of entities and their attributes, but also of automatically generating problem-solving produc- tion rules from these hierarchies. This is performed by presenting experts with a variety of 'cases' and using the repertory grid technique to elicit traits of these cases, giving a solution to the case and rating solutions against each trait. The method basically represents a form of 'machine induction' (abstraction of general rules from specific cases) which will be examined in the next section.

It should be noticed that repertory grid techniques have had most success in the elicitation of knowledge about solving classification and diagnosis problems, rather than problems of synthesis such as planning and design. Whether automated knowledge acquistion techniques can be successfully developed for these latter types of problems is open to some doubt.

16.4.3 Knowledge elicitation by inductive reasoning from examples

Serious study has been given to the possibility of circumventing the knowledge engineering 'bottleneck' by moving rules from the expert's head to a computer representation through the language of examples rather than explicit articulation. A new 'route map' for knowledge acquisition, shown in Figure 16.11, has been proposed by Michie, (1987).

Apprentices generally gain knowledge by observing the problem-solving activities of the master through a series of tutorial examples, and

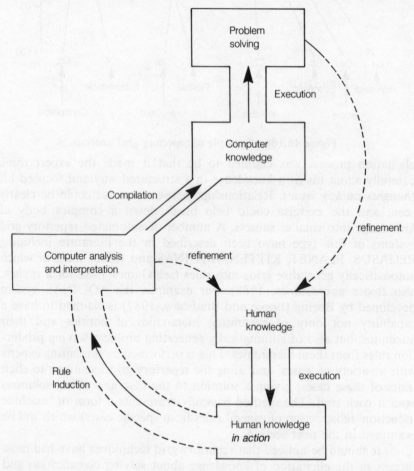

Figure 16.11 Use of rule induction to bypass the Feigenbaum bottleneck.

reconstructing or inferring the master's general problem-solving strategy from the specific decisions taken in each example. Knowledge aquisition by machine induction requires the specification in terms of the characterising *attributes*, of a set of tutorial example problems, together with the specific decision taken by the expert on each example, and an algorithm for inductive inference. The purpose of the algorithm is to generate a set of rules that will not only produce the same decision for each example as was produced by the expert, but will also hopefully produce the same decision as would be produced by the expert for other similar problems not in the example set. A 'similar problem' is here defined in the sense of being describable by the same set of attributes. This is an iterative process in that any examples for which the currently generated rule set gives answers which are incorrect (i.e., do not agree with the answer that the expert would have given) can be used to refine and improve the induced rule set by a further application of the induction algorithm. Quite obviously, the quality of the induced rules will be dependent on the quality of the induction algorithm and the extent to which the set of training examples are representative of the full range of cases likely to be encountered. If the training set does not contain enough information, or if the algorithm makes poor generalisations or is oversensitive to 'noise' in the example set, an inadequate set of rules will be induced.

16.4.4   The ID3 algorithm

A good example of a machine induction algorithm is the ID3 algorithm developed by Quinlan (1982). ID3 uses a training set of examples which are characterised by a list of attributes having either truth or numerical values, and membership of a particular class which represents the categorisation of that example as made by the expert. In the original versions of the algorithm, only two classes were permitted (e.g., in diagnosis examples a given set of symptoms described by attribute values might be diagnosed by an expert as either attributable or not attributable to one particular class of disease). Subsequent versions of ID3 have extended this to allow multiple classes.

The procedure used by ID3 is to start with a subset of examples that are already classified. The inductive algorithm then selects the attribute that has the most success in discriminating individual classes, and partitions the data into sets with common values of that attribute (for attributes with continuous values cut-off points are chosen for subdividing the examples into subsets). ID3 uses a measure of the discriminating power of an attribute based on Shannon's Information Statistic, although different measures such as the chi-squared statistic have been suggested since.

As an illustration, let us consider a set of production jobs that must be separated into the classes of expedite subcontract or no action on the basis of the job attributes days past due, customer and product type. An example set of classifications (performed by the production scheduler) is shown in Figure 16.12. Each attribute has three possible values, and can partition the jobs into three subsets. The Information Statistic for an attribute measures the extent to which a particular value of the attribute is invariably associated with a particular classification of the job. Computation of the value of the information statistic for each attribute indicates that the product attribute has the most success in correctly classifying jobs, with Widgets being invariably subcontracted, Sprogs invariably expedited, and Grommets invariably left with no action.

Once the examples have been partitioned into subsets using the most discriminating variable, each subset is again partitioned based on

Days past-due	Customer	Product-type	Class
0 – 5	Amtex	Widget	expedite
> 10	Actol	Sprog	expedite
> 10	Zipex	Grommet	leave
> 10	Actol	Widget	subcontract
0 – 5	Zipex	Widget	expedite
5 – 10	Zipex	Grommet	leave
0 – 5	Actol	Grommet	subcontract
5 – 10	Zipex	Widget	subcontract
> 10	Amtex	Widget	subcontract
5 – 10	Amtex	Sprog	expedite
0 – 5	Actol	Sprog	leave
0 – 10	Amtex	Grommet	leave

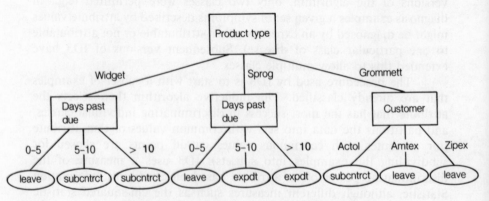

Figure 16.12 An example of rule induction.

the most discriminating of the remaining variables. The process is repeated recursively until each subset contains examples of only one class. This results in a decision tree which can then be used to classify new examples. An example of a rule resulting from the tree in 16.12 is: if Product-Type is Sprog and days-past-due > 10 then expedite. When an example is found which is misclassified, ID3 adds this example to a so-called 'refutation set' since it will have tutorial value in developing a better rule. When the refutation set has grown to a prespecified size, the entire decision tree is discarded and redeveloped from scratch on the original example set together with the refutation set. This process is repeated until the current decision tree has been tested on a sufficiently large number of examples without finding a refutation to satisfy some termination condition. If the attributes are exhausted before the tree is complete, there will be contradictory examples inthe training set which must be handled by introducing additional attributes.

ID3 originally performed well on classifying chess problems and on other problems where the data is clear cut and free from noise. Noisy data, however, tend to lead to decision trees that fit the training set but which do not generalise to handle new examples. One other problem that has been identified in ID3 is its lack of ability to treat uncertain or imprecise data, although this could be rectified. Another problem with ID3 lies in the restrictiveness of the representation language of the discrimination tree, whose nodes represents tests with only two branches and which can only be simple comparisons of variables with constants. Compound tests and comparison of one variable with another are not allowed.

Although inductive algorithms can be used to generate rules very quickly from a set of examples, the quality of induced results on other examples depends very much on the quality of the training set. Also, for problem domains of any complexity, the induced decision tree is somewhat of a black box as far as the human expert is concerned, with the internal rules not necessarily mapping on to any way of structuring the problem that the expert would naturally adopt. This can to some extent be overcome by factoring the problem up into a number of smaller subproblems and applying induction separately to each one. This is the basis of the system RULEMASTER developed at the University of Edinburgh (Michie, et al, 1984). Like the repertory grid, however, machine induction is really only suitable for classifaction and diagnostic problems and not for developing plans of action.

16.4.5   Integration of knowledge acquisition techniques

It is possible that some form of automated knowledge acquisition or machine learning will be an important part of the future development of knowledge-based systems for the factory floor or design office, whether these are based or repertory grids, machine induction, or some other technique. However, it will be important that these are somehow integrated with other forms of knowledge acquisition. Lu (1986) has proposed a nine level framework for integrated knowledge acquisition in the engineering and manufacturing domains of which a modified form is shown in Figure 16.13.

At the lowest level of this framework, the **task** level, are the individual engineering and manufacturing tasks such as design, process planning, production planning and control, and maintainance. It is assumed that one very important knowledge elicitation task will be the capture of 'deep' knowledge of the structure and behaviour of the entities comprising the above domains. Since the majority of this knowledge will be well structured, this can be performed using a combination of conventional systems analysis approaches, augmented with such techniques as repertory grid analysis. Representation of this knowledge, at the next higher level, the **model knowledge base** level, would be within the object-oriented paradigm, with explicit representation of entity *behaviour* as well as structures giving the capability for the *simulation* of individual domain tasks. The **information engine** can then simulate and predict various interesting behaviours of different combinations of domain entities for different inputs, using this object-oriented representation. These simulation results can then be combined with results from actual observation and experience to generate a set of cases, examples and counter-examples. These serve as inputs to the **induction engine** which uses some form of induction algorithm such as ID3 to generate efficient generalised heuristic rules from the individual cases and examples. These rules are then added to **surface knowledge bases** which also contain heuristic rules elicited directly from manufacturing domain experts. Obviously, some form of consistency checker will be required to analyse the compatability of the rules obtained from machine induction and rules obtained directly from domain experts. The resulting surface knowledge bases then serve as conventional knowledge-based systems at the application level to provide specific pieces of advice or to automate certain tasks as appropriate.

This framework is characteristic of more general trends in AI research to find knowledge representation schema based on deep knowledge, and to 'compile' efficient problem-solving heuristics from this deep knowledge rather than eliciting it directly from experts. However, the rather restricted ability of current machine induction techniques presents problems for the effective implementation of such an approach. In the shorter term, a more feasible alternative is perhaps one in which domain experts themselves play a much more active role in structuring and encoding their own knowledge using appropriate computer assistance (as in Greene's AI Circles approach), thereby short circuiting both knowledge engineers and inductive algorithms.

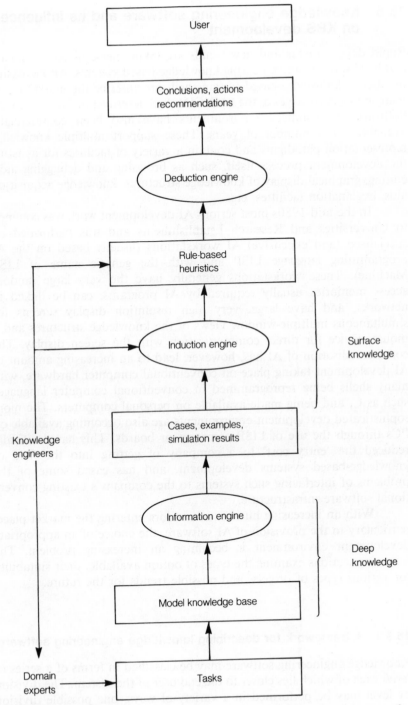

Figure 16.13 Lu's schemea for integrated knowledge acquisition in manufacturing organisations.

16.5 Knowledge engineering software and its influence on KBS development

Rapid developments and new trends are taking place in both software and hardware for implementing knowledge-based systems. An increasing number of knowledge-based system shells are entering the market place, many being derivatives of the EMYCIN shell described in Chapter 15. AI Software Development Environments have also been commercially available for a number of years. These support multiple knowledge representation paradigms and contain a variety of facilities for assisting the development process itself, such as browsing and debugging aids, editing, graphical display of knowledge structures, knowledge acquisition aids, explanation facilities, etc.

In the mid-1980s most serious AI development work was confined to Universities and Research Establishments and was performed on specialised (and expensive) AI workstations (usually based on the AI programming language LISP and with the generic name of LISP Machine). These workstations generally have the very large random access memories usually required by AI programs, can be linked in networks, and have large, very high resolution display screens for simultaneous multiple-window views of the knowledge structures and a mouse device for direct communication with the screen display. The commercialisation of AI has, however, lead to an increasing amount of AI development taking place on conventional computer hardware, with many shells being reprogrammed in conventional computer languages such as C, and being made available on personal computers. The more sophisticated development environments are also becoming available on PCs through the use of LISP co-processor boards. This has drastically reduced the 'entry cost' to a company of getting into the field of knowledge-based systems development, and has eased some of the problems of interfacing such systems to the company's existing conventional software infrastructure.

With an increasing number of vendors entering the market place, particulary in the provision of AI software, the choice of an appropriate development environment is becoming an increasing problem. The following sections examine the types of option available, their suitability for various types of project, and possible trends for the future.

16.5.1 A framework for describing knowledge engineering software

Knowledge engineering software may be classified in terms of a series of *levels* each of which lies closer to the end user of the system. The division by level may be performed in a variety of ways, one possible division being shown diagramatically in Figure 16.14. At the top level lies the

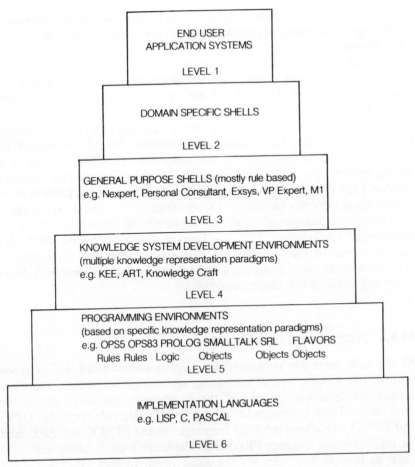

Figure 16.14 A framework for describing knowledge engineering software.

specific application system using domain knowledge on an operational basis to solve real-world problems. At the lowest level are the basic programming languages in which such systems are implemented. At intermediate levels are various types of knowledge system building tools or shells, some of which are suitable for use only by experienced AI programmers, and others suitable for direct encoding of knowledge by domain experts or end users.

16.5.2 Implementation languages

At the lowest level are the basic implementation languages which allow efficient running of large AI programs. These include not only the AI oriented language of LISP, but also other languages such as C and Pascal which support dynamic data structures and have been used to implement knowledge-based systems (particularly smaller implementations on personal computers).

LISP is the language which has been used most widely in the USA, and a variety of 'dialects' have been developed originating from different research laboratories. Thus MACLISP, the earliest version, was developed at MIT, subsequently being extended with the addition of a comprehesive support environment into ZETALISP. INTERLISP developed by the Xerox Corporation was another dialect containing an elaborate programming support environment, including editing and debugging features, and was designed to support incremental development of LISP programs. FRANZLISP was developed at the University of California at Berkeley for the UNIX operating environment. Since 1985, a standardised version of LISP has replaced the other dialects in the commercial marketplace. This has been named COMMON LISP, and was developed at Carnegie-Mellon University to provide compatibility across a wide range of computers and to standardise the proven features of several major LISP implementations.

16.5.3 Programming environments

At the next level are programming environments which are oriented towards one specific type of knowledge representation paradigm and are usually 'implemented' in one of the implementation languages at the level below. These languages include the production rule languages OPS5 and OPS83, the object-oriented languages SMALLTALK and SRL, and the logic-oriented language PROLOG. The latter is often 'compared' with LISP as though they were on the same level. In fact LISP is a more general purpose language than PROLOG which is specifically a logic programming language, although it can also be used to implement rule- and object-oriented representations.

The OPS family of languages were developed at Carnegie-Mellon University. OPS5, which contains powerful pattern-matching capabilities for matching rules against data, and a forward chaining interpreter, has been implemented in several dialects of LISP. It has been used as the basis for quite a wide variety of knowledge system implementations in the manufacturing field, including Digital's XCON system. OPS83 is intended to integrate rule-based and procedural styles of programming in a PASCAL-like language with the addition of the rule-oriented programming constructs from OPS5.

SMALLTALK is a programming language for object-oriented representation developed in the Xerox Palo Alto Research Centre in the 1970s and early 1980s. In addition to the standard object-oriented programming constructs of class organisation, inheritance, embedded procedures and message passing, the SMALLTALK environment consists of a graphical interactive user interface driven by a mouse and utilising a high resolution graphics display screen. SMALLTALK-80 is a commercial version of SMALLTALK developed by Tektronix. SMALLTALK V and SMALLTALK 286 are inexpensive, user-friendly versions available for PCs.

SRL is another language for object oriented representation developed at Carnegie-Mellon University, and implemented in LISP. It includes a facility for user-definable relations, meta-level knowledge and multiple contexts. Much of the evolution of SRL occurred during the ISIS project (see Chapter 12). A dialect of SRL — SRL/1.5 — is implemented in FRANZLISP and runs under UNIX. SRL is also used under the name CRL as the one of the basic knowledge representation languages in the integrated environment KNOWLEDGE CRAFT (see below).

PROLOG is very popular in Japan and Europe. It is used as one of the basic languages for the Japanese Fifth Generation Computer Project. A number of implementations of PROLOG exist including QUINTUS PROLOG, MPROLOG, ARITY PROLOG and Turbo PROLOG, most being available on a PC. Some versions of PROLOG are implemented in LISP, but there is a possibility that the basic constructs of PROLOG will be embedded directly in computer hardware to improve its performance, thus effectively changing its status to an implementation language.

POPLOG is a programming environment developed in the UK containing LISP, PROLOG and POP11 (a language similar to LISP) which share common data structures. This too is available on PC.

16.5.4 Knowledge system development environments

Above the level of application languages we find **knowledge system development environments** which can provide a comprehensive and integrated set of tools and facilities for knowledge representation, display, reasoning, acquisition and explanation, as well as editing and debugging tools. Multiple knowledge represention paradigms are usually included and these are integrated in the sense that data structures are commonly accessible, allowing production rules to be fired by patterns of data stored in an object-oriented representation, for example. The architecture of a typical knowledge system development environment, which would normally be available on a LISP machine, is similar in its lower levels to the architecture used to describe KE software and is shown in Figure 16.15.

At the bottom level lies the language (in this case COMMON LISP) in which the system is implemented. Above this lie the application languages corresponding to the various knowledge representation para-

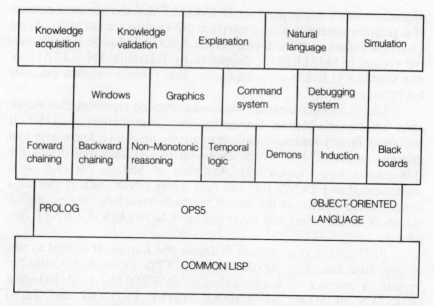

Figure 16.15 Architecture of a typical knowledge system development environment.

digms. Typically, logic-based, rule-based and object-oriented paradigms would be represented, and would have access to common data structures built up in the COMMON-LISP ground environment. The object-oriented representation language would generally support user-definable relations. Multiple forms of inferencing would generally be included, including forward and backward chaining, non-monotonic and temporal reasoning, induction, demons, and blackboard-based reasoning for multiple knowledge sources. To facilitate programming in the application languages, a set of **program development** tools are provided, which typically would include a multiple-window graphical display of knowledge structures, including a browsing facility, a graphics editor for modifying knowledge structures, a command system for the management of multiple tasks and user interfaces, and a debugging system for tracing through reasoning processes to diagnose errors. For higher levels of development support and to facilitate interaction with the final users of the application system, a set of **application tools** might include a knowledge acquisition system, a knowledge validation system, an explanation system (which explains lines of reasoning), a natural language interface, and a simulation system.

The support environment described here has features that are typically found in such systems as KEE (developed and marketed by Intellicorp), KNOWLEDGE CRAFT (developed and marketed by the Carnegie, Group) and ART (developed and marketed by the Inference

Corporation). Smaller scale support environments are also available containing a subset of these features.

There is a trend for these support environments, including the more sophisticated ones, to become available on personal computers. However the number and variety of the facilities they offer makes them complex to use, and this does not make them suitable for use in the rapid prototyping of simple end-user application systems by personnel who are not experienced in AI programming. They are perhaps more suitable for the development of very large, complex application systems in which experimentation with several different knowledge representation paradigms is required, or for the developement of knowledge system shells.

16.5.5 Knowledge-based system shells

A very large number of knowledge system shells are commercially available, at increasingly low prices. Most of these are based on the rule-based paradigm (similarly to the EMYCIN shell) and typically offer facilities (depending on price) of:

- forward and backward chaining
- certainty factors
- 'how' and 'why' explanations
- inference tracing
- on-line knowledge base editor
- saving of cases
- hooks to databases, graphics packages and conventional programs
- rule induction facilities

Some of these shells are quite primitive in that they only allow simple attribute-value pairs in the 'facts' database on which the rules are fired. This significantly limits their representational power in problem domains where multiple instantiations of similar types of object exist. More sophisticted shells allow object-attribute-value triplets and thus support more of a database representation of the facts. Most of these tools are mainly suitable for diagnostic, consultative and *simple* procedural tasks. They would not generally be suitable for complex procedural tasks such as planning or scheduling which might involve more sophisticated reasoning strategies and the use of meta-rules. The pragmatic issues of interfacing knowledge system shells with existing databases and procedural algorithms have motivated the implementation of many shells in conventional programming languages such as C and PASCAL, and the provision of 'hooks' to make the interfacing easier.

16.5.6 Application specific shells

At the next level closer to the final end user, we have **application specific shells** which are coming into increasing prominence in the market place. An application specific shell is oriented towards a specific type of application that requires standard types of reasoning process and merely needs customisation in terms of entering the appropriate domain-specific knowledge, and fine-tuning the inference procedures. Many of the general purpose shells which do little more than provide forward and backward chaining within the rule-based representation paradigm, are strongly oriented towards classification or diagnostic problems. However, other types of application specific shells based on different representation paradigms, and using more sophisticated inference procedures may be developed for design and synthesis problems, planning problems, scheduling problems, prediction problems, or monitoring and control problems. If any domain knowledge can be identified that might be generally applicable for many different implementations of the system, then this knowledge might be embedded in the shell. For example, a mechanical design application shell might have some basic engineering knowledge embedded in it, and would be customised by adding more detailed knowledge of engineering principles particularly applicable in the engineering domain in which it was to be used.

16.5.7 End-user application systems

At the top level we have the end-user system itself, which will be tailored to the specific environment in which it is required to operate, and will contain all the appropriate domain knowledge which allows it to solve domain-specific problems. Since this must interface directly with users who are themselves unlikely to be knowledge engineers or programmers, it at this level that the majority of effort into user-interface design should be invested, with explanation capabilities, natural language dialogues, graphical displays, possibilities for different degrees of user participation in the problem-solving process, etc.

16.5.8 Evolving roles in KBS development

Sprague and Carlson (1982) have classified DSS personnel in terms of 'manager', 'DSS builder' and 'DSS toolsmith'. The manager in this classification is the end user of the DSS. The DSS builder is the individual who configures the DSS from the available building blocks, and who must be familiar both with the manager's problem and with DSS technology. The DSS toolsmith develops the new technology, software and languages required for the DSS builder to produce specific DSS in a short time frame.

Different individuals with knowledge-based systems technology can be classified in a similar way. **End users** of the system will normally be concerned only with using level 1 (the application system itself) and perhaps building level 1 systems from level 2 and 3 support environments. The **knowledge engineer** will be concerned primarily with building (in conjunction with domain experts if an expert system is involved) level 1 or 2 systems from level 2, 3 and 4 support environments or languages. The **knowledge toolsmith** is concerned with building level 3 and 4 support environments using level 5 and 6 languages.

16.6   From implementation to integration

The availability of low cost, user-friendly shells that integrate easily into existing conventional software environments has provided a spur to the development of knowledge-based systems in an incremental fashion, with many companies currently taking this approach. These types of tool allow the knowledge engineer to be bypassed, and domain experts in various professional fields, having little or no computer programming skills, have successfully developed working models of subsets of their own expertise. At a lower level, programming environments provided by TURBO-PROLOG, SMALLTALK V and OPS83 are sufficiently easy to use that more technically oriented domain experts (including manufacturing and industrial engineers) with some computer experience have proved capable of using them effectively in the development role. These types of tool have the advantage of greater flexibility than simple rule-based shells, and indeed Greene in his advocacy of the 'AI circles' approach recommends them as suitable tools to be used by such circles.

In spite of encouraging signs of rapidly increasing effective utilisation of simple tools, and the potential elimination of the knowledge acquisition bottleneck by the active participation of domain experts in developing their own systems, the achievement of true manufacturing integration using shared knowledge requires rather more than the implementation of a series of stand-alone knowledge-based systems, even if these can be interfaced to existing company databases. The next chapter examines the specific issue of integration of knowledge-based systems both with each other and with existing company infrastructures from a technical and social perspective.

Chapter 17
Integrating Knowledge-based Systems

17.1 Introduction

17.2 Procedural integration of knowledge-based systems

17.3 Task decomposition and goal integration

17.4 Socio-technical integration of knowlegde-based systems

17.1 Introduction

The previous chapter discussed some of the issues concerned with the development of knowledge-based systems in 'stand-alone' mode. Most of the early prototypes were in fact developed as stand-alone systems, and much of the existing 'wisdom' on implementation has evolved from stand-alone developments. In a manufacturing organisation, however, the maximum productivity leverage is unlikely to come from stand-alone KBS implementations. Indeed, this would be contrary to the general spirit of computer-integrated manufacturing. In order to realise the full potential of the KBS approach, knowledge-based systems must be effectively integrated, both with the rest of the organisation and with each other. This implies that KBS must not only be physically interfaced with other computer and software systems, but must also be semantically and logically interfaced in terms of their interdependent tasks.

The physical interfacing of KBS with other computer systems will be greatly facilitated by the emergence of communication protocols such as MAP and TOP and will not be considered in further detail here. We can define three higher level types of required integration as:

(1) **Procedural** integration in which knowledge-based systems which are connected to manufacturing databases, MRP systems, or other KBS using common data have a consistent interpretation of the meaning of that data.

(2)   **Goal** integration, in which the individual knowledge-based tasks
       are ensured to be consistent with, and the knowledge embedded in
       the systems to be brought to be on these tasks are ensured to be
       adequate for, the achievement of overall organisational goals; this
       implies that individual knowledge-based systems can act synergis-
       tically in *cooperative* mode.

(3)   **Socio-technical** integration in which knowledge-based systems are
       effectively and harmoniously integrated with humans in the
       organisation in such a way as to achieve a synergy of the individual
       capabilities of people and computers.

The first two types of integration are broadly equivalents of the
integration types of the same name described by Miller, Rosenthal and
Vollman (1986) in their investigation into the current extent of linkages
between individual 'islands of automation', described in Chapter 2. The
third type of integration raises another very important set of issues
concerned with human factors and societal impacts of knowledge-based
systems in organisations.

The three types of integration will now be considered in turn.

17.2   Procedural integration of knowledge-based systems

17.2.1   General

Although some localised KBS may only require access to local data,
much of the information required for KBS applications is of the type that
would generally be stored in existing company databases or information
systems. For example, a knowledge-based production scheduling system
will require a list of the orders to be scheduled and the characteristics of
these orders in terms of items, quantities and due dates. It will also
require the routing information for each order. The former information
might be maintained by an existing MRP system, or an order entry
system implemented on a transaction-oriented database, possibly of the
relational type. The latter information might be stored in the routing file
of an MRP system, or in a separate manufacturability database. In either
of these cases, to avoid costly duplication of data entry and storage, it will
be essential for the scheduling system to be capable of directly accessing
the existing data. Hence a critical area of the technical integation of
knowledge- based systems is the **integration** or **coupling** of knowledge-
based systems to existing manufacturing and production management
databases.

Knowledge-based systems will also require to operate in a *cooper-*

ative mode and must exchange messages and information to ensure that common goals are being achieved. This can either be in the form of a blackboard architecture in which messages are stored in the form of an 'agenda' in a commonly accessible database, or by the direct passing of messages. The former will again require a coupling of knowledge bases and databases while the latter will require some form of protocol and common syntax and semantics for the interpretation of messages. This is treated in more detail in the section on goal integration.

17.2.2 Integration of knowledge bases and databases

For the purposes of discussing the integration of knowledge bases and databases in a manufacturing organisation, consider the schema shown in Figure 17.1 for a company with a heavy investment in *conventional* database systems. The company might typically have:

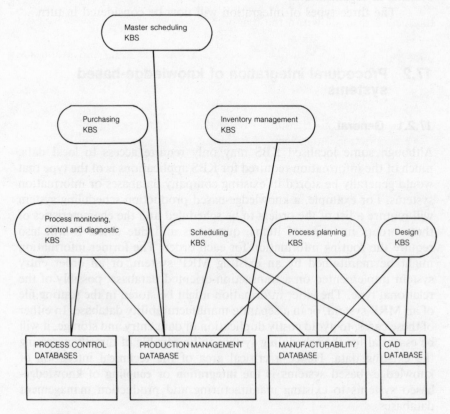

Figure 17.1 Database access requirements of manufacturing KBS.

(a)   a production management database containing order, inventory and costing data; this may also contain Bill-of-Materials and Routing data maintained separately from the CAD and manufacturability databases.

(b)   a manufacturability database of possible process plans for each item produced;

(c)   a CAD database containing the design details and characteristics of individual components, subassemblies, and final assemblies;

(d)   a production resource database containing inventories of existing production resources and their technical capabilities; this could possibly be integrated with the production management database;

(e)   process-monitoring and diagnostic databases (which may be localised in machine cells) and which store current and historical operational data for all production facilities and processes, for control, maintenance and diagnostic purposes.

A set of KBS applications that such a company might plan to implement, together with linkages to the databases with which they would need to interact, is also shown in the diagram. These might include:

(a)   a design KBS that needs to interact with the CAD and Manufacturability databases.

(b)   a process-planning KBS that needs to interact with CAD, manufacturability and production resource databases.

(c)   a production-scheduling KBS that needs to interact with the production management database and possibly with the CAD, manufacturability, and production resource databases (an FMS scheduling KBS would also require to access the associated process monitoring database).

(d)   maintenance/diagnostic KBSs that need to interact with the process monitoring and diagnostic database.

(e)   master planning, purchasing, and inventory control KBSs that need to interact with the production management database.

Each of these individual KBS applications will require access to a mixture of *local* data that will be stored in local databases which can be completely integrated into the KBS, and *external* data stored in one or more of the databases in Figure 17.1. For example, the scheduling KBS might maintain data on tentative capacity reservations locally, whereas firm reservations might be recorded in the production management database.

Many different types of coupling of varying strengths between databases and knowledge-based systems are conceptually possible. The coupling techniques used in any particular application will depend on such things as the quantity of data required by the KBS that is stored in existing databases or information systems, whether these databases are centralised or distributed, the number of different KBSs that will require access to the same data, whether KBSs will require only to access or to both access and update databases, and who will be responsible for maintaining and updating the knowledge bases.

The methods of coupling that will be considered here are derived from Brodie, and Mylopoulos (1986) and are as follows:

(1)   Use of a special application program to serve as a 'bridge' between the database and the knowledge base.

(2)   The enhancement of existing databases with more sophisticated knowledge representation models: knowledge layers are built directly on top of existing databases, and individual KBS applications can be embedded within the knowledge layer, or interact with the databases through the knowledge layer.

(3)   The enhancement of knowledge bases with DBMS capabilities; data is stored and maintained within the knowledge base which essentially replaces the existing databases. The resulting new types of integrated knowledge/database system combine the semantic expressiveness and reasoning power of knowledge bases with the efficiency and mass storage capabilities of databases.

The first two of these approaches are evolutionary in nature, in that knowledge-based systems are added to computer systems already in place. The third alternative is somewhat more revolutionary in that it would involve the complete replacement of existing conventional systems. Each of these alternatives will now be examined in more detail.

17.2.3   Bridges between databases and knowledge bases

Coupling of databases and knowledge bases using a 'bridge' between the two will require an application program that itself contains embedded knowledge about the conceptual schema of the database, the knowledge structures in the knowledge base, and the mapping from one to the other. This will enable it to 'translate' data into a form compatible with the knowledge base, and to translate 'output' of the knowledge base into a set of update statements on the database. Data can thus be downloaded between database and knowledge base, and vice versa.

For example, a production rule-based system written in OPS5 uses the RETE match algorithm to match data elements against the conditional parts of production rules. The RETE match algorithm assumes that all data elements are in main memory. Hence the matching of rules against data stored in external databases will require a translation program to download all data items that might match the production rule set currently active, and the translation of this data into appropriate OPS5 working memory elements. The translation program will require knowledge of the mapping between data entity and attribute names in the conceptual database schema and element classes and attributes in OPS5, and must be able to retrieve values from the database, and initialise OPS5 working memory elements. In DEC's R1 Computer Configuration Expert System, information on the 9000 individual components that can be configured (each having between 25 and 125 attributes) is stored in DEC's DBMS system. Knowledge of the required interface between R1 and the DBMS is itself stored as a subset of R1's rule base (Fox and McDermott, 1986).

In cases where data is being downloaded from a relational database to an object-oriented knowledge base, the mapping from data to knowledge structures can be quite complex. Data structures available in a relational database are usually much less expressive and more tightly constrained than the corresponding structures in an object-oriented knowledge base. For example, the object-oriented knowledge representation paradigm supports complex data types, together with notions of class membership and inheritance, which are not a feature of relational databases.

17.2.4   KEEconnection — an example of a general purpose data-konwledge bridge

An important class of knowledge engineering tool appearing on the market is the *general purpose* database-knowledge base bridge. Typical of this class of tool is Intellicorp's KEEconnection (Intellicorp, 1987). This provides a software bridge between relational databases using the SQL query language, and object-oriented knowledge-based systems developed using Intellicorps's Knowledge Engineering Environment, KEE. The following section gives a brief description of the mechanisms by which coupling of the data and knowledge bases takes place in KEEconnection, and the facilities offered by the system.

KEEconnection contains three software modules for **mapping**, **translation**, and **data communications** which automate most of the process of building the database — knowledge base connection.

In the **mapping** step, KEEconnection automatically reads the database's data dictionary and creates a set of KEE knowledge base objects called 'class units' which have a one-to-one correspondence with the set of relational database *tables* selected by the user as being those which are to provide data for the knowledge base. The rationale here is that a single relational table in the database will often represent an entity that would correspond to a KEE object. For each *column* of the relational table (i.e., each attribute of the entity), KEEconnection creates a *slot* in the KEE class unit. These class units serve as *templates* for objects which will be used subsequently to store data downloaded from the database to the knowledge base. At the same time, a separate *mapping* knowledge base is created to store information about the mapping of tables and columns to class units and slots. The default-mapping knowledge base stores 'connections' between each template class unit and the corresponding relational table, and between slots in each template unit and columns in each relational table. Data type conversions can also be specified in the mapping knowledge base. Thus, numerical values in the database might for example be converted to string values in the knowledge base. When tables of relational data are downloaded to the knowledge base, KEEconnection creates a 'child' of the template class object for each row of data, and enters the column values into each child's slots.

An example of a default mapping is shown in Figure 17.2a. This shows a database consisting of two relational tables, one representing the entity **part** and the other representing the entity **machine**, both having the attributes shown. In the default mapping, template class units corresponding to each table would be created with slots corresponding to the table columns. A default mapping knowledge base would also be created which stores this mapping of tables to objects and columns to attributes.

The user can now change the default mappings using the KEE graphic editor. This allows both the default template class units in the application knowledge base, and the default mapping knowledge base which maps data into these template class units from the database to be modified to provide mappings other than a direct table-to-object, column-to-slot mapping. The types of mapping that are supported are:

(1)   Mapping of multiple-relational tables to a single object class (equivalent to a relational JOIN).

(2)   Mapping of one relational table to several object classes.

(3)   Mapping of multiple columns of a relational table into a single object slot.

(4)   Mapping of a single column of a relational table to several object slots.

(5)   Transformation of column values into complex data structures (including other objects).

(6)   Transformation of data values into new values, either from database to knowledge base (e.g., by statistical analysis) or from knowledge base to database (e.g., by reasoning).

These mappings impart additional structure and semantics to the data, and the mapping knowledge base may in a loose sense be regarded as raising the 'knowledge content' of the data.

TABLE **PART**

P-Identifier	Machine	Lead-Time
P104	M21	2
P105	M21	3.5
P137	M34	4

TEMPLATE UNIT **PART**

Slot: P-Identifier
Value: (unknown)
Slot: Machine
Value: (unknown)
Slot: Lead-Time
Value: (unknown)

TABLE **MACHINE**

M-Identifier	Type	Cost/Hour	Capacity
M21	Mill	104.3	50
M22	Mill	130.0	50
M34	Drill	80.2	50

TEMPLATE UNIT **MACHINE**

Slot: M-Identifier
Value: (unknown)
Slot: Type
Value: (unknown)
Slot: Cost/hr
Value: (unknown)
Slot: Capacity
Value: (unknown)

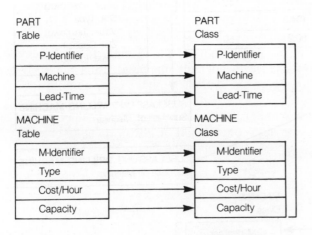

Figure 17.2a

As an example of how the default mapping may be altered by the user, consider the class unit part in the knowledge base containing a slot named machine which in the default mapping is the same data type as the corresponding column in the relational database. In the KEE application knowledge base, we may require the data mapped into this slot to be *instances* of the class machine rather than the string value of the machine identifier. By using a graphic mapping editor, the user can change the mapping knowledge base to indicate that values from the machine column of the part table should be changed from string values to KEE class units of type machine when downloaded into machine slots.

The machine table in the relational database may also contain data relating to several different types of machine (milling machines, drilling machines, etc.). The KEE application may require that different types of machine are represented as subclasses or specialisations of the more general class machine (Figure 17.2b). This involves creating one new template class unit for each subclass of the machine template (e.g., subclasses drilling-machine, milling-machine etc.) and mapping the machine table to these subclasses through a set of *membership conditions* which classify rows of the machine table based on the value in the type column, and are specified in the mapping knowledge base. The required changes to the default template class structures and the mapping knowledge base are again made by the user, employing the graphic editor.

KEE connection uses the mapping knowledge base for the automatic generation of SQL statements to retrieve data from the target database when such data is requested by the KEE application. The

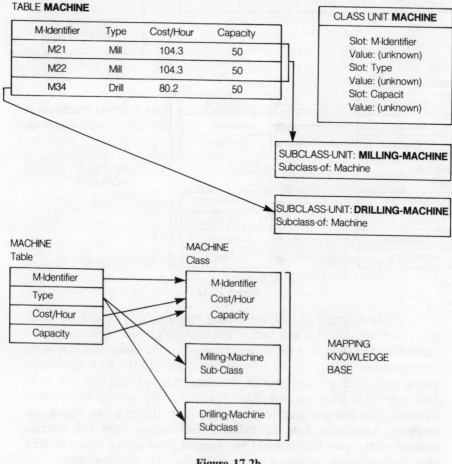

Figure 17.2b

retrieved data is downloaded and transformed into units and slot values, again according to information in the mapping knowledge base.

The conditional parts of KEE production rules (which are themselves KEE objects) may contain instructions to download data if they are matched by putting an instruction in the rule's download after premise slot. Although this does not directly match the rules' conditional parts against data in external databases, it can guide the problem-solving process of a production rule-based KBS by controlling the downloading of external data against which further rules might be matched.

By creating a series of mapping knowledge bases, KEEconnection can couple a single KBS application to several different external databases, provided they are relational and use the SQL retrieval language. Thus a system such as KEEconnection could be used to couple the individual KBS's in Figure 17.1 to the appropriate databases provided the former were based on KEE knowledge structures and the latter were relational. This has the advantage of providing a relatively cheap *incremental* approach to the integration of knowledge-based systems into the environment, that does not involve restructuring or reorganisation of existing databases with massive amounts of data reentry. There are, however, a number of potential disadvantages with this approach, namely:

- the frequent necessity to download data from external databases is a heavy performance overhead; the cost of search increases dramatically when most of the data is not in main memory; however, the dynamic reasoning capabilty of a KBS makes it difficult to predict and download in one 'shot' all the data required for a particular problem.

- the external databases (particularly the CAD database) may not all be relational in nature; special-purpose bridging programs would need to be developed in these cases.

- the necessity for many separate knowledge bases to store information about several different database schemas could lead to integrity problems on schema modification unless excellent and tightly controlled communications between individual database and knowledge base administrators were maintained.

17.2.5 Enhancing databases with a knowledge interface

A more ambitious strategy for the integration of knowledge bases and databases is to enhance existing database systems by providing a **common semantic interface** to individual company databases which enforces a consistent semantic interpretation of the data contained within them.

The semantic interface, which would take the form of an integrated global database schema, would be relatively tightly coupled to each individual database, and could be implemented in a distributed fashion, provided the global view was maintained. Individual knowledge-based systems could then request the required data from distributed databases in terms of the semantics defined in the common interface, rather than being required to tailor requests in terms of the specific structure of each individual database.

There has been a considerable amount of work in global schema integration in the field of conventional data management, much being based on the entity-relationship model. The Computer Corporation of America, for example, has developed a system called MULTIBASE (Smith *et al*, 1981) which is a collection of individual heteregeneous distributed databases, integrated by means of a global schema. Objects and relationships in the data models of the individual databases are mapped to objects and relationships in the global schema in such a way as to resolve data inconsistencies. A run-time query processing system maps user queries from the global schema to the local schema of the appropriate individual database, decides how to retrieve the data, and issues the appropriate commands. KADBASE (Rehak and Howard, 1985) is a more recent project at Carnegie Mellon University concerned with interfacing users to a number of databases. This has a knowledge-based system interface which converts user queries into a common internal query language for processing by a Network Data Access Manager which uses a global schema to locate where the data is stored. A knowledge- based database interface then translates the queries into the query language of the database being accessed.

Global database schemas that have been developed for integrative purposes are generally more semantically expressive than the schemas of the individual databases being integrated. For example, Navathe, Elmasri and Larsen (1986) describe an integrating schema based on what they call the Entity-Category-Relationship (E-C-R) Model which extends the basic E-R model to include generalisation hierarchies and subclasses, and uses explicit structural constraints on relationships to specify how entities may participate in them. Entity and relationship sets in individual E-R schema are integrated by repeated integration of pairs of similar entity sets from different databases or 'views' by establishing domain equalities and semantic correspondences between attributes. For example, the domains of two entity sets in different databases may be:

(1)   Identical (they refer to the same set of real-world objects)

(2)   Contained (one is a subset of the other)

(3)   Overlapping (they have some members in common)

(4)   Disjoint (they have no members in common)

Entity sets from different databases which have identical domains may be merged in the global schema taking as attributes the union of the attributes in each database, with the merging of attributes having the same semantic meaning. Contained and overlapping domains are merged using the notion of generalisation and subclasses. For example, the entity set machine in a production management database may include non-productive equipment such as generators, whilst the same entity set in a manufacturability database may only contain productive-machinery; in this case the more generalised entity set machine is created in the global schema with subclasses production-machine and other-machine). A similar procedure is followed for the integration of relationships which are classified by their *degree* (number of entity sets participating), the *role* of the relationship, and the *structural constraints* associated with it. Relationships of the same degree and role may be merged (with different structural constraints leading to the addition of extra entity classes). Relationships of different roles may be classified in terms of containment, overlap and disjoint and merged in generalisation hierarchies accordingly. Relationships of different degree may be mergeable, conditionally mergeable or not mergeable.

Other extensions of the expressive power of the entity-relationship model that make it more suitable for the development of global database schemata have been developed in the form of **semantic data models** (for example, King and McLeod, 1985) which use constructs such as aggregation, class membership and a distinction between objects and events in order to model domain semantics more effectively. This work has been briefly described in Chapter 4. However, these approaches have originated mainly in the area of conventional data processing and therefore tend to be oriented towards the representation of large numbers of instances of a small number of data types, as might be found in a production management database. As has been previously observed, CAD and manufacturability databases are liable to contain a much wider variety of data types and relationships, and so a semantic interface that is appropriate for developing an integrated view of CAD, manufacturabilty and production management data will require to be oriented towards the representation and manipulation of data that is highly amorphous in nature. The types of database suitable for these applications are themselves likely to be semantically sophisticated and capable of supporting complex data types. The Semantic Association Model, SAM (Su, 1986) is typical of the type of data model currently being developed for CAD/CAM applications. SAM employs complex data types such as **vector, ordered-set, compute** and **rule** and seven types of association between entities defined as membership, aggregation, interaction, generalisation, composition, cross-product and summarisation. Another example is POSTGRES (Stonebraker and Rowe, 1986), a relational DBMS that has been extended to allow object management and complex data typing whilst retaining the underlying simplicity of the relational approach.

Clearly, the sophisticated types of representation possible with data models such as SAM and POSTGRES will demand correspondingly sophisticated models for integrating such databases. It is in this area of development that a potentially highly fruitful merging of AI and Database technology is currently taking place, through the use of the knowledge representation paradigms of AI as a basis for developing integrated semantic interfaces to complex, heterogeneous distributed databases.

The logic-based paradigm has received a considerable amount of attention for this particular role. The close relationship between propositional and predicate logic and the relational data model was, for example, one of the main motivating factors in the choice of the relational data model and the PROLOG programming language as the basis for the Japanese Fifth Generation Computer project. Relational data tables can be expressed as implicitly conjoined sets of logical propositions, and a relational data schema can be expressed in terms of general predicates using universal and existential quantification, as shown in the example in Figure 17.3.

The distinction between the schema (the **intention** of the database) and the data itself (the **extension** of the database) is essentially removed in this form of representation. Expression of relational data schema in first-order logic provides a convenient means for the expression and enforcement of integrity constraints, providing further motivation for the use of this paradigm for data schema management through the coupling of logic-based systems to relational databases. The relative ease with which a schema description represented in terms of predicate logic can be modified is also important for heterogeneous

Relational representation:

Part#	Qty	Machine
P103	46	M42
P108	20	M46
P120b	100	M46

Machine	Capacity
M42	50
M46	50

Predicate logic representation

hasqty(P103, 46)   procmachine(P103, M42)   hascapacity(M42, 50)
hasqty(P108, 20)   procmachine(P108, M46)   hascapacity(M46, 50)
hasqty(P120b, 100)   procmachine(P120b, M46)

part(x) <— hasqty (x, y)
part(x) <— procmachine(x, y)
machine(x) <— hascapacity(x, y)

Figure 17.3 Predicate logic representation of relational tables.

engineering databases to which new data structures must be frequently added.

However, predicate logic is capable, of expressing and formalising data modelling constructs of far more complexity than that of the relational model. Logic programming can, for example, be used to represent general semantic networks (Deliyanni and Kowalski, 1979) and has the added advantage that data does not have to be strictly typed. This places the logic-based paradigm as a strong contender for use in developing a knowledge-based global schema capable of providing an integrated, consistent semantic view of databases which themselves use complex semantic constructs and data types.

The use of logic programming to formalise database schemata also has other advantages. Normal databases generally make what is known as the **domain closure** and **closed world** assumptions which state that the universe of discourse (that part of the real world represented by the database) contains only those object and relationship instances which are actually recorded in the database. Objects and relationships not explicitly recorded in the extension of the database are assumed not to exist in the real world. In a logic representation of a conventional database, rules involving universal and existential quantifiers would be used merely to express integrity constraints. Domain closure and closed world assumptions are obviously rather restrictive, and a logic-based formalisation presents the possibility of using inference rules to deduce the existence of objects and relationships not explicitly stored in the database. A **deductive database** is a database which contains factual assertions (data), a set of rules which define what explicit facts can or must be stored (integrity constraints) and a set of rules for the deduction of implicit facts *not* explicitly stored (inference rules), as a finite and homogeneous set of well-formed formulae. Database queries involving deduction (inference of facts not explicitly recorded) are implemented by the automatic construction of proof plans, as for example, in the resolution/refutation method used in PROLOG. Integrity constraints, which are themselves expressed as predicates, can be combined with heuristics for semantic query optimisation to produce the most efficient strategy for answering a given query, and to provide more information than a simple list of values satisfying the restrictions by detecting, for example, semantically meaningless queries. In deductive databases, extra precautions must be taken when updating the database to ensure that new facts do not contradict the implications of the deduction rules, *in addition* to satisfying integrity constraints.

The deduction possibilities implied by taking a logic-based model for the global schema description opens the possibility of implementing knowledge-based systems within the language of the global schema itself. This effectively means we are enhancing existing databases by embedding knowledge-based systems in the global schema developed to achieve semantic and logical integration of individual databases.

Extensions to individual databases in the form of the superposition of a logic-based schema to facilitate integrity checking, to provide a deductive capability and to perform semantic query optimisation have been widely reported. For example, an interface of a relational database with PROLOG has been described by Marque-Pucheu *et al* (1984). The Knowledge Manager, KM-1 (Kellog, 1986) has a sophisticated interface between a logic-based deductive processor implemented on a Xerox 1100 Lisp machine, and a Britton-Lee IDM-500 Relational Database machine. In this system non-deductive queries are translated directly into the appropriate set of retrieval statements for the relational database, whilst for deductive queries, proof plans are produced which result in data access strategies for answering the posed queries. The logic-based paradigm has also been successfully used to implement schema descriptions underlying CAD databases. For example, ROSALIE (Cholvy and Foisseau, 1983) is an object-oriented CAD database using a semantic data model employing classes, relationships, functions and rules. It also uses a logic representation of the data model for deductive queries.

17.2.6   Combined knowledge/data bases

The integrative solutions between knowledge and databases discussed so far have been oriented towards maximising the utilisation of existing database technology with its highly developed facilities for efficient storage and manipulation of large volumes of similarly structured data, including efficient retrieval techniques, concurrency and security control, and backup facilities. These solutions are, as far as possible, also concerned with utilising existing company data files by providing interfaces to knowledge-based systems, rather than by necessitating complete data reentry, and again imply an *incremental* or *evolutionary* approach to KBS implementation. However, as has been previously indicated, the large scale implementation of Knowledge-Based systems creates opportunities for major rationalisation of an organisation's operating philosophy, procedures, and distribution of decision-making responsibility, and hence also of the data and information on which this is based. Indeed, the importance of **variety reduction** through rationalisation has already been stressed as a prerequisite to maximising the chances of successful and effective large scale implementation of knowledge-based systems. Thus the *evolutionary* approach is not always necessarily the most appropriate.

In cases where a *revolutionary* approach to change is adopted (complete reorganisation and rationalisation of the manufacturing operation), the possibilty arises of using new generations of system which combine the best of both existing knowledge base and database technologies to create integrated knowledge/data base management systems utilising data files restructured from a new top-down viewpoint. These types of system would combine the representational and reasoning capabilities of current knowledge bases with the high volume data handling capability of existing data bases to provide *commercially acceptable* levels of performance and operationally essential features such as backup, concurrency control and security that are not achieved by current generations of system. A survey of the issues involved in achieving this synthesis is the subject of a book edited by Brodie and Mylopoulos (1986).

In this approach, the conventional functions of Data Base Management Systems such as efficient data retrieval and manipulation, integrity maintenance, concurrency control, secondary storage management, restrictions on data access and update authority become subsumed as components in an integrated **Knowledge Base Management System**. A possible architecture for such a system has been proposed by Manola and Brodie (1986) and is shown in Figure 17.4.

The components of this knowledge base consist of the following:

(a) A global knowledge manager (GKM) serving as a general coordinator and planner, and consisting of two knowledge base components, a monitor/interpreter and a scheduler/optimiser, using knowledge contained in the GKM knowledge base. It also contains an internal DBMS.

(b) A unified I/O interface enabling system components to produce integrated displays.

(c) Two categories of knowledge source: application-oriented knowledge-based systems (e.g., scheduling KBS, process planning KBS, etc.) and data type processors with specialised data repositories for different types of data.

(d) Interfaces which provide translation where necessary between the knowledge sources and the GKM.

This type of approach has the advantage that not only does it provide efficient data access to individual knowledge-based systems, but also that the types of data management facility hitherto the main province of DBMS technology can potentially be applied to the management of *knowledge* rather than merely to the management of *data*. Knowledge must be stored in the form of sets of symbols, and can itself be viewed at the 'symbol' level (Newell, 1982) in the sense that different 'chunks' of knowledge need to be classified and stored in such a way that they can be efficiently retrieved when required, must be subject to backup, maintenance, possible restrictions on access, etc., in the same way as data. The view of knowledge as data (albeit of a complex type) requiring

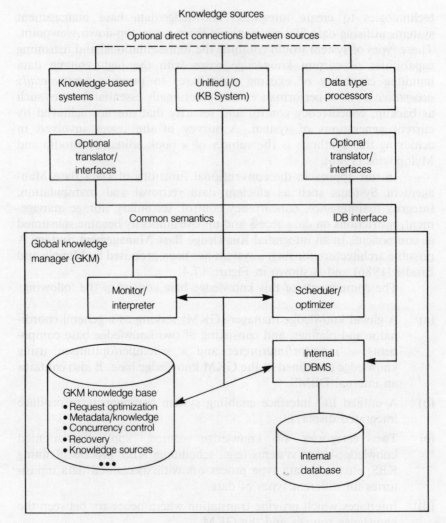

Figure 17.4 A knowledge base management system.

data-like management opens new and comprehensive sets of requirements for future generations of Knowledge Base Management Systems which will need more sophisticated forms of technology than those used in current DBMS. Research into the incorporation of complex data types such as spatial data, active procedures etc. into DBMS is likely to lead to advances in this area. 'Integrity maintenance' for knowledge (more usually termed 'truth maintenance') is another key area which is the subject of intensive research. When knowledge is added to a knowledge base, checks must occur to establish whether the new piece of knowledge conflicts with the existing knowledge and appropriate steps must be taken to resolve the conflict. This is another function that a KBMS will be required to perform.

Conversely to the 'knowledge as data' implications for the enhancement of the knowledge management capabilities of KBMS, the use of knowledge representation paradigms as bases for more sophisticated data modelling can help to overcome some of the representational limitations of conventional databases. The enhancement of data semantics is an obvious advantage that has already been discussed at some length. Additional advantages derive from the possibility of representing data that is vague, uncertain, or incomplete. The domain closure and closed world assumptions of the finite, conjunctive relational model, although convenient for data access, update and integrity maintenance, are unrealistic in their inability to map the many uncertainties inherent in real-world factory data. Use of knowledge representation paradigms for the representation of data allow for the *quality, inherent uncertainty*, or *inherent vagueness* of the data to be included in the representation through such things as uncertainty factors or fuzzy set membership. The database can also be allowed to exist in temporarily inconsistent states to facilitate troubleshooting of the actual factory problems that might have lead to the inconsistencies. A database with these facilities can not only generate answers to specific questions but also supply evidence or arguments for or against these answers. This is likely to be of much greater value than a simple factual answer to the user who is operating in an environment in which unreliable reports and uncertain facts abound.

Some of these facilities are starting to emerge in the latest releases of certain of the Knowledge Engineering Environments described in the previous chapter. Fox and McDermott (1986) describe some of the work on SRL (the Schema Representation language that forms the basis of Knowledge Craft) to enhance it with database capabilities, and also discuss issues of synchronisation and security. Representation of uncertain and incomplete data is becoming recognised as a crucial issue, and commercial hardware chips are already available on the market with the ability to reason using fuzzy logic. As stated by Fox and McDermott, the full integration of Knowledge and Database technology is a problem whose 'time has come'. Although the problems are formidable, commercially viable integrated knowledge/data base management systems are likely to become a reality in the very near future.

17.3   Task decomposition and goal integration

If it is assumed that the tasks for which knowledge-based support is to be provided are all autonomous, the implementation of individual knowledge-based systems could proceed relatively independently with the progressive addition of knowledge-based support to those responsible for performing each task, to increase efficiency and effectiveness potentially up to the level of complete task automation. In actual organisational environments, however, it is not reasonable to assume merely that using KBS to make existing tasks more efficient will represent the best possible usage of KBS technology in increasing organisational synergy. Large knowledge bases have the potential to redistribute knowledge throughout the organisation, making it generally more *available*. Individual knowledge based systems have the potential to use this knowledge to take over certain tasks previously performed by humans, thus freeing the available human cognitive resources for other tasks for which the unique capabilities of the human brain are better suited. Thus the type of overall task decomposition on which an existing organisational structure is based may not provide the most synergistic means for goal achievment when due regard is paid to the possibility of relaxing previous constraints on knowledge availability and knowledge and information processing capacity associated with various functional organisational positions.

The process of managing a manufacturing operation may effectively be regarded as a multi-agent cooperative problem-solving task, in which individual agents have different knowledge about different aspects of the overall situation, some of which will be shared and some of which will be private. In order to establish how knowledge bases and knowledge-based systems can most effectively be used, the key questions that need to be asked are:

(1)   Given the new possibilities for the distribution and application of knowledge implied by the large scale introduction of knowledge-based systems, what is the best form of overall task decomposition and delegation of decision making to individual problem-solving agents for the achievement of overall organisational synergy?

(2)   For each problem solving agent, how can that agent's task best be shared between human and computer.

(3)   What knowledge will each agent need for the performance of its task? What types of knowledge need to be *common* (i.e., shared between individual agents) and what types of knowledge are local (only required by one individual agent)? How will knowledge *consistency* be maintained?

(4)   What types of communication need to take place between individual agents? Which other agents will need to be informed about the results of a particular problem-solving activity and how will this occur? How will an agent acquire knowledge it needs but does not have?

17.3.1 Task decomposition

The principles of good organisational design allied with the principles of cybernetics outlined in Chapter 3 suggest that the overall organisational task should be divided in such a way as to achieve the maximum possible degree of autonomy of individual subtasks, and that these subtasks should not be so complex that their **variety** cannot be matched by the variety of the regulating mechanism brought to bear by the agent responsible for performing them.

Types of interdependence between subtasks may be classified as either **pooled** interdependence, **sequential** interdependence or **reciprocal** interdependence (Thompson, 1967). **Pooled interdependence** is where subtasks do not directly depend on each other, but the overall health and survival of the organisational entity (and hence the survival of agents performing the subtasks) depends on the adequate performance of each subtask. An example would be a group of independent product lines in a product-organised company. **Sequential interdependence** is where one agent must complete a task or some section of it before the next can start. Obvious examples are the sequential stages of manufacturing in a functionally divided company: design must precede production; machining of components must be completed prior to assembly. **Reciprocal interdependence** involves a close degree of cooperation between agents. For example, the concept of design for manufacture suggests a certain amount of give-and-take between designers and process planners to develop products that are easily and economically manufacturable.

As was pointed out in Chapter 3, traditional manufacturing organisations normally subdivide and compartmentalise tasks in order to reduce their variety to a level that can be handled by a single controlling agent. However, the resulting tasks often have quite strong degrees of sequential and reciprocal interdependence, and good coordination between tasks is often difficult to achieve, particularly in organisations in which strict hierarchical relationships are maintained. One of the principal beneficial effects of the introduction of knowledge bases and knowledge-based systems is in the potential increase they give to the *variety* available to the individual agents who are controlling the subtasks. Higher concentrations of knowledge can be brought to bear at lower levels of the organisation on tasks in which they are needed. This opens up the possibility of aggregating certain types of reciprocally and sequentially independent subtask, and putting them under the control of a single human agent, whose ability to dispose sufficient variety for their performance is augmented by the **knowledge-focusing power** of globally available knowledge bases and local knowledge-based systems. Alternatively, these types of task may be better coordinated between individual human agents by the ready availability of common knowledge (in the form of sets of constraints for example) from a shared knowledge base, and/or a message passing either directly or by a blackboard.

Consider again the subtasks of product design and process planning. Both these tasks are of sufficiently high variety for the unaided human that they are normally assigned to different organisational units. However, close coordination is required between the two to ensure economically manufacturable designs. As an example of the first type of architecture, the availability of knowledge-based systems such as IMDA described in Chapter 15 can serve as 'knowledge amplifiers' to increase the disposable variety of a single human agent to the extent that one individual might be assigned both tasks, thereby achieving the necessary degree of coordination between the two without having to rely on hierarchical communication. A further interesting possibility is the notion of series of **cooperative knowledge-based systems** under the control of a single human agent, where each KBS is responsible for part of the task that previously required a separate human agent. A design/process-planning KBS might have two cooperative knowledge-based systems, a design expert and a process planning expert with a single human agent monitoring and participating in each task, particularly at the cooperative interface.

The alternative and more passive form of variety amplification for increasing task coordination is to use a common knowledge base for the communication of constraints between subtasks. Consider, for example, the reciprocally interdependent tasks of process planning and scheduling in a job shop. The process planner will require knowledge of the machines available, their technical capabilities and their current loadings to develop a plan which can be feasibly executed by the due date of the order. The scheduler who is responsible for ensuring this plan is implemented may be faced with a machine breakdown amd will require information on which alternative machines may be used. A common knowledge base containing information both about machine loadings and about possible alternative machines for a particular operation would facilitate the coordination of these tasks. This common knowledge might also contain information such as the fact that a particular machine tends to produce a large number of rejects of a particular class of part and therefore should only be used for that part type in exceptional circumstances. This helps to ensure integration of the two tasks by basing decisions on **consistent premises** as well as using consistent data. Examples of these different architectures are shown in Figure 17.5.

17.3.2   Division of task between human and computer

Knowledge-based systems also require to be effectively integrated with human problem-solving ability to achieve the maximum possible degree of synergy between human and machine. Some of the issues concerned

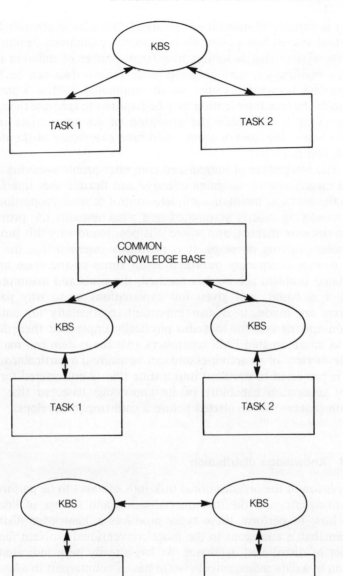

Figure 17.5 Different forms of task integration using knowledge-based system.

with this have been covered in Chapter 10. A general rule is that the lower the level of the organisational task, the more of the task can be delegated to automated decision making systems. A crucial assumption here is that tasks have been designed in such a way that the degree of variety representable in an automated knowledge-based decision making system is capable of matching the variety that can be generated within the actual system being controlled. A poorly maintained flexible manufacturing system that is subject to a large number of different types of random malfunction may generate more variety than can be handled through the knowledge stored in an automated control system, and continuous human intervention may be required to generate the requisite variety. This would mean the provision of an appropriate interface through which the human agent could take over some of the decision-making functions.

The integration of human and computer problem-solving capabilities is largely one of designing effective and flexible user interfaces, in which the user can maintain complete control of what proportion of the problem-solving task is automated and what remains the province of human decision making, and where it is possible to vary this proportion as problem solving develops. It is obviously essential that the human agent is kept adequately informed at all times of the stage at which automated problem solving has reached, the goals and assumptions on which it is based, and given full explanations as to why particular decisions are made. It is also important, particularly for automated decision-making systems that also physically implement their decisions (such as an automated FMS controller), that the system can maintain a 'metalevel view' of its activities and can be aware if a particular situation is (or is projected to develop) into a state that is not catered for by the variety generation capability of its knowledge base, so that human decision makers can be alerted before a catastrophe develops.

17.3.3 Knowledge distribution

The division of the organisational task into subtasks to be performed by different agents, and the institutionalisation and storage of knowledge about how to perform these tasks produces a **knowledge distribution** problem that is analagous to the more conventional problem facing the designer of distributed databases. As has already been indicated, every function in a data management system has its counterpart in a system for knowledge management. In the same way that we make the distinction between 'common' data stored either in a centralised database or in accessible distributed databases with a global semantic interface, and private data which are maintained and accessed only by their owning subunits, we can also talk about 'common' knowledge (accessible to everybody, or to selected groups of agents) and 'private' knowledge concerned only with local problem solving and accessible to the agent tasked with solving the problem. In the interests of controlling the potentially proliferating complexity that would result from 'everybody having access to everything', individual problem-solving agents will generally be restricted only have access to the knowledge of the overall problem that they require. In other words, the amount of private knowledge will be considerably greater than the amount of common knowledge. This gives rise to problems of **knowledge consistency**. An individual agent may well generate or change its private knowledge base during its problem-solving task that makes its view of the world inconsistent with that of other agents. We can distinguish three possible types of knowledge inconsistency: inconsistent beliefs or assumptions about the **current state of the world**, inconsistent **knowledge semantics** and inconsistent or conflicting **problem-solving goals**. In the corresponding database problem, we have proposed the solution of a global schema or common semantic interface which at least maintains the consistency of data semantics, and could also check its integrity. The problem for the case of a distributed knowledge base is considerably more complex, and would require a powerful knowledge representation meta-language (similarly to the notion of logic as a database meta-language). The task of the agent assigned to detecting and resolving knowledge inconsistencies would be exceedingly complex (for example, the problem of detecting goal inconsistencies would involve complex inferencing procedures and a considerable amount of meta-knowledge) and possibly would be of higher variety than any current or immediately forseeable knowledge-based system is capable of generating. A more feasible solution would be to allow individual agents to resolve inconsistencies between themselves by direct communication and feedback.

17.3.4   Direct communication

Problem-solving activities of individual knowledge-based systems can also be integrated by direct communication as well as by having access to shared data and knowledge. The latter is of course a form of indirect communication analogous to the use of blackboard architecture in systems such as PLATO/Z, where the blackboard represents the common part of the knowledge base. However, work on cooperative problem-solving systems has generated a number of concepts which are useful for the analysis of how individual decision-making agents in manufacturing companies — be they humans, intelligent systems, or both acting in some augmented mode — can cooperate in the interests of achieving overall organisational goals through direct communication. These concepts are concerned with **commitment** and **contract negotiation**.

In order to achieve coordination of sequentially or reciprocally interdependent tasks, individual agents must form *agreements* with one another to perform certain tasks. However, merely exchanging intentions with one another is not generally enough for cooperative work, as pointed out by Rosenschein (1985). Davis and Smith (1983) developed a framework based on 'contract nets' in which it was assumed that task distribution between a group of individual problem solvers can be regarded as a form of contract negotiation, and they proposed a set of data structures for the communication and manipulation of these contracts. As the complexity of the overall organisational task increases, so does the necessity for more communication, and for the entering into a greater number of commitments, and agents can lose track of the agreements to which they have been committed. Koo and Cashman (1987) have extended the work of Davis and Smith to the monitoring as well as the management of contracts in the COMTRAC-M language designed specifically for manufacturing environments.

COMTRAC-M allows individual contracts between agents to be specified as one or more **terms**, where one term of the contract specifies a particular **task** to be performed (an action, group of actions, or a goal) the **asker**, the **doer**, and the **time** by when the result is to be delivered. Different agents can fill different roles of asker and doer in different terms of the same contract. Terms can also have **qualifications** (conditions that must be satisfied before or after the obligations in the term are fulfilled), and **justifications** (the reasons behind the corresponding term, which can include beliefs and assumptions both factual and deduced, which may relate to terms in other contracts). Sets of terms in a contract can thus be displayed as **qualified commitment nets** (directed graphs in which nodes represents terms and arcs represent qualification relations). An example of such a commitment net is shown in Figure 17.6.

Terms in a contract are normally **negotiated** between two agents. In the negotiation process, one agent (say A) makes a request to another agent (say B), who can accept or reject this request, or make a counter proposal. If B accepts the request, or makes a counter-proposal that is

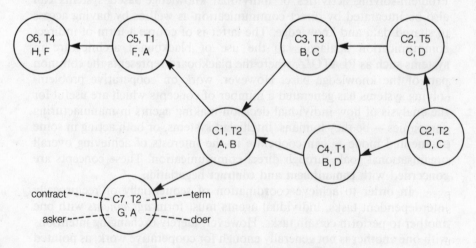

Figure 17.6   A commitment net in COMTRAC—M.

acceptable to A, then A and B have committed themselves to a contract and can cooperate to carry out the responsibilities stated in it. Each term in a contract forms part of a stored **activity network** which represents the overall task plan. The content of the various proposals and contracts at various stages may either be stored in a global database shared by all agents, or may be stored locally by individual agents.

The management of agent commitments is facilitated by means of a set of operators. An agent can **summarise** its commitments. It can **trace-up** qualification links in commitment nets to find other agents whose tasks may affect its own performance. It can **query** other agents for information. It can **trace-down** a commitment net to find which agents will be affected if a contract in which it is participating is breached or delayed. It can also signal these affected agents so that they can modify their plans accordingly.

COMTRAC-M requires that a semantically consistent common vocabulary for task domains should be specified, and should be clear enough for agents to reason about agreements, whether the agents are humans or automated problem solvers.

There are no described implementations of COMTRAC-M, which appears to be largely in the experimental stage. However, this type of system would clearly be of great value in managing, for example, the communications between independently operating scheduling agents which form the basis of the ISTOP philosophy described in Chapter 12.

17.4 Socio-technical integration of knowledge-based systems

17.4.1 General

Introduction of knowledge-based systems implies major technological change. Technological change in organisations is not something that is new, and the social effects of technological changes in general have been intensively studied over a number of years, starting with the 'socio-technical systems' framework of Trist (1963). In many cases it has been found that, although the characteristics of a new system from a purely technical point of view may be faultless, the system simply does not live up to its expectations and that this is due to inadequate attention to the psychological and social factors connected with the introduction of such systems. Resistance to change is an endemic part of human nature, and if steps are not taken during the technology implementation process to understand and thereby minimise this resistance, the chances of achieving successful implementation will be greatly reduced.

17.4.2 Lessons from conventional MIS implementations

The number of published KBS implementations is still relatively small, and very little research has been done on the effect that the types of problem mentioned above might have on the KBS implementation process. However, intensive studies have been performed of the manifestations of these problems in relation to conventional Management Information System implementations (for example, Dickson and Wetherbe, 1985) and have indicated a number of major factors which will determine whether and to what extent the implementation of a new system will be accepted or rejected. Some of the major conclusions of this research will be summarised in this section. This will be followed in a subsequent section by an examination of the specific characteristics of KBS implementations and the extent to which lessons from MIS implementation research may be applicable.

Dickson and Wetherbe have identified a number of major factors that will determine whether and to what extent new computerised information systems are likely to be resisted:

(1) **Disruption of established departmental boundaries.** Introduction of new systems often result in changes to existing organisational structure, perhaps involving mergers between departments (e.g., stock control and purchasing). This type of change may be resisted by individuals who may resent any changes in how and with whom they work.

(2) **Disruption of the informal system**. New computerised information systems may alter communication patterns to the extent that existing informal communication networks may be disrupted. These informal channels may have become a 'way of life' for the organisation and may fulfill important social needs, so there may be resistance to more formal channels set up by the new system.

(3) **Group cohesiveness leading to resistance to outsiders.** The implementation team of systems specialists, who are likely to be outside consultants or internal specialists with little experience of the area in which the system is being implememented, may be resisted because they are not part of the 'local' team who may have worked together for many years and may see them as 'outsiders'.

(4) **Reduction in job responsibility.** The new system may be perceived as leading to a loss of responsibility, or of personal power and influence.

(5) **Reduction in job security.** It may be perceived that the system will pose a threat to job security by automating hitherto human-performed tasks and making staff redundant.

(6) **Information possessiveness.** The system may make information

which is jealously guarded (because its private possession confers expert authority on the possessor) available to others. This can also eliminate the possibility of blaming poor performance on lack of information.

(7) **Organisational climate.** If open communications and a climate of trust is generated by top management, resistance to a new system is likely to be reduced. If top management are aloof and unwilling to communicate details and objectives of the new system, or if the organisational climate is inflexible, implementation is likely to be hindered.

In a manufacturing context, the majority of large MIS implementations have been concerned with MRP or MRP2 systems. As indicated in Chapter 2, the rate of successful implementation of these systems has been low, although many technical and human factors have obviously contributed to this. However, human factors of the type described above have been attributed to most of the failures in all situations where the technical aspects of the system were favourable.

The frustrations associated with the implementation of new computerised information systems can manifest themselves in a variety of ways. Dickson and Simmons (1970) have identified **aggression**, **projection** and **avoidance** as three common forms of frustration. **Aggression** is an active expression of frustration and may take the form of sabotage, in which individuals may deliberately input false or misleading information to the system, or even cause physical destruction of system components. **Projection** is where individuals blame their own poor performance, or their own errors, on the presence of the system. **Avoidance** is where individuals simply fail to use the system, or ignore its output or recommendations in favour of their own information sources or decision heuristics. These types of manifestation have been more recently described by Dickson and Wetherbe as constituting the 'tactics of counter-implementation'.

Individuals at different levels of the organisation will generally adopt different types of tactic against a system whose implementation is being insensitively handled. Operating personnel who may be required to work directly with the new system and must accustom themselves to new procedures are more likely to exhibit aggression toward the system. Operating management will be affected through changes in departmental boundaries and organisational communication channels, and by the fact that data and information that were previously kept on a private basis now suddenly become more freely available. Operating management are likely to exhibit all three forms of frustration. It has frequently been observed that top management tend to avoid contact with computer systems, possibly out of feelings of insecurity about computers. This is consistent with Mintzberg's (1973) findings that higher level managers have a strong preference for oral over other forms of information.

Dickson and Wetherbe have identified a set of factors which can contribute towards the overcoming of implementation problems. These are summarised below:

(1)   **User orientation.** If a system is strongly oriented towards user needs, both in design and implementation, then it is more likely to succeed. If it fails to satisfy user needs, then users are likely to quickly revert to previous 'informal' systems.

(2)   **User involvement and participation.** It has become almost axiomatic that a successfully implemented information system requires end-user participation in the system design, with the user making a major input to decisions on the type of information the system provides, and any job redesign involved.

(3)   **Communication and education.** The objectives and characteristics of the proposed system should be clearly communicated to all those who will be affected by it, with regular updates on how the development of the system is progressing; those affected should also receive intensive education and training programs on the nature and usage of the new system.

(4)   **Redefined performance evaluation methods.** New information systems may modify the nature of certain tasks to the point where previous methods of performance evaluation are no longer applicable. New tasks and evaluation procedures must be accompanied by incentives to encourage employees to cooperate, and the new method must be clearly explained so that individuals know exactly how they are being evaluated.

(5)   **New challenges.** To reduce the feelings of insecurity, redundancy, or loss of job responsibility that may accompany the introduction of a new information system, the potential challenges made possible by the new system should be publicised. For example, when the more mundane tasks are taken over by the computer system, staff have more time to devote their energies to more challenging and creatively rewarding tasks.

Of great importance in establishing an organisational climate conducive to the fostering of the above factors is a wholehearted commitment by top management to the success of the implementation project. This has been identified as the most important **single** factor associated with successful MIS implementations (Meredith, 1981), although in many cases it may be difficult to achieve, particularly in organisations where the top management has a predominantly financial or accounting background and insist on detailed cost justifications for the new system.

The potential benefits of systems which improve information flow and availability derive largely from their contribution to organisational synergy, which does not lend itself to objective quantification of the type normally required by accountants. In many cases, top management commitment must be an act of faith.

Ginzberg (1981) has suggested that two types of commitment are required: commitment to the project itself, and commitment to the more general process of organisational change which will inevitably be associated with introduction of any new information system. If a commitment to change is already present (e.g., in an organisation implementing a major rationalisation program in an attempt to move towards JIT), it is more likely that there will be commitment to the successful implementation of individual systems which are consistent with this broader aim.

17.4.3 Lessons from DSS implementation research

Much is being written about the human aspects of the implementation of Decision Support Systems. DSS are more closely linked to the personalised ways in which people (particularly managers) use data and information to arrive at decisions than are MIS which essentially only collect, manipulate and redistribute information. The personalised nature of DSS has resulted in iterative design based on the rapid prototype-user feedback cycle becoming an accepted feature of the DSS implementation process, and the importance of involving the user in the design has been magnified to the extent that some researchers have advocated the user should exercise total control of the project from conception onwards. Brightman and Harris (1984) have indicated some of the ways users have contributed to successful DSS implementations, and this does indeed cover the whole spectrum of activity (Figure 17.7).

An area of DSS research has been in the matching of individual DSS to the *cognitive style* of the user. Different individuals appear to use different subjective methods of organising information during the decision-making process. McKenney and Keen (1974) have used a two-dimensional representation of cognitive style in which individuals vary along an **information gathering** axis and an **information evaluation** axis (Figure 17.8). The information gathering axis runs from *preceptive* (those people tending to infer generalisations about the environment from the available data) to *receptive* (tending to derive specific knowledge from the data). The information evaluation (or analysis) axis runs from *systematic* (tending to use a structured, deductive approach to analysis) to *intuitive* (tending to use trial and error strategies, or acting spontaneously on the basis of new information).

Examples of User Participation in DSS

---

1. Planning Phase
   a. The user initially suggests that the model bebuilt.
   b. The user participates in initial discussions prior to building the model.
   c. The user evaluates the potential cost-benefit ratio for building the model.
   d. The user defines the goals of the model.

2. Design Phase
   1. The user is the team leader in building the model.
   2. The user obtains necessary data to build the model.
   3. The user makes suggestions for improving the model.
   4. The user "smoothes the way/runs interference" during the model design
   phase.

Figure 17.7

Whereas conventional MIS are more suitable to receptive, systematic styles, one of the challenges of early DSS was to try and develop systems which supported the more preceptive and intuitive type of decision maker. To the extent that different people do display different

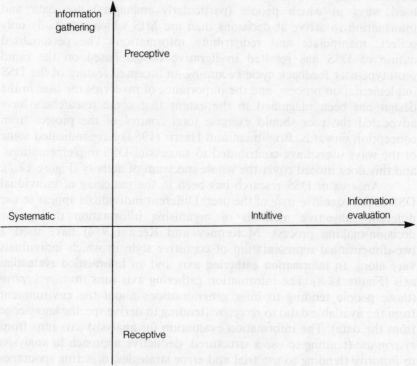

Figure 17.8   Cognitive styles of DSS users.

(and distinguishable) decision-making styles (which is contentious) this has only occurred to a very limited extent, and the majority of DSS are still based on notions of systematic analysis and deduction. Alter (1980) has indicated that many DSS are not in fact used by those for whom they were intended, and that many higher level managers either ignore their DSS or delegate its use to assistants. Ambiguity about the identity of the end user obviously creates additional problems about tailoring the system to user needs.

Another important issue emerging from experiences of implementing DSS is the very sensitive and potentially problematical relationship between DSS development personnel and traditional Data Processing departments. The notions of personalised, iterative design of the former run totally counter to traditional DP development cycles, and this lead to most early DSS being developed independently of DP departments, who reacted unfavourably to a trend that they saw might reduce their own power and status. However, the increasingly widespread usage of personal computers and the general trend towards 'end-user computing' are forcing the more conservative DP departments to come to terms with the situation, and the increasing emergence of 'information centres' (departments providing a comprehensive centralised support service to users who wish to write their own computer applications) is radically changing the organisational structure related to computer technology of many companies.

17.4.4 Human aspects peculiar to KBS implementation

The introduction of knowledge-based systems into an organisation may be expected to be associated with many of the human problems associated with the introduction of MIS. KBS are even more likely to result in the disruption of existing departmental boundaries and informal systems, with profound changes to individual task responsibilities. Quite clearly, the prerequisites of establishing a good organisational climate with mutual trust and open communications about the nature and purpose of the new system, and the importance of involving those affected by the new system in its design, are equally valid for KBS implementation. There is, however, an important feature of widespread KBS introduction that is not necessarily associated with the introduction of MIS. Whereas the introduction of a management information system tends to encourage **centralisation** of decision making and control by facilitating the upward flow of information, the introduction of knowledge-based systems, although in principle capable of supporting either centralisation or decentralisation, will tend to encourage the **decentralisation** of decision making by bringing more knowledge to bear on problems at lower organisational levels. This is particularly likely in manufacturing environments in which decentralised decision making is almost essential in order to achieve a 'variety match' in the cybernetic sense, between problems and regulating systems. Thus, rather than removing responsibility from operating personnel through the automation of their tasks (as might be feared), KBS are likely to result in increased responsibility at this level, with many of the coordinating and exception decision-making functions of middle management now devolved to personnel on the shop floor, whose information processing and decision making capability (i.e., their capability of matching the *variety* of shop floor problems) is augmented with knowledge-based systems. This will result in flatter organisational hierarchies, with a corresponding reduction in the number of middle management personnel.

This type of organisational restructuring will not necessarily be achieved smoothly. Although it may be possible for middle management to be gradually phased out, shop floor personnel may not take kindly to increased job responsibilties and accountability unless these are accompanied by some form of extra reward, remuneration, or the possibility of career advancement. A massive 'reskilling' of the workforce will also be required, which will involve intensive training programs. Attitudinal changes towards job responsibilities will also be necessary. To some extent these may result from increases in job depth and responsibility giving to employees a greater sense of involvement with their work, and of their own value, a phenomenon which has been observed in a number of top performing companies (Peters and Waterman, 1982) and is one of the supporting philosophies of the JIT approach. The 'AI Circles' approach advocated by Greene (Section 16.2.4) is one way of exploiting this phenomenon. However, this is a problem that will need to be examined very carefully.

Introduction of KBS opens up the possibility of **electronic monitoring and supervision** of operating personnel's performance. Since work is performed on-line, individual decisions can be recorded, stored and subsequently analysed for their quality. This capability will need to be handled with extreme sensitivity, since the resulting connotations of increased control may negate the motivational aspects associated with increased job depth.

The encapsulation of various types of professional expertise in knowledge-based systems will not necessarily imply the redundancy of the human experts themselves, merely that they will be able to spend more time on other activities such as research and development, and on the elaboration and expansion of expert knowledge bases, rather than on the *routine* application of their expert knowledge. This aspect would need to be stressed, to reduce the feelings of insecurity that such professionals might otherwise feel in being expected to 'give up' their perhaps jealously guarded expertise.

Whether KBS, when developed, remain unused as has been the case with many DSS, will be a function of the types of user interface provided, and whether task restructuring and KBS integration allows any *possibility* of effectively performing the task *without* recourse to the KBS. DSS are themselves intended to assist a particular user in a personal way in the performance of an existing task. A KBS is not necessarily geared to the personal characteristics of an individual user. However, the provision of a sophisticated 'intelligent' interface should make it easier for all potential users to operate, and the redesign of the task it supports may very well make KBS usage an integral part of the task itself. For example, a production scheduler may only receive information about which jobs are required to be scheduled from the scheduling KBS. This will already necessitate some interaction with the KBS, and it might then be much simpler to proceed to use the KBS facilities to schedule the jobs, than to perform the task manually.

The appearance of the knowledge engineer as a new class of professional will be an obvious trend. However, it is likely that with the development of more sophisticated knowledge acquisition tools, and an emphasis on domain experts directly encoding their own knowledge, the role of the knowledge engineer may change from that of knowledge acquisition and knowledge base development to trouble shooting and knowledge base maintainance. With the increasing importance of this particular type of expertise, a redistribution in power is likely from marketing and finance departments to the department charged with the coordination of Information and Knowledge Systems development and maintenance. This shift of power is unlikely to occur without opposition from those whose power base is reduced.

We may conclude that the path to large-scale KBS implementation and integration in manufacturing companies will not be easy, and will almost inevitably be accompanied by a major program of fundamental organisational change and restructuring which perhaps will make the physical appearance of the KBS themselves almost incidental. As stated in Chapter 2, the remaining technical problems to KBS integration can almost certainly be overcome. The human and organisational problems are perhaps much more intractable. Human beings are only capable of assimilating change at a certain rate, and current rates of technological advance have far outstripped our ability to make effective use of them.

CHAPTER 18
Epilogue — Current Trends and Future Directions

The whole field of knowledge engineering and knowledge-based systems is in a state of rapid flux. Whereas up to the mid-1980s Artificial Intelligence was a topic that was little discussed outside of Universities and Research Establishments, the past few years has started to see an apparent exponential growth in the number of systems actually fielded and operationally running in industry. The major computer companies, including DEC, NCR and IBM are particularly active in applying this type of technology to their own operations. Whether the majority of such systems are paying their way is still uncertain. However, what does seem clear is that the majority of companies are adopting the 'start small' approach, and are developing simple systems for relatively straightforward and well-structured subtasks, using rule-based shells. It is unlikely that these types of application per se will have a profound effect on organisational performance. As we have seen, the increased automation of existing structured or semi-structured tasks, if these are based on a traditional division by function with sequential decision making at the various phases of material and design flow, is simply not sufficient to reach the full degree of synergy potentially achievable.

In addition to the development of individual knowledge-based systems, whether this is performed by AI circles or by specialised knowledge engineers, there are at least two other essential ingredients needed for a successful recipe for achieving this synergy. First, organisational restructuring must occur based around simplified, rationalised product lines. The traditional organisational barriers imposed by the persistence of the classical management philosophy of reductionism, must be broken down, and there must be a grouping on a product basis, within single knowledge-based system, of individual pieces of knowledge previously generated, maintained and applied within the strict confines of watertight functional departments. Second, rather than functioning as independent, autonomous applications, individual knowledge-based systems should be regarded as 'nodes' in a knowledge 'network', with real-time information exchange not just on predefined items of operational detail, but on unstructured and ill-defined issues that relate to higher level organisational goals. For this purpose the presence of human judgement in each knowledge node is essential, and for the immediate future, a knowledge node would ideally consist of a small group of humans augmented in their knowledge processing power with a knowledge-based decision-support system, which collectively integrates the disparate types of knowledge about a given set of activities requiring close coordination, and enables these activities to be performed as a coherent whole.

Whether any organisation has yet come near to successfully achieving the knowledge network ideal is at present doubtful. The implementation of such a concept is likely to be an ongoing evolutionary process, which never actually attains a state of completion. There is evidence that a number of companies are some way along the evolutionary road. For example DEC, who pioneered knowledge-based systems implementation with the operational installation of the XCON system, are well on the way to developing a 'knowledge network', in conjunction with researchers at Carnegie Mellon University, for the integration of sales, engineering, configuration, manufacturing, distribution and field service. The network configuration is shown in Figure 18.1, in which it can be seen that these individual systems are sequentially interconnected in that the flow of information from one system to another corresponds to the traditional flow of materials and information. The requirements of developing knowledge systems with acceptable response times has resulted in most of these systems being rule based, and employing surface heuristics for reasoning and problem solving. Any common model of the organisation that they employ is therefore implicitly embedded in the types of information they are allowed to exchange, and the embedded rules that manipulated this information. Research on distributed knowledge sources working on different aspects of a common task and communicating either directly or by a blackboard or both, is a rapidly growing area, and issues of contract negotiation and commitment between autonomous agents is receiving increasing attention. This field is converging and overlapping with research on the 'neural network' model of computing, which is a contender to replace the strictly sequential von Neumann processing architecture of conventional computers. Much of the research on distributed intelligence has been oriented towards full task automation, and has been concerned with the distribution of knowledge, within a single KBS, between structured and detailed tasks at the hardware control level (e.g., Robotics or automatic FMS scheduling as in the PLATO/Z system). However, there is much scope for the use of the results of this research in developing distributed knowledge networks at the production management level, where the knowledge nodes consist of a combination of humans and knowledge-based decision-support systems, rather than being fully automated decision- making agents. An example of this approach is the philosophy of the ISTOP system described in Chapter 12.

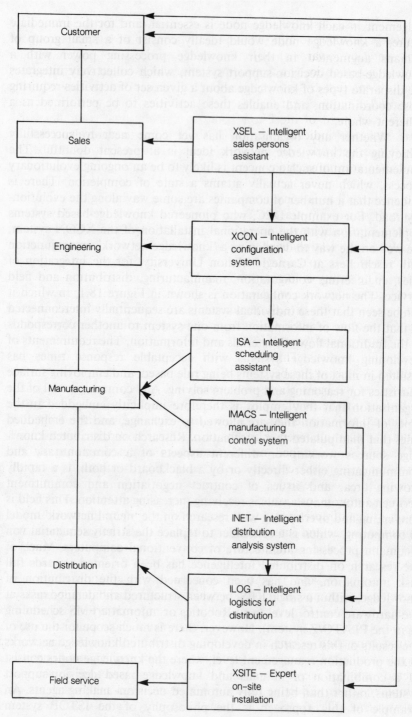

Figure 18.1 DEC's 'knowledge network'.

In these less-structured, production management tasks, it is obviously desirable to aim to move away from a pure surface knowledge representation towards an object-oriented organisational knowledge base containing semantically rich structural information about the entities and relationships that collectively constitute the organisation. However, the ever-present requirement for processing speed, coupled with the existing heavy investment of most companies in conventional computer hardware seems to indicate that in the short term, the prevalent type of knowledge network will be based on surface heuristics and direct structured communication.

The implementation of knowledge-based systems using hardware and software that is conventional by today's standards will clearly be a relatively short-term practice, since what is unconventional today will be conventional tomorrow. In the longer term, new generations of computer hardware will certainly enable object-oriented databases containing large volumes of data to be implemented with acceptable levels of performance. The ability of local rule-based systems to interact with a common 'deep' knowledge base would reduce the level of direct communication required, and what direct communication did take place could be at a higher conceptual level, since the underlying common deep knowledge base could be used by each system to interpret and resolve ambiguous or conflicting messages. This could allow such things as resolution of goal conflicts, which would be problematical in rule-based systems communicating on the basis of message interpretation ability restricted to that embedded in the available rule set. A possible trend will be towards distributed object-oriented databases, in which individual information about, for example, specific groups of machines and parts, are localised in databases maintained on distributed computer hardware by the corresponding manufacturing cells. The cell itself would, in the distributed database, be regarded as a composite object which could interact with other objects (e.g., other cells, superclass objects, etc) as in a normal object-oriented representation. The difference would be the possibility of human influence and intervention in the pattern of the interaction, and the ability of the complete system effectively to perform 'parallel processing'.

The 'when' and 'how' of the general implementation of the next generation of computer hardware which allows such an approach to occur is uncertain. Clearly the upgrading to new hardware would present a good opportunity for companies that had not already done so to start restructuring their organisation and management philosophy in such a way as to take maximimum advantage of the opportunities and potential offered, and not merely to transfer their existing practices to the new computer system. Effective planning will be required as to just how this restructuring will take place, and this must be initiated well before the investment in computer hardaware is actually made. Ironically, many of the knowledge-based tools that would greatly facilitate this planning are such that they could only be effectively available *after* the new implementation was well under way.

The slow response times of complex knowledge-based systems and the resulting adverse effects on their commercial acceptability is a problem that should be greatly reduced with new computer hardware. Computers based on parallel processing are likely to play an increasingly important role in raising the performance level of knowledge-based systems, even making centralised object-oriented databases a viable possibility. Blocks of tightly coupled memory elements can be used to divide search algorithms into separate parts and process each part simultaneously. Parallel processing is particularly appropriate for PROLOG because the built-in inference mechanisms of the language are suited to parallel search. This technique forms part of the basis of the Japanese Fifth Generation Computer Project. Computers using parallel architectures are appearing on the general market place, although they have not yet been extensively used in AI applications.

The possibility of increasing performance by embedding knowledge-based systems in microprocessor chips has also been investigated. A problem here is that knowledge is difficult to update, hence this technique is only applicable to static knowledge domains. Possible applications exist in process control and machine diagnostics, where although complex, the required knowledge is stable. For these applications KBS chips might be 'hard-wired' to the process or equipment concerned. Other applications exist in domains where a large proportion of the knowledge is static and can be stored on a chip (e.g., basic engineering knowledge) with more knowledge being added to additional random access memory in the normal way.

Trends in software development are likely to see a reduction in the number of general purpose KBS shells, and a corresponding increase in the number of application specific shells for such activities as design, planning and scheduling. These are likely to be provided with sophisticated user interfaces, making it possible for unskilled users to enter domain-specific knowledge directly. The knowledge acquisition bottleneck is likely to stimulate the development of increasingly sophisticated automated knowledge acquistion tools which will form a part of this user interface. This would be expected to result in a trend away from the knowledge engineer acting in the knowledge acquisition and system building role, towards a role more connected with *knowledge maintenance* (e.g., ensuring the consistency of knowledge stored in various distributed knowledge bases).

As a concluding comment, it might be stressed yet again that the major barriers to achieving knowledge-based integration of manufacturing are not likely to be technical but organisational. Many manufacturing companies are still blindly following the precepts of functional scientific management in which the individual is a cog in a large, clumsy and inefficient wheel. The transition from the machine analogy of cogs and wheels to the organic analogy with flexible knowledge networks is, however, not necessarily counter to basic human instincts. As H. Chandler Stevens writes in his poem *The Networker's Creed*:

> I'd rather be a node in a network
>   than a cog in the gear of a machine
> A node is involved with things to resolve
>   while a cog must mesh with cogs in between.

References and Bibliography

Ackoff, R. L. 'Management misinformation systems', *Management Science* 14 (4) (1967), pp147–56.

'The future of operational research in past,' *Journal of the Operational Research Society*, 30 (1979), pp93–104.

Ackoff, R. L. and Emery, F. E. *On purposeful systems*, London, Tavistock, 1972.

Allen, D. K. *An introduction to computer-aided process planning*, SME-CASA CAPP Symposium, Orlando, 1986.

Alter, S. L. *Decision support systems: current practices and continuing challenges*, Reading, MA, Addison-Wesley, 1980.

Anthony, R. N. *Planning and control systems: a framework for analysis*, Harvard University Graduate School of Business Administration, Studies in Management Control, Cambridge, MA, 1965.

Ashby, W. R. *An introduction to cybernetics*, New York, Wiley, 1958.

Astrahan, M. M. and Chamberlin, D. D. 'Implementation of a structured English query language', *CACM* 18 (10) (1975), pp580–88.

Baker, K. R. *Introduction to sequencing and scheduling*, New York, John Wiley, 1974.

Bartlett, S. Cole, C. L. and Jain, R. 'Expert system for visual solder joint inspection', IEEE Third Conference on AI Applications, Kissimmee, Florida, Feb. 1987.

Beer, S. *Decision and control*, London, John Wiley, 1966.

The heart of the enterprise, London, John Wiley, 1979.

Bennet, J. S. and Englemore, R. S. 'SACON: a knowledge-based consultant for structural analysis', Proc 6th International Conference on Artificial Intelligence, Tokyo, 1979, pp47–49.

'Experiences using EMYCIN' in Buchanan, B. and Shortliffe, E. H. (eds) *The MYCIN experiments of the Stanford heuristic programming project*, Reading, MA, Addison-Wesley, 1984.

Bensana, E., Bel, G, and Dubois, D. 'OPAL: A multi-knowledge-based system for industrial job shop scheduling', *International Journal of Production Research* 26 (5) (1988), pp795–818.

Berenji, H. R. and Khoshnevis, B. 'Use of artificial intelligence in automated process planning', *Computers in Mechanical Engineering* 5 (2) (1986), pp47–55.

Bertalanffy, L. von. 'The organism considered as a physical system' (1940), reprinted in Bertalanffy L. von. (1968) *General system theory*, New York, Braziller.

Bitran, G. and Papageorge, T. 'Integration of manufacturing policy and corporate strategy with the aid of expert systems', in Michael Oliff (ed) *Intelligent manufacturing*, Reading, MA, Addison Wesley, 1987.

Bitran, G. R. and Chang, L. 'A mathematical programming approach to a deterministic Kanban system', *Management Science* 33 (4), 1987.

Bonczek, R. Holsapple C. and Whinston A. *Foundations of decision support systems*, New York, Academic Press, 1981.

Boose, J. H. and Bradshaw, J. M. 'Expertise transfer and complex problems: Using AQUINAS as a knowledge acquisition workbench for knowledge-based systems', *Int. J. Man-Machine Studies*, 26 (1987), pp3–28.

Boothroyd, G. and Dewhurst, P. *Design for assembly — a designer's handbook*, Department of Mechanical Engineering, University of Massachusets-Amherst, 1983.

Bourne, D. A. 'CML: A meta-interpreter for manufacturing', *AI Magazine 7*, (4) (1986), pp86–96.

Brightman, H. J. and Harris, S. E. 'Building computer models that really work', *Managerial Planning*, Jan-Feb 1984.

Brimson, J. and Downey, P. J. 'Feature technology: a key to manufacturing integration', *CIM Review*, Spring 1986, pp21–26.

Brodie, M and Mylopoulos, J (eds) *On knowledge base management systems*, New York, Springer-Verlag, 1986.

Brown, D. C. and Chandrasekaran, B. 'Knowledge and control for a mechanical design expert system', *Computer* 19 (7) (1986) pp92–100.

Brownston, L., Farrell, R., Kant, E., Martin, N. *Programming expert systems in OPS5*, Reading, MA, Addison-Wesley, 1985.

Bruno, G. Elai, A. and Laface, P. 'A rule-based system to schedule production', *IEEE Computer* (1986), pp32–39.

Bu-Hulaiga, M. I. and Chakravarty, A. K. 'An object-oriented knowledge representation for hierarchical real-time control of flexible manufacturing, *Int. J. Prod. Res. 26*, (5) (1988), pp777–93.

Buchanan, B. G. and Shortliffe, E. H. *Rule-based expert systems: the MYCIN experiments of the Stanford heuristic programming project*, Reading, MA, Addison-Wesley, 1984.

Buffa, E. S, Armour G. C, and Vollman, T.E. 'Allocating facilities with CRAFT', *Harvard Business Review* 42 (2) (1964), pp136–159.

Bundy, A. 'Intelligent front ends' in M. A. Bramer (ed) *Research and development in expert systems*, Cambridge University Press, 1985.

Butcher, J. and Yu, C. 'JIT — then AI', in Michael Oliff (ed) *Intelligent manufacturing*, Menlo Park, Benjamin/Cummings, 1988.

Buzzacott, J. A., and Yao, D. 'Flexible manufacturing systems: review of analytical models', *Management Science* 32 (1986), pp890–905.

Cahill, C. and Demers, A. 'Using knowledge technology to gain a competitive edge in manufacturing through predictive control', in Michael Oliff (ed) *Intelligent manufacturing*, Menlo Park, Benjamin/Cummings, 1988.

Chapman, D. 'Nonlinear planning: a rigorous construction', Proc. International Joint Conference on Artificial Intelligence, 1985.

Chen, P. R. 'The entity-relationship model: towards a unified view of data', *ACM TODS*, 1, (1976), 9–36.

Cholvy, L. and Foisseau, J. 'ROSALIE: A CAD object-oriented and rule-based system', *Information Processing '83*, pp501–505, Amsterdam, North Holland, 1983.

Churchman, C.W. *The design of inquiring systems,* Basic Books, 1971.

Clocksin, W. F. and Mellish, C. S. *Programming in Prolog*, Berlin, Springer-Verlag, 1980.

Codd, E. F. 'A relational model of data for large shared data banks', *CACM 13* (6) (1970), pp377–87.

Dagli, C. H. and Stacey, R. 'A knowledge-based system for selecting control charts', *Int. J. Prod. Res.* 26, (5) (1988), pp987–96.

Date, C. J. *An introduction to database systems* 3rd Edition, Reading, MA, Addison-Wesley, 1981.

Davis, E. H. and Goedhart, J. L. 'Integrated planning frontiers', in Michael Oliff (ed) *Intelligent manufacturing*, Menlo Park, Benjamin/Cummings, 1988.

Davis, J. and Oliff, M. D. 'Requirements for the integration of manufacturing planning islands using knowledge-based technology', in Michael D. Oliff (ed) *Expert systems and intelligent manufacturing*, New York, North Holland, 1988.

Davis, R. 'Diagnostic reasoning based on structure and behaviour', *Artificial Intelligence*, 24 (1984), pp347–410.

Davis, R. and Smith, R. G., 'Negotiation as a metaphor for distributed problem solving', *Artificial Intelligence*, 20, (1983), pp63–109.

Dayal, U., Blaustein, B. et al 'The HiPAC project: combining active databases and timing constraints', *SIGMOD Record* 17 (1) (1988), pp51–70.

de Kleer, J. 'An assumption-based truth maintainance system', *Artificial Intelligence* 28, 1986.

de Kleer, J. and Williams, B. C. 'Diagnosing multiple faults', *Artificial Intelligence* 32 (1987), pp97–130.

de Marco, T. *Structured analysis and system specification'*, Englewood Cliffs, NJ, Prentice-Hall, 1978.

De, S., Nof, S. Y. and Whinston, A. B. 'Decision support in computer integrated manufacturing', *Decision support systems 1* (1985), pp37–56.

Deliyanni, A. and Kowalski, R. A. 'Logic and semantic networks', *CACM*, 22, 2 (1979), pp184–192.

Descotte, Y. and Latombe, J. C. 'GARI: A problem solver that plans how to machine mechanical parts', Proc. 7th IJCAI Conf. (Vancouver 1981), pp766–772.

'Making compromises among antagonistic constraints in a planner', *Artificial Intelligence* 27 (1985), pp183–217.

Dickson, G. W. and Simmons, J. K. 'The behavioural side of MIS', *Business Horizons*, 13, 4, (1970), pp59–71.

Dickson, G. W. and Wetherbe, J. C. 'The management of information systems', New York, McGraw-Hill, 1985.

Dilts, D. M. 'Integration of computer integrated manufacturing databases using artificial intelligence', in Michael D. Oliff (ed) *Expert systems and intelligent manufacturing*, New York, North Holland, 1988.

Dixon, J. R and Simmons, M. K. 'Computers that design: expert systems for mechanical engineers', *Computers in Mechanical Engineering*, 2 (3) (1983), pp10–18.

Doyle, J. 'A truth maintainance system', *Artificial Intelligence*, 12 (1982), pp231–72.

Dubois, D. and Stecke, K. E. 'Using Petri nets to represent production processes', Proceedings of IEEE Conference on Decision and Control, Dec. 1983, p1062.

Duchessi, P. 'The conceptual design for a knowledge-based system as applied to the production planning process', in B. Silverman (ed) *Expert Systems for Business*, Reading, MA, Addison-Wesley, 1987.

Dunn, M. S. 'Computerised production process planning for machined cylindrical parts', Proc. 19th Numerical Control Soc. Tech. Conf (Dearborn) 1982, pp162–73.

Duggan, J. and Browne, J. 'ESPRIT Project 477: Production activity control design and implementation', *Proceedings of ESPRIT Technical Week, 14th–17th Nov. 1988*, Amsterdam, North Holland.

Dwivedi, S. N. and Klein, B. R. 'Design for manufacturing makes dollars and sense', *CIM Review*, Spring 1986, pp53–59.

Dyer, M. D and Flowers, M. 'EDISON: An engineering design invention system operating naively', *International Journal of Artificial Intelligence Engineering*, 1, (1), (1986), pp36–44.

Ebner, M. L., Lindgren L. H. and Vollman, T. E. *The IMPS system: its scope and applications*, Working Paper, Manufacturing Engineering Department, Boston University, 1986.

Elleby, P, Fargher, H. and Addis, T. R. 'Reactive constraint-based job-shop scheduling', in Michael D. Oliff (ed) *Expert systems and intelligent manufacturing*, New York, North Holland, 1988.

Ernst, G. and Newell, A. *GPS: a case study in generality and problem solving*, New York, Academic Press, 1969.

Erschler, J. and Esquirol, P. 'Decision-aid in job-shop scheduling: A knowledge-based approach', Proc. of the 1986 IEEE Conf. on Robotics and Automation, San Francisco, 1986, pp1651–6.

Evans, G. W., Karwowski, W. and Wilhelm, M. R. *Applications of Fuzzy Set Methodology in Industrial Engineering,* Amsterdam, Elsevier, 1989.

Farinacci, M. L., Fox, M. S, Hulthage, I. and Rychener, M. D. 'The development of ALADIN, an expert system for aluminium alloy design', in T. Bernold (ed) *Artificial intelligence in manufacturing*, Amsterdam, North Holland, 1986.

Feigenbaum, E. A. 'The art of artificial intelligence: themes and case studies in knowledge engineering', 5th International Joint Conference on Artificial Intelligence, Cambridge, MA, 1977.

Flitman, A. M. and Hurrion, R.D. 'Linking discrete event simulation models with expert systems', *Journal of the Operational Research Society* 38 (8) (1987), pp723–33.

Fox, M. 'Constraint-directed search: A case study of job-shop scheduling', PhD Thesis Computer Science Department, Carnegie-Mellon University, 1983.

Fox, M. S., and Baykan, C. A. 'WRIGHT: an intelligent CAD system', *SIGART Newsletter* 92 (1985), pp61–62.

Fox, M. S. and McDermott, J. 'The role of databases in knowledge-based systems', in Brodie, M. and Mylopoulos J (eds) *On knowledge base management systems*, New York, Springer-Verlag, 1986.

Fox M. S. and Smith, S. F. 'ISIS: a knowledge-based system for factory scheduling', *Expert Systems* 1 (1) (1984), pp25–49.

Frost, R. A. 'Binary relational storage structures', *Computer Journal* 23 (3) (1982), pp358–367.

Futo, I '*Combined discrete/continuous modelling and problem solving*', T O'Shea (ed) ECAI 84, Amsterdam Elsevier, 1984.

'Knowledge acquisition: developments and advances', in Michael D. Oliff (ed) *Expert systems and intelligent manufacturing*, New York, North Holland, 1988.

Gaines, B. and Boose, J. (eds) *Knowledge acquisition for knowledge based systems*, London, Academic Press, 1988.

Gairola, A. 'Design for assembly: a challenge for expert systems', in T. Bernold (ed.) *Artificial intelligence in manufacturing*, Amsterdam, North Holland, 1987.

Galbraith, J. *Designing complex organisations*, Reading, MA, Addison-Wesley, 1973.

Gallagher, C. G. and Knight, W. A. *Group technology methods in manufacture*, Chichester, Ellis Horwood, 1986.

Giannesini, F., Kanoui, H., Pasero, R. and van Caneghem, M. *Prolog*, Reading, MA, Addison-Wesley, 1986.

Ginzberg, M. J. 'Key recurrent issues in the MIS implementation process', *MIS Quarterly*, 5, 2, 1981.

Glover, F., Hultz, J. and Klingman, D. 'Improved computer based planning techniques Part I', *Interfaces* 8 (4) (1978), pp16–25

Goldbogen, G. *et al* 'Comparison of two knowledge representation paradigms for diagnosis of complex analytical instruments', in Michael D. Oliff (ed) *Expert systems and intelligent manufacturing*, New York: North Holland, 1988.

Goldbogen, G., Hoernes, P., McCool, A., and Lim, A. 'Expert systems for extracting features from a CAD database', in Michael D. Oliff (ed) *Expert systems and intelligent manufacturing*, New York: North Holland, 1988.

Goldrath, E. 'The unbalanced plant', APICS 1981 Conference Proceedings, pp195–9.

Greene, R. Tabor, *Implementing Japanese AI techniques* , New York, McGraw-Hill, 1990.

Hakami, B. and Newborn, J. 'Expert system in heavy industry: an application of ICLX in a British Steel Corporation Works', *ICL Technical Journal*, November 1983, pp347–59.

Hall, R. W. *Zero inventories*, Homewood, Ill, Dow Jones-Irwin, 1983.

Hardy, S. 'Expert systems for diagnosis', in *Expert systems for advanced manufacturing technology*, Detroit, ESD/SMI* 1987, pp301–308.

Harrington, J. R. (1973)

Hart, A. *Knowledge acquisition for expert systems*, London; Kogan Page, 1986.

Hart, P. E. 'Directions for AI in the eighties', *ACM SIGART Newsletter*, 79 (1982), pp11–16.

* Engineering Society of Detroit/Society for Machine Intelligence

Hawryszkiewycz, I. T. 'Automated tools for database design', Proceedings of the Pan-Pacific Computer Conference, Melbourne, Australia, 1985.

Hayes-Roth, F., Waterman, D. A. and Lenat, D. *Building expert systems*, Reading, MA, Addison-Wesley, 1983.

Helferich, O. K., Espel, C. J. and Taylor, L. A. 'Expert systems: logistics applications in support of materials planning and production', in Michael D. Oliff (ed) *Expert systems and intelligent manufacturing*, New York, North Holland, 1988.

Henderson, M. R. 'Automated group technology part coding from a three dimensional CAD database', ASME winter meeting: Knowledge-based expert systems and manufacturing, Anaheim, December 1986.

Herrod, R. A. 'Industrial applications of artificial intelligence', IEEE Western Conference on Expert Systems, Anaheim, CA, June 1987.

Holt, C. C., Modigliani, F., Muth, J. F. and Simon, H. 'A linear decision rule for production and employment scheduling', *Management Science* 1 (1953), pp1–30.

Hull, R., and King, R. 'Semantic database modelling: survey, applications and research issues', *ACM Computing Surveys* 19 (3) (1987), pp201–260.

Hummel, K. E. and Brooks, S. L. 'Symbolic representation of manufacturing features for an automated process planning system', ASME Winter meeting: Knowledge-based expert systems in manufacturing, December 1986.

Hummel, K. E. and Brooks, S. L. 'Using hierarchically structured problem-solving knowledge in a rule-based process planning system', in Michael D. Oliff (ed) *Expert systems and intelligent manufacturing*, New York, North Holland, 1988.

Intellicorp, 'KEEconnection: a bridge between databases and knowledge bases', Intellicorp, Mountain view, CA, 1975

Iri, M. 'On the synthesis of loop and cut set matrices and the related problems', in K. Kondo (ed) *RAAG Memoirs*, 4, 1968, pp376–410.

Ishikawa, K. 'Guide to quality control', Asia Productivity Organisation, 1976.

Jackson, M. A. *Principles of program design*, New York, Academic Press, 1975.

Kanet, J 'Knowledge based scheduling systems', Second International Conference on Expert Systems and the Leading Edge in Production Planning and Control, Charleston, SC, 1988.

Karmarker, U. S. 'Lot sizes, lead times and in-process inventories', *Management Science 33* (3) (1987).

Karwowski, W. and Evans, G. W., 'Fuzzy concepts in production management: a review', *Int J. Prod. Res*, 24 (1) (1986), pp129–147.

Keen, P. G. W. and Scott Morton, M. *Decision-support systems: an organizational perspective*, Reading, MA, Addison-Wesley, 1978.

Kelly, G. *The psychology of personal constructs*, New York, Norton, 1955.

Kellog, C. 'From data management to knowledge management', *IEEE Computer* 19, (1) (1986), pp75–84.

Kempf, K. 'Artificially intelligent tools for manufacturing process planners', in Michael Oliff (ed) *Intelligent manufacturing*, Menlo Park, Benjamin/Cummings, 1988.

Kent W. 'Fact based analysis and design', in *Entity relationship approaches to software engineering*, New York, North Holland, 1983.

Kerr, R. M. and Walker, N. 'ISTOP: preliminary specification', Information Concepts Confidential Technical Report, Sydney, 1988.

'FACSIM — preliminary specification', Information Concepts, Sydney, 1988.

'A job-shop scheduling system based on fuzzy arithmetic', Proc. 2nd Int. Conf. on Expert Systems and the Leading Edge in Production and Operations Management, Hilton Head Island, 1989.

Kickert, W. *Fuzzy theories on decision making*, Leiden, Martinus Nijhoff, 1978.

King, R. and Mcleod, D. 'Semantic database models', in *Database design*, pp115–150, New York, Springer Verlag, 1985.

Klingman, D. and Phillips, N.V. 'An intelligent decision-support system for integrated distribution planning', in Michael Oliff (ed) *Intelligent Manufacturing*, Menlo Park, Benjamin/Cummings, 1988.

Koo, C. C. and Cashman, P. 'A commitment-based communication language for distributed manufacturing' in 'Knowledge-based expert systems for manufacturing', Proceedings of the ASME winter meeting, Anaheim, November 1986.

Kosy D. W., and Wise, B. P. 'ROME: a reason-oriented modelling environment', *SIGART Newsletter* 92 (1985), pp102–104.

Kowalski, R. *Logic for problem solving*, New York, North Holland, 1979.

Kumara, S.R.T, Kashyap, R. L. and Moodie, C. L. 'Expert system for industrial facilities layout planning and analysis', *Computers in Industrial Engineering* 12 (2) (1987), pp143–152.

Kusiak, A. 'Scheduling flexible manufacturing and assembly systems', in K. Stecke and R. Suri (eds) Proc of the 2nd TIMS/ORSA Conference on Flexible Manufacturing Systems, New York, Elsevier, 1986.

'KBSS: A knowledge-based system for manufacturing scheduling', IFIP WG 5:7 Working conference on knowledge-based production management systems, Galway, Ireland, 1988a.

'EXGT-S: A knowledge-based system for group technology', *Int. J. Prod. Res.* 26, (5) 1988b, pp887–904.

Kusiak, A., and Chow, W. S., 'Efficient solving of the group technology problem', *Journal of Manufacturing Systems* 6 (1987), pp117–124.

Lecocq, P. 'An expert systems application to increase the flexibility and the efficacy of real-time FMS controllers', in Michael D. Oliff (ed) *Expert systems and intelligent manufacturing*, New York, North Holland, 1988.

Lu, S. C-Y. 'Knowledge-based expert systems: a new horizon of manufacturing automation', in 'Knowledge-based expert systems for manufacturing', Proceedings of the ASME winter meeting, December 1986.

Lee, K. and Gossard, D. 'A hierarchical data structure for representing assemblies: Part 1', *Computer Aided Design* 14 (1985), pp79–107.

Lewin, K. 'Frontiers in group dynamics: concept, method and reality in social science', *Human Relations* 1 (1) (1947), pp5–41.

Luby, S. Dixon John, R. and Simmons, M. K. 'Creating and using a features data base', *Computers in Mechanical Engineering*, November 1986, pp25–33.

Manola, F. and Brodie, M. L. 'On knowledge-based system architectures', in Brodie, M. and Mylopoulos J. (eds) *On knowledge base management systems*, New York; Springer-Verlag, 1986.

Marque-Puchen, G., Martin-Gallauxiaux, J. and Jomier, G. 'Interfacing PROLOG and relational database management systems', in *New applications of databases,* pp225–44, London, Academic Press, 1984.

Martin, J. and McClure, C *Structured techniques: the basis for CASE,* Englewood Cliffs, NJ, Prentice-Hall, 1988.

McDermott, J. 'R1, The formative years', *AI Magazine,* Summer 1981, pp21–30. 'R1: A rule-based configurer of computer systems', *Artificial Intelligence* 19 (1982a), pp39–88.

'XSEL: A computer sales person's assistant', in J. E. Hayes, D. Michie and Y. H. Pao (eds) *Machine Intelligence 10,* London: John Wiley, 1982b.

McKenney, J. L. and Keen, P. G. W. 'How managers' minds work', *Harvard Business Review,* May-June 1974.

Melkannof, Michael K. 'The CIMS database: goals, problems, case studies and proposed approaches outlined', *Industrial Engineering* November 1984, pp78–93.

Meredith, J. R. 'The implementation of computer-based systems', *Journal of Operations Management,* October 1981.

Meyer, R. J. *AI and expert systems: in pursuit of CIM,* CIM Technology, February 1987, pp CT15–CT17.

Michie, D. 'Current developments in expert systems' in proceedings of the second Australian conference on applications of expert systems', Sydney, May 1986.

Michie, D., Muggleton, S., Reise, C. and Zubnick, S. 'Rulemaster: A second generation knowledge engineering facility', in First Conference on Artificial Intelligence Applications, Denver, December 1984.

Miller, J. G., Rosenthal, S. R. and Vollman, T. E. *Taking stock of CIM,* Manufacturing Roundtable Research Report Series, 1986.

Mina, I. 'UMXD: a diagnosis expert system for manufacturing' expert systems for Advanced Manufacturing Technology, Detroit, ESD/SMI, 1987, pp281–294.

Minsky, M. *Matter, mind and models in semantic information processing,* Cambridge, MA, MIT Press, 1968.

Mintzberg H. 'The nature of managerial work', New York, Harper and Row, 1973.

Morton, T., Lawrence, S., Rajagopalan, S. & Kekre, S. *Sched-Star: A price-based shop scheduling model,* Graduate School of Business Administration, Carnegie-Mellon University, 1987.

Morton, T. E., and Smunt, T. L. 'A planning and scheduling system for flexible manufacturing', in Kusiak, A. (ed.) *Flexible manufacturing systems: methods and studies,* Amsterdam, North Holland, 1986.

Navathe, S., Elmasri, R. and Larson, J. 'Integrating user views in database design', *IEEE Computer,* January 1986, pp50–62.

Nau, D. S. and Chang, T. C. 'Hierarchical representation of knowledge in a frame-based process planning system', Computer Science Dept, University of Maryland, 1985.

Newell, A. 'The Knowledge Level', *Artificial Intelligence* (18) 1 (1982) pp87–127.

Newell, A., and Simon, H. *Human problem solving,* Englewood Cliffs, NJ, Prentice-Hall, 1972.

Nijssen, G. M. 'From databases to knowledge bases: a technical comparison', in King, P. H. J. (ed) *Databases: state of the art report,* London, Pergamon Press, 1984.

O'Connel, A. M. 'Expert maintainance personnel now available', Expert Systems for Advanced Manufacturing Technology, Detriot, ESD/SMI, 1987, pp199–207.

O'Grady, P. and Lee, K. H. 'An intelligent cell system for automated manufacturing', *Int. J. Prod. Res.* 26 (5) (1988), pp845–61.

O'Grady, P. J. 'The control of automated manufacturing systems', New York, Chapman Hall/Kogan Page, 1987.

Orlicky, J. A. *Material requirements planning*, New York, McGraw-Hill, 1975.

Ow, P. S., Smith, S. F., and Howie, R. 'A cooperative scheduling system', in Michael D. Oliff (ed) *Expert systems and intelligent manufacturing*, New York, North Holland, 1988.

Pels, H. J. and Wortmann, J.C. 'Decomposition of information systems for production management', in S. Augustin, R. Gundling and J. Ohanian (eds) *Decentralized production management systems*, Amsterdam, North Holland, 1985.

Peters, T. J. and Waterman, R. H. *In search of excellence,* New York, Harper and Row, 1982.

Quillian, M. R. *Semantic memory in semantic information processing*, M.Minsky (ed), Cambridge, MA, MIT Press, 1968.

Quinlan, J. R. 'Semi-autonomous acquisition of pattern-based knowledge', in D Michie (ed) *Introductory readings in expert systems*, New York, Gordon and Breach, 1982.

Rasdorf, William J. 'Extending DBMS's for engineering applications', *Computers in Mechanical Engineering*, March 1987, pp62–9.

Reddy, Y. V. 'Epistemology of knowledge-based simulation', *Simulation* 48, (4) (1987), pp162–6.

Reddy, Y. V. R., Fox, M. S. and Husain, N. 'The knowledge-based simulation system', *IEEE Software*, 3 (1986), pp26–37.

Rehak, D., and Howard, C. 'Interfacing expert systems with design databases in integrated CAD systems', *Computer Aided Design*, 17, (9) (1985), pp443–454.

Reitman, W. 'Artificial Intelligence, Expert Systems and Operations Management: A long term view', in Karwan, K. R. and Sweilgart, J. R. (eds) *Proc. 2nd Int Conf. on Expert Systems and the Leading Edge in Production and Operations Management*, College of Business Administration, University of South Carolina, 1989.

Rosenschein, J. S., and Genesereth, M., 'Deals among rational agents', *Proceedings of International Joint conference in Artificial Intelligence*, 1985 pp91–9.

Ross, D. 'Structured analysis: a language for communicating ideas', *IEEE Transactions on Software Engineering*, pp16–34, January 1977.

Sacerdoti, Earl D. *A structure for plans and behaviour*, New York, Elsevier, 1977.

Savory, S. 'FF: A Nixdorf expert system for fault finding and repair planning — an outline description', in T. Bernold and G. Albers (eds) *'Artificial intelligence: towards practical application'*, Amsterdam, North Holland, 1985.

Schonberger, R. *Japanese manufacturing techniques: nine hidden lessons in simplicity*, New York, Free Press, 1982.

Shannon, C. E. 'A mathematical theory of communication', in D. Slepian (ed)*Key papers in the development of information theory'*, New York, IEEE, 1948.

Shaw, M. J. 'Knowledge-based Scheduling in flexible manufacturing systems: an integration of pattern-directed inference and heuristic search', Int. J. Prod. Res. 26, (5) (1988), pp821–844.

Shaw, M. J. P. and Whinston, A. B. 'Applications of artificial intelligence to planning and scheduling in flexible manufacturing', in A. Kusiak, (ed) *Flexible manufacturing systems: methods and studies*, Amsterdam, North Holland, 1986.

Silverman, Barry G. *Expert systems for business*, Reading, MA, Addison-Wesley, 1987.

Simon, H. *The new science of management decision*, New York, Harper and Row, 1960.

Skinner, Wickham. *Manufacturing and corporate strategy*, New York, John Wiley, 1978.

Smith, J. M. *et al.* 'Multibase — integrating heterogeneous distributed database systems', *AFIPS National Computer Conference Proceedings*, 50, 1981, pp487–99.

Smith, S. F. 'A constraint-based framework for reactive management of factory schedules', in Michael Oliff (ed) *Intelligent manufacturing*, Menlo Park, Benjamin/Cummings, 1988 .

Smith, S. F., Fox, M. S. and Ow, P.S. 'Constructing and maintaining detailed production plans: investigations into the development of knowledge-based factory scheduling systems', *AI Magazine*, 7, (4) (1986), pp45–61.

Smithers, T. 'The Alvey large scale demonstrator project Design to Product', in T. Bernold (ed) *Artificial intelligence in manufacturing*, pp251–261, Amsterdam, North Holland, 1987.

Sprague, R. and Carlson, E. *Building effective decision support systems*, Englewood Cliffs, NJ, Prentice-Hall, 1982.

Stecke, K. E. 'Design, planning, scheduling and control problems of flexible manufacturing systems', *Proceedings of the TIMS/ORSA Conference on FMS*, (1984) pp22–27.

Stelzner, M., Dynis, J., and Cummins, F. *The SIMKIT system: knowledge-based simulation and modelling tools in KEE, Intellicorp*, 1987.

Stonebraker, M. and Rowe, L. A. 'The Design of POSTGRES', in *Proceedings of The International Conference on the Management of Data ACM*, New York (1986), pp340–55.

Stuart, J. D. and Vinson, J. W. 'TURBOMAC: An expert system to aid in the diagnosis of causes of vibration-producing problems in large turbomachinery', Proc. Conf. Computers in Mechanical Engineering, Amer. Soc. Mech. Eng., Boston (1985), pp319–25.

Stuart, J. D. *et al.* 'TITAN: An expert system to assist in troubleshooting the Texas Instruments 990 minicomputer system', in Kamal N. Karma (ed) Proc. Expert Systems in Government Symposium, IEEE Comp. Soc., McLean, VA. (1985), pp439–446.

Su, S. Y. W. 'Modelling integrated manufacturing data with SAM', *IEEE Computer* 19 (1) (1986), pp34–49.

Subramanyam, S. and Askin, R. 'An expert systems approach to scheduling in flexible manufacturing systems', in A Kusiak (ed) *Flexible manufacturing systems: methods and studies*, pp243–256, Amsterdam, North Holland, 1986.

Taguchi, G., 'Introduction to quality engineering', Asian Productivity Organisation, 1986.

Thompson, James D. *Organisations in action: social science bases of administrative theory*, New York, McGraw-Hill, 1967.

Trist, E. L. *et al. Organisational choice*, London, Tavistock, 1963.

Tsichritzis, D. and Lochovsky, Frederick H. *Data models*, Englewood Cliffs, New Jersey, Prentice-Hall, 1982.

Tulkoff, J. 'Lockheed's GENPLAN', Proc. 18th Num. Control Soc. Conf. (Dallas) (1981) p417.

Turban, E. *Decision support and expert systems*, New York, Macmillan, 1988.

Tversky, A. and Kahneman, D. 'The framing of decisions and the psychology of choice' *Science* 211 (1981), pp453–458.

van Melle, W., Shortliffe E. H. and Buchanan, B. 'EMYCIN: a knowledge engineer's tool for constructing rule-based expert systems', in Buchanan, B and Shortliffe, E. H. (eds) *Rule-based expert systems: the MYCIN experiments of the Stanford heuristic programming project*, Reading, MA, Addison-Wesley, 1984.   *on loan 2/6 science*

Vollman, T. E., Berry, W. L., and Whybark D. C. *Manufacturing planning and control systems*, Homewood, Illinois, Dow Jones-Irwin, 1988.   *TS176.V63 1988*

Waterman D. A. *A guide to expert systems*, Reading, MA, Addison-Wesley, 1986.

Wight, O. *MRPII unlocking America's productivity potential*, Williston, VT, Oliver Wight Limited Publications, 1981.

Winston, P. H., *Artificial intelligence* (second edition), Reading, MA, Addison-Wesley, 1984.

Wirth, N. 'Program Development by Stepwise Refinement', *CACM* (1971) 14, (4), pp221–227.

Woo, T. C. 'Interfacing solid modelling to CAD and CAM: data structures and algorithms for decomposing a solid', *Computer Integrated Manufacturing*, November 1983, pp39–45.

Woodworth, R. S. and Schlosberg, H. *Experimental psychology*, pp192–223, New York, Henry Holt, 1955.

Wright, P. K. and Bourne, D. A. *Manufacturing intelligence*, Reading, MA, Addison-Wesley, 1988.

Yourdon, E. and Constantine, L. *Structured design*, Englewood Cliffs, NJ, Prentice-Hall, 1979.

Yoshiura, H., Fujimurs, K. and Kunii, T. L 'Top-Down Construction of 3-D Mechanical Object Shapes from Engineering Drawings', IEEE Computer 1984, pp32–39.

Young, R. L., O'Neill, D. M., Mullarkey P. W. and Grinch P. C. 'An object-based architecture for manufacturing parts routing', IEEE 3rd Conf on AI Applications, Kissimmee, Florida, Feb 1987.

Zadeh, L. 'Fuzzy Sets', *Information and control* 8 (1965), p338.

Zimmerman, H-J., Zadeh, L. A. and Gaines B. R., *Fuzzy sets and decision analysis*, Amsterdam: North Holland, 1984.

Subject Index

accounting data 362
actuator 49, 50
AGV 258, 277
ALADIN system 299
Alvey program 315
application
  generator 285, 294
  languages 385
  network 288, 292
  specific shells 388,428
APT (NC programming language) 34
  see also NC programming
    languages
AQUINAS (repertory grid, Boeing)
  375
ARL (Abbreviated Rule Language)
  332
ART (Inference Corporation) 385,
  386
AI (Artificial Intelligence)
  Circles, 260, 323, 362, 380, 389,
    424
  computer languages 224, 380
  planning techniques 188–90,
    217
  software development
    environments 382 *see also*
      Knowledge CRAFT
  systems in Japan 362
Ashby's law of requisite variety 50–2,
  265
assertions
  logical 147–50, 154, 159, 162
    see also axioms
assumption-Based
  Reasoning 190, 216
  Planning 190
  Truth Maintenance systems 314,

316, 342 *see also* Truth
  Maintenance systems
attenuator 51
attributes 81–105, 141, 165, 275,
  300–2, 369, 374, 377, 401
automatic 229
axiom set 157, 159
axioms 149–53, 160 *see also*
  assertions

Backtracking 118, 133
  dependency directed 190
batch
  production 29
  quantity
    economic 15
  scheduling 212
  size 14, 23, 207, 208, 217, 223,
    234–6, 278
  policy 234–5
Bayesian
  approach 139
  reasoning 314
beam Search 120, 213, 234
bill of Materials 22, 71, 232, 287–8,
  325, 328, 330, 364, 393
  processor (BOMP) 17
Binary Relations Model 91, 104–5
binary relations 104, 105, 108
blackboard architecture 137, 213,
  228, 256, 260–2, 392, 410, 413,
  425
bottleneck resources 22, 24, 205,
  207, 216, 249, 251, 255–7, 279,
  288, 290, 369
Boundary Representation BREP 302,
  309
Box Jenkins model 206

443

Author Index